EDUCATING SCHOLARS

EDUCATING SCHOLARS

DOCTORAL EDUCATION
IN THE HUMANITIES

PN Many thanks for your help so many year ago

Ronald G. Ehrenberg, Harriet Zuckerman,
Jeffrey A. Groen, and Sharon M. Brucker

[signatures]

PRINCETON UNIVERSITY PRESS   PRINCETON AND OXFORD

Library of Congress Cataloging-in-Publication Data

Educating scholars : doctoral education in the
humanities / Ronald G. Ehrenberg . . . [et al].
p.   cm.
Includes bibliographical references and index.
ISBN 978-0-691-14266-1 (hardcover : alk. paper)
1. Humanities—Study and teaching (Higher)—United States.
2. Doctor of philosophy degree—United States.   3. Andrew W. Mellon
Foundation.   4. Scholars—United States.   5. Learning and
scholarship—United States.   6. Universities and colleges—United States—
Graduate work.   I. Ehrenberg, Ronald G.
AZ183.U5E35   2009
001.2—dc22   2009010082

British Library Cataloging-in-Publication Data is available

This book has been composed in Adobe New Baskerville by
Princeton Editorial Associates Inc., Scottsdale, Arizona

Printed on acid-free paper. ∞

press.princeton.edu

Printed in the United States of America

1 3 5 7 9 10 8 6 4 2

———————— For ————————

Randy Ehrenberg
Robert K. Merton
Melissa Groen
Eric Brucker

Husbands, Wives, Closest Friends

Contents

CONTENTS

Appendixes

Figures

Tables

_____ *Preface and Acknowledgments* _____

THE FIRST CHAPTER of this volume lays out the origins of The Andrew W. Mellon Foundation's Graduate Education Initiative (GEI): how it came into being and then evolved over the next decade. Many of the problems that prompted it—the long and far-from-predictable time it took for graduate students in the humanities to earn their degrees, the costs incurred by both students and institutions, and the concerns of faculty members about the process—remain in place. Indeed these are perhaps more urgent now as the economic difficulties universities face introduce new constraints on graduate education and limit opportunities for new PhDs as they begin their careers.

This book is the product of efforts by many individuals beyond the four authors. We were very fortunate to have the help of superbly competent graduate students at Cornell and Columbia universities, who worked hard on various aspects of the project. At Cornell, Joseph Price contributed to the research reported in Chapters 7, 9, and 10; Eric So, to Chapter 6; and Joshua Price, to Chapters 9 and 10. Scott Condie and Albert Liu assisted in the development of the ever-expanding database and helped with the research reported in Chapters 4 and 8, respectively. Elizabeth Needham Waddell found time while doing her dissertation at Columbia to work on the design of the questionnaire for the Graduate Education Survey and to shepherd it though its preparation for online and paper administration in conjunction with the staff at Mathematica Policy Research, Inc.

Our project director and a senior survey researcher at Mathematica, Laura Kalb, helped polish the questionnaire and dealt with the complex problems of locating respondents, getting the survey into the field, and keeping track of returns. She also helped achieve the very high response rate that gives us confidence that the data are in fact representative. Geraldine M. Mooney, vice president of Mathematica as well as managing director of methodology and development in its Surveys and Information Services Division, gave us the benefit of her long experience in mounting surveys in the field of higher education.

We are greatly indebted to the provosts, deans, and faculty members in the 54 departments (or programs) in the 10 universities that were part of the GEI. They planned in detail how it would be organized in each department and guided its realization. They reported each year to the Foundation, often diplomatically, about the ups and downs of the Initiative in their institutions. Some generously participated in various conferences on the GEI and helped us understand how it worked out on the ground.

Most offered advice and some, suitable criticism. All took their responsibilities to the GEI, and for collecting the necessary data, very seriously.

The 10 universities that participated in the Initiative also contributed by assigning members of their excellent research staffs to collect and process data for the GEI. Over a full 16 years, they faithfully provided information that permitted this longitudinal study of more than 30,000 students to proceed. They endured questions about how the data were being assembled, how the variables were being defined, and why various reports did not square, and they willingly corrected inconsistencies in the files. We are also grateful to the provosts, deans, and research staffs at the three universities that were not beneficiaries of the GEI but were nonetheless willing to contribute their institutional records to improve our control-group data. Their assistance was exceptionally important.

Other colleagues were of great importance to the research. Sarah E. Turner, now University Professor of Economics and Education at the University of Virginia, played multiple roles in the GEI. At the outset, she helped design the data-collection methodology while she was a research associate at the Mellon Foundation. Some years later, she was infinitely generous in giving advice on analysis of the evidence and went on to comment extensively on early drafts of the manuscript. George H. Jakubson, associate professor of labor economics at Cornell University, played a crucial role in designing the analysis for Chapters 4 and 6. We also received help from colleagues too numerous to mention, from a variety of institutions, in the form of comments and occasional chiding on papers we gave at seminars and conferences as well as meetings of the Council of Graduate Schools and the Association of Graduate Schools.

We are grateful to one anonymous reviewer, who gave us an extraordinarily insightful reading and advice on the manuscript and its structure. This reviewer performed well beyond the call of scholarly duty and is clearly an exemplary member of the academic community.

Several colleagues at the Mellon Foundation put up with the trials that come with participation in a very-long-term research enterprise. Susanne Pichler, the Foundation's highly skilled research librarian, helped answer ceaseless questions, from the detailed to the general, about higher education. Joseph S. Meisel devoted his best critical capacities to the ongoing enterprise and never ceased to encourage us toward its completion.

All four authors are indebted to Darrie O'Connell and Martha G. Sullivan. Assistants to Ronald G. Ehrenberg at Cornell University and to Harriet Zuckerman at the Mellon Foundation, respectively, Darrie and Martha coordinated our schedules, made sure multiple versions of the manuscript were under control, and generally kept things moving with great effectiveness and good spirits. Thanks are also due to Sharon Brucker's assistants, Daniel Thompson at the University of Michigan and Janine

Calogero at Princeton University. Without fail, they provided a range of services—from database construction to conference organization and general support—that kept Sharon grounded as she grappled with the gathering and presentation of the data.

We also acknowledge our great debt to the board of trustees of the Mellon Foundation, which underwrote the GEI in the first instance as well as the research on which this analysis is based. William G. Bowen and Neil L. Rudenstine, whose own studies led to the creation of the GEI and who launched it while they were, respectively, president and executive vice president at the Foundation, are uniquely significant contributors to this study. Bill Bowen oversaw the GEI from its beginnings and made it one of the Foundation's signature programs during the course of his tenure there. Never once, however, did he depart from the disinterested position he took at the outset, namely, that the GEI as a prototype required "careful monitoring and full publication of whatever lessons are learned."[1] He and his successor, Don M. Randel, the Foundation's current president, permitted us full autonomy. Likewise, the Foundation's board did not impose any limits on what the book or its offshoot papers were to say or how they were to say it. As a consequence, any views, findings, conclusions, or recommendations expressed in this book are those of the authors and do not represent those of The Andrew W. Mellon Foundation. We are exceptionally grateful for the freedom we have been given.

Appreciation also goes to the U.S. Bureau of Labor Statistics, where Jeffrey A. Groen serves as a research economist, for permitting him to work on the study. However, the views expressed in this book are solely those of the authors and do not reflect the views of the Bureau.

Our publisher, Princeton University Press, deserves special thanks for excellent guidance and careful production under tight time constraints. We are especially indebted to Kathleen Cioffi, production editor; Charles T. Myers, senior editor; and Peter J. Dougherty, director of the Press. Peter Strupp and the staff of Princeton Editorial Associates Inc. managed the copyediting and production. Each of them made publishing with the Press a distinctly satisfying professional experience.

The text of *Educating Scholars* is almost entirely new. Parts that have appeared elsewhere include portions of Chapters 1, 2, and 12. These chapters are substantial expansions of material that appears in Ronald G. Ehrenberg, Harriet Zuckerman, Jeffrey A. Groen, and Sharon M. Brucker, "Changing the Education of Scholars: An Introduction to the Andrew W. Mellon Foundation's Graduate Education Initiative," in Ronald G. Ehrenberg and Charlotte V. Kuh, eds., *Doctoral Education and the Faculty of the Future* (copyright 2009 by Cornell University; used by permission of

---

[1] Andrew W. Mellon Foundation, *Annual Report,* 1991, p. 11.

the publisher, Cornell University Press). Parts of Chapters 4 and 5 are a revision of material that appeared in Jeffrey A. Groen, George H. Jakubson, Ronald G. Ehrenberg, Scott Condie, and Albert Y. Liu, "Program Design and Student Outcomes in Graduate Education," *Economics of Education Review* 27 (April 2008): 111–24 (copyright 2007 by Elsevier Ltd.). Chapter 6 is a revision of material that appeared in Ronald G. Ehrenberg, George H. Jakubson, Jeffrey A. Groen, Eric So, and Joseph Price, "Inside the Black Box of Doctoral Education: What Program Characteristics Influence Doctoral Students' Attrition and Graduate Probabilities?" *Educational Evaluation and Policy Analysis* 29 (June 2007): 134–50 (copyright 2007 by the American Educational Research Association).

Abbreviations

CGS   Council of Graduate Schools
DGS   director of graduate studies
GEI   Graduate Education Initiative
GES   Graduate Education Survey
GRE   Graduate Record Examination
NRC   National Research Council
RA   research assistant
SYC   student-year cost
TA   teaching assistant
TTA   time-to-attrition
TTD   time-to-degree

CHAPTER 1

Introduction

Gratitude is mostly due to the ways in which the Mellon grant impelled change. Signing on to the Mellon grant required faculty to reconsider their collective responsibilities and forced them to devise new requirements and monitoring procedures. Although impressionistic evidence will be cited, faculty and students will easily attest that the cultures of their graduate groups have changed with new expectations and sense of mission.

—Graduate dean of a participating
university in 1996[1]

When I began my grad career, there were formal steps early in the program, but there was no further program designed to encourage students to make progress in dissertation writing or to prepare them for professional work. The department began to have a more consistent program for encouraging progress in the early '90s. Perhaps a response to a Mellon Foundation grant.

—Student in English who began graduate
school in 1985 and left in 2001

IN 1991, THE Andrew W. Mellon Foundation launched what would become the largest effort ever made to improve graduate education in the humanities in the United States. The Graduate Education Initiative (GEI) was "to achieve systematic improvements in the structure and organization of PhD programs in the humanities and related social sciences that will in turn reduce unacceptabl[y] high rates of student attrition and

---

[1] The quotations introducing this chapter and those that follow are drawn from annual reports sent to The Andrew W. Mellon Foundation on the Graduate Education Initiative and from the Graduate Education Survey (GES) of students. See Chapter 2 for detailed descriptions of the reports and the GES.

lower the number of years that the typical student spends working towards the doctorate."[2] At the time, the humanities were, it is fair to say,
uneasy not only because their central intellectual presuppositions remained in contention but also because their standing in American universities was uncertain.[3]

During the preceding decades, from the mid-1960s onward, "theory"
in its many varieties had flourished in many fields of the humanistic disciplines and had also found advocates in some of the social sciences as
well. Only departments of history, philosophy, and the "hard" social sciences remained relatively immune to these developments. Debates continued about the contributions various theoretical perspectives made to
the interpretation of texts and evidence and the epistemological and
political issues they raised. Inevitably, they also centered on the place of
theory in graduate education, on what the humanities were for, what
students should know, what skills they should command, and whether
"the canon" should survive and if so, how it should be constituted. In the
process, the graduate curriculum grew and became more diverse, not
only in response to the succession of new theoretical perspectives being
introduced but also because a multiplicity of new subject matters had
emerged.[4] By 1991, however, contention had mostly abated, although the
objectives of humanistic inquiry and what students should be taught remained undecided.

In the preceding decades, other significant trends were also discernible.
Interest in the humanities among undergraduates, as gauged by the percentage of students majoring in these fields, had dropped to a low of
about 10 percent in the mid-1980s and rebounded very mildly to 12 percent in 1990s.[5] The number of PhDs awarded in the humanities had
fallen steadily from a high of 4,873 in 1973 to a low of 2,749 in 1988, a re-

[2] Andrew W. Mellon Foundation, "Foundation Announces a Major New Program in
Graduate Education," press release, March 25, 1991.

[3] "Humanities and related social sciences" is so unwieldy a term that hereafter when we
refer to the humanities, we intend to include the composite of fields being represented.
These are art history, English, classics, comparative literature, all foreign languages, history,
musicology, philosophy, and religion, along with anthropology and political science, two
fields residing in the social sciences but parts of which (cultural anthropology and political
theory) draw on methodological and theoretical perspectives from the humanities. The array of hybrid fields—such as medieval studies, Asian studies, Africana studies, women's studies, and ethnic studies, with their strong multidisciplinary commitments—was already developing, but at the time these were not yet standard components of the humanities.

[4] The state of play in the humanities at the time is well summarized in the essays in Alvin
B. Kernan, ed., *What's Happened to the Humanities?* (Princeton, NJ: Princeton University Press,
1997).

[5] Kernan (1997), p. 248, Figure 1.

duction of 49 percent in 15 years.[6] At the same time, intense competition for resources in universities required that graduate programs justify their value and utility. The humanities had a particularly difficult time satisfying demands that they prove they had both.[7]

Educating Scholars recounts the history of the GEI and seeks to gauge critically how effective it turned out to be. Intended as a prototype, the GEI was both a social experiment and a major research project. The GEI was not an effort to change the content of the curriculum. Nor was it an attempt to increase the number of students who took graduate degrees. It was decidedly not an effort to change faculty members' views about their disciplines or their research.

Rather, the GEI had other objectives, as the language of that official press release indicated. It sought specifically to improve the effectiveness of graduate education in the humanities, that is, to use available resources in such a way that larger numbers of scholars would be educated in briefer periods of time while maintaining or even improving the quality of the education being offered. Two measures of effectiveness, attrition rates and the average time it took for students to get the PhD, were selected as key indicators.

Over a 10-year period (1991–2000), the Foundation provided over $58 million to 54 humanities departments at 10 major universities to support the departments' efforts. An additional $22.5 million was provided to these universities in the form of endowment and challenge grants as the GEI ended to help them sustain the progress that had been made with the help of GEI grant funds. Including funds the Foundation provided in the form of planning grants and grants for data collection and data management, all in all the Foundation devoted almost $85 million to supporting the GEI.

As we describe the GEI's successes and its failures, the influence of larger forces at work in graduate education at the time (and now) will become clear. The faltering job market and competition among departments for gifted students both affected the outcomes of the GEI. Inevitably, *Educating Scholars* is also a tale of unanticipated consequences that emerged as the intervention unfolded. Because the students who were the focus of the intervention would go on to lives after graduate school, the book also describes the careers new PhDs made as they began work

[6] See "Doctorate Recipients in the Humanities, 1970–2007" in *Humanities Indicators, 2008* (Cambridge, MA: American Academy of Arts and Sciences). http://www.humanities indicators.org.

[7] Lynn Hunt, "The Tradition Confronts Change: The Place of the Humanities in the University," in *The Humanist on Campus*, ACLS Occasional Paper 44, 1998, p. 3. http://archives.acls.org/op/op44hunt.htm.

in the academy, and it follows the histories of those who left graduate school without earning degrees.

This chapter first lays out the history of the Graduate Education Initiative, its rationale, and how it came into being. It reviews other interventions now under way and other research on related matters. Then it turns to the principal findings of our research, and finally it describes the plan of the book.

THE GRADUATE EDUCATION INITIATIVE: ITS HISTORY, RATIONALE, AND DESIGN

Worries about an array of issues in graduate education, including its slow pace, were brewing long before Bernard Berelson began research in the 1950s on the "controversial" state of American graduate education.[8] The questions he addressed ranged from the fundamental, that is, what graduate education was for (to prepare teachers or researchers), to the more advanced, including the quality of institutions producing PhDs, the purposes of the dissertation, and the reasons why students take so long to earn their degrees. He also sought to determine whether there were going to be enough PhDs to teach the oncoming waves of students likely to enroll in colleges and universities in the future.

Berelson's study was in a sense a grandparent of the GEI research. More directly ancestral was an important study of the current and future supply of PhDs by William G. Bowen and Julie Ann Sosa, *Prospects for Faculty in the Arts and Sciences,* published in 1989. Based on a careful analysis of evidence—including trends in faculty retirement, class size, and doctoral production—they projected a severe shortage of doctorate recipients in the arts and sciences who would be qualified to teach in the nation's colleges and graduate schools.[9] This shortage would be caused, they said, by a large number of anticipated faculty retirements, increases in college enrollments, and the rising nonacademic employment of new doctorate recipients. Moreover, Bowen and Sosa projected that the shortage would occur in all arts and science fields and would become serious in the humanities by the end of the 1990s.

In 1988, Bowen became president of The Andrew W. Mellon Foundation, which had a long-standing interest in the humanities in higher ed-

---

[8] Bernard Berelson, *Graduate Education in the United States* (New York: McGraw-Hill, 1960), p. 1.

[9] William G. Bowen and Julia Ann Sosa, *Prospects for Faculty in the Arts and Sciences* (Princeton, NJ: Princeton University Press, 1989).

ucation. Hence it was not surprising that he and Neil L. Rudenstine, then the executive vice president of the Foundation, would begin to think about how it might assist programs of doctoral education in the humanities and how the projected shortage of PhDs might be alleviated.[10] To get a better fix on the state of graduate education, they undertook a detailed analysis of PhD production in the United States in the arts and sciences and their component fields. This resulted in a second important book, *In Pursuit of the PhD*.[11]

Bowen and Rudenstine observed that the humanities, in comparison with the sciences and social sciences, were plagued by especially high attrition rates, which approached 50 percent or more, and by especially long time-to-degree (TTD), a shorthand term for the interval between the time students begin degree programs and the time they complete their degrees. (See Chapter 2 and Appendix C for various ways of measuring TTD.) By the late 1980s, median registered TTD in the humanities had risen to approximately nine years, even in some of the most highly regarded programs in the nation.[12]

High attrition rates and long TTD in the humanities, they concluded, resulted in part from the inadequate financial support graduate students received. They also concluded that simply increasing available funding was not likely to help much. Careful research on the outcomes of major multiyear national fellowship programs—including those sponsored by the Danforth Foundation, the National Defense Education Act fellowship program, the National Science Foundation, and the Woodrow Wilson National Fellowship Foundation, as well as the Mellon Foundation itself, all of which were focused on assisting individual graduate students with predictable long-term support—demonstrated that these programs had markedly "limited success . . . in reducing attrition and time-to-degree."[13] Put simply, despite these programs being highly competitive and supporting students with exceptionally impressive academic records, fellowship recipients did not have appreciably higher rates of completion than their classmates, nor did they have substantially shorter TTD.[14]

[10] Bowen, an economist, had been president of Princeton University from 1972 to 1988. Rudenstine, an expert on English literature, had been provost at Princeton; after serving at Mellon from 1988 to 1991, he was president of Harvard University from 1991 to 2001.

[11] William G. Bowen and Neil L. Rudenstine, *In Pursuit of the PhD* (Princeton, NJ: Princeton University Press, 1992).

[12] Ibid., Chapter 6.

[13] Ibid., p. 228.

[14] Ibid., Chapter 11. At the same time, the fellowship programs made important contributions to recruiting talented students to graduate study and to supporting them during its duration.

Other major fellowship programs provided funding not to students but to universities. These programs included the Ford Foundation's ambitious effort, begun in 1976 at six universities. It aimed at instituting a four-year PhD program, but it failed to produce the intended results at four of the six universities, and even at the other two the achieved reductions were slight.[15] These findings were sobering and led Bowen and Rudenstine to think that neither funding students individually nor turning money over to universities without involving departments was a successful recipe for improving doctoral education in the humanities.

Their research also revealed that the scale of university departments, that is, the number of students in annual entering cohorts, significantly affected completion rates and TTD, independent of the financial assistance students received. For example, fellowship recipients who studied in smaller departments were on average more likely to complete their degrees and to do so more quickly than recipients of the same fellowships who studied in larger departments. Such differences were not attributable to differences in the quality of faculty in larger and smaller departments.[16]

The importance of scale implied much about the significance of departments in graduate training—for example, the connection of scale with the vitality of graduate-student life and the attention students received. In addition to scale, Bowen and Rudenstine's research pointed to the importance of departmental organization and culture. Among the obstacles for students, they cited unclear expectations about how long it "should" take to earn the degree, the absence of timetables, a proliferation of course options, elaborate and sometimes conflicting requirements, intermittent (or insufficient) advising and monitoring, and, in certain disciplines, disagreements among faculty members about epistemological fundamentals and thus about what doctoral programs should teach. If a serious attempt were to be made to increase the effectiveness of graduate programs, more financial support would be needed, and departments would need to reconsider the design and organization of their doctoral programs. These conclusions resulted in the GEI being focused on departments—a major departure from both individual fellowship support and support given to universities.

Furthermore, these programmatic changes were to be linked to funding decisions, so that students could be considered for funding if they met the expectations their departments had instituted, including time-

---

[15] David Breneman later did a thorough review of the Ford program and noted the absence of any attention to attrition—in his view, an opportunity lost. See Bowen and Rudenstine (1992), especially pp. 212–14, on the Ford program.

[16] Ibid., pp. 146–47, 216.

tables for achieving specified steps toward the degree. Funding was to be "conditional," not guaranteed; competition was to prevail among students. This, it was thought, would motivate all students, even those who failed to receive support.

Taken together, such changes, Bowen and Rudenstine reasoned, could reduce attrition (especially late attrition) and shorten average TTD. These are not simply matters of academic bookkeeping. Rather, high attrition rates and long TTD clearly countered the interests of degree seekers. It was less often recognized that they also countered the interests of universities. In both instances, individuals and institutions were making large investments in graduate education that were not yielding their desired outcomes. With the approval of the Foundation's board of trustees, the decision was made to use Mellon's resources to undertake an intervention that, if it proved successful, might be used by others seeking to improve the "effectiveness" of graduate programs. That the GEI might also increase the number of PhDs who graduated from leading programs would be beneficial as well, since such an outcome would contribute to solving the faculty staffing problem at U.S. universities that was projected to occur at the end of the 1990s. It would be "a sensible way to begin to prepare," and even if these projections did not materialize (and we now know they did not), the GEI would nonetheless have highly positive outcomes.[17] Furthermore, because making significant changes in the academy almost always takes time, it was anticipated at the outset that the GEI would operate for 10 years, that is, unless it became evident after five years that it was going seriously awry.

The Foundation invited 10 universities to participate in the GEI. All were promised annual grants that would be applied to increasing financial aid for students in departments they chose and for other improvements aimed at reducing attrition and increasing completion. For their part, the universities and the departments would have to agree to propose plans for redesigned graduate programs.

The recipient universities were selected using one apparently simple criterion. They were to be the 10 universities that had attracted the largest number of winners of the Mellon Foundation's much-sought-after portable fellowships in the humanities. This single criterion was in fact highly correlated with important institutional attributes. It reflected the preferences of carefully vetted Mellon fellows who, owing to the terms of

---

[17] Ibid., p. 289. That jobs remained scarce throughout the period of the GEI was a source of some resentment among students and faculty members who believed the Bowen and Sosa projections and were disappointed to find they did not prove out. "Why hurry" they countered, "when the jobs aren't there?" In Chapter 9, we review the validity of this conclusion and find it erroneous.

the fellowship, could choose to go to any university that would accept them, since their tuition and living costs were covered.[18] The fellows' choices were to serve as a "market test." Excellent students would "vote with their feet" and select the universities they considered most desirable for graduate study. The 10 universities were the universities of California at Berkeley, Chicago, Michigan, and Pennsylvania, and Columbia, Cornell, Harvard, Princeton, Stanford, and Yale universities. That these universities were also generally thought to have first-rate faculties, demanding programs of study, and alumni who had contributed significantly to their disciplines was consistent with using the Mellon fellows' preferences in choosing the GEI participants. Although the graduates of these 10 universities (and of the three added for the purposes of having a control group in the study) seemed to constitute a small slice of those earning doctoral degrees in the humanities, this was not the case. These 13 institutions graduated 18 percent of all PhDs awarded in the humanities, far more than their share of the total number of doctoral programs.

Once selected, the participating universities were invited to nominate four to six departments in the humanities to receive GEI awards. The universities and departments that agreed to participate in the GEI were asked to determine not only how they wished to use the funds the Foundation awarded to them but also how their programs should be changed. Such changes were to be tailored to the needs of the departments and their universities. Inasmuch as most participating departments developed their own strategies (or "treatments") to improve their PhD programs, it was understood that treatments would vary considerably across departments.[19] Moreover, it was understood that they would also vary over time, as strategies that appeared to be working would be continued, those that appeared counterproductive would be discontinued, and new strategies might be adopted. Giving the participants such latitude was consistent with the Foundation's general policies of not interfering with grantees, but, as we shall indicate, the GEI was far from a uniform intervention. Rather it involved a great array of programmatic changes, thus making an assessment of its effects quite problematic.

However, the programmatic changes the departments and universities undertook, although highly varied, had to be consistent with the general objectives of the GEI and its guidelines. Putting a high priority on im-

---

[18] The Mellon Fellowships in the Humanities provided multiyear support but did not cover all years in graduate school. Universities usually supplemented them so that fellows could count on full support.

[19] In Chapter 3 we note that the plans submitted by all departments at certain universities were the same, while at other universities they varied. We assumed that university administrators in the first instance were more directive than in the second.

proving effectiveness, lowering attrition, shrinking TTD, redesigning programs, and funding graduate students in line with helping them move expeditiously toward completion of their degrees were not matters for negotiation. Furthermore, agreeing to provide data annually on a predetermined set of indicators was a quid pro quo for participation. At the same time, it was understood that participants retained control over what was taught, the criteria to be used in judging students' work, how professors would supervise their students, and how university administrators were to decide on policies relevant to the GEI.

Did these terms undermine the independence of the universities involved? Were they excessively prescriptive, even "bullying," as foundations are sometimes accused of being?[20] We think not. Not only was the Foundation flexible in approving university decisions that did not quite comply with the "rules" (for example, permitting fellowships to be awarded after the sixth-year deadline if students had to master multiple languages or spend long periods on the field), there was no compulsion that departments participate—although the desire to improve the funding students could receive was surely a powerful incentive to universities and departments to comply. It will become evident that some faculty members continued to be at best ambivalent about and at worst resistant to the objectives of the GEI and the means of achieving its objectives— signs of the freedom faculty members enjoyed in pursuing their work as they saw fit. In light of a widespread sense that foundations use their resources to achieve ends to which they (rather than their grantees) are committed, calling attention to the very considerable leeway the grantees had in designing the GEI according to their particular requirements, and the primary roles institutions and departments had in how it functioned, seems to the point.

The details of data collection for the GEI are reviewed in Chapter 2. Since they are an integral part of the GEI's history and rationale, we also summarize them here. From the beginning of the GEI, measurement of the intervention's effects would be central to the enterprise. The Foundation wished to keep abreast of how the intervention was proceeding so that adjustments, if needed, could be made along the way. It also wished

---

[20] Charles T. Clotfelter, "Patron or Bully? The Role of Foundations in Higher Education," in Ray Bacchetti and Thomas Ehrlich, eds., *Reconnecting Education and Foundations: Turning Good Intentions into Educational Capital* (San Francisco: Jossey-Bass, 2006), pp. 211–48. See also the early critique of private foundations by Waldemar A. Nielsen, *The Big Foundations* (New York: Columbia University Press, 1972). A recent book in a similar genre is Bill Somerville with Fred Setterberg, *Grassroots Philanthropy: Notes of a Maverick Grantmaker* (Berkeley, CA: Heyday, 2008). A more sober essay on foundations is Joel L. Fleishman, *The Foundation: A Great American Secret—How Private Wealth Is Changing the World* (New York: Public Affairs, 2007).

to let the participants know how they were doing and, more important, wanted them to gather relevant information so that, when the time came for an assessment of the GEI's successes and failures, others in the future might benefit from what had been learned.

The assessment would examine the effects of the GEI on attrition and TTD, as well as changes in the organization of graduate programs that might be responsible for any observed effects. With this in mind, annual data were collected by the institutions and provided to the Foundation on all PhD students that entered the 54 departmental PhD programs that the 10 universities had chosen as participants. Descriptive data were collected annually on every student's progress in each of these departments until each of them had graduated or terminated his or her studies. The data collection covered the 10 years prior to the start of the GEI, during its tenure, and up through 2006. Information, made suitably anonymous by using identification numbers in place of the names of entering students, was gathered on their background characteristics (their Graduate Record Examination [GRE] test scores, gender, race and ethnicity, citizenship, and prior master's degrees). The universities also reported on the types of financial support that students received each year they were pursuing the doctorate and their academic status each year (left, continued, or graduated).

Moreover, soon after the GEI began, the Foundation realized the need for data on a set of control departments (in order to determine whether changes observed during the GEI period were in fact attributable to the Initiative or were the result of events affecting other departments and universities as well). Similar data were then collected for all students who were enrolled in PhD programs at a set of 47 control departments during the same period. Some of these control departments were at the 10 universities at which the GEI was already in place; the rest were at three other universities that were of comparable academic standing but had not received funding from the GEI: the University of California at Los Angeles, the University of California at San Diego, and the University of North Carolina at Chapel Hill.

In 2002 and 2003, having assembled institutional data on students' progress over two decades, along with the often-revealing annual reports from each participating department, it became abundantly clear to the Foundation that these in and of themselves were insufficient for understanding how the GEI worked. The decision was made to conduct a survey (the Graduate Education Survey [GES]) to obtain the views of all doctoral students who began their study in departments participating in the GEI and in control departments between 1982 and 1997. It would tell far more than we knew about students' experiences in graduate school, their assessments of the education they received, and their employment after leaving graduate school, either with the degree or without it. Not only did the GES achieve a remarkably high response rate of 74 percent, it provided data on aspects of doctoral education never studied before on such a scale or with such precision.

RECENT RESEARCH AND EFFORTS
TO IMPROVE GRADUATE EDUCATION

The GEI and the research on which this book is based did not occur in a vacuum. Earlier research (for example, on rates of attrition and its determinants as well as on TTD) influenced the GEI and its design. Similarly, in the 15 years since the GEI began, some of the other efforts made to improve graduate education have been shaped by the GEI. To place this book in context, we briefly summarize those interventions and publications most pertinent to the GEI's objectives.

Maresi Nerad and her colleagues, first at the University of California at Berkeley and later at the University of Washington, have been studying the post-PhD employment of degree recipients, potential improvements in doctoral education throughout the period, and the opinions of former students about the value of their graduate programs, using administrative data, surveys of doctoral recipients, and interviews of students, faculty, and administrators.[21] Their work has highlighted the important roles played by financial support, department culture, advising, and the setting of clear expectations for students. Their surveys of doctoral recipients in a number of fields have provided information on the life-cycle employment patterns of doctoral recipients, although so far their publications have not reported on the educational and employment experiences of doctoral candidates who failed to earn their degrees.[22]

---

[21] See, for example, Maresi Nerad, *Doctoral Education at the University of California and Factors Affecting Time-to-Degree* (Oakland, CA: Office of the President of the University of California, 1991); Maresi Nerad and Debra Miller, "Increasing Student Retention in Graduate and Professional Programs," *New Directions for Institutional Research* 92 (Winter 1996): 61–76; and Nerad and Miller, "The Institution Cares: Berkeley's Efforts to Support Doctoral Students in the Humanities and Social Sciences with Their Dissertations," *New Directions for Higher Education* 99 (Fall 1997): 75–90.

[22] Maresi Nerad and Joseph Cerny, "From Rumors to Facts: Career Outcomes of English Ph.D.s," *Communicator* 32 (Fall 1999): 1–11; Nerad and Cerny, "Improving Doctoral Education: Recommendations from the 'Ph.D.s Ten Years Later' Study," *Communicator* 33 (March 2000): 6; Nerad and Cerny, "Postdoctoral Appointments and Employment Patterns of Science and Engineering Doctoral Recipients Ten-Plus Years after Ph.D. Completion: Selected Results from the 'Ph.D.s Ten Years Later' Study," *Communicator* 35 (August–September 2002): 1–11; and Renate Sadrozinski, Maresi Nerad, and Joseph Cerny, *PhDs in*

A number of economists, including the first author of this book, have tried to model formally the role that financial factors play in influencing attrition and TTD and then to estimate the magnitudes of these relationships.[23] Empirical studies have also been undertaken on graduate education in the United States and abroad.[24] *The Education of Historians for the Twenty-First Century*, a comprehensive study conducted by the American Historical Association's Committee on Graduate Education, includes the results of a survey of graduate history departments.[25] The findings the committee reports mirror many of those in this book, concerning, for example, predoctoral examinations, program size, funding, and departmental culture, while also taking up subjects we do not address, such as professionalization and premature professionalization of graduate students, graduate assistants and unions, new technologies, teacher training, and interdisciplinarity and theory.

Other research has focused particularly on attrition and its causes. Chris Golde's studies draw on interviews, specifically with 68 doctoral students who failed to complete their degrees. Eighty-five percent of them studied in four departments (biology, English, geology, and history) at one major university.[26] In one paper, she describes interviews with three students in great detail and points to the effects of students' failure to be integrated into the academic and social life of their departments on their departures from graduate school.[27] Advising, or lack of it, also played an important role in each case.

Barbara Lovitts's work on the causes of attrition draws attention to the social structure of graduate programs and especially to the lack of opportunities students have for integration into their departments. She also

---

Art History: Over a Decade Later (Seattle, WA: Center for Research and Innovation in Graduate Education, 2003).

[23] Ronald G. Ehrenberg and Pangiotis G. Mavros, "Do Doctoral Students' Financial Support Patterns Affect Their Times-to-Degree and Completion Probabilities?" *Journal of Human Resources* 30 (September 1995): 581–609.

[24] Eskil Wadensjö, "Recruiting a New Generation," in Lars Engwall, ed., *Economics in Sweden: An Evaluation of Swedish Research in Economics* (London: Routledge, 1992), pp. 67–103. See p. 83 for information on the very, very long average TTD in Sweden in that field.

[25] Thomas Bender, Phillip M. Katz, Colin Palmer, and the Committee on Graduate Education of the American Historical Association, *The Education of Historians for the Twenty-First Century* (Urbana: University of Illinois Press, 2004).

[26] Chris M. Golde, "How Departmental Contextual Factors Shape Doctoral Student Attrition," PhD dissertation, School of Education, Stanford University, 1996, and Golde, "The Role of the Department and the Discipline in Doctoral Student Attrition: Lessons from Four Departments," *Journal of Higher Education* 76 (November–December 2005): 669–700.

[27] Chris M. Golde, "Should I Stay or Should I Go? Student Descriptions of the Doctoral Attrition Process," *Review of Higher Education* 23 (Fall 2000): 199–227.

contends that high attrition rates are not due to admission of students incapable of earning the degree. A sociologist, Lovitts surveyed over 800 students at two universities, including those who completed degrees and those who had not. She also carried out interviews with those who left school and with a sample of faculty members.[28] In subsequent research, she focused on obstacles students encounter in writing the dissertation and stressed the importance of faculty members making explicit to their students the implicit criteria used in assessing dissertations.[29]

In a study of doctoral students at 21 universities, Michael Nettles and Catherine Millett surveyed 9,000 who had completed at least a year of doctoral study in 1997, and they combined these data with entries in dissertation abstracts and the Survey of Earned Doctorates and with data from the 21 universities to determine which of these students had earned degrees by 2001.[30] Based on their survey data, they identified a number of the themes that are addressed in this volume: the role of financial support in completion of the degree, the importance of socialization, students' research productivity while enrolled in doctoral programs, TTD, completion rates, and group differences in outcomes. Students who had dropped out prior to the start of their second year were excluded from Nettles and Millett's sample, and thus they could not analyze the determinants of early attrition. The study provided no information on the experiences students had after completing their degrees or after leaving graduate school.

With the support of a number of private foundations, the National Research Council (NRC) and the Council of Graduate Schools (CGS) have been deeply involved in research on doctoral education. As earlier worries about long TTD began to be overshadowed by or joined with concerns about high rates of attrition, CGS's annual meetings became a venue for presentations of research on attrition and its relationship to admissions.[31] These concerns led to the organization of two national workshops on the study of attrition and the factors that might contribute to it. The first, sponsored by the NRC in 1996, was followed quickly by the second, held in 1997 and sponsored by the National Science Foundation.[32] A third workshop was part of the process of designing the CGS's PhD

---

[28] Barbara E. Lovitts, *Leaving the Ivory Tower* (Lanham, MD: Rowman and Littlefield, 2001).

[29] Barbara E. Lovitts, *Making the Implicit Explicit: Creating Performance Expectations for the Dissertation* (Sterling, VA: Stylus, 2007).

[30] Michael T. Nettles and Catherine M. Millett, *Three Magic Letters: Getting to Ph.D.* (Baltimore, MD: Johns Hopkins University Press, 2006).

[31] Peter Diffley, "Selection and Attrition," *Communicator* 38 (November 2005): 3–8.

[32] National Research Council, *The Path to the Ph.D.: Measuring Graduate Attrition in the Sciences and the Humanities* (Washington, DC: National Academies Press, 1996), and Alan I.

Completion Project; it focused on identifying the data necessary for studying and monitoring attrition and for a better understanding of factors associated with it.[33] A fourth workshop, organized in 2005 by the Center for Education at the NRC, concentrated exclusively on the effects of financial aid on the quality of doctoral education received by students in science, technology, engineering, and medicine.[34]

Intended to answer the fundamental question of the purpose served by graduate education, the Carnegie Initiative on the Doctorate (CID) was a five-year project sponsored by the Carnegie Foundation for the Advancement of Teaching and paid for by the Atlantic Philanthropies. Begun in 2002, the CID encouraged 84 departments in six fields (chemistry, education, English, history, mathematics, and neuroscience) to reconsider the functions served by graduate education and to align them more effectively with the requirements they impose in graduate training and the practices they follow. Beginning with the supposition that the fundamental purpose of doctoral education was to create *stewards of the discipline*—people "who will creatively generate new knowledge, critically conserve valuable and useful ideas, and responsibly transform those understandings through writing, teaching and application"—the participating departments were asked to think critically about what they do and why they do it, and to identify changes that should be made to educate stewards of their disciplines and to build "intellectual communities."[35] Furthermore, they were asked to institute program changes consistent with their goals and to devise and assess the changes they made that would lead to strategies to improve doctoral education both in participating departments and more generally. One important product of the CID is a set of critical essays by distinguished leaders in each of the six fields on their views about the future of doctoral education and its evolution.[36] Future publications from the Carnegie Foundation will summarize the results of this effort.

Rapoport, *Summary of a Workshop on Graduate Student Attrition* (Washington, DC: National Science Foundation, December 1998).

[33] Council of Graduate Schools, *Ph.D. Completion/Attrition Workshop* (Airlie, VA, April 2003).

[34] National Research Council, Center for Education, Workshop on "STEM Doctoral Students: How Finance Mechanisms Influence the Quality of Their Education," Washington, DC, June 22, 2005.

[35] Chris M. Golde, "Preparing Stewards of the Discipline," in Chris M. Golde and George E. Walker, eds., *Envisioning the Future of Doctoral Education: Preparing Stewards of the Discipline* (San Francisco: Jossey-Bass, 2006), pp. 3–22.

[36] Chris M. Golde and George E. Walker, eds., *Envisioning the Future of Doctoral Education: Preparing Stewards of the Discipline* (San Francisco: Jossey-Bass, 2006).

Finally, in 2002, CGS began its PhD Completion Project. The fundamental assumptions on which this project is based are (1) that the vast majority of students entering PhD programs have the academic ability to complete degrees and (2) that the high attrition rates endemic in graduate education are to a large extent due to institutional factors, that is, to those which administrators and faculty members can control. These include the selection and admission of students, mentoring and advising, financial support and its structure, programs' social environments, research experiences, and curricular processes and procedures—many of these being factors that the GEI also emphasized. The CGS project has been supported at various stages by the Ford Foundation, the National Science Foundation, Pfizer Inc., and the Alfred P. Sloan Foundation.

Unlike the GEI, which focuses on departments, the focus of the CGS project is on graduate schools and graduate deans and the roles that they can play in fostering intervention strategies to improve doctoral education in the fields of science, engineering, and mathematics as well as in the humanities and social sciences. A total of 45 universities are involved either in creating intervention strategies and pilot programs, in evaluating the impact of these programs, or as research partners.[37] One recent publication from the CGS project presents data on 10- and 7-year completion and attrition rates based on data submitted by 24 of the participating universities on cohorts of students who entered their PhD programs between 1992–93 and 1997–98.[38] A second publication summarizes what is known about attrition and completion and addresses policies that might be effective in reducing the former and increasing the latter.[39] Evidently, interest in the effectiveness of doctoral programs and in the broader issue of their objectives has only increased since the beginning of the GEI; much remains to be learned about these subjects.

SUMMARY OF PRINCIPAL FINDINGS

This volume describes the effects of the GEI on students' careers in graduate school, on the progress they made (or did not), and on the gradu-

[37] The project, which has been shepherded by CGS President Debra Stewart, is described at http://www.phdcompletion.org and in Daniel D. Denecke, Helen S. Frasier, and Kenneth E. Redd, "The Council of Graduate Schools' Ph.D. Completion Project," in Ronald G. Ehrenberg and Charlotte V. Kuh, eds., *Doctoral Education and the Faculty of the Future* (Ithaca, NY: Cornell University Press, 2008), pp. 35–52.

[38] Council of Graduate Schools, *Ph.D. Completion and Attrition: Analysis of Baseline Demographic Data from the Ph.D. Completion Project* (Washington, DC, 2008).

[39] Council of Graduate Schools, *Ph.D. Completion and Attrition: Policy, Numbers, Leadership, and Next Steps* (Washington, DC, 2004).

ate programs of the participating departments. Drawing on the data the
13 universities provided and on students' responses to the GES, we also
take up the effects on their careers during and after graduate school of
three large-scale developments affecting graduate education in the humanities: the deteriorating job market, the intensification of competition
among graduate departments for students deemed most promising, and
changes in financial-aid regimes. When our analyses draw on statistical
models, technical details are relegated to an appendix. The book is intended to be accessible to a broad range of readers interested in the humanities and graduate education while also meeting appropriate standards of analytic rigor.

In describing our findings here and in the remainder of the book, readers will note that we often use causal language in describing the outcomes
of statistical analysis; for example, we remark that increased financial aid
"led to" reductions in attrition. Such statements are, strictly speaking,
probabilistic, not causal, although in places we do try to infer causality.
Readers who are unfamiliar with this kind of analysis may find it helpful
to remember that high correlations do not definitively prove that a causal
relationship exists, but that the chances it does are great if we have ap-
propriately modeled the process that led to our estimating equations.

The book addresses a host of questions about doctoral education in the
humanities in major universities and the students who study for the doctoral degree. In Chapter 12, we draw together the main findings reported
in the chapters that follow. Here we report only those we think are of particular importance.

First, did the GEI and the changes in graduate programs that it stimulated produce higher rates of completion and lower rates of attrition?
Based on careful statistical analysis, the answer is yes. Completion rates
rose and attrition rates declined, on average. However, changes we observed in the GEI departments can be understood properly only if we
compare them to changes occurring at the same time in departments we
chose to serve as controls. It turned out that changes in the GEI departments were only modestly better than those in the control departments.
We also found that some GEI departments did very well on these measures of effectiveness and some did quite poorly, raising questions about
why the GEI was so effective in some departments but not in others. Did
students who earned degrees under the GEI regime earn them more
quickly on average than those in control departments? They did, but
again the observed improvements were small. As we found with respect
to rates of completion and attrition, average TTD dropped quite dramatically in some departments but not at all in other departments. It is
clear that the next order of research business is additional analysis of the
histories of those departments that achieved major improvements along

with those that retrogressed. In short, the GEI was associated with improved completion rates, lower attrition rates, and shorter TTD, but such improvements were not large and were not uniformly distributed.

What did improved financial support do for graduate students? We found that more support was associated with increased probabilities of students completing their degrees; furthermore, when we examined the outcomes of different patterns of financial support (how much of which kinds of support students receive and when), we also found that more support was associated with higher rates of completion. However, even students given the most generous financial support (holders of fellowships for many years) had high attrition rates. Hence attrition is not due exclusively to inadequate financial aid. Furthermore, we found that improved financial support clearly reduced early attrition. (By early attrition, we mean the number of students leaving between their first and fourth years.) However, we did not find that reduced attrition rates were matched by higher completion rates. Instead we found that attrition rates increased among students who were in or beyond their fifth year of graduate study. This is directly contrary to the GEI's intent of reducing attrition overall and particularly of reducing late attrition, which is costly to both students and institutions. Furthermore, we found that the percentage of students who neither graduated nor left school after their fifth year of study increased markedly. What could account for this altogether unanticipated outcome?

It would appear that the increasing prevalence of guaranteed multiyear funding (financial aid that students are promised for their first three to five years) reduced early attrition but did not increase rates of completion, nor did it shorten TTD. It is important to note that guaranteed funding is not consistent with the GEI policy of making financial aid past the first year conditional on meeting timetables—a more demanding requirement than simply achieving "satisfactory performance." Ironically, there is evidence that the GEI contributed to the spread of guaranteed packages—a second unanticipated consequence observed in our research.

The GEI had as one of its objectives the reduction of heavy teaching obligations, so common among graduate students in the humanities. Did it have this effect? It did. During the GEI, the probabilities that students would serve as assistants for six semesters or more were significantly reduced, falling more precipitously in GEI departments than in the controls. But does lengthy service as a teaching assistant (TA) contribute, as many observers think, to long TTD? It does. Serving as an assistant for six semesters or more delays completion of the degree; but, on average, the majority of students teach for fewer semesters. Moreover, in a finer-grained analysis in which we compared serving as a TA to various other financial-aid arrangements, we found that the effects of being a TA were more complicated. They depend on how long students teach, the extent and nature of their duties, what other types of financial support they receive, and in what sequence they receive that support.

We noted that attrition rates fell among students early in their graduate careers, but climbed later on. At the end of 10 years, 40 percent of students who began graduate study had left without degrees. This suggests that considerable attrition occurs between students' 5th and 10th years. Members of this group, of course, are the much-written-about ABDs, or those leaving with "all but dissertation." Whether one describes them as numerous or not depends on the value put on students' time, the education they receive during graduate study, and the institutional resources they consume. Our research indicates that attrition rates overestimate the actual extent of attrition: 31 percent of those counted as having left graduate school earned PhDs or other professional degrees, and an additional 50 percent finished with master's degrees—some no doubt awarded "in course" (automatically awarded for passing candidacy) but valuable nonetheless on the job market. Moreover, it is no surprise that, given their abilities, the employment experiences of those who leave graduate school depart substantially from the stereotype of the unemployed or taxi-driving graduate-school dropout. Three years after leaving school, their employment rate topped 96 percent, and most had professional or managerial jobs.

Finally, in exploring the employment of those who received degrees, the deteriorating job market is in clear evidence in the employment histories of successive cohorts of PhDs. Fewer and fewer of them received tenure-track positions upon leaving graduate school. However, the majority of those who started out in non-tenure-track positions found tenure-track positions in three years' time, and the chances of their doing so have not changed with time. However, the combination of shrinking probabilities of finding tenure-track jobs immediately and the stable probabilities of moving into them later means that successively smaller proportions of graduates managed to get on the tenure track three years after earning their degrees.

Are those who finish their PhDs quickly more likely to get better jobs? Or are PhDs in these fields like good wine, in that they take time to become fully mature and productive scholars? Again, this apparently simple question does not have a simple answer. Students who finish their degrees in five or six years do no better in the job market, and are no more likely to get tenure-track jobs, than those who finish in seven years. However, PhDs in the humanities (unlike good wine, apparently) do not improve after seven years: those who finished in more than seven years were less likely than faster completers to obtain tenure-track positions.

And finally, did the programmatic changes associated with the GEI make any difference in completion and attrition rates and TTD? They did, but, taken one at a time, their effects were not strong. At the same time, students who reported on the GES that departmental expectations were clear—that they were told how long the degree should take and what requirements they must meet—were significantly more likely to finish. By contrast, those who reported that their departments' expectations were unknown or ambiguous were more apt to leave. Furthermore, the data speak to the significant role faculty members play in students' careers. The presence of particular faculty members influences where students elect to study; students who reported that a faculty member was interested in their work had a higher probability of finishing, as did those who benefited, in their view, from good advising. Conversely, those who said advising was poor were more apt to leave. Were these instances of retrospective rationalization or of truth telling? Probably some of each.

A READER'S GUIDE TO *EDUCATING SCHOLARS*

Chapter 2 presents the data on which this study is based and the methods of analysis that we have used. The institutional and survey databases are described as are various measures and their relative benefits. (A listing of the variables gathered from the institutions is provided in Appendix A, a copy of the survey instrument is provided in Appendix B, and a detailed description of the measures, their calculation, and recommended uses is given in Appendix C.) Chapter 3 introduces the departments that participated in the GEI and were central in the intervention. It shows how similar they were at the outset in certain respects and how much they differed in others. It also recounts in some detail the history of the GEI in six illustrative departments. Since most departments were given considerable leeway in introducing changes (what we later call "innovations") they themselves considered most useful, and since they were encouraged to emphasize in their annual reports the pitfalls they encountered, we had the opportunity to determine whether the GEI "worked" and which innovations among many the departments made had actually improved effectiveness.

Chapter 4 reports the outcomes of our analyses of the GEI's influence on rates of attrition and completion and on TTD. Since some of the control departments were located at the same universities as the treatment departments, we were concerned that "treatment contamination" might have occurred. Were control departments at the 10 universities subject to some of the same influences as the treatment departments, and was there

evidence that the control departments emulated the treatment departments? If so, our findings on the effects of the GEI would understate its
real influence. We address that issue in this chapter.

Patterns of financial support received by students, both prior to and
during the GEI, are the subject of Chapter 5. The roles that different
types of financial support (fellowships, assistantships, and other assistance) play in determining attrition and completion probabilities are analyzed in this chapter.

In Chapter 6, we turn to analyses of the survey data on students' ap-
praisals of their PhD programs. We use these data to analyze the effects
the GEI had on students' perceptions of their departments. The GES data
are then merged with data provided by the institutions (data that are analyzed in the previous two chapters) in order to identify those characteristics of graduate programs that influenced the probabilities that students
would leave or graduate.

We find that students' attrition and completion probabilities depend
not only on the financial support that they receive but also on a group of
programmatic attributes that presumably can be changed at relatively low
cost. Hence the analysis in this chapter provides a road map of relatively
inexpensive changes that can be made by those interested in reducing
students' rates of attrition and increasing their rates of completion.

Chapter 7 addresses a matter of continuing concern among students,
their professors, and administrators. Do marriage and childbearing affect
the chances men and women have of completing their degrees and of doing so promptly? Although these questions are not at issue in the GEI,
they are important. As a result, we made sure the student survey would
yield data on students' marital status when they entered graduate school
and whether they had children at the time. In light of the increasing numbers of women earning PhDs in all fields and their very significant rep-
resentation in the humanities, having an understanding of the relationships linking gender, marital status, and parenthood and the collective
impact of all three on completion and TTD is likely to become increasingly important in the years ahead. Gender differences on average favor
men, but we find these differences are due solely to the fact that married
men do better than single men and single women. Marriage benefits men
but does not do the same for women.

Chapter 8 presents data on attrition and its timing. Drawing on our survey data, we explore the reasons why it occurs and its effects on those who
experience it. As far as we are aware, these data on post-attrition educational and occupational achievement of former graduate students are
unique. We describe the reasons they gave for leaving graduate school
and what happened to them afterward. Of some interest is that the oc-

cupational achievements of those who left doctoral programs long after having begun are no worse or better than the achievements of those who left early on.

The early-career outcomes of PhD recipients in the humanities are addressed in Chapter 9. It examines the determinants of PhDs' chances of getting on the tenure track immediately after earning the degree, including the roles played by TTD and having published during graduate school. Having published increases a PhD's chances of getting a tenure-track position within three years of the degree. But taking as long as eight years to get the degree (or longer) has the opposite effect; it reduces the chances of getting a tenure-track position within three years of graduation.

Since a prime goal of PhD programs is to prepare graduate students to contribute to the production of knowledge, Chapter 10 analyzes the publication records of PhDs in the humanities while they were in graduate school and during their early careers. Not explicitly part of the GEI, the extent to which students publish is nonetheless of interest in light of its possible contribution to long TTD. We found variation in rates of publication among ethnic and racial groups as well as between U.S. citizens and foreign-born students, and we provide some explanations for them.

Chapter 11 deals with the challenges encountered in implementing and evaluating the GEI. We have learned more than we anticipated about how interventions in graduate education should be introduced and about some of the pitfalls that develop in the process. The wisdom we have gleaned is summarized for those who seek to make changes of the sort that this book describes.

The concluding chapter, Chapter 12, summarizes our findings about the effects of the GEI and the lessons they hold more generally for doctoral education in the humanities. It highlights the implications our findings have for future efforts to improve graduate education, not only in the humanities but in other fields, and for attempts to evaluate them.

PART I

Data, Methods, and Context

CHAPTER 2

Data Collection, Outcome Measures, and Analytical Tools

> The need for such "demonstration" [of com-
> pliance with the GEI guidelines] will require us,
> in turn, to strengthen our [own] data gathering
> and analytic capabilities on graduate student
> progress and degree completion, a commitment
> of staff resources and energies to institutional re-
> search that we are pleased to make for such a
> purpose . . . and will pose a continuous prod to
> our academic departments to reexamine their
> policies and expectations with regard to time-to-
> doctorate and to take positive steps to reduce it
> among their students.
> —Provost at University X, 1996

THIS CHAPTER describes the raw materials on which this study is based, the measures it uses, and the analytic procedures it employs. It is divided into three parts. First, it focuses on the varieties of data on which the study draws. It spells out how the quantitative data on students and the qualitative reports from faculty members and administrators were collected. Part and parcel of the Graduate Education Initiative (GEI), these data constitute a substantial share of the evidence on which this study draws. This part also describes the Graduate Education Survey (GES) of students that was intended to complement the heavily demographic and descriptive data collected from the GEI's institutional participants. The results of the survey shed light on graduate students' experiences as they moved through their training. The second part of the chapter takes up an array of potential measures of students' progress and how they are calculated. It suggests uses that can be made of these measures (and their limitations) in order to facilitate the work of others who may wish to judge for themselves aspects of graduate education that are addressed here. Finally a brief introduction is provided to the principal statistical techniques we use in the study, aimed at readers who are unfamiliar with them.

DATA COLLECTION: QUANTITATIVE AND QUALITATIVE

The GEI differed markedly from other interventions in graduate education quite apart from the attention it gave to departments. Its design was
shaped by empirical research, its ongoing execution was monitored by
annual data collection, and its assessment has been heavily data driven.
Furthermore, unlike the majority of such interventions, assessment did
not wait until the Initiative ended. Statistical analysis was done annually
so that the Foundation and the participants were continually kept informed about what was happening. As we noted, baseline data were gathered for pre-GEI cohorts beginning in 1980. Furthermore, the universities agreed to provide various kinds of information each year, including
detailed accounts of the progress made by every student who entered GEI
departments through 2006—a full 15 years after the GEI began—to allow sufficient time for its effects to be registered accurately.

From the outset it was clear that the reporting and storage of data
would have to meet strict standards of confidentiality. All reports from
the universities on individual students came to the Foundation stripped
of students' names. For its part, the Foundation pledged that data would
not be published unless it was sufficiently aggregated that no individual
could be identified. Protection of privacy extended in the same way to
students' responses to the GES. Respondents were promised that their
identities would be protected in connection with any information provided to their home departments or institutions. The Foundation also
pledged that data on individual departments or universities would not be
published in any way that would make them identifiable.

Data Provided Annually by Departments and Institutions

When students began graduate school, descriptive information was
recorded on their GRE scores, the institutions from which they obtained
their bachelor's degrees, and the dates of their undergraduate degrees.
Then annual reports were submitted on students' academic progress, including the key outcome variables: completion, attrition, and time-to-
degree (TTD). (See Appendixes A and C for a complete list of individual
descriptors and outcome variables.) The universities were also asked to
report annually on the financial support they provided to the departments in the form of student aid. This information was requested in part
to make sure the GEI was incremental rather than substitutional support
and in part to keep track of the total amount of aid departments and students were receiving. In return, the Foundation provided the universities
with annual detailed statistical summaries on each of their participating

departments and comparisons with departments in the same fields at other universities.

From 1991 onward, departments—usually department heads or directors of graduate studies—responded to questions the Foundation raised about their PhD programs, about the changes they were making and how they were faring in realizing plans to reshape their programs.[1] Assembling information about departmental efforts was necessary if effects were to be assessed and the successes identified, as would be the case in testing any prototype. As a consequence, Mellon staff went to considerable effort to capture in detail all program changes or "innovations" made over the course of the GEI and then to summarize them so that effects could be compared. Chapter 3 reviews these innovations in detail and describes the experiences of six departments as they instituted the GEI. (In particular, see Table 3.7 and the associated discussion.)

As in all efforts to introduce change, there were discrepancies between what the actors (here, the departments) said that they planned to do and what they actually did—not surprising, since the GEI was such a long-term proposition. These discrepancies are also described in Chapter 3.[2] The vignettes presented there illustrate how creative and committed many faculty members and students were in trying to improve graduate education, along with the disappointments, failures, and frustrations some faculty members experienced in instituting the GEI and in response to it. They also recount the encouragement and support some senior administrators lent to their departments and the GEI.

Initially, the impact of the GEI on attrition rates and TTD was to be gauged by comparing outcomes for students who had enrolled in doctoral programs in the prior decade to those for students who enrolled in these programs after the GEI began. This standard pre-post design took appropriate account of the large differences in starting points that existed among departments before the GEI was put in place. It made intellectual and organizational sense not to compare departments to one another, but only to their own prior performance. However, it did not take long to realize that observed changes in, say, attrition rates or TTD could be attributable to circumstances other than the GEI that affected graduate education at large. The circumstance cited most often to account for

---

[1] Foundation staff were well aware that these reports reflected the aspirations, preferences, and idiosyncrasies of the faculty members who wrote them. Nonetheless they proved remarkably informative—and many were engaging reading as well.

[2] Students' perceptions of the changes that departments made also differed from what the departments said they were doing. In the next section we discuss the GES that was undertaken for the Foundation in 2002 and 2003 to obtain, among other things, direct information on students' perceptions of their doctoral programs.

lower-than-hoped-for completion rates and longer TTD was the deteriorating labor market for PhDs in the humanities. Clearly the effect of this
large-scale external influence could not be estimated using the pre-post
comparison. A design that compared the GEI departments with others in
the same fields that were not its beneficiaries was needed if the effects of
these larger changes were to be taken into account.

As a result, the Foundation returned to the 10 universities for additional
data on students in departments in the humanities that were *not* participating in the GEI, that is, those that neither received GEI funding nor had
made changes in their programs but which shared the same university context. These departments, following standard experimental nomenclature,
were labeled "control" or "comparison" departments, whereas the GEI beneficiaries were labeled "treatment" or "participating" departments. Comparing the progress students made in treatment and in control departments, when holding constant other variables that might be expected to
influence measured outcomes but that differ across departments and over
time, would, we thought, give us a means of gauging the effects of the GEI.[3]

Just five of the GEI universities had sufficiently detailed information on
control departments and agreed to provide it. The historical records of
the other five were simply not up to the task. Persuaded that it was critical to have data on a sufficient number of students who could serve as
controls, the Foundation sought information from other universities that
had not received Mellon funds but that had contributed significantly to
the production of PhDs in the humanities. Not all that were asked had
the required data, but three were able to provide it: the University of California at Los Angeles, the University of California at San Diego, and the
University of North Carolina at Chapel Hill.[4] This procedure for assembling a control group was far from perfect, but it was better than having
control data limited to the five institutions with both treatment and control departments.

Table 2.1 lists the 54 treatment departments and programs that participated in the GEI and the 47 comparison programs that were identi-

---

[3] In later chapters we consider the effects of "diffusion" of the GEI on the outcomes of
treatment and control departments. For example, some deans and provosts became such
enthusiastic supporters of the GEI that they intentionally improved conditions in departments that were not directly benefiting from the GEI. They provided additional internal
funds to nonparticipating departments in exchange for these departments making GEI-like
changes in their programs. Foundation staff were pleased by these efforts to spread the effects of the GEI. At the same time, it became evident that we had to determine if our estimates of the effects of the GEI were influenced by such "treatment contamination."

[4] One of the three institutions needed and received a small sum of money to defray the
cost of limited data collection; otherwise the control data were provided gratis.

fied after the Initiative began. Ideally, we would have wanted equal numbers of departments in each discipline represented in both treatment and control groups. But since 9 of the 10 GEI universities had included their English departments, and 8, their departments of history, too few departments in these important disciplines were available to serve as controls. Thus the treatment group is more heavily weighted with departments of English and history than is the control group. By contrast, six departments of comparative literature are included, only two of which are treatment departments. Table 2.1 provides information on the departmental composition of all 54 treatment and 47 control departments. After eliminating treatment departments that were too small or had no comparable controls, the analyses that follow compare data from 51 treatment and 46 control departments.[5]

Graduate Students and the Graduate Education Survey

Departmental reports on programmatic changes and on new "climates of opinion" or "cultures" were illuminating and provocative. But they could not capture systematically how students responded to the GEI, whether they understood the Initiative's intentions or took note of the associated changes departments introduced. Such information was central since the structure of the GEI depended heavily on clarifying students' expectations about the appropriate length of time for the PhD, conveying clearly the deadlines and other requirements they were to meet, indicating the strictness departments would exercise in enforcing them, and explaining the conditions affecting the allocation of financial aid. Getting a fix on students' perceptions, as well as on their progress, seemed critical to understanding whether the GEI actually worked as it was meant to. The GES grew out of the need to gauge students' expectations, to identify their perceptions of departmental requirements, and to determine what they thought about them.[6]

The survey was also an opportunity to learn more about graduate students and their experiences than the quantitative data institutions reported annually could reveal. For example, in accounting for the effects of the GEI it would be helpful to know the nature and extent of students'

---

[5] We elected to eliminate from the analyses that follow two treatment departments for which no controls could be identified (medieval studies and ethics) and the three East Asian studies programs, which had such small enrollments that they would not provide meaningful results.

[6] In order to measure the change in those perceptions, we compared the responses of students in the pre- and post-GEI cohorts.

TABLE 2.1

Treatment (T) and Comparison (C) Programs in the Graduate Education Initiative

Field (number of treatment, comparison programs)	Berkeley	Chicago	Columbia	Cornell	Harvard	Michigan[a]	Penn	Princeton	Stanford[b]	Yale	UCLA	UCSD	UNC
Anthropology (6,4)	T			C	T	T[c]		T	T	T	C	C	C
Art history (6,3)	T		T[d]	C	T	T[d,e]		C	C	T	C		C
Classics (3,5)	T			C		C	T	C		C	C		C
Comparative literature (2,4)			T	C		C		T[c]		C	C		
East Asian studies (1,2)								C		T	C		
English (9,3)	T	T	T	T	T	T	T	T	T	C	C	C	
Ethics (1,0)								T					
History (8,3)	T	T		T[d]		T	T	T[f]	T	T	C	C	C
Medieval studies (1,0)				T[d]									
Music (3,6)		T	T	C		C		C	C	T	C	C	
Philosophy (4,5)		T	T	C		T[d]		C	T	C	C	C	
Political science (4,5)				T	T		T	T	C	C	C	C	C
Religion (2,3)				C	T		T		C		C		
Romance languages (2,4)			T	C		C		T[d,g]	C				C
Total (54,47)[a]	5,0	4,0	6,0	5,7	5,0	8,3	5,0	7,5	4,5	5,5	0,11	0,6	0,5

[a]Two interdisciplinary Michigan programs—anthropology and history, and American culture—were treatment programs starting in 1997–98. These programs are reflected in the number of treatment programs at Michigan (8) and in the overall number of treatment programs (54), but they are not reflected in the totals for any of the fields shown in the table. These Michigan programs, along with Cornell's medieval studies program and Princeton's ethics program, have been excluded from the evaluation of the GEI because of a lack of control programs in these fields.

[b]Stanford departments started treatment status one year later.

[c]Ended treatment status in 1995–96.

[d]Added as a treatment program in 1996.

[e]Includes classical art and archaeology as well as art history (added as treatment program in 1996).

[f]Includes history of science.

[g]Includes German and Slavic languages.

time commitments, how much they taught, how much they worked outside their departments, and their financial circumstances apart from the funds they received from their institutions. Since reducing attrition was a key element of the GEI, the survey could provide a more nuanced account of why students left. It could also shed light on degree completion —on students' decisions on when to finish, and why. We also wanted to know how much supervision students got from their advisors and how satisfactory they found it. Finally, we were interested in learning about students' publication histories while in graduate school and afterward (publication being a significant aspect of the education of scholars) and where they worked after leaving their programs or completing their degrees.

The GES queried all PhD students who entered treatment and control departments between 1982 and 1996. The survey was designed by Foundation staff and conducted by Mathematica Policy Research.[7] Between November 2002 and October 2003, 18,320 individuals were surveyed and 13,552 responded, producing a remarkably high and reassuring response rate, for a retrospective survey, of 74 percent. (See Appendix A for further details on response rates and Appendix B for a copy of the questionnaire.)

Many of the questionnaire items that were related to students' graduate school experiences were intended to correspond to the departmental innovations reported in Table 3.7. Taken together, the institutional databases and GES results are a unique description of graduate education and graduate students in the humanities covering two decades. These data are the bases for the analyses on which we report in the chapters that follow.

OUTCOME MEASURES AND THEIR CALCULATION

Five outcome measures serve as the backbone of this study. They are calculated from data the institutions provided on individual students and were aggregated to provide information on groups of many kinds (e.g., men and women, departments, disciplines, institutions, time periods, and treatment and control groups) and degree recipients and program leavers. Two of these measures gauge the time it takes to complete the PhD, two focus on the extent and timing of attrition, and a fifth, student-year cost, calculates the "total number of years invested in doctoral study

---

[7] A more complete description of the GES, including how it was administered and how Mathematica achieved such a high response rate, is found in Laura Kalb and Emily Dwoyer, *Evaluation of the Graduate Education Initiative: Final Report* (Princeton, NJ: Mathematica Policy Research, February 27, 2004). A copy of the report is available in the library of The Andrew W. Mellon Foundation.

by all members of an entering cohort [in a department or institution or some other collectivity] divided by the number of doctorates earned by the cohort."[8] It is a means of conveying the magnitude of the costs universities incur in the process of producing a single PhD.

These measures each merit further comment because they are so central to this study. Others seeking to gauge the "effectiveness" of graduate programs may find such comments helpful since together, and separately, the measures have shortcomings that call for caution when using them to assess graduate programs. Most important among these shortcomings is that the measures fail to capture those significant outcomes of graduate study that do not lend themselves to ready quantification. A brief list of these would include the sharpening of students' analytic skills, increasing their ability to formulate questions and to differentiate between those that are important and those that are not, improving their research skills and capacity to evaluate evidence, and enhancing the clarity of their writing and speaking. These measures do not capture the mastery students gain over bodies of knowledge. They say nothing about the future scholarly prospects for graduates of these programs. And they do not begin to estimate how much universities actually invest in graduate education.

This said, in their place, these measures are useful and convey how likely students are to complete their degrees and how long it takes them to do so. They also convey something of the costs universities incur in the process. The following descriptions draw heavily on Bowen and Rudenstine's analysis.[9] Appendix C considers each measure in greater detail and describes its drawbacks, calculation, and alternate forms.

Time-to-Degree

This much-used indicator registers both the investments of time students make on average in earning their degrees and also the resources, measured in years, which institutions have invested in them. TTD can be mea-

---

[8] Bowen and Rudenstine (1992), p. 163. As they note, the approach they devised turned out to be "essentially identical" to one David Breneman proposed more than two decades earlier in his dissertation; David W. Breneman, "The Ph.D. Production Process: A Study of Departmental Behavior," Ph.D. dissertation, Department of Economics, University of California at Berkeley, 1970. This would not be the first or the last time that the same measures were created or the same discoveries made independently of one another; Robert K. Merton, "Singletons and Multiples in Science," in *The Sociology of Science: Theoretical and Empirical Investigations* (Chicago: University of Chicago Press, 1973), pp. 343–70.

[9] Bowen and Rudenstine (1992). See Chapter 6, "Completion Rates and Time-to-Degree: Concepts and General Patterns," and Chapter 9, "Student-Year Cost and Its Components."

sured three ways: by the length of time elapsed between entering graduate school and completing the degree (elapsed TTD), the time spent between earning a bachelor's degree and the PhD (total TTD), and the duration of registration of students who sought the PhD (registered TTD). Each of these measures addresses a particular aspect of TTD, and all must be calculated for members of the same entry cohorts, rather than for the same completion cohort, that is, all those who completed their degrees in a given year. TTD for completion cohorts is greatly biased by "fairly rapid and pronounced swings in the sizes of entering cohorts," a phenomenon well known to demographers but one that is only now being widely recognized by educational researchers.[10] It is much easier to collect data on completion cohorts (all one need do is average the time spent on the degree by those who present themselves for degrees at a given time), but the bias this approach introduces is not trivial. For example, Bowen concluded that calculations based on completion cohorts significantly overestimated average TTD in both the 1960s and the 1970s and also led to overestimates of increases in TTD over the decades, leading to even greater alarm than the findings justified.

All such measures (including completion and attrition measures) are affected by the comprehensiveness of the information on which they are based, even if they are calculated on entering cohorts. They are always dependent on the date of measurement since they are based only on what is known at a given time about degree recipients or school leavers. They inevitably fail to reflect the fact that cohort members who had not completed their degrees at the time the measurement was taken might do so in the future or might never finish. In this study, we use the mean TTD from matriculation to completion for specific entry cohorts. It is, for our purposes, more telling than the total interval between the bachelor's degree and the PhD or registered TTD (since some students are not registered while still working on their dissertation). We were not able to use TTD for comparisons between earlier and later cohorts since more recent cohorts will have (by definition) shorter TTD (see Appendix C). There is clearly no correct answer for how long it *should* take for graduate students to earn the PhD in the humanities or other fields. Many contingencies, such as the extent of advance preparation departments require, will affect the time spent on degrees, as will departmental demands for field work or study abroad, the number of languages students need

[10] Bowen and Rudenstine (1992), p. 116. The nature of bias introduced by changes in cohort size is thoroughly described in William G. Bowen, Graham Lord, and Julie Ann Sosa, "Measuring Time to the Doctorate: Reinterpretation of the Evidence," *Proceedings of the National Academy of Sciences USA* 88 (February 1991): 713–17, which is reproduced in Appendix D of Bowen and Rudenstine (1992).

to master, and the acquisition of other scholarly skills, such as paleography or numismatics. The GEI settled on a "norm" of six years as "reasonable" and assumed that some flexibility would be needed in the GEI's administration. As we shall see, actual TTD differed considerably from that norm in the GEI in treatment and control departments.

Cumulative Completion Rate

The cumulative completion rate measures the share of students in an entering cohort who have finished their degrees by a given year. It is a summary measure that combines information on how long students have taken to earn degrees and what share of them have done so. It shows when completion occurs and the marginal increases that occur through time. Unlike entering cohorts of medical and law students, all of whom tend to finish at one time, cohorts of graduate students complete the PhD gradually over time; this is reflected in cumulative completion rates that increase and then level off as all students who will eventually complete their degrees actually do so. This measure requires substantial investments in data collection because information must be maintained for all students in a given entering cohort. Cumulative completion rates do not permit distinctions to be drawn between the number of students who continue to be registered at a given time and have not completed their degrees and the number who have left graduate school. It is possible to calculate a truncated completion rate that indicates the share of students who finish by a given year. This measure is useful in comparing completion rates across earlier and later cohorts. An alternative measure for making comparisons across time periods is "half-life," which measures how long it takes for half of all students who entered at any given time to finish.

Time-to-Attrition and Cumulative Attrition Rate

Like TTD, time-to-attrition (TTA) should be calculated only for entry cohorts. Using the number of students who leave in a given year as the basis for the calculation will introduce bias owing to rapid swings in the size of entering cohorts, similar to the bias introduced when TTD is calculated for completion cohorts. TTA is central to this study since it matters a great deal not only what share of students ultimately leave before finishing their degrees but also how long they remain before leaving. The assumption underlying the GEI was that attrition should be reduced overall, but just as important, or even more so, was the idea that if attrition is to occur it should do so earlier in students' careers rather than later on. This view is not universally shared. There are those who believe that even students who ultimately leave graduate school after a long time benefit greatly from it. Be that as it may, TTA and cumulative attrition rates are useful indicators for universities because they signal that university resources, including financial aid, are being consumed without the degree being awarded.

Calculating TTA and cumulative attrition rates requires that data be collected for all entering students until they either leave or graduate. Although attrition, in principle, should occur only once (putting aside those limited cases of students who return after being away for decades), in practice it is an ambiguous phenomenon. Both those who leave graduate school and their institutions cannot be sure that the leaver will not return at some time in the future. And even those who believe they have left for good can sometimes change their minds and return. It can take several years for a student who has not registered to be officially declared to have left. This delay in identifying leavers often leads to underestimates of the rate of attrition, since some fraction of those considered continuing students have already left.[11] If the leavers remain in the database as continuing students and only several years later are inaccurately recorded as having left in that later year, TTA will be overstated. Truncated attrition rates can also be calculated, and they show the share of students who have left by a given year.

Student-Year Cost

Critics of long TTD and high rates of attrition point, as we have noted, not only to the costs students bear but also to the costs borne by institu-

---

[11] At the extreme, the ambiguity of attrition is institutionalized in the rules of Columbia University (and perhaps other institutions), which permits graduate students who have long been gone to return and earn their degrees "extra muros," that is, by presenting scholarly work done outside the university in place of the dissertation. "At any time within ten years from the date of the award of the M.Phil. degree and subject to approval for continuation toward the Ph.D. degree by the department or Ph.D. program chair, a recipient of the M.Phil. degree who has not continued studies in residence at the University may present to the Dean, in lieu of a sponsored dissertation, a substantial body of independent and original published scholarly material toward completion of the requirements for the Ph.D. degree. The publisher of the material must be a recognized scholarly publisher in the field, rather than a vanity press. A recipient of the M.Phil. degree who has not continued studies in residence at the University is not entitled to regular guidance or supervision by the Faculty." http://www.columbia.edu/cu/gsas/sub/dissertation/rules/extra-muros/index.html (accessed January 22, 2009).

tions for "producing" a PhD in the humanities. Long degree times reflect years of effort by faculty and staff as well as the investment of other institutional resources (financial support and facilities). Most administrators and faculty members are, of course, aware of these costs, and some consider them reasonable given the contribution highly educated individuals make to the culture, the economy, and the academy. However, other costs are involved that are rarely considered. These are associated not with those who earned degrees but with all of the other students who entered the PhD program in the same cohort but who left or "languished," that is, neither left nor earned the degree.

In order to measure and then compare the magnitude of these costs, we use as a fifth outcome measure the student-year cost (SYC), which represents the number of years associated with the production of one "new" PhD.[12] This measure requires three calculations. The first is familiar: the mean number of years it takes for PhDs from a given cohort or several cohorts to complete the PhD (usually the mean TTD). If SYC is to be compared for two or more time periods or two or more groups, it must be truncated to a specified number of years.[13] In the following chapters, when we calculate SYC, TTD is truncated at 11 years. In other words, the comparison is limited to the mean TTD for all students who complete their PhDs by the end of the 11th year of study. The second calculation SYC requires is the mean number of years spent in a program by students who leave the program, that is, the mean TTA. A third calculation is included that accounts for those students who have neither left nor completed their degrees by the end of the 11th year. This allows the total to reflect the institutional resources consumed by students who remain or "languish" beyond the year chosen for truncating the measurement. In this case, all students who have neither finished nor left their programs

[12] This measure was first suggested by Breneman (1970) as a measure of efficiency. Bowen and Rudenstine (1992), pp. 163–74, devoted a chapter to SYC. And more recently, Harvard University's graduate school calculated it as part of an internal evaluation of the resource investment made by its graduate departments; Scott Jaschik, "'Collision Course' for Graduate Education," *Inside Higher Ed*, August 28, 2008. Yet this measure has not been commonly used because of the extent of the data needed for its calculation.

[13] To demonstrate the importance of truncation, consider a comparison as of 2003–04 of TTD for students who began in 1982 and 1993. Since students who began in 1982 could potentially have a 21-year TTD, whereas students who began in 1993 could only have a maximum TTD of 11 years, the more recent entrants will always have a shorter TTD. Thus, if we include only persons who completed in 11 years or less and only include entering cohorts up to 1993–94, we will have a measure of mean TTD that represents comparable averages for the pre- and post-GEI time periods. In our analyses, TTD, TTA, time-to-candidacy, and time from candidacy to completion are all based on truncated means.

by the end of the 11th year are counted as having cost the institution 11 years of resources.

All three means are multiplied, respectively, by the number of students in each of the three categories, and then the sum of these products is divided by the number of PhDs produced from the relevant entering cohorts. Thus SYC, which is the sum of investments in years the university has made in each group, estimates the number of years of student (or faculty) time or institutional resources spent on all of the students in the entering cohort in order to produce a PhD from that cohort.[14] The years spent in each category represent its share of the SYC. Each of these categories is likely to be affected by efforts to reduce TTD and similarly by efforts to reduce attrition—especially by efforts to reduce late attrition.

SYC is especially useful in evaluating the effectiveness of PhD programs because it captures in one measure the effects interventions have on several different outcome measures that are usually examined independently: the number of PhDs produced, the number of students who leave the program, the number of students who earn a PhD but take longer than 11 years (or any other number of years one uses in truncating), the number who leave early versus those who leave late, the degree times of those who graduate, and the number of students who languished in the program beyond a given number of years. Although each of these outcomes is important, when they are viewed separately or even in pairs the interactions among them are often lost to view. These missed interactions include unintended consequences resulting from planned interventions (for example, the denial of teaching-assistant opportunities in years beyond the sixth in hopes of freeing student time to hasten completion, and the unintended consequence of students without funding working at unrelated jobs, taking longer to finish or not finishing at all) or from external changes in the larger academic environment (for example, the increasing use of guaranteed financial-aid packages and their unanticipated correlations with languishing).[15]

Other outcomes of graduate programs we examine are the graduates' job histories, treated in Chapter 9, and the scholarly productivity of students and graduates, treated in Chapter 10.

---

[14] One weakness of this analysis is the omission of the benefits that students who do not earn the PhD glean from their graduate education. For a more complete discussion of this measure, including its strengths and weaknesses as well as the details of the computations, see Bowen and Rudenstine (1992), Chapter 9.

[15] Versatile as SYC is, it too has limitations. For example, it does not capture the changes in institutional and departmental investments in students at different points in their careers.

ANALYTICAL TOOLS

This book is intended to be accessible to readers lacking a technical background in statistics. The text emphasizes findings, not methods, and the technical details of the statistical methods that are used are relegated to an appendix. However, because many of the findings are based on statistical analyses, this section provides readers with brief and intuitive descriptions of some of the methods and concepts used in the analyses that follow.

When trying to estimate the effect of an intervention (such as the GEI) on an outcome (such as rates of attrition from PhD programs), researchers must consider the fact that, in addition to the intervention (the GEI), other influences (variables such as students' academic ability, cohort size, or gender) may be independently correlated with measured outcomes and may also vary across observations (individuals or departments) and over time. The use of *multivariate linear regression* models allows researchers to estimate the effect of the intervention, after taking into account other variables that are hypothesized to affect the outcome. Such models also allow the separate effects of other explanatory variables on the outcome to be estimated. If appropriate statistical assumptions are satisfied, the estimated effects of each variable on the outcome that researchers obtain are *unbiased* estimates of the true effects of each variable —that is, these estimates are correct on average.

The estimates of the effects of the GEI and other variables on outcomes that we examine devolve from multivariate statistical models. These estimated effects are, as the term implies, only estimates; they are not known with certainty. In addition to providing estimates of effects, these models also provide estimates of the *standard error* of each estimated effect. The standard error is a measure of the lack of precision of an estimate: the larger the standard error, the less precise the estimate. A rough rule of thumb for identifying a "real" (or nonrandom) effect is that when the absolute value of an estimated effect is equal to or greater than twice its estimated standard error (this ratio is called the t statistic), the researcher can reasonably conclude that the effect of the explanatory variable on the outcome is significantly different from zero. This rule of thumb is based on statistical assumptions about the form of the underlying distribution of error terms in the model. When we report the size of effects in the text, we typically do so only for those estimated effects that are significantly different from zero.

When the outcome variable of interest is not continuous, that is, can take on the values of only one or zero (or yes or no)—for example, completing a doctoral degree in a given period or not—the multivariate linear regression model must be modified to ensure that the estimates that are obtained are correct, on average, and to permit statistical testing of hypotheses. There are various ways to make these modifications; two that we use are called *logit* and *probit* models. Each is a nonlinear model, and the estimates obtained from each model can be transformed to provide estimates of the effect of the GEI, or of a one-unit change in any of the explanatory variables, on the outcome of interest. When we report estimated effects from these models in the text, we report the transformed estimates, sometimes referred to as *marginal effects*.

In a number of chapters, we present models of student outcomes involving not two but three alternatives. These models involve changes or transitions in students' careers over a one-year period among those who have already completed a given number of years in a PhD program. For example, when we seek information on the effects of the award of a fellowship to students in their sixth year on what occurs in the seventh year, three outcomes can ensue: students can complete the program, continue in the program, or drop out. The probabilities of these three alternatives, or *competing risks,* must sum to one since they represent all of the possible options that each student confronts. In such situations (more than two mutually exclusive outcomes), we estimate a generalization of the logit model called the *multinomial logit* model, and the estimates reported in the text are those of the impact of the GEI on the cumulative probabilities of completing the program or dropping out of the program by the end of each period.

Within the regression models described, we use what economists have come to call a *difference-in-differences* approach to estimate the effects of the GEI on outcomes. To explain this approach, it is useful to compare it to two other approaches that in general do *not* provide valid estimates. Comparing outcomes in treatment departments before and after the GEI was introduced would not yield accurate estimates of the GEI's effects. As we noted, other influences on student outcomes, such as labor market conditions for new PhDs and the academic ability of entering PhD students, may have changed after the GEI began. Similarly, focusing on the period that the GEI was in effect and comparing outcomes of students in treatment departments with outcomes of students in departments that did not receive GEI funding (control departments) would not yield accurate estimates of the effect of the GEI because there may be differences between the two kinds of departments owing to characteristics of their students (or the characteristics of the departments or universities) that we cannot measure and thus fully account for, and which may be the real causes of the observed differences in outcomes between the two kinds of departments at a given time.

In contrast, the *difference-in-differences* approach involves making both sets of comparisons—over time and between treatment and control departments. It is useful to think of this approach as involving two steps. First, the difference in outcomes between the period before the implementation of the GEI and the period after the implementation of the GEI is computed for treatment departments, as is the difference in outcomes between the two periods for control departments. Second, the difference between these two differences (hence the term *difference-in-differences*) is calculated; this is our estimate of the impact of the GEI on outcomes. For example, if the proportion of entering first-year PhD students who completed their degrees in eight years or fewer increased by 0.30 between the two periods at treatment departments and increased by 0.20 at control departments, then our estimate of the impact of the GEI on the proportion of PhD students who completed their degrees in eight years or less would be 0.10 (0.30 − 0.20).

Although much of the analysis in this book address the overall effects of the GEI, Chapters 5 and 6 focus, respectively, on the impact of the GEI that operated through the changes it induced in financial support of graduate students and those it induced in the characteristics of graduate programs. The GES provides data on almost a hundred characteristics of graduate programs. Many of these characteristics are highly correlated with each other, and no statistical analysis that attempted to include all of them would have any hope of disentangling the effects of changes in the individual characteristics on doctoral program outcomes. So instead, in Chapter 6, we use a statistical method called *factor analysis* to cluster these individual characteristics into a small number of factors (for example, financial support patterns, departmental culture, and advising), and then we estimate the effect of the GEI on each factor and then the effect of each factor on attrition and completion in different departments.

These six tools—linear regression models, the measurement of standard errors, estimations of marginal effects and competing risks, calculations of difference-in-differences, and factor analysis—are used in the chapters that follow to gauge whether the GEI had its intended effects and more generally to discover how significant various changes in the organization of doctoral programs and the funding of students proved to be. In a narrow sense, this study assesses how well the GEI served to improve the effectiveness of graduate programs. But more broadly, it is an exploration of the organization of doctoral programs and those attributes of the programs that are consequential, both negatively and positively, for the students who seek degrees. The next chapter introduces the departments that participated in the GEI and describes the experiences six of them had in reorganizing their programs over the decade of the GEI.

The Departments

> The most important differences between our ex-
> perience and our predictions have been in the rel-
> ative importance of pre-dissertation field work
> and dissertation completion awards. Pre-disserta-
> tion field work support has proven particularly im-
> portant. . . . Our overall conclusion is that there
> are indeed critical periods in a graduate student's
> career when progress is vulnerable. In the light of
> experience we would adjust our sense of their rel-
> ative importance by highlighting pre-dissertation
> support in particular.
>
> —Graduate chair of an anthropology
> department, 1996

THIS CHAPTER introduces the departments that participated in the Graduate Education Initiative (GEI). It describes the changes they planned,
the challenges in implementing those changes, and the successes and failures that resulted. It is intended to complement the intensively statistical
analysis of changes in completion rates and time-to-degree (TTD) in the
next two chapters and the multivariate analysis of the effects of particular program elements in Chapter 6. First, we describe key attributes of the
treatment departments before the advent of the GEI in simple quantitative terms; then we turn to how they "looked" five years into the GEI.[1]
Next, detailed vignettes recount the experiences of six departments in
designing GEI-related "innovations" and in implementing them, so as to
convey the complex mechanisms affecting whether the GEI did or did
not have its desired effects. Third, we describe broader aspects of departmental and institutional cultures and weigh their influence on selected departmental outcomes.

---

[1] Ideally, the control departments would have been studied in the same way, but the absence of comparably detailed qualitative information on their histories for the same period
made the comparison impractical. Later chapters that explore the overall effects of the GEI
compare both the treatment and control departments on a variety of dimensions.

Departments are central in graduate education from the time students enter universities to the time they leave, with or without degrees. They were, as we noted, central also to the GEI, which called for improving and restructuring the financial aid students would receive and also for redesigning graduate programs, thus locating the intervention squarely in departments. The decision to focus on funding and on departmental programs drew on a detailed historical study of earlier attempts to improve the funding of graduate students and to shorten TTD. None of those earlier attempts had considered in detail how the funding of students should be tied to their accomplishments, nor had they highlighted the unique significance of departments. The focus of the GEI was also based on empirical research that showed how important departmental attributes were in determining whether or not students earned the doctoral degree. Outlined in the prior chapter, this research made it clear that if changes were to be made, bypassing departments would be unrealistic and counterproductive.

Participation in the GEI called for departments to review their graduate programs and to introduce changes they considered likely to increase completion rates and reduce TTD.[2] More specifically, each department was to identify its own norm for TTD (preferably as close to six years as was realistic) and the timetables students should meet on the way to earning the degree. Department members were to consider programmatic changes that would help students meet requirements, improve advising and monitoring, and enforce rules concerning the progress students were expected to make. In connection with the redesign of graduate programs and the establishment of goals and timetables, financial aid—including the awarding of fellowships, assistantships, summer funding, and dissertation support—was to be given only to students who met the schedules the departments had set. These changes would, it was thought, produce the outcomes the GEI was intended to foster.

Having individual departments make decisions about the changes they would introduce in their programs and in the use of Mellon funds made political sense, but it also made the GEI interventions and, as we found, the resulting outcomes almost as varied as the departments themselves. Variation in outcomes due to departmental plans was compounded by major differences among the 10 universities participating in the GEI: in the scale of graduate programs (that is, the number of students departments admitted), in wealth, in commitment to professional training, and

---

[2] As we shall see, some university administrations played a very strong role in determining the changes that were to be made. This was evident from the uniformity of departmental proposals and plans for using Mellon funds across all disciplines and without regard to department size and departmental practices. Other proposals were far more varied.

in governance. At the same time, some uniformity prevailed: each of the 10 universities accepted the GEI's objectives and each received the same amounts of money annually.

The GEI had one additional feature highly relevant to the departments and to gauging improvements in their effectiveness. Because the GEI was intended to improve the educational experiences of *all* students, not just those who had benefited from the Mellon funds or from programmatic changes, its impact would be judged by its effects on all students in a department. This was in distinct contrast to other efforts to assess interventions, which typically focused only on those individuals directly affected by the intervention. This method of assessing the GEI's impact was chosen based on the assumption that even those students who had not received financial aid or other GEI benefits would profit from their departments' improved programs and be motivated to meet deadlines in the hope of gaining future funding.

THE DEPARTMENTS PRIOR TO THE GEI

The stage is set with a description of the 45 treatment departments before the GEI was instituted.[3] Table 3.1 highlights how different they were at the outset in some respects and how similar they were in others. Although the 10 universities all had the objective of educating scholars, they did not share the same views about how that goal should be accomplished. For example, they differed markedly in scale and in the number of students they chose to admit each year.[4] Table 3.1 divides the depart-

[3] Although there were 54 treatment departments overall (see Table 2.1), this chapter describes only 45 departments. Nine departments were excluded from this analysis because they were dropped from the GEI, they entered the GEI five years after it began, or their identity would be disclosed since no other department in the discipline was a participant in the Initiative.

[4] Generally, decisions about the size of departments and the amount of financial aid to be made available are made by the graduate deans, whereas the departments have the obligation to choose among applicants and, if full funding is unavailable, to propose allocations to the deans. Such decisions rested at the time on the amount of financial aid that could be deployed, whether all students should be funded, and how confident institutions were in their ability to identify the "best" students right out of college. Three institutions among the 10 made it a practice to accept more entering students than could be supported on the grounds that doing so would provide really able students whose records were less than stellar an opportunity to prove themselves once in graduate school. This policy placed the risk firmly on students, challenging them to perform rather than asking the institution to invest in them. Since then, institutions with the largest entering classes have cut back admissions and now attempt to support all or almost all of the students they accept, in part as

ments into three groups, based on their scale since that measure had proved so powerful in earlier research on completion rates: small (those having fewer than 10 students on average in their entering cohorts in each year from 1982–83 through 1985–86); medium-sized (those having between 10 and 16.4 students per year in their entering cohorts in those years), and large (those having 16.5 or more students entering per year). Table 3.1 makes clear that departments were quite similar on a number of dimensions regardless of their size. Differences in their demographic profiles—including the proportions of women, U.S. citizens, and African Americans—and in mean GRE verbal scores are notably small. Indeed, but for the variation in relative numbers arriving with master's degrees (lower in small departments) and in GRE math scores (higher in small departments), the similarity in averages is quite striking.[5]

However, the similarity in means calculated by averaging the departmental means in each category conceals a great deal of variation both among size categories and within them. For example, although the average share of women students is much the same irrespective of department size, that average includes a low of 19 percent in a medium-sized political science department and a high of 77 percent in a large English department. Similarly, the average share of students who were U.S. citizens is quite uniform across departments of differing size, but the range of mean values is considerable: 62 percent at the low end and 97 percent at the high end. Similarly, the mean share of African-American students in entering cohorts ran between 2 and 3 percent for each of the three size categories, but among the individual departments it ranged from 0 to 10 percent. It follows that the size of a given department, by itself, predicts very little about the department and the attributes of students enrolled at the start of the GEI, with one significant exception.

The financial support that departments commanded before the GEI was strongly and negatively correlated with departmental size. The bottom four rows of Table 3.1 are based on institutional data reported to the Foundation.[6] A much larger share of first-year students in small departments

---

a response to competition for able graduate students and in part to make their use of resources more efficient. A number of other considerations also affect the number of graduate students universities admit; these range from estimating the number of teaching assistants needed to cover undergraduate courses to maintaining a critical mass of students in various subspecialties.

[5] Students in philosophy had particularly high GRE math scores, and departments of philosophy were generally small.

[6] Each year the universities provided such data to the Foundation. In this sense, they are the best evidence available on institutional support of graduate students in the humanities. However, they do not systematically include the stipends paid by outside fellowships. Some institutions collected such data; others did not.

TABLE 3.1

Financial and Student Characteristics of Participating
Departments Prior to the GEI

	Department Size		
	Small	Medium	Large
Number of departments	14	16	15
Mean size of entering cohorts	6.3	13.7	29.4
Student-characteristic profile of departments			
Percent with prior master's degree	21.8	27.8	29.1
Mean verbal GRE	669	661	666
Mean math GRE	636	600	607
Percent women	46.9	48.8	47.9
Percent U.S. citizens (and permanent residents)	82.8	81.1	87.6
Percent African American	2.9	1.8	2.9
Financial-support profile of departments			
Percent of entering students with first-year fellowship	71.5	49.9	49.1
Percent with summer support at least one year	42.4	35.9	27.9
Mean per-student funding	$12,621	$11,744	$9,372
Mean total dollars of financial aid per year (all students)	$488,814	$937,504	$1,627,582

Notes: "Percent with summer support at least one year" is based on years 1–6 only and on students who completed at least six years and have valid data on summer support for the first six years. Size groups based on average size of entering cohorts from 1982–83 through 1985–86. Small: <10; medium: 10–16.4; large: ≥16.5. Total financial support includes fellowships, assistantships, tuition grants, and other support, but does not include external support. All dollar amounts are in 1991 dollars. Financial-support data reflect spending for academic years 1988–89 through 1990–91. Student characteristics reflect entering cohorts 1982–83 through 1985–86.

had fellowships (71.5 percent) than in large departments (49.1 percent). Moreover, students in smaller departments received more support on average ($12,621) than those in large departments ($9,372)—about 1.3 times the amount.[7] In addition, a larger share of students in small departments had summer support for at least one year. This difference is not the outcome of large departments having less money to spend overall—indeed, the mean total dollars of pre-GEI financial support was greater for large

[7] These means, however, do not capture the overall range of difference in stipends, which varied from less than $8,000 to over $14,000, or 1.75 times as much.

departments ($1.6 million) than for small departments ($0.49 million)—
but the result of their having to spread it over much larger numbers of students; student support was thus on average far poorer.

Consistent with the observed differences in demographics and financial resources among departments of different sizes, there was also great
variation in their completion rates, TTD, and student-year cost (SYC).
Table 3.2 presents pre-GEI cumulative completion rates for students at
the end of their 7th, 8th, and 11th years of graduate school according to
the size of their departments and according to field.

Cumulative completion rates focus attention on rates of completion of
all students in a given cohort, not only on the time it took for those who
graduated. They permit comparison of rates for different groups and
time periods if cohorts are similarly defined.[8] The table shows that only
37 percent of students prior to the GEI had completed degrees by the
end of their eighth year of graduate school. But when these data are dis-
aggregated by department size, the mean 8-year cumulative completion
rate for the small departments (42 percent) is much higher than the
means for the medium-sized and large departments (36 percent and 33
percent, respectively). Within size categories the variation is also considerable.[9] Overall, individual departments' pre-GEI 8-year cumulative completion rates range from a low of 9 percent to a high of 77 percent. The
mean 8-year cumulative completion rate also varies widely among disciplines, ranging from a low of 22 percent in comparative literature to a
high of 42 percent in political science, but the ordering of disciplines
does not lend itself to easy generalization.

In light of the emphasis in the early plans for the GEI on completion
in six years as a "norm," it may seem odd that data for rates of six-year
completion are not reported. The reason for this exclusion is that only
15 percent of students had completed their degrees by the end of the
sixth year. The table shows that by the end of the 7th year, about 26 percent (that is, another 11 percent) had finished; by the end of the 8th year,

---

[8] As described in Appendix C, the cumulative completion rate is the percentage of students in an entering cohort who have completed the PhD degree by the end of a given year
—in this instance, the 8th year since beginning the PhD program—including all those who
completed in earlier years. Later on we use TTD rather than cumulative completion rate as
a measure, because TTD focuses attention on duration rather than completion. Comparisons of TTD, in order to be meaningful, must specify the elapsed time during which the
calculation has been relevant—for example, for all those who received degrees in n years
or fewer.

[9] One medium-sized department had an 8-year cumulative completion rate of 57 percent, far higher than the 22 percent rate of one of the small departments. Likewise, one of
the large departments achieved a 54 percent rate, higher than the rates achieved by several
small or medium-sized departments.

TABLE 3.2

Cumulative Completion Rates in Participating Departments Prior to the GEI

	Number of Entering Students	Mean Cumulative Completion Rate by End of Given Year (%)		
		Year 7	Year 8	Year 11
All departments	3,063	26	37	51
Department size				
Small	355	28	42	54
Medium	834	27	36	49
Large	1,874	24	33	49
Field				
Anthropology	214	26	38	53
Art history	193	17	28	43
Classics	58	22	37	53
Comparative literature	92	19	22	38
English	1,035	30	39	52
History	737	28	40	55
Music	114	27	41	52
Philosophy	144	29	36	48
Political science	352	34	42	55
Religion	65	22	34	47

Notes: Calculated for 1982–83 through 1985–86 entering cohorts. Small: <10; medium: 10–16.4; large: ≥16.5.

as we noted, about 37 percent had finished; and by the end of the 11th year, the completion rate had increased to 51 percent. This datum calls attention to the low completion rates even in these very strong universities, and also to the extent of progress that would have to be made to bring their mean TTD anywhere near the six-year figure.

Table 3.3 uses the same data to show how students who entered in the pre-GEI period (1982–83 through 1985–86) and earned their degrees divided their time between coursework and the dissertation.[10] The table also shows the total time they took to earn the degree and the time spent in graduate school by students who left without degrees.[11] The GEI was

[10] The coursework period is defined as the elapsed time between entry and advancement to candidacy. The dissertation period is defined as the elapsed time between advancement to candidacy and completion of the PhD. Generally departments determine the criteria students must meet to advance to candidacy.

[11] Mean time in years is traditionally called TTD. However, it is important that if comparisons regarding the TTD are made across time periods the actual calculation be a truncated TTD. That is, it should be calculated as the mean time in years it has taken entering students who entered the PhD program *n* years earlier to complete the degree. For the

TABLE 3.3
Mean Time Spent in Stages of PhD Programs in Participating
Departments Prior to the GEI (years)

	Coursework and Exams[a]	Dissertation[b]	Entry to PhD (TTD)	Entry to Attrition (TTA)
All departments	3.30	4.11	7.29	3.42
Department size				
Small	3.63	3.74	7.25	3.37
Medium	3.18	4.20	7.30	3.78
Large	3.10	4.34	7.32	3.14
Field				
Anthropology	2.80	4.85	7.56	3.69
Art history	3.34	4.49	7.64	4.14
Classics	4.25	3.31	7.56	3.31
Comparative literature	3.87	3.62	7.15	3.04
English	3.13	4.13	7.14	3.47
History	2.62	4.68	7.22	3.23
Music	3.98	3.40	7.25	3.29
Philosophy	4.15	2.90	7.06	2.86
Political science	2.53	4.55	7.04	3.76
Religion	4.12	3.54	7.46	2.72

Notes: Calculated for 1982–83 through 1985–86 entering cohorts. Small: <10; medium: 10–16.4; large: ≥16.5. Mean times are computed using times of 11 years or less.

[a]Measured from entry to advancement to candidacy.

[b]Measured from advancement to candidacy to completion.

intended to compress both periods, to shorten both the time spent preparing for exams and that spent on the dissertation. Later in this chapter, we report on how much compression actually occurred and when it occurred.

Confining our attention to those who finished their degrees within 11 years, the pre-GEI TTD was 7.29 years for all participating departments, with the differences by size of department being comparatively small.[12] But the component times of TTD varied considerably more among de-

---

calculations in this chapter, we truncate TTD at 11 years. In other words, those whose TTD is longer than 11 years are not included in the calculation of a mean time.

[12] TTD was just under that (7.25 years) for small departments and just over that for medium-sized (7.30) and large (7.32) departments. Although the means by size group exhibit only small differences (and are not statistically significant), TTD for individual departments ranged from 5.8 to 8.6 years. Nonetheless, the means show interesting tendencies.

partments differing in size. The length of time students spent in course-work and exams was longest in the small departments (3.63 years), but the time they spent writing the dissertation was the shortest (3.74 years). By comparison, students in large departments completed coursework and exams sooner on average (3.10 years) but took longer to complete the dissertation (4.34 years). This may indicate less assiduous supervision by faculty members in large departments, although other variables, such as the disciplinary composition of large and small departments, could also have produced this outcome.[13] Mean time-to-attrition (TTA) also differed by department size; students in large departments leave earlier than those in small or medium-sized departments (on average a half year earlier), for reasons examined in Chapter 7. The mean TTA for the individual departments in the pre-GEI period ranges from a low of 1.49 years to an alarming 6.35 years.

Table 3.3 also calls attention to the similarities among the fields in TTD (ranging from 7.04 for political science to 7.64 for art history). But despite the small differences among the fields in overall TTD, the lengths of each of the two component periods of the doctorate do differ, reflecting perhaps their distinctive regimes of graduate study. It is no surprise, for example, that students in anthropology, art history, and history spent more time on average on the dissertation than students in other fields. Anthropologists often spend long periods doing field work, and this is registered in the time they spend after completing coursework and getting the degree—longer than in any other field. Art historians and historians are expected to work from sources in museums, archives, and libraries, and this explains the 4.49 and 4.68 years that on average elapse between completing coursework and earning the degree. However, political scientists also spend considerable time on the dissertation (4.55 years), and whereas some do archival research, others do not. These observed differences between disciplines lend themselves to ad hoc speculation—but in the absence of good evidence on the actual sources of the differences, further conjecture would be unwarranted.

Comparisons of SYC among departments and disciplines are also revealing. Table 3.4 shows, for each of the three size categories, the mean value of the total SYC and its components before the GEI was instituted. Looking first at the total SYC (last column), small departments have much lower SYC (12.11 years) than either large (13.30) or medium-sized (13.46) departments. However, the amount of time spent by completers

---

[13] The predominance of English and history departments among participating departments must be kept in mind in interpreting overall averages. These departments comprise 17 (9 and 8, respectively) of the 45 departments and have larger numbers of students on average than departments in the other fields.

TABLE 3.4
Mean Student-Year Cost Prior to the GEI

	Completers[a]	Leavers	Languishers[b]	Total[c]
All departments	7.34	3.22	2.42	12.98
Department size				
Small	7.40	2.71	2.00	12.11
Medium	7.28	3.98	2.20	13.46
Large	7.35	2.97	2.98	13.30
Field				
Anthropology	7.84	2.55	3.14	13.53
Art history	7.54	5.06	3.09	15.69
Classics	7.63	3.49	0.75	11.87
Comparative literature	7.32	4.52	2.10	13.93
English	7.10	3.16	2.36	12.62
History	7.29	2.04	2.46	11.79
Music	7.25	3.55	2.00	12.80
Philosophy	7.11	4.72	2.89	14.72
Political science	7.00	2.00	3.07	12.07
Religion	7.56	3.60	2.46	13.62

Notes: Calculated for 1982–83 through 1985–86 entering cohorts. Small: <10; medium: 10–16.4; large: ≥16.5.

[a]This is equivalent to the mean TTD for the given cohort, truncated at 11 years.

[b]Languishing students are those who have not completed their PhDs or left by the end of their 11th year since entry.

[c]Years spent in a program by all entering students divided by number of PhDs granted.

was slightly more in small departments (7.40 years) than in medium-sized (7.28) or large (7.35) departments. Why, then, was the total SYC in small departments so much lower? The explanation lies in the limited time spent in small departments by those who left and by those who languished. Compared to small departments, medium-sized departments spent more time on school leavers (1.27 years more) and large departments used more of their resources on those who languished (0.98 year more). Said another way, the high costs of leavers in medium-sized departments and of languishers in large departments played a major role in the greater total SYC in medium-sized and large departments relative to small departments. This suggests that attention should be paid to identifying methods of reducing attrition and languishing if the effects of department size are to be minimized.

The data on SYC for the various disciplines are equally intriguing. Although the difference among disciplines in the time spent by completers is less than a year at maximum, the length of the other two components differs a great deal. Art history departments invested an average of 5.06

years in those who eventually left, followed fairly closely by departments of philosophy, which invested 4.72 years in leavers; departments of art history and political science invested considerable time in languishers.

Overall, the average investment in leavers—reflecting a combination of the relative number of students who left before completing their degrees and the resources they consumed—was larger (3.22 years) than that in languishers (2.42 years). Furthermore, those languishers might, at least in principle, have gone on to complete their degrees beyond the 11-year cutoff point. The results of disaggregating SYC into its components raise an important question. If these results were replicated in the post-GEI period, should reducing TTD continue to receive the emphasis it has had in efforts to reduce the overall costs of producing a PhD? Or might it make more sense to encourage higher completion rates and to front-load attrition, that is, to compress attrition as much as possible into the early years of graduate school?

HOW FINANCIAL SUPPORT AND OUTCOMES CHANGED

So far, this chapter has dealt mainly with the state of the departments before the GEI was under way. In this section, our focus is on changes—in financial support and in outcomes—that occurred in the years following its introduction. In the absence of the kind of multivariate analysis of treatment and control departments that comes later in this volume, the remainder of this chapter—with the exception of the following description of the GEI's effects on financial aid—should not be viewed as analyses of cause and effect. Rather we offer here observations about events ordered in time that suggest certain connections are present but do not amount to claims of causality. Over the decade of the GEI, the large grants the 10 universities received substantially increased the financial support they could give graduate students in the participating departments. Table 3.5 demonstrates how substantial those increases were. In the five years following the institution of the GEI, it increased the annual support available per student by 11.1 percent, 9.9 percent, and 8.2 percent in the small, medium-sized, and large departments, respectively. Larger shares of entering students received fellowship support and larger shares of students received summer support of a year or more, irrespective of department size. This had the unintended effect of greatly improving the competitive edge of the participating departments in admissions and in financial aid, a matter to which we will return later.

Table 3.5 also shows that the differences in financial aid that originally existed between small (and rich) departments and large (and relatively poor) departments before the GEI were maintained or increased by its

TABLE 3.5
Financial Support Pre- and Post-GEI

	Pre-GEI (1982–83 through 1985–86)			Post-GEI (1991–92 through 1996–97)		
	Small	*Medium*	*Large*	*Small*	*Medium*	*Large*
Percent of entering students with first-year fellowship	71.5	49.9	49.1	84.8	79.5	62.7
Percent with summer support at least one year	42.4	35.9	27.9	92.0	80.0	76.2
Mean annual total dollars of financial support (all students)	$488,814	$937,504	$1,627,582	$580,460	$1,133,872	$2,083,304
GEI as percentage increase in mean annual total dollars	12.3	10.8	9.9	—	—	—
Mean per-student annual financial support	$12,621	$11,744	$9,372	$13,629	$13,118	$10,135
GEI as percentage increase in mean per-student annual financial support	11.1	9.9	8.2	—	—	—

Notes: "Percent with summer support at least one year" is based on years 1–6 only and on students who completed at least six years and have valid data on summer support for the first six years. Size groups based on average size of entering cohorts from 1982–83 through 1985–86. Small: <10; medium: 10–16.4; large: ≥16.5. There are 14 small, 16 medium-sized, and 15 large departments. Total financial support includes fellowships, assistantships, tuition grants, and other support, but does not include external support. All dollar amounts are in 1991 dollars. For first-year support and summer support, entering cohorts included as labeled above columns. For dollars of financial support, departmental expenditures are calculated for academic-year budgets (pre-GEI = 1988–89 through 1990–91; post-GEI = 1991–92 through 1996–97). The "percentage increase" figures are placed in the "pre-GEI" columns even though they were calculated using data for both periods.

advent. The GEI increased the mean dollars available by 12.3 percent in the small departments and by 9.9 percent in the large departments. In actual dollars, per-student funding was raised to $13,629 and $13,118 in the small and medium-sized departments and to $10,135 in the large ones.[14] The maintenance of differences we observe between small, medium-sized, and large departments flowed from the way GEI funds were allocated. Each university was given the same dollar amount in an-

---

[14] In 1999–2000 the small departments' mean stipend was $21,078, whereas the medium-sized departments provided $15,889 on average and the large departments provided only $11,065.

nual grants to cover approximately four to five departments; no consideration was given to the number of enrolled students or the number of departments the institutions elected to include in the Initiative.[15] This formula made it nearly inevitable that departments with more students would receive less per capita and would see smaller increases due to the GEI. Be that as it may, the GEI's goal of improving the amount of financial aid students received was without question met. The issue of whether those improvements were responsible for higher completion rates and briefer degree times are dealt with in Chapters 5 and 6.

Table 3.6 focuses on the extent of the changes in departmental outcomes after the GEI, according to size and discipline. The table presents the changes in departmental 8-year cumulative completion rates, measured by percentage-point differences, and the changes in departmental mean TTD and the components of that total time. Cumulative completion rates increased overall after the GEI, as intended, by an average of 8.4 percentage points. Small departments showed an increase of 9.8 percentage points as against increases of 8.2 and 7.4 percentage points in large and medium-sized departments, respectively.

Again, averages conceal marked internal variation. Changes in 8-year cumulative completion rates of over 30 points occurred in many departments (for example, from 20 percent to 50 percent), but the rates barely changed at all in others, and there were also some departments in which completion rates decreased. Mean TTD fell somewhat in small and medium-sized departments, by about six months and two months, respectively, but it rose by three months in large departments. Such changes do not amount to much in relative terms when TTD runs between seven and eight years. However, six departments managed to drive average completion times down to six years.

Table 3.6 provokes two additional comments. The first concerns changes occurring in the time it took students to complete their coursework and exams and then finish the dissertation. After programmatic changes associated with the GEI were implemented, reductions occurred in the interval between entry and advancement to candidacy in departments of all sizes and in every discipline.[16] However, the mean amount

---

[15] The logic underlying this decision had two components. First, it satisfied the principle of equity. Had grants been prorated according to size, institutions that made sure not to admit more students than could be financed would be penalized whereas those that had decided not to match growth with resources would benefit. It is not clear that the same decision would be made now. After the end of the GEI, larger endowment grants were made to institutions that had limited resources than to those that were relatively well endowed.

[16] The underlying departmental data show that mean times-to-candidacy were reduced in 35 of the 45 departments, and in 16 departments they were reduced by half a year or

TABLE 3.6

Change in Departmental Outcomes from Pre-GEI to Post-GEI Time Periods

	Mean Change in Departmental 8-Year Cumulative Completion Rate (percentage points)	Mean Change in Time Spent (years)[a]			
		Coursework and Exams[b]	Dissertation[c]	Entry to PhD (TTD)	Entry to Attrition (TTA)
All departments	8.4	−0.30	0.05	−0.31	0.36
Department size					
Small	9.8	−0.33	−0.18	−0.51	0.59
Medium	7.4	−0.25	0.15	−0.18	0.01
Large	8.2	−0.31	0.15	0.26	0.49
Field					
Anthropology	0.9	−0.35	0.24	−0.16	0.39
Art history	14.0	−0.58	0.09	−0.39	−0.66
Classics	10.3	−0.40	−0.20	−0.69	−0.64
Comparative literature	26.1	−0.39	0.39	0.15	1.78
English	6.2	−0.10	−0.02	−0.19	0.04
History	3.5	−0.07	0.00	−0.11	0.50
Music	13.8	−0.02	−0.76	−0.98	0.50
Philosophy	3.8	−0.46	0.57	−0.16	1.22
Political science	9.1	−0.14	0.03	−0.23	0.52
Religion	13.5	−0.45	0.35	−0.24	2.38

Notes: Small: <10; medium: 10–16.4; large: ≥16.5. Pre-GEI = 1982–83 through 1984–85; post-GEI = 1991–92 through 1993–94.

[a]Computed using times of 11 years or less.

[b]Measured from entry to advancement to candidacy.

[c]Measured from advancement to candidacy to completion.

of time spent on research and writing dissertations either increased slightly or remained the same.[17] This suggests that programmatic changes the GEI stimulated in the first stage of graduate study were effective or that faculty members had more influence on students' progress when they were close at hand. In the dissertation phase, however, the changes that were introduced—for example, in dissertation advising and monitoring—

more. Overall reductions in dissertation-writing time were, as we noted, not as large on average, but they occurred in 22 of the 45 departments, and in 9 a reduction of half a year or more occurred. As a whole, the time students took to get their degrees was reduced in 30 departments, and 7 of these achieved reductions of more than a year. See Appendix Table E.3.1 for the minimum and maximum outcomes in the pre- and post-GEI periods.

[17] Only music is an outlier in this respect. Time spent on the dissertation was reduced by 0.76 year, quite a large reduction compared to those in other disciplines.

seem to have been less effective. Perhaps the dissertation phase itself is marked by so many difficulties that it is hard to effect change in it. These interpretations are consistent with students' comments from the Graduate Education Survey (GES) about the contrast in their experiences between these two phases of work toward the degree. One student lamented: "Completion of coursework happened quickly and smoothly. Writing the dissertation was laborious and lonely. The department offered no formal institutionalized help at this stage." Another was similarly "at sea": "I see now, in retrospect, that my program was almost entirely unstructured, and that there was no formal guidance whatsoever in the research and dissertation enterprise. It is not surprising that I faltered at this stage: I hadn't a clue what I was doing. There was no group forum for discussing problems and no guidance, either collective or individual."

The dissertation phase is further complicated by students being absent from campus, either for the purposes of their research or to take income-producing jobs. Communication with advisors may become sporadic, which is all the more problematic for students who are not quite sure what they are doing and are vulnerable to the isolation that often marks the dissertation-writing period. As we will see in Chapter 6, the attitudes faculty members convey about how speedy dissertation completion should be play a role in the time students take to finish the dissertation phase of their careers.

Table 3.6 also prompts an observation concerning changes in rates of attrition and its timing. One objective of the GEI was to reduce attrition overall and another was to structure programs so that the attrition that did occur took place earlier rather than later. However, contrary to expectation, the mean elapsed time from entering graduate school to attrition actually increased after the GEI, on average, by slightly more than a third of a year. Later, we will explore the causes of this important, unexpected, and far from heartening correlate of the GEI. The last column of Table 3.6 shows that TTA increased in all fields except art history and classics. Such increases in TTA are indicators of further delay in attrition rather than its acceleration.

As with the data we reported earlier, the means in Table 3.6 cannot convey the variation in change within categories: many departments in each of the size groupings were able to reduce their TTA significantly—by two years or more.

Since dispersion is so central a part of the analysis reported thus far, it may be useful to study an example of it in some detail. Figure 3.1 highlights how much dispersion there was among participating departments in both the direction of *change* in 8-year cumulative completion rates and its extent (measured by changes in percentage points) after the GEI. This figure arrays all the departments in order of extent of change in cumu-

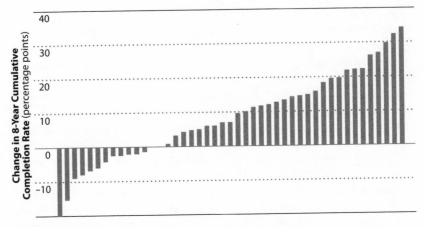

Figure 3.1. Percentage-Point Change in 8-Year Cumulative Completion Rate from Pre-GEI to Post-GEI Time Periods, Arrayed for Participating Departments

lative completion rates. The left side of the figure shows that six departments were backsliders: their completion rates declined by more than 5 percentage points. The next dozen (going from left to right) neither increased nor decreased by more than 5 percentage points in either direction. But completion rates in 27 departments rose by more than 5 percentage points, and in 10 departments completion rates increased by 20 percentage points or more. Of the latter group, four were large departments; five of those whose completion rates decreased were small departments. Thus, although department size is associated with changes in departmental completion rates, the connections are weak; there were departments in each of the three categories that improved and some that retrogressed. On balance, however, more departments showed improved completion rates than declining or static rates, and their rates increased by far more than the declines measured in other departments. Judged on this criterion, the GEI was associated with change in the intended direction.

Last we turn to changes in SYC following the GEI.[18] Figure 3.2 compares the overall costs in student years per PhD produced and changes in the component parts of SYC. Overall, SYC decreased from 12.58 to 11.44 years, a change of slightly more than 1 year. As the figure shows, most of the change was due to reductions in TTD among those who earned degrees within 11 years. It fell from 7.27 to 6.98 years. However, the figure also shows that the GEI shortened the number of years spent by students

---

[18] See Chapter 2 for the calculation of SYC and a description of its potential value to administrators. For the pre-GEI levels, see Table 3.3.

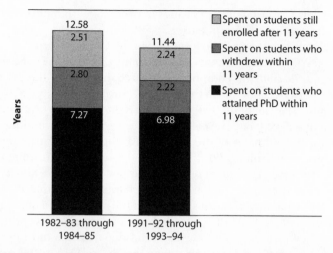

Figure 3.2. Student-Year Cost in Participating Departments during the Pre-GEI and Post-GEI Time Periods

Notes: Pre-GEI time period is represented by the 1982–83 through 1984–85 entering cohorts (N = 2,218 and average cohort size = 16.4). Post-GEI time period is represented by the 1991–92 through 1993–94 entering cohorts (N = 2,309 and average cohort size = 17.1).

before they left and also shortened the number of years spent by students who "languished" as long as their 11th year.[19] Thus, using the SYC as a measure of effectiveness—that is, calculating the "savings per PhD" of time and resources multiplied by the number of PhDs who graduated in the post-GEI time period—the GEI was associated with significant savings of student and faculty time. Put another way, the reductions in SYC for the three cohorts that started graduate school after the GEI, from 1991–92 through 1993–94 (the cohorts for whom we have 11 years or

[19] Since we know from the data presented in Table 3.6 that the mean TTA actually increased from the pre-GEI to post-GEI time periods, we might wonder how the cost in years associated with students who left could show a decrease. The answer reflects the complexity of this calculation. The reduction in cost in years for students who left the program can be affected by the number of students leaving and the number of PhDs produced as well as the mean time in years spent in the program by those who leave. Furthermore, the numbers in Table 3.6 were based on department means and thus gave equal weight to each department. By contrast, the calculation of SYC is based on degrees and thus gives greater weight to larger departments, which had greater decreases in TTA and greater reductions in numbers of students who left. In addition, in Figure 3.2 the change in overall SYC also represents a significant reduction in the years spent on students who completed the PhD and fewer students (relative to the number of PhDs produced) "languishing" beyond the 11th year.

more of data), translate into a savings of over 1,800 student years (or faculty years, or years of resource use).

The extent of dispersion now familiar in the GEI data turns up in calculations of SYCs for departments and disciplines. Despite the wide range in the magnitude and the components that changed from the pre-GEI to post-GEI periods, 27 of the 45 treatment departments reduced SYC by one year or more. Fifteen of these departments reduced SYC by over four years.

These descriptive data reveal some patterns to keep in mind when interpreting the estimates of the overall GEI impacts that are reported in the chapters that follow. Positive effects that occurred in some departments were counterbalanced or even swamped by negative effects occurring in other departments. Early in this chapter we saw that the participating departments varied considerably in the number and demographic composition of students they enrolled and in the generosity of financial support they provided. The participating departments did not start as equals. These different starting points may be related to the extent of change they would experience.

PROGRAMMATIC CHANGES MADE BY DEPARTMENTS

Treatment departments, as we observed earlier, embarked on a great variety of programmatic changes or "innovations" that were to improve the quality of graduate education and its effectiveness. Based on a content analysis of the original proposals and the yearly reports that the Foundation received, Table 3.7 lists the innovations departments introduced and groups them into 10 principal categories. (Categories of change are listed in column 1; specific changes included in each category are listed in column 2.) The specific changes adopted by six sample departments are indicated in the remaining columns to illustrate how varied the changes were. As the numerous "N" entries in cells indicate, few of the changes listed were made by more than three of the six sample departments.[20] (The footnote to Table 3.7 describes the meaning of cell entries other than "Y" for yes and "N" for no.)

The first set of innovations listed deals with clarifying departmental expectations. Most departments felt it was necessary to be very specific about timetables for satisfactory progress toward the degree during their orientation of new students; five of these six sample departments re-

[20] The sample consists of two departments of history, one of English, one of political science, and two of other disciplines, as indicated by the column headings in Table 3.7. Per agreement with the participating departments and universities, the university names have been suppressed.

TABLE 3.7

Interventions Implemented as Part of the GEI in Six Sample Departments

Innovation	Description/Purpose	English A	History B	History C	Political Science D	Other Humanities[a] E	Other Humanities[a] F
Expectations	Clarify timetables	Y	Y	Y	N	Y	Y
	Clarify TTD expectations	N	N	Y	N	N	Y
	Clarify advancement to candidacy and prospectus deadlines	Y	N	Y	Y	Y	Y
Advising	Required schedule	Y	Y	Y	N	Y	N
	Formal group advising	Y	N	N	N	Y	N
Monitoring	Earlier review	Y	N	Y	Y	Y	Y
	Faculty submit dissertation progress reports	Y	N	Y	Y	N	N
Group workshops or colloquia	To reduce isolation	Y	Y (plan)	N	Y	N	N
	To prepare prospectus	Y	N	Y	Y	N	Y
	To start dissertation	N	N	N	Y	N	N
	Dissertation writing/feedback	Y	Y (plan)	Y	Y	Y	N
	Early seminar or field work	N	N	N	N	N	N
	Collaborative work	N	Y	N	N	N	N
Curricular changes	Job/profession preparation	N	N	Y	N	N	N
	Coursework requirements	Y	N	Y	N	Y	Y
	Writing requirements	N	N	N	Y	N	N
	Timing for advancement to candidacy	N	N	Y	Y	Y	Y

(continued)

TABLE 3.7 (*Continued*)

Innovation	Description/Purpose	English A	History B	History C	Political Science D	Other Humanities[a] E	Other Humanities[a] F
	Nature of advancement to candidacy	Y	N	N	Y	Y	Y
	Prospectus required to advance to candidacy	N	N	Y	Y	N	Y
	Reduce language requirements	N	N	N	N	N	N
	Modify incomplete policy	Y	Y	Y	Y (1997)	N	Y
	Limit length of prospectus	N	N	Y (1997)	Y	Y	N
	Courses graded	Y	N	N	N	Y	N
	Preliminary fields identified earlier	N	Y	Y	N	Y	Y
	Deadlines for submitting dissertation chapters	Y	N	Y	Y	Y	N
Uses of GEI funding (percent)	Summer language	0	0	9	5	0	0
	Summer travel or field work	9	22	25	50	0	0
	Pre–advancement to candidacy	0	0	0	0	0	20
	Post-advancement to candidacy or dissertation start-up	13	26	0	20	2	0
	Finishing dissertation	78	52	66	25	98	80
Tuition policy	Tuition increases after six years	N	N	N	N	Y	N
	Guaranteed multiyear packages	Y	Y	Y	Y	N	Y
Enforcement of rules	Funding conditional on timing	Y	Y	N	Y	Y	Y
	Limit years funded	Y	N	Y	N	N	Y

	Final-year support conditional on completing specific number of chapters	Y	N	N	Y	Y
	Cannot register if miss deadlines	N	N	N	N	N
	No further funding (including TA) if dissertation defense not scheduled by end of dissertation write-up year	N	N	Y	N	N
	No TA if prospectus not on time	N	N	Y	N	N
	Postdoc available if schedule defense by end of dissertation write-up year	N	Y	Y	Y	N
TA changes	Reduce time as TA	Y	Y	Y	Y	N
	Enhance TA experience or design own course	N	Y	N	N	N
Structural changes	Improve training for teaching	N	N	N	N	N
	Define summer tasks	Y	N	Y	Y	Y
	Add placement advisor	Y	N	N	N	N
	Reduce size of entering cohorts	Y	Y	N	Y	N
	Match better with available mentors	N	N	N	Y	Y

Notes: "Y" indicates that a department implemented the named innovation. "N" indicates that a department did not adopt the innovation as part of the GEI, although it may have been a policy already in place. "Y (plan)" indicates that a department had indicated that it planned to implement the innovation, but did not subsequently mention that it had actually been adopted. "1997" in a cell indicates that the department did not make the change until that year. Percentages appearing in rows for "Uses of GEI funding" represent the mix of uses for which GEI funding was used in each department, totaling 100%.

a"Other humanities" includes disciplines for which we have fewer than four participating departments: classics, comparative literature, music, philosophy, religion, and romance languages.

ported that they did so. The other two innovations in this set indicate whether these departments had clarified their TTD expectations and their deadlines for advancement to candidacy and submission of a dissertation prospectus. Only two of these departments claimed to do the first, but five worked on clarifying and setting deadlines for candidacy and prospectus submission. Many students who entered graduate school before the GEI complained in the GES regarding the absence of clear expectations about the length of the degree when arriving in graduate school; for example: "I innocently thought that I was signing up for a 4 year program, only to be told on the first day of orientation (by a bitter student) that the average was 8, and that many of us would never finish."

The next set of innovations deals with advising. For example, four of the six departments required students and their advisors to schedule regular meetings, and two instituted formal meetings of students and groups of advisors. Another set of innovations relates to faculty monitoring and reviews of students' work. Five of these six departments instituted earlier reviews of the progress students were making, and three required faculty members to submit regular reports on students' progress on their dissertations. Although few students mentioned these specific policies, they reiterated the importance of faculty advisors in their graduate school experience. In response to the open-ended query in the GES—"Please tell us about the experiences you had in graduate school that bore the most heavily on your progress towards your degree"—more mentioned their faculty advisors than any other factor; for example: "My advisor was the most important factor in [my] receiving . . . good training & getting a job. He had relatively few advisees and spent a lot of time working with me, reading papers and giving advice." Another comment illustrates a view most shared about the relative importance of good advising: "I was fortunate to work with an advisor who was supportive and who emphasized above all else the quality of our work so when I went looking for a job, I had a good dissertation, and a project that was good enough to lead directly to a book, a publishable manuscript, and a tenure track position. This was even more important than sufficient funding."

In light of the often solitary nature of humanistic research and writing, departments adopted another set of innovations that were intended to reduce the isolation in which graduate students usually pursued their dissertations. These included establishing group workshops or colloquia for students at various stages of the dissertation. Four of the departments established such workshops to aid students in preparing their dissertation prospectuses; one established a workshop to help students get started on the dissertation. Students found they benefited from these workshops. "The most helpful innovation," one wrote, "[was] the dissertation writing groups—students working on . . . similar topics who read and criticized

each others work-in-progress under the direction of common dissertation director." The dissertation was apparently sufficiently challenging
that one former student wrote: "Another thing that helped was a group
workshop on methodology led by someone administrative rather than academic which showed very practical, systematic ways to work on dissertation and keep track of chapters, pages etc without getting bogged down
too much in endless intellectual questions that were making people's dissertations get out of control in time and length."

Although several departments mentioned the need for a workshop
that would prepare students for job searches, few followed through on
that intention. Among these six, only one department claims to have done
so. We do not know whether department efforts to help students on the
job market have expanded since then. It is likely that they have. Yet the
survey indicates that students often bemoaned the lack of such preparation: "My own graduate study was conducted by my teachers as though
there were no job market to consider, no publication-record to establish,
no *teaching*, in short, about what a job candidate needed to know and how
to obtain that knowledge. There were no mock-job talks in the department when I went there. I had no idea what a placement office might be
for. My teachers were (and remain) brilliant scholars, but poor convey-
ors of professional information."

Curricular changes were also frequent. Four of the six departments al-
tered their coursework requirements as might have been expected, given
the complex, even baroque, requirements many departments had before
the GEI. A number changed the timing of advancement to candidacy, required a dissertation prospectus for advancement to candidacy, required
students to identify earlier than before the fields in which they would take
their preliminary examinations, or established deadlines for submitting
dissertation chapters. One department's report commented on changing
the nature of the prospectus review it had required and the impact of the
new format on the quality and efficiency of the experience:

The faculty regards most of them [the GEI changes] as beneficial, even when
they have entailed losses as well as gains. For example, removing the anxiety-
fraught aura of an examination from the prospectus meeting has caused
students to come forward for it much sooner and has enabled them to use
the occasion itself, as well as their preparation for it, more constructively
than in the past. It is true that most prospectuses nowadays are less polished,
contractual-looking documents than they used to be. But when one compares
the former system with the present one, it is clear that the time it used to take
to fashion the old prospectus is now devoted more profitably to the dissertation
itself, that a prospectus need not and probably should not aspire to definitive-
ness, and that on balance this change is therefore a distinct improvement.

Among the other curricular changes shown in Table 3.7, departments introduced changes in their grading policies, including the number of "incomplete" grades that were permissible. They also introduced new rules tying financial aid to the number of years students had been in residence, limiting the number of years students would receive support, and not permitting students to be teaching assistants (TAs) if their prospectuses had not been submitted on time; three of the six reduced the time students could spend as TAs.

Departments also reported how they planned to use the amplified funds they received from the GEI. Many planned to use the funds to support summer activities. Some devoted funds to support summer study so that language requirements could be passed. Some provided funds for students to travel to do preliminary research on their proposed dissertation subjects, so that the feasibility of projects could be tested. For their part, students reported on the survey that summer support helped them move to candidacy at a faster pace: "The Mellon Foundation gave my department nine summer grants (for students in my year), and this money meant that I spent the summer before my qualifying exams not having to hold a job: I could concentrate on exam preparation and writing my dissertation prospectus. As a result my 3rd year was efficient and I moved quickly to writing the dissertation."

We will return to the extent, timing, and targeting of financial aid for graduate students in Chapter 5. Here it is important to note that all six sample departments used GEI funds for dissertation-writing fellowships, perhaps the most important but most often unsatisfied need in graduate student support. (Indeed, every one of the 45 treatment departments increased the funding available for dissertation support.) Five of the six departments used the great majority of the funds that they received from the GEI to help students complete their dissertations.[21] Students who had such support attributed their ability to complete the dissertation to it. And finally, all but one of the six departments, presumably in response to competitive pressures, increased the number of years of funding they would guarantee students at the time of admission. As we noted earlier, this was not a change intended by the architects of the GEI, although it might be argued that guaranteed multiyear funding would increase completion rates and decrease TTD. The evidence on its effects indicates otherwise and therefore bears the further discussion it will receive later. However, students reported that such guaranteed funding has benign effects on department life; it engenders esprit de corps among

[21] The fifth department, the political science department, had supported most of its students with fellowships during the dissertation-writing year even before the GEI began and thus did not need substantial funds for that purpose.

students and reduces financial worries so that they can focus on their studies; for example:

> Secure finances made the world of difference, both in freeing me to work on my courses and then [on my] dissertation and [they] also . . . improve[ed] the atmosphere in the department. Part of why we could be such a supportive community for each other (a key factor in overcoming the loneliness or feelings of inadequacy that seem to be inherent in PhD programs, at least in the humanities) was because we were not competing with each other for funding.

Department policies also included efforts to increase enforcement of rules to tie funding to satisfactory progress through the program. For example, three of these sample programs set a limit on the maximum years of funding that students could receive, and three gave a final year's support only to students who had already satisfactorily completed two chapters of their dissertations. In response to concerns that students were spending too many years as TAs and that work as a TA was slowing down their progress, three departments limited the amount of time students could spend working as TAs.[22] One department tried to enhance the TA experience by providing more mentoring and setting up a program that permitted students to design their own courses.

Finally, these departments instituted a number of other structural changes in their programs. Three departments explicitly defined what they expected students to accomplish during summers, one added a placement advisor, two (as directed by their universities) said that they planned to improve their programs by reducing the size of their entering cohorts, and two said that they would try harder to admit only students whom they could match with mentors with similar interests.

VIGNETTES: PROPOSED DEPARTMENTAL CHANGES AND IMPLEMENTATION CHALLENGES

From the outset of the GEI, the changes that departments made and how they were carried out were expected to be "custom tailored" and thus to vary—and vary they did. The following six vignettes are intended to convey some of that variety. They also describe how department members and university administrators responded to the GEI and how the changes

---

[22] Those familiar with the financial pressures graduate students face know that such rules do not always reduce the amount of time they spend teaching, because those studying at institutions in urban areas could often easily find part-time teaching opportunities at nearby academic institutions.

they made evolved over the program's lifetime.[23] They show the richness (or lack of it) of the proposed changes, the creativity (or lack of it) they evinced, and the commitment (or lack of it) that faculty members and students mustered in response to the GEI's intentions and the new resources it provided. Each of the six departments has its own story, as the brief subtitles for each vignette indicate.[24]

Department A: Reduction in Size and Shift in Culture

This large department of English began a self-review several years before the GEI was introduced as part of the graduate school's program of periodic assessment of departments. Faculty members concluded that students took too long after prelims to complete their PhDs and that too many students left after they had achieved candidacy. The department was also concerned about the large number of graduate students officially in residence and about its high student-faculty ratio. The review led to new policies being instituted (before the advent of the GEI) that sent a clear message to faculty and students that their current long TTD was unacceptable.

Faculty members attributed the department's long TTD to the students' heavy instructional responsibilities. Students taught so much because no other financial aid was available. The faculty (and others) worked with the

---

[23] In choosing the six departments we sought ones that exemplified the types of program innovations the Foundation sought. The full array of such changes is listed in Table 3.7. Moreover, we chose departments whose proposals and reports were rich enough in detail that we could glean from them how the program design had taken shape and how the implementation had proceeded. Finally, we included those departments that were self-aware enough to be keen observers and evaluators of their own progress.

[24] In order to avoid the possibility that any individual department can be identified, the designation of "other humanities" is used for those fields that have fewer than four participating departments: classics, comparative literature, music, philosophy, religion, and romance languages. In later chapters, we say more about the impact of disciplinary cultures on graduate training. In the vignettes, we avoid using the idiosyncratic and varied terminology departments use to describe various stages and tasks of graduate work. In particular, the paper students write to prepare for dissertation research is called the prospectus even though the various departments use many terms (qualifying essay, dissertation proposal, prospectus); the exams and meetings that take place as a requirement for advancement to candidacy are called "prelims" although in practice they are also called qualifying exams, general exams, or orals. Teaching and research responsibilities are referred to as TA or RA although departments also may use the term graduate student instructor. The faculty member in charge of the graduate program is referred to as the director of graduate studies (DGS).

graduate dean to make significant changes in all aspects of its program—in admissions, advising, financial aid, and curriculum. Reducing the teaching load students had to assume and reducing the overall size of entering classes were two significant changes the faculty sought. At the same time, it made interest in teaching one criterion for admission. A program of teacher training for all second-year students was added, so that all students could effectively assume instructional responsibilities and then reap their benefits when entering the job market. The department also increased faculty involvement in students' teaching performance by designating a number of faculty members as teaching supervisors.

These changes were complemented by a major overhaul in the extent and types of financial aid the university and the department provided. Much more financial aid was awarded, students were not permitted to teach for more than three years, and students in their second and sixth years received stipends but had no teaching responsibilities. Summer support became available to students for preparation of dissertation prospectuses or for travel needed for dissertation research.

Reducing the size of entering cohorts enabled first-year courses to be taught as seminars rather than as lectures, which allowed for closer monitoring of students' progress. A new rule required that all coursework and language requirements must be completed before students could take prelims (reflecting the establishment of a new, more rigorous policy regarding incompletes).[25] Prelims were restructured to cover three subfields rather than the four that had been required earlier and were designed to serve as a bridge between coursework and the dissertation research to follow. The time allowed (expected) between prelims and prospectus was shortened from a year to six months. This was facilitated by interdepartmental dissertation-planning workshops held by the graduate school for students beginning to work on the dissertation prospectus. In addition, new dissertation seminars were added in which students and faculty members participated. The director of graduate studies (DGS) wrote the Foundation: "The Mellon-supported doctoral dissertation seminars have an enormous impact on our students, both in terms of [their receiving] substantive collegial feedback and in terms of [their] morale. I even think that my colleagues are looking noticeably livelier as a result."

Entering students were assigned advisors who were to continue until dissertation sponsors were named. The department created a student information database, which facilitated reviews of students' work by all faculty

---

[25] Policies on "incompletes" usually state the time by which work must be completed to change a grade of "incomplete" to a letter grade. They also indicate how "incompletes" on students' records affect their eligibility for advancement to candidacy.

members. It also instituted additional meetings of the DGS with each second-year student to discuss plans for prelims, including possible topics to be covered, the shape of the overall exam, and potential examiners.

These changes, combined with more readily available information from the improved student database, facilitated monitoring and the enforcement of expectations concerning students' timely progress. They also created a sense that each cohort of students was, so to speak, in the same boat. In fact, cohort identification was emphasized in student meetings and even by means of e-mail groups. Set in motion before the GEI began, these changes represented just the sort of reorganization the framers of the GEI hoped would be instituted.

Yet the best-laid plans sometimes go awry. As the department began to implement these changes, the goal of having students advance to candidacy by the middle of their fourth year was thwarted. In the first year, several of the most sought-after examiners went on long-planned leaves. Then it became clear that the three-year limit on student teaching conflicted with the timing of the "Mellon [dissertation] write-up" fellowship, which was to be an incentive for students in their sixth year to work on their dissertations after completing three years of teaching. This arrangement discouraged those exceptional students who had done their three years of teaching but were ready to write their dissertations in their fifth year from "claiming" the write-up fellowship despite their being ready for it. If they took the fellowship early and failed to finish that year, the rules would prohibit them from serving as TAs in order to finance their last (sixth) year.

This department's annual reports to the Foundation reveal that attempts were made to minimize the effects of these stumbling blocks. The chairman wrote the Foundation, saying:

> The shorter time mandated from beginning of candidacy to the dissertation proposal has transformed the rhythms of graduate education for all students. Students now know from day one that they must plan the intellectual trajectory of their professional training with care and precision. The consensus is that keeping students on time begins early and [needs] close monitoring of incompletes and progress. The reviews combated students' tendencies to delay talking to potential examiners until he/she had fully worked out a proposal. Furthermore, keeping students on track early and addressing problems before they become insurmountable improves completion rates. Year [that is, cohort] specific meetings and e-mail lists have been of particular use in keeping students informed of expected tasks and deadlines. Demanding that all course and language requirements be completed prior to the prelim seems to be an effective impetus and enforcement mechanism because prelims are seen as a more serious, funding-implicative deadline. Having those minor requirements out of the way facilitates timely progress on the disser-

tation itself. Once the dissertation has begun, routine progress reports and dissertation workshops are useful and effective, but reducing the TTD depends as much, if not more, on insuring that work on the dissertation begins as soon as possible.

New plans were also laid to assist students who had finished their degrees, or were close to completion, in searching for jobs. A placement advisor was assigned to assist new PhDs in making a timely exit from the university, with the result that the department's placement record was among the best in its field in the country. This in turn bred "an atmosphere of confidence" within which the students could pursue their degrees.

Another outcome, mentioned in this department's report, was the increase in the number of applicants for admission and the eventual improvement in the quality of students in its entering cohorts. This point was made in most departmental reviews and is corroborated by the rising GRE scores of post-GEI cohorts. This improvement was said to reinforce (or in some cases to make possible) the changes in the program and the enforcement of deadlines and more stringent rules. Later on, we observe that the improvement in GRE scores of the treatment departments was never an intended outcome of the Initiative. (Members of departments outside the treatment group reminded us that the GEI had put them at a relative disadvantage in recruitment.) And finally, from the Foundation's perspective, the department was fortunate to have the principal drafters of the plan continue to lead the department for a number of years and to have other faculty members serve on a committee that evaluated its effectiveness.[26] This continuity built a group of knowledgeable people who could be tapped for future leadership.

This department's leadership combined support for the program with continued concern over long TTD, an ongoing departmental review, and a well-thought-out, comprehensive plan that resulted in the outcomes faculty members were seeking. Student and faculty morale was reported to be enormously improved. As the leadership hoped, the absolute number of PhDs the department graduated actually rose, despite the dramatic reduction in the number of entering students. This outcome was made possible by lower attrition rates and improved completion rates. The 8-year cumulative completion rate doubled from 15 percent before the GEI to 30 percent for the students who began in the first five years after the GEI was instituted (1990–91 through 1995–96). The consonance of this department's objectives with those of the GEI, the changes it instituted, and the adaptations it made enabled the department to achieve its

---

[26] Mellon staff has been and continues to be much aware of both continuity and change in the departmental members who were responsible for keeping the GEI in motion.

goals more effectively than almost all of the other departmental participants in the GEI. As it happens, this department's experience was not
unique. The provost at Department A's institution declared in a letter ac-
companying the original proposal that one of its objectives would be to
reduce the size of entry cohorts and improve financial aid, while increasing or maintaining the scale of doctoral production—a goal that was
achieved in all five participating departments in that university. Furthermore, a total of 10 departments across several institutions managed to
increase the absolute number of PhDs who earned degrees while reducing the number of entrants. An additional two departments kept constant
their number of entrants but increased the number of degree recipients.

Department B: Elaborate Plans, Little Follow-Through

When it was chosen for participation in the GEI in 1990, faculty members
and students in this medium-sized history department carried out a serious review of graduate training. Over a period of two months, they evaluated the effectiveness of the department's program, identified trouble
spots, and made recommendations for both academic and financial
remedies. Students fielded their own questionnaire with faculty assistance and followed up with additional interviews. The recommendations
the department made were based largely on the students' inquiry, and
they dealt with the students' concerns.

In the students' view (the following is drawn from the report on the
findings of their survey and interviews), progress toward the degree was
most seriously impeded by (1) their having to spend too much time as
TAs (this included the number of terms they had to serve, the size of
classes they taught, and their having to teach outside their fields of con-
centration) and (2) their stipends, which were so small that many suf-
fered considerable financial anxiety. However, the students also said that
teaching was one of the most gratifying aspects of graduate training, and
they were disturbed that teaching at the institution was undervalued in
general and in particular by their own professors. Many said that providing TA training would be one of the most important changes the department could make. (3) Students also reported being frustrated by
"post-prelim drift." They said they were "treading water" after their exams and suggested that this was due in large part to a lack of clarity about
the standards their dissertations were expected to meet. Was it to be a major five- to six-year effort leading to a lasting contribution to the field or
a two- to three-year project demonstrating the author's capacity to conduct major research? (4) In accord with their lack of clarity about the dissertation, the students suggested that the department offer an informal
workshop following the preliminary exam for all students on how to con-

struct dissertation proposals. (5) The students never mentioned wanting additional "mentoring" per se, but all agreed on the need for more supervision and guidance. (6) They also asked for clarification of the "norms" and rules. (7) And finally, they wanted a place in which faculty and students could talk frequently and informally—"perhaps a lounge."

The students' report even included a description of an "ideal" graduate life cycle. It recommended that first-year students receive a stipend without having to work in exchange, but that the year include some pedagogic activity, such as attending a TA workshop, observing an undergraduate course, and then developing their own strategies for covering the material. Years 2 and 3 would combine teaching, coursework, and studying for exams. Required exams would be completed by the end of year 3. A dissertation prospectus workshop would take place once or twice a year. Dissertation prospectuses would have to be approved by the dissertation committee by the end of year 3 in order for students to receive preferred funding in year 4. This funding would consist of a Mellon start-up fellowship during the first semester of that year to free up time to begin research; in the second semester, service as a teaching assistant would be required. Finally, in years 5 and 6, students would receive fellowships to support dissertation research and writing.

The department's proposal to the Foundation identified the transition between coursework and dissertation research as the critical point in a graduate student's career. In order to smooth this transition, the department would use GEI funds for a fourth-year fellowship—as the students recommended—that would be given after the prospectus had been approved. It would enable one semester to remain free of other obligations, so the students could devote themselves to the crucial early stages of dissertation research.

The students' interest in teaching was reflected in many other innovations the department introduced: a semester fellowship in the fourth year would be followed by a semester's service as a TA, which would encourage connections to be made between research and teaching. For example, students might design a course related to their research, which they might later teach. The proposal's section on teaching also recommended hiring a graduate student to take charge of TA training. Again in line with the students' recommendations, the department's proposal for funding called for dissertation write-up fellowships that would support the final year of dissertation research. And finally the proposal included a large investment in summer funding, permitting students to continue their studies and then to serve as TAs during the year.

A dissertation research seminar, in which students would present chapters they were writing, was instituted and was to serve a variety of purposes: it would teach research methods, provide students with the experience of discussing their research, impart some professional socialization, and increase students' social ties. The department's proposal summarized the nonfinancial changes it planned: it would (1) reduce the time students spent as TAs; (2) provide a clear timetable for students at each of the major stages of graduate study; (3) attempt to fix the same timetable in the minds of the faculty, thus making it more likely that they would hold students to it; (4) hold weekly colloquia to discuss and critique work in progress; and (5) institute training for job interviews.

As with other departments that took part in the GEI, the actual implementation of these plans changed as faculty members learned from experience and new students were recruited. In 1997, the department decided to alter the structure of its first-year exam. The new exam had two parts: the first would be taken at the beginning of the second semester. It was to be a "relaxed" meeting with a faculty committee charged with evaluating a student's strengths, weaknesses, and plans. The second part was to take place at the end of the second semester and was to be a more formal evaluation, based on seminar papers the student had written. It was to yield a decision on whether the student should continue toward the PhD. The "minor" fields that students would study were also to be identified so that students could begin to prepare early. Prelims were to be completed before the summer of the third year, provided all "incomplete" grades on record had first been resolved. If the student passed the prelims on time, she or he would be eligible for a Mellon start-up grant in the first semester of the fourth year.

In practice, many students received start-up grants even though they were still studying for their prelims. In 1997–98, however, anticipating a reduction in overall funds available for fellowships, the graduate school eliminated the start-up semester grants. That year the department countered with a proposal that the graduate school put in place a postdoctoral lectureship for new PhDs, which would be an incentive to hasten completion and serve as a financial safety net for those who had completed their degrees but had no job.

The department was convinced that the Mellon fellowships enhanced the program and facilitated students' progress. Their reports to the Foundation contained highly positive evaluations of the changes. The following statements are drawn from these reports:

> The GEI made the department more competitive with peer institutions for promising graduate students because of the improved financial packages it could offer.

> Not having to serve as TAs before their exams motivated students to prepare for prelims and boosted their morale along the way.

> The Mellon start-up fellowship offered valuable time for planning and launching dissertation research. Its elimination in 1997–98 lengthened TTD.

The Mellon completion fellowship provided essential time for finishing dissertation research and writing. The proportion of students whose progress through the program was "on time" increased.

The Mellon fellowships enabled faculty to enforce more effectively the expectation that students would finish in their sixth or seventh years—even in the face of a weak job market.

These rosy accounts do not describe the difficulty the department had in implementing the intended innovations. It began to reduce delays in the "problem years" between exams and dissertation research with great enthusiasm. But it focused exclusively on two objectives: reducing the time its students spent teaching and preparing them for teaching careers. It did add strategically timed fellowships and made a few major curricular changes. As time passed, departmental reports contained little mention of other planned changes, nor did they mention faculty commitment to the new regime or increasing the clarity of expectations (for example, about the prospectus). Despite the department's intensive self-examination, most of its changes drew on student proposals rather than on those from the faculty. The graduate school supported the GEI but did not contribute further incentives. Rather, it eliminated one of the main elements of financial aid, and one that the department thought was effective.

Department reports gave no hint that financial support was granted on the condition that students were making timely progress. The department's 1999 report stated "the package we offer (5 years guaranteed) is very competitive (with peer institutions). The fact that we offer it to everyone is a key to the morale and non-competitiveness among our graduate students." Yet some faculty members expressed their concern that "excessive pressure to complete the dissertation during the Mellon Completion year can produce poor work and sloppy research which, in the long run, is not in the student's interest." The report added that "time constraints militate against truly brilliant and important work." Meanwhile, the department's completion rates were discouraging. The original 8-year cumulative completion rate of 44 percent rose briefly to 47 percent for cohorts entering in 1989 and 1990 but then fell back down to 36 percent for students in the 1991–92 through 1995–96 entering cohorts.

This department had useful ideas about improving its programs, but it did not follow through and did not receive the kind of support from the graduate school that would have made its plans effective.

Department C: United Effort, Successful Outcome

A year before the GEI began, the graduate school in this university introduced new policies aimed at reducing TTD and increasing completion rates. Those policies established a six-year norm for earning the degree and prohibited students from registering if they had not advanced to candidacy by their fourth year. Incompletes were to be granted reluctantly, and dissertation write-up fellowships were introduced. A teaching postdoctoral fellowship was made available to students who graduated within six years but had not found academic jobs. By exercising its authority to control registration and the allocation of financial support, the graduate school had done a good deal of "heavy lifting" to support and encourage departmental deadlines. Thus this large department of history began the GEI with the enthusiastic backing of the dean and with significant financial support.

The department undertook its own review and concluded, as had other departments, that "students have too large a teaching load," that they were "too committed" to teaching and thus spent time on teaching at the expense of their own research; that two or more foreign languages were required but no time was available to learn them; and that "the field requires original archival research—usually entailing extended periods away from campus." These were not the only problems that were identified, but the department elected to concentrate on these three because additional funding would go far toward solving them. The department concluded that other reforms could significantly hasten students' progress without large infusions of new money. These had to do with greater integration of requirements and advising and with instituting the long-term goal of a completed dissertation within six years. It also recognized the tendency to treat each stage of the graduate training as separate from the others. Students worked first on courses, then on prelims and the prospectus, and finally on the dissertation, with the result that many did not think seriously about writing a dissertation until late in their third year of study.

As a consequence, the department decided on making changes the faculty thought could facilitate students' movement from one stage to the next and would help them map out how they would meet the department's new goals for progress. First, a more aggressive advising program was instituted, and entering students were told that they should be planning and working on all their degree requirements right from the start. Dissertation advisors were encouraged to help students choose dissertation topics that could be completed within two to three years and to spend more time monitoring their students' writing progress.

To encourage students to move more expeditiously through their training, the department designed a series of "strategy workshops" that focused on planning coursework so that it would lead to efficient preparation for oral exams (in this department, the equivalent of qualifying exams); how to read for orals; how to select a dissertation topic that could be completed in two to three years; how to avoid becoming bogged down in the often lonely final stage of dissertation writing; and finally how to compete effectively in the job market. It institutionalized these discussions so that all students would begin thinking about moving from one stage to the next at the earliest appropriate times. The department planned to produce a series of written documents from the workshops that could be distributed to students as guides. It put in place first- and second-year faculty reviews in order to identify students who might have to struggle to complete their degrees. It also insisted that faculty members state whether "[they] would be willing to direct a dissertation with this student." If no one was willing, the student would be more closely monitored. To reduce delay in the writing of the prospectus and minimize the power of any single faculty member to slow a student's progress, three-member committees were established. Annual progress reports were instituted for students who had been admitted to candidacy, and satisfactory results on these were a prerequisite for registration for the following fall term.

Consistent with the graduate school's official norm of completing the degree in six years, faculty members elected to reduce the expected length of the dissertation in the hope of conveying to students that "the dissertation is intended as an apprenticeship and not a life's work." Requirements for completing the prospectus were moved back from the spring of the third year to the fall, and a finished prospectus was required for candidacy to be granted.

The department's proposal to the Foundation indicated that it planned to use GEI funding for (1) dissertation-writing fellowships, to free students from having to support themselves for that year and to serve as an incentive to choose a project with a more realistic and less extended timetable; (2) grants for language study in the summer; and (3) grants for research travel. Although most other research grants were awarded for an academic year, this department argued that if the students could have these trips funded during the summer they would not miss activities (for example, colloquia or the prospectus preparation seminar) that occurred during the regular school year.

As time passed, this department made few changes in its original plans. One workshop, the dissertation colloquium, was discontinued and replaced by a program of "job talks" based on completed dissertation chapters, which stemmed from an initiative by the graduate student association. The department deemed this student-designed program strikingly successful. It also added a new post, associate director of graduate studies; the associate director's task was to aid students at every stage of the job-seeking process. Furthermore, in response to a request from the graduate student association, it created a faculty-student liaison committee.

The department reported to the Foundation that "in scrutinizing its procedures more systematically, the department has become increasingly aware of its collective responsibility to offer its students more than just coursework and dissertation supervision." Accordingly, it continued its efforts to monitor students' progress more carefully and to provide workshops and guidance to make the passage from student to (employed) scholar as expeditious as possible. The department reported that "It has taken the responsibility of tracking the progress of its students very seriously and this has prodded the department to take a much more active role in seeing its students through the long and difficult years of their apprenticeships."

The programmatic changes this department made involved no major alterations in curriculum, no revamping of the structures of exams or course requirements, no significant redefinition of requirements for advancing to candidacy (although, as we noted, the required deadline for prospectus completion was moved up), and no institution of required workshops or colloquia. However, the size of entering cohorts was reduced, financial aid was modestly increased, newly targeted funds for language study and research were provided, and the department monitored its students more conscientiously.[27] The department's 8-year cumulative completion rate rose from 35 percent for the pre-GEI cohorts to 62 percent for the students who entered between 1991–92 and 1995–96.

Why was the department so successful in increasing its students' completion rates? At this reading, we cannot point to a single critical innovation. However, taken together, the innovations clearly represented major alterations in the way the department went about its business. The graduate school and the department had consistent objectives and took consistent actions, based on changes in policy the graduate school itself had made before the GEI began. As a consequence the department was ready to consider making its own changes before the GEI began. It had already decided to target financial aid on what its members had decided were certain problematic transitions in graduate study, and the graduate students themselves were involved in these decisions. And the faculty remained diligent in meeting its obligations to its students. This department proved successful in substantially improving its completion rate. That it (and other departments) did so demonstrates that such an outcome is possible.

Department D: Instability in Program Design, Emphasis on Summer Support

Three years before the start of the GEI, the faculty of this medium-sized political science department reviewed its graduate program, and that as-

---

[27] The mean size of entering cohorts went from 29 to 24.

sessment led to several major curricular changes.[28] Workshops, seminars, and both research and dissertation colloquia were added, as were a limited number of writing requirements in the first two years. The timing and structure of the dissertation prospectus were changed by requiring that it be part of the preliminary examinations; the monitoring of first- and second-year students was improved; and formal reports on the dissertation progress of advanced students were instituted. Expectations for "prelims" were described in a detailed brochure (reviewed by students as well as faculty members); it dealt with the purpose and format of the exams, how students should prepare for them, and how the exams would be evaluated.

The proposal submitted to the Foundation for the GEI called for the establishment of a required "Mellon Summer Seminar" for students who had advanced to candidacy. Its primary objective was to help students get an early start on their dissertations. The department's proposal explained that "In previous years, students finished their prelims in May and often did not begin to think seriously about their dissertations for several months thereafter. The summer workshop was intended to shorten, if not eliminate, this delay by applying both 'carrots and sticks.' Students who enrolled in the workshop received a summer stipend of $3,000. In exchange, they committed themselves to attend a nine-week series of workshops that met for two hours each week."

As part of the workshops, students had to make periodic substantive reports on the progress of their dissertation research. They also had to comment in detail on the reports made by other students. These reports were taken seriously—one student was threatened with expulsion from the seminar and loss of his stipend unless his work improved.

The department also added "Mellon Seminars" that were held every four weeks; attendance at these was mandatory for Mellon fellowship recipients. These seminars were not required of other students at the same stage of their work, perhaps reflecting the department's misunderstanding of the GEI's objective of improving the graduate experience for all students in a department, not just those who received Foundation funding.

Finally, the department intended to allocate 60 percent of the financial support it received from the GEI to funding students' participation in its new Mellon Summer Seminar. Twenty percent would support summer language study or field work travel during the first two years, and another 20 percent was to be provided to a small number of unfunded students in the form of dissertation write-up fellowships. This budget allocation departed considerably from those submitted by other depart-

---

[28] The size of entering cohorts in this department averaged 15 prior to the GEI and decreased only slightly (to around 14) over the period of the GEI.

ments. In those, the majority of GEI funds were used for dissertation write-up fellowships and for fellowship stipends to relieve students of multiple teaching obligations. One must conclude that fellowship support in this department was ample enough that the Mellon money could mainly be assigned to "add-ons" rather than basic student aid.[29]

The annual reports the department submitted to the Foundation showed that most of these proposed changes were amended—fairly dramatically—within the first five years of the GEI. In 1992–93, the department dropped the requirement that the prospectus be part of prelims. Prospectus writing would begin during the Mellon Summer Seminar and be completed within three months of taking the exam. Then in 1997–98 the Mellon Summer Seminar was discontinued—not because it was ineffective, but because its faculty leader was no longer able to teach it. Originally, the dissertation workshops had required students to present their own work, but later, outsiders made presentations on topics of interest to dissertation writers, and still later, the workshop was transformed into a publication-and-placement seminar, focusing on how to publish and how to interview for jobs. In 1997–98 the original workshop, which had been discontinued, was replaced by "post-prelim research seminars" for each subfield the department offered. Designed to keep students focused on their dissertations, these seminars met biweekly and were attended by faculty and students. The department considered these seminars so successful that they were transformed into a course, in which students who had completed prelims were required to enroll for one year.

The professor who led the Mellon Summer Seminars (before they were discontinued) believed that there were two reasons why the workshops expedited progress on students' dissertations and also improved their quality. First, he wrote, they established firm deadlines for completion. Second, they exposed students to more diverse reactions to their work than they would otherwise have received. As a result, students revised poorly conceptualized projects or, in some cases, abandoned them altogether. One student entered the workshop undecided about which of two dissertation topics to pursue and found the opportunity to discuss both of them very helpful in his ultimate decision. The students said "it was extremely valuable in providing a supportive and helpful group of colleagues during the most difficult stage of dissertation formulation."

Members of this department were quite engaged in designing and redesigning its program, and students' views were taken into account. How-

---

[29] The data on fellowship support for this department are imperfect but show that before the GEI was instituted and provided additional funding, 55 percent of the students had fellowships in their fifth year and 34 percent in their sixth year, a number far higher than that in many departments.

ever, because of continuing program changes, no clear or consistent set of interventions was established whose impact could be assessed. Even the allocation of funds changed when the Mellon Summer Seminars were discontinued and only 20 percent of the funds went to dissertation start-up support. The 8-year cumulative completion rate for those who would have been midway through their graduate program when the GEI began (and were thus eligible for the early years of the summer seminar) rose from 49 percent for the pre-GEI cohorts (students who began between 1981–82 and 1985–86) to 68 percent for entrants who began between 1986–87 and 1990–91.

Later cohorts (students who began in 1991–92 and later) entered when the curricular changes just described were already in place and when the additional write-up fellowships, which were created as part of the GEI, would have been available for fifth- and sixth-year students. However, the high rate of completion by the end of the eighth year that we observed for the 1986–87 through 1990–91 entering cohorts was not maintained by the next group of cohorts. The department's completion rate for the 1991–92 through 1994–95 entering cohorts fell back to 61 percent—still considerably higher than its pre-GEI figure but down somewhat from the 68 percent for the intervening cohorts. Immediate improvement in completion rates upon the introduction of the GEI followed by some backsliding is not unique to this department.[30] We suspect that the original enthusiasm for the GEI's interventions waned among faculty members and students and, in this department, the discontinuation of the Mellon Summer Seminar and the frequent redesign of the dissertation workshops might have seemed confusing and capricious to students and perhaps even contributed to the observed reduction in the completion rate.

Department E: Conditional "Carrots"

This vignette describes a large department in a discipline labeled "other humanities." The department began the design phase of the GEI after a university-mandated review and two internal studies of its program in 1985 and 1987. In response to these assessments, it made two major changes in its program before the GEI began. Language requirements

---

[30] One reason for backsliding may be the fact that departments initially awarded Foundation funds on a competitive basis to a few individuals in the form of large fellowships, but in later years they tended to spread Foundation funds among a much larger number of individuals, thereby reducing the size of the awards and the competition involved in their allocation. Details are provided in Joseph Price, "Gender Differences in Response to Competition," *Industrial and Labor Relations Review* 61 (April 2008): 320–33.

and requirements for the prospectus were reduced in order to decrease the time students took to advance to candidacy. These same reviews led to the conclusion that the department's course and field coverage requirements served the students well.

The department's proposal for the GEI was written by a faculty committee and modified to reflect students' reactions. The program changes it proposed reflected the department's concern that, even though earlier changes had streamlined the pre-examination phase of the program, most students still had to rely on teaching or outside part-time employment for support after passing their exams; both of these added responsibilities delayed dissertation work. The department asserted that students needed a "boost" just after their exams and that "post examination malaise has in fact been a crucial factor in the creeping upwards of time-to-degree."

The department's new program included better funding for students in the post-examination phase on the condition that it be restricted to students who had made timely progress (hence the label for this vignette). This change marked the end of an earlier departmental commitment to provide all students with financial assistance and teaching appointments. The new policy would offer less generous packages of guaranteed multi-year support; funding from Mellon GEI awards would not be automatically provided; and students were told that funding in later years would depend on timely progress. The department's proposal stated its views on the virtues of timely completion: "We believe that it is in the matter of pacing that departmental standards are most clearly asserted and that the 'good time' calendar is thus a truer and fairer form of quality control than further oaths on the part of advisors."[31] This "good time" calendar called for the following timetable: no more than two years from master's exam to prelim, no more than one semester from prelim to prospectus meeting, and no more than one semester from initial prospectus meeting to prospectus completion.

The centerpiece of the department's curricular redesign was the addition of the Mellon Dissertation Colloquium, which was intended to speed up the dissertation. The colloquium would meet during the first and next-to-last weeks of each term, and faculty would participate. All candidates would be required to present their first and second dissertation chapters. In accord with the policy of rewarding timely progress, students who followed the "good time" timetable and had a completed chapter ready for presentation would receive a dissertation write-up fellowship for

---

[31] The "oaths" refer to a common practice of basing a dissertation fellowship on a faculty member's assurance that a student had progressed sufficiently to be able to complete the dissertation within one year.

the first semester of the colloquium; an additional semester's fellowship was to be given conditional on completion of a second chapter. These fellowships would free the recipients from teaching responsibilities while they were writing their dissertations. As a further incentive, a differential tuition plan was instituted, with tuition for the first three years of candidacy set lower than tuition for subsequent years. Moreover, students were required to register continuously.

As the new program proceeded, faculty members recognized that the revised timetable was more demanding than might be desirable. Some adjustments were made to remove obstacles to timely progress; for example, advising for first-year students was intensified and the required master's exam was replaced with a second-year review during which the student, his or her advisor, and two other faculty members would assess the student's progress, intentions, prior academic experience, mastery of languages, critical theoretical skills, and historical knowledge. The second-year review was intended to define students' next steps and to shape the specific prelim exam they would take. In addition to testing students' broad knowledge, this meeting would direct them to their dissertation subjects. The department recognized that there was a balance to be achieved between the short-term goal of exam preparation and the longer-term objective of completing the dissertation. At the end of the meeting student and advisor would agree on a "contract" that would list the remaining specific courses to be taken and the reading to be done for the preliminary exam, and also allow the student to emerge with a sense of possible dissertation topics.

Such intensified advising was designed to replace a "hurdle" (the master's exam) with an experience that would encourage faculty members and students to develop an intellectual relationship and that was not so formidable that students would delay its scheduling. Furthermore, limits were set on the length of prelims and the prospectus to help students "see these efforts as finite and manageable rather than infinite and apocalyptic."

Later reports from the department described further adjustments it made in its original plans. Perhaps the most important was the decision to reduce the number of students it admitted. The average size of entering cohorts was reduced from about 20 to about 12, changing it from a "large" department to one of "medium" size. At no time, however, did the department waver in its commitment to the key elements of the philosophy underlying its original proposal. Leadership in the department did not change. Its DGS would continue to be involved in admissions and the allocation of fellowships; the assistant director would be expected to lead the dissertation colloquium. The chairman wrote in one of his annual reports to the Foundation that

The awareness of the possibility of obtaining a Mellon dissertation writing fellowship has "percolated" through all levels of our grad program. Students make plans for the shape of their program with it in mind. Sometimes students shift into higher gear in preparing for exams and in finishing coursework precisely to remain eligible for a year's support. Even when students make choices, say to go abroad, they do so with a real sense of how that decision translates into cost. The presence of the Mellon fellowships has increased the level of intellectual seriousness. It shortens the time-to-degree for many (though not all) and usually in most acceptable ways.

This department also made financial aid in the later years of graduate study conditional on students' timely progress. To help them meet the conditions it specified, the expected timeline students should follow was clearly stated and requirements were adjusted to remove unintended hurdles. This department began the GEI with a very low 8-year cumulative completion rate—just 13 percent of its students finished within eight years. That rate increased to 33 percent for the cohorts that entered between 1991–92 and 1994–95. In this instance, as in others, there was far more room for improvement than in those cases in which completion rates were reasonably strong initially.

Department F: Waste No Time and Use the Summers

This small "other humanities" department began to improve its program two or three years before the GEI began. It had recruited several new and energetic faculty members and brought in a cohort of students who were better prepared and more amply funded. In 1989, in response to renewed concerns about long TTD and late attrition, the graduate school led a major planning effort that included data gathering and analysis of the determinants of TTD and attrition in all humanities departments. Its findings were shared with all departments, and discussions took place about changes that would make PhD programs more effective. The graduate school also conducted a summer dissertation workshop as a pilot project to test the hypothesis that students who had completed two years in the graduate program could formulate workable dissertation prospectuses. The hypothesis proved correct, and the workshop became a major element in Mellon proposals from all departments in this institution. The discussions fostered by the graduate school resulted in a Seven-Point Common Plan. The elements to be included in all departments' proposals were as follows:

- Advertise department strengths to ensure a good fit with student aspirations;

- Define the norm for TTD as four years, with a five-year maximum;
- Introduce students to research in an area of their choosing from the beginning of graduate study;
- Identify early those students unlikely to be able to complete the program;
- Redesign foundational courses to link them with research techniques, and move pedagogical initiation from the first year to the second or third year;
- Use fellowships rather than TAs in the first year; and
- Make summers an integral part of the doctoral program, and schedule credit-bearing activities in the summers following the first and second years.

Although each department interpreted the plan slightly differently, the departments' participation in the design process seemed to ensure commitment and even enthusiasm. In the Foundation's view, the proposals were based on good evidence. Department F's DGS described its proposed plan as follows:

> We completely revised our program. In particular we streamlined our sequence of exams, giving students fewer hoops to jump through and thus less occasion for dragging things out; we introduced clear expectations that the summers be used for certain defined purposes; we instituted a stricter incomplete policy for coursework; and we required much earlier identification of the dissertation topic. Less formally, we underwent a shift in . . . culture and students began to get the message that funding would be linked to steady progress and that we had faith that they could complete a PhD in 5–6 years.

In particular, Department F laid out a specific timeline for coursework and qualifying exams and consolidated and redesigned the collective reading lists that guide students in studying for exams. These changes and others were published in a new pamphlet aimed at clarifying the department's expectations of students. It also required students to participate in a workshop in the summer of their second year aimed at developing a practicable dissertation proposal. The workshop carried course credit, and most students received a $2,000 stipend to permit them to concentrate on their proposals and, if needed, to travel to archives to establish the feasibility of their projects before they were started. Early identification of a topic was expected to enable students to integrate dissertation preparation with coursework and enable the department to design the qualifying exams to complement more closely the research interests of individual students. Advisors were assigned to all entering students. Those advisors would submit annual reports on the student's progress to a committee charged with student reviews and with screening out those unlikely to finish the PhD in a timely manner.

Financial support was divided between stipends for the summer dissertation workshop and fourth- or fifth-year dissertation fellowships. The department indicated that the closer monitoring, the earlier identification of topics, additional funding, and the clear timelines "worked," noting in a report that "attrition has been diminished because the students now have greater confidence that they can finish in a reasonable time and the department can provide more stable funding."

The department made few modifications as it introduced these changes. The single deviation from the plan was instigated when it became clear that students could not be expected to complete the PhD in four years. It then became more common for the Mellon fellowship to be given in the fifth year and for students to graduate soon after. The department also found that it could not initially offer the summer workshop as a formal course because it attracted too few students. But the size of the entering cohorts was increased (by just one or two students per year), and this provided a sufficient number of students for the workshops and seminars and also led to a greater sense of cohesion among students. In 1995 the department spearheaded a series of profession-wide discussions of curriculum, but those changes centered on content rather than the structural questions that were addressed in the 1991 revision.

If the following report correctly reflects the views of both faculty members and students, they seem to agree completely that timelines for exams and proposal completion were no detriment to intellectual quality:

> The Program is yielding dissertations of improved quality. Emphasis on timely completion insures the currency of the dissertation work with less chance for the methodology and the research to get out of date. Also dissertation writing is becoming a less isolated experience. More attention is now given by faculty committees to the dissertation proposals which have become part of the qualifying exam. Thus more people than just the supervisor are involved at the conceptualization stage of the dissertation. In many cases, the dissertations are treating narrower topics, but the increased interaction of the student with more faculty and with fellow students through the summer workshop produces a more diverse approach.

In the department's view, the most important elements of the redesigned program were: the active use of summers, including attending the summer dissertation workshop; streamlined exams; and earlier identification of dissertation topics. Evidently, the importance of the summer workshop was made crystal clear to the students. According to the GES, only 7 percent of the students in the pre-GEI cohorts said they were required to prepare a prospectus during a summer workshop; by contrast, 77 percent of those who began in 1991–92 or later reported doing so. The message plainly got through. The department's summary report was enthusiastic: "The Mellon grant has not just fostered procedural reforms, but changed and boosted the very spirits of the program. Faculty commitments to the programs are now strong; students are also more secure, not just in the easing of their financial worries, but in participating in programs that have definite trajectories and time frames—the sixth year is now thought of as 'overtime.' That is an entirely new norm."

In fact, commitment to the new norm showed up in marked changes in outcome measures for this department. None of the students who entered the program before 1991–92 completed the PhD within seven years, and only 33 percent did so within eight years. Those who entered the revised program in 1991–92 and beyond completed at the rate of 47 percent by the end of the seventh year and 53 percent by the end of the eighth year, a difference of 20 percentage points in a relatively brief time period. The mean TTD was reduced from 8.6 to 6 years. Mean TTA dropped from 4 to 2.3 years. It appears that the clear commitment, by both the department and the graduate school, to enforcing the timelines and providing funding to make that faster pace possible, as well as the efforts of new faculty members in the department, combined to produce visible success in achieving the desired outcomes.

THE ROLES PLAYED BY DEPARTMENTAL CULTURE AND INSTITUTIONAL STRUCTURE IN EFFECTING CHANGE

So far, the plans departments made, their efforts to put them into effect, and their histories have occupied our account. These are plainly important. But departments also have their own cultures, consisting of shared values, attitudes, beliefs, preferred modes of operation, and not least intellectual perspectives that color day-to-day and long-term operations. They also exist as parts of larger institutions, which themselves have distinctive cultures, histories, modes of organization, and resources. Like it or not, departments are subject to institutional decisions and oversight. From the very beginning of the GEI, differences in departmental cultures and in the institutional contexts in which they were located were evident in the original proposals and persisted in annual reports and the site visits foundation staff made to the participating universities. In this section, we highlight four aspects of culture and structure (two departmental and two institutional) that affected the GEI's success and departmental effectiveness.

Departmental Culture: Enthusiasm for GEI Goals

Reports and actions made clear that many faculty members embraced the idea that TTD and attrition should be reduced. Others, however, did not, expecting that shortening TTD would produce insufficiently prepared students and poor dissertations. One department report stated: "the department prefers a properly trained student rather than an undertrained student who is on time." Some faculty members were skeptical and some were outright hostile. In particular, the goal of reducing TTD was viewed with suspicion in those disciplines that required the mastery of multiple languages (especially "esoteric" ones), multiple scholarly skills (such as paleography), and intensive archival or field work for the dissertation. One anthropology student voiced this opinion—one very typical of faculty in his department: "I am proud of being a true intellectual as opposed to the poor fools who are now made to jump hoops through a short-circuited system of 'quickie education.' Long live my mostly European educated non-American mentors who supported my endeavors and who have always stood for high quality intelligence high quality scholarship and therefore high quality education."

At the extreme, one excellent and powerful department invited to participate in the GEI by its university simply elected not to do so. It had no wish to change its practices to accord with what the GEI would have required. In some cases, although there was no active disagreement with the goals of the GEI, the faculty simply lacked the enthusiasm for the necessary changes or the continuity of leadership that could make them happen. Attrition was largely viewed as a problem of individual students and rarely one for which departments might be responsible. From their comments in the GES, it was clear that the students "heard" the faculty's views and reflected them in their own attitudes toward a speedier pace of work.

Departmental Culture: Appetite for Change and Prior Experience

In some departments, the very idea of changing the program came as a shock. Resistance to changing the "ways we have always done things" militated against acceptance of the GEI, which was perceived as intrusive and thus illegitimate by definition. However, the vignettes make it clear that a number of departments and graduate schools had already put new policies in place before the GEI, and these prepared the ground for the Mellon program. In their proposals and later reports, departments described themselves as concerned about high attrition rates and long TTD and as already searching for ways to improve. And for some, the newly available GEI funds (and the self-examination required as part of the proposal process) served as a wake-up call to faculty members to identify changes from which their programs could benefit. For them, the GEI provided an impetus, a focus, and resources that encouraged them to redesign their programs.

For example, one senior administrator wrote: "The great enthusiasm for the program is shared by faculty and students in the participating graduate departments. The notable support is only in small part attributable to the funds available for final-year fellowships. Gratitude is mostly due to the ways in which the Mellon grant impelled change." Another characterized the impact as follows: "I would summarize the Mellon effect most broadly in two ways. Foremost, the Program has made faculty throughout the university far more conscious of the basic questions concerning graduate education. We have been unsettled from our habitual ways and made to think newly about our ultimate goals and our every practice."

Institutional Structure: Top-Down Influence and Governance

The proposals the universities submitted and the annual reports from the departments made it clear that the graduate schools at some universities were far more engaged in shaping the program in a top-down fashion than in others. In some instances, the departments apparently had little input into the institutional proposal and thus had comparatively little opportunity to contribute creatively (or otherwise) to the changes that would occur in their programs. Two of the departments described in the preceding vignettes were located in institutions with highly engaged administrations. This model was evidenced in uniform departmental proposals, near-uniform budgets for each department, and uniform statements of expected goals for TTD and attrition required of all departments that would participate in the GEI—whatever their previous records had been. Three of the 10 universities submitted such proposals covering a total of 13 departments. Students in those departments understood the mixed messages from department and graduate school. One student reported: "Conversation with the Dean of the graduate school on more than one occasion led me to conclude that there is no agreement between the graduate school and the department about times-to-completion. Whereas 7–8 years is considered normal in the department, the graduate school estimates 5 years to be the expected time-to-completion. For 98 percent of us this is totally unrealistic." In the remaining seven institutions, the departments had significant influence on the proposed plans, but these were nonetheless centrally administered. We expected the sense of "ownership" of the proposed changes to be greater when the departments were more intensively engaged in their creation.

Institutional Structure: Supportive Enforcement

In all 10 universities, the graduate schools and graduate deans supported the GEI. (After all, they elected to participate.) In some, they were especially forceful. They encouraged departments to make changes that depended on and took advantage of the graduate school's capacity to provide university-level incentives—"carrots and sticks"—aimed at helping students finish in a timely manner. The graduate schools (or in some instances the provosts or the deans) in these institutions used the opportunity the GEI presented to change a variety of practices aimed at speeding degree completion for all graduate students. For example, they limited the terms during which students could occupy university housing, they changed tuition regimes so that long-registered students were required to pay larger rather than smaller tuition fees, and they stepped up requirements for annual reporting on the progress students were making on their dissertations.[32] Graduate deans exercised authority as supportive enforcers, so to speak, and took some of the heat off the faculty for changes the GEI introduced. They provided the resources such changes required. The importance of serving as an outside authority and monitor (or what some perceived as a "policeman") was well stated by one department head: "It's hard to get some (not all) faculty to help in enforcing deadlines, but we keep trying. Faculty generally take what they perceive to be the students' side, as no doubt they should. Coercive measures come best from above."

Relating Departmental Culture and Institutional Structure to Student Outcomes

Did these different departmental cultures and institutional structures affect completion rates? To answer this question, each department was assigned a code of "yes" or "no" for each of the four contextual variables just described. The classification was based on the departments' original proposals, their annual reports, and observations during site visits and conferences. The classification scheme was clearly subjective, but care was taken to prevent those who assigned the classifications from knowing the outcome measure. Then we used multivariate linear regressions to relate these four variables to the change over time (pre-GEI to post-GEI) in

---

[32] The institution- or humanities-wide changes in universities introduced additional ambiguity into our efforts to compare the student outcomes in treatment and control departments.

departmental completion rates.[33] (See Appendix Table E.3.2 for the coding schemes for each of these variables.)

We expected that each of these variables describing culture and structure would affect the magnitude of the change in several outcomes. Since the pattern of results was consistent for all outcome measures, we focus here on the effect of these variables on the change in a department's 8-year cumulative completion rate from the pre-GEI period (cohorts that started in years 1982–83 through 1985–86) to the period after the introduction of the GEI (cohorts that started in years 1991–92 through 1994–95). These results provide striking evidence that variables describing departmental culture are associated with improvements in completion rates.

In departments in which faculty members were enthusiastic about and "bought into" the importance of reducing TTD, we found completion rates improved about 10 percentage points more than they did in departments whose faculty had not "bought in."[34] Those departments that had already begun to redesign their programs prior to the GEI also exhibited greater improvements in 8-year cumulative completion rates. Departments that had already been considering or had begun to make changes to reduce TTD showed an almost 15-percentage-point-greater increase in their 8-year cumulative completion rates than those that began the GEI with no such prior experience. These differences may be due to the faculty's prior experience or to the fact that it takes a long time for changes in programs to be instituted and to produce changes in faculty and student expectations. They may also reflect delays in the institution of change. Although departments said they made changes in 1991, in later reports it became clear that many of these changes were not actually put into place until 1993 or 1994. Thus, although multiple explanations may be offered for the observed changes, it is nonetheless evident that a statistically significant correlation exists between the two aspects of departmental culture—pre-GEI concern about TTD and departmental

[33] The detailed results of the analysis are presented in Appendix Table E.3.2 in terms of regression coefficients in equations with the following dependent variables: change in cumulative completion rates for the 7th, 8th, and 11th years and change in SYC. That table lists the variables included to control for other important factors influencing the change in completion rates. Multivariate linear regression is described in Chapter 2.

[34] For example, if the mean 8-year cumulative completion rate for those departments in which the faculty had not "bought in" went from 34 percent for the pre-GEI cohorts to 39 percent for the post-GEI cohorts (an increase of 5 percentage points), then the mean 8-year cumulative completion rate for departments in which the faculty had "bought in" increased from 34 percent in the pre-GEI cohorts to 49 percent for the post-GEI cohorts (an increase of 15 percentage points).

agreement on the value of reducing TTD—and improved 8-year cumulative completion rates.

At the same time, neither of the institutional variables were statistically associated with improved 8-year cumulative completion rates. Since the sample consisted of only 10 universities, it could be argued that the number of observations was too small for proper statistical evaluation. Furthermore, the observed volatility in the size and direction of the effects suggests that if these attributes of university structures are connected to completion rates, much more precision is needed to measure them.

Although these efforts to measure the effects of innovations associated with the GEI in various outcome measures were fraught with complications, it does appear that differences in the cultures of departments contribute significantly and independently to the effects of the GEI. It may be that the departmental outcomes depend more on the degree of commitment to goals on the part of those implementing the change than on the specific choice of innovations to be implemented. Or it may be that the magnitude of the commitment to the goal interacts with the initial choice of innovations, or that efforts made to tinker with those innovations as their impact (or lack of it) is determined have an independent influence. If such interactions between faculty "buy-in" or commitment and choice of innovations exist, they would further complicate the identification of effective innovations. The difficulty of finding sufficiently sensitive indicators of complex social phenomena and measuring them effectively is an all-too-familiar problem in research in the social sciences. The statistical analyses in Part II, especially in Chapter 6, attempt to address these challenges.

SUMMARY

When the GEI began, the 54 departments in 10 universities that participated in the Initiative differed in important respects—including their sense that change was needed in how they educated scholars. Therefore, it is not surprising that the impact on measurable outcomes in these departments varied widely. In more than half of the departments, significant increases in completion rates occurred during their decade-long participation in the GEI. In most departments, attrition rates declined, and declining attrition was associated with the expected concomitant increase in completion. But in a few departments, declining attrition actually led to increases in the share of students who "languished," that is, had neither left nor earned their degrees after 10 or 11 years of graduate study. In many departments, overall TTD was reduced, but often by only a few months. In most cases, the reduction in TTD came from reductions in the time students spent before advancing to candidacy; only small reductions are evident in the time spent researching and writing the dissertation. Nonetheless, overall the departments participating in the GEI experienced a savings of many years of both student and faculty time. Those savings were largely attributable to increased completion rates rather than to appreciable reductions in the time doctoral recipients spent in earning their degrees.

This chapter combines qualitative observations with quantitative data and explores the connection of the qualitative characteristics with measurable change. However, many changes reported by departments are not easily measured. Even in departments with negligible changes in completion rates, faculty and chairmen spoke glowingly about improved morale, changed expectations regarding the nature and timing of qualifying exams, and, in some cases, changed expectations about the nature of the dissertation. Even factoring in the skepticism that reports to foundations must evoke, it appears from the departments' vantage points that real improvements did result. Perhaps they were more subtle than our measures could detect, or sufficient time had not elapsed for measurable changes to appear.

In short, the departments' reports show that they thought the exercise was worthwhile. Regardless of the changes in quantifiable outcomes (or their absence), most departments reported improvements in the quality of their programs, in the esprit of their students and faculty, and in their sense that it was useful to have the opportunity (or pressure) to redesign and rethink their programs.

One chair of a religion department wrote:

There is no question in our minds that the Mellon funding has prompted us to scrutinize our doctoral programs and to pay particularly close attention to the issue of student progress. The innovations have had a positive effect on the quality of our graduate education. Although it can be intangible and not easily made concrete, a climate of expectation for more rapid progress through the program has definitely occurred.

Perhaps the chair of an English department best sums up the consequences of the GEI:

How has Mellon affected the culture of the whole department? To summarize what I said already, the Department is attracting and keeping better students. The level of intellectual exchange, in class and beyond class, has gone up with the level of trust that the students are working in an environment that is relatively free of money worries. This change has turned our Department into something closer to the scholar's ideal atelier, a creative space where participants work together to encourage the best work they can. More than ever, students feel empowered by our forms and processes. One sees a striking difference in the degree of engagement in the program. Students clamor for participation in decision-making on a variety of levels: admissions, hiring, curriculum. This has made for a highly vigorous, charged atmosphere in which students and faculty alike take part with vigor in the process of preparing the next generation of professors.

PART II

Influences on Attrition, Completion, and Time-to-Degree

CHAPTER 4

The Impact of the Graduate Education Initiative on Attrition and Completion

> The sensible thing financially and emotionally
> would have been to get through the program quick-
> ly, but the scholar in me was all too prone to for-
> get about the issue of time.
>
> —Student in art history who entered
> in 1991 and completed PhD in 2001

THE PREVIOUS CHAPTER includes information on how attrition and completion rates changed in departments that took part in the Graduate Education Initiative (GEI) between the period prior to the start of the GEI and the period during which the GEI was in effect. Although such analyses are suggestive of the impact of the GEI, they ignore the possibility that the observed changes may have been caused by factors other than the GEI. These include changes in the characteristics of the entering students (such as test scores, race and ethnicity, gender, marital status, and citizenship status) and changes in labor market conditions. To more accurately estimate whether the GEI did in fact influence attrition and completion probabilities, one must more formally model the processes by which students leave their programs, continue in their programs, or graduate from them, and exploit the data that were collected as part of the GEI about the students enrolled in treatment and control departments.

This chapter provides estimates of the impact of the GEI on attrition rates, completion rates, and time-to-degree (TTD).[1] It does this for the entire period of students' doctoral study and separately for the periods prior to and after admission to candidacy. We also compute how the GEI influenced the cost, in terms of student years, per doctoral degree granted. Our analyses are based on the systematic data on student progress collected annually from both the departments that participated in the GEI

---

[1] Some of the material presented in this chapter is a nontechnical summary and extension of material presented in Jeffrey A. Groen, George H. Jakubson, Ronald G. Ehrenberg, Scott Condie, and Albert Y. Liu, "Program Design and Student Outcomes in Graduate Education," *Economics of Education Review* 27 (April 2008): 111–24.

and the control departments. The data allow us to track the progress of each student who started a PhD program in these departments over a 21-year period spanning the introduction of the GEI. The availability of data on students enrolled in comparison departments allows us to control for external forces (such as the job market for humanities PhDs) that affect students enrolled in all PhD programs.

To preview the main findings of these analyses, we estimate that, on average, the GEI had modest impacts on student outcomes in the expected directions: reducing attrition rates, reducing TTD, and increasing completion rates. The overall impacts of the GEI appear to have been driven in part by reductions in cohort size and increases in student quality. The following two chapters present analyses of the roles that changes in financial support patterns and changes in doctoral program characteristics played in generating these findings.

We also find that the GEI reduced attrition from PhD programs prior to students being admitted to candidacy, increased the percentage of students who were admitted to candidacy, and reduced attrition during the period that students were writing dissertations. However, it did not appear to increase completion rates for those admitted to candidacy. Put another way, the GEI increased the percentage of entering students who were still pursuing the PhD many years after entry, a phenomenon that we call "languishing." Finally, it appears that the GEI at best caused only a small reduction in the cost, in terms of student years, for each PhD produced. The benefits of the GEI in terms of reduced student-year costs due to reduced attrition were offset by increases in these costs due to increased languishing.

DATA AND METHODOLOGY

The analysis in this chapter is based on 85 treatment and control departments in 10 fields, as shown in Table 4.1. These departments accounted for 18 percent of all PhDs awarded nationally in these fields from 1980 to 1991, according to data from the Survey of Earned Doctorates. Among departments ranked in the top 10 of their fields by the National Research Council, the departments in our analysis represent 50 percent of PhDs awarded nationally. Treatment and control departments can be compared prior to the GEI using measures from the 1995 National Research Council study of doctoral programs.[2] Treatment departments are

---

[2] Marvin L. Goldberger, Brendan A. Maher, and Pamela E. Flattau (eds.), *Research Doctorate Programs in the United States: Continuity and Change* (Washington, DC: National Academies Press, 1995).

TABLE 4.1
Treatment and Control Departments Analyzed in Chapter 4

Field	Treatment	Control
Anthropology	Columbia, Harvard, Princeton, Stanford, Yale	Cornell, North Carolina, UCLA, UC-San Diego
Art history	Harvard, Michigan, Princeton, UC-Berkeley, Yale	Cornell, Stanford, UCLA
Classics	Michigan, Pennsylvania, UC-Berkeley	Cornell, North Carolina, Princeton, Yale, UCLA
Comparative literature	Cornell, UC-Berkeley	Michigan, Princeton, UCLA, Yale
English	Chicago, Columbia, Cornell, Harvard, Michigan, Pennsylvania, Stanford, UC-Berkeley, Yale	Princeton, UCLA, UC-San Diego
History	Chicago, Cornell, Michigan, Pennsylvania, Princeton, Stanford, UC-Berkeley, Yale	North Carolina, UCLA, UC-San Diego
Music	Columbia, Pennsylvania, Yale	Cornell, Michigan, Princeton, Stanford, UCLA, UC-San Diego
Philosophy	Chicago, Columbia, Stanford	Cornell, North Carolina, UCLA, UC-San Diego, Yale
Political science	Chicago, Cornell, Harvard, Princeton	North Carolina, Stanford, UCLA, UC-San Diego, Yale
Religion	Columbia, Harvard	Princeton, Stanford, Yale

Note: Overall, there are 44 treatment departments and 41 control departments in the analysis sample for this chapter.

more highly ranked: the typical treatment department is ranked in the top 10, whereas the typical control department is ranked in the second 10 (average rankings of 8.2 versus 14.3). In addition, treatment departments are larger than control departments, in terms of both the number of faculty (averages of 32.4 versus 25.0) and the number of PhD students (averages of 101.3 versus 61.5). These differences in size reflect in part the fact that treatment departments are more heavily represented in fields, such as English and history, that tend to have larger departments compared to the other fields in our study.

The student-level data cover all students who started PhD programs in these departments in entering cohorts between 1982–83 and 2002–03. Our sample includes 22,994 students, including 14,488 from treatment departments and 8,506 from control departments. Among students who began doctoral study well before the GEI commenced (the 1982–83

through 1985–86 entering cohorts), 53 percent graduated, 45 percent left
the program, and 3 percent were still pursuing the PhD 17 years after entry. The bulk of the attrition occurred during the first four years in the
program (Figure 4.1). Looking at the distribution of attrition, 30 percent
of all who left the program did so in the first year and 69 percent of all
who left did so in the first four years. The modal years for completing the
PhD were years 6, 7, and 8, which together represent 49 percent of all completions in these cohorts. There is a significant right tail in the distribution, with 10 percent of those who complete taking 12 years or more.[3]

We use an evaluation design that takes account of pre-GEI differences
between the outcomes of PhD students enrolled in treatment and control departments. We identify the impact of the GEI by comparing the
change in student outcomes that occurred in treatment departments to
the change that occurred in control departments. The use of annual data
on student progress allows us to model the impact of the GEI in terms of
year-to-year transition probabilities. Our model involves student transitions over a one-year period among students who have already completed
a given number of years in a PhD program. Over the next academic year,
each of these students can complete the PhD, continue in the program,
or leave the program. Appendix D, Section 1, presents a summary of our
model (which economists call a competing-risk duration model) and the
empirical methodology we employ.

After estimating the model, we use simulations to compute the impacts
of the GEI on the cumulative probabilities of attrition and completion by
each year.[4] The simulations are based on the estimated parameters of the
model and data on students who entered treatment departments after the
GEI was implemented. For each of these students, we use the student's
characteristics and the model parameters to predict the student's transition probabilities for each year in program, supposing that the student survived to that year. Then we use these transition probabilities to predict the
student's probabilities of attrition, completion, and continuation in each
year. Finally, we use these probabilities to compute cumulative probabilities of attrition and completion by the end of each year in program.

For each student in the simulation, we predict two sets of these probabilities. The first assumes that the student was never subject to the GEI, and
the second assumes that the student was always subject to the GEI. The difference between the two sets of predictions is an estimate of the effect of
the GEI on the student. These differences are then averaged across stu-

[3] Median (mean) TTD for these cohorts is 8 (8.16) years and median (mean) time-to-
attrition is 3 (3.98) years.
[4] The cumulative probability of an event occurring by year t is the probability that the
event has occurred by that year.

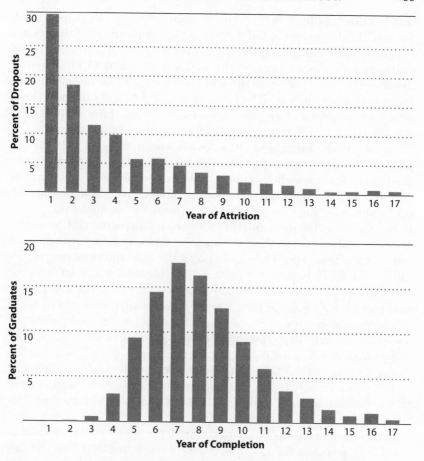

Figure 4.1. Distribution of Attrition and Completion, 1982–83 through 1985–86 Entering Cohorts

dents to produce our overall estimates of the effects of the GEI on attrition and completion. We compute the impact of the GEI on mean elapsed TTD using the cumulative completion rates predicted from the model, as described in Appendix D, Section 2.

MAIN FINDINGS

Impact of the GEI on Outcomes: Baseline Estimates

We present two sets of estimates from our baseline model, which includes explanatory variables for student gender, race and ethnicity, and citizenship but does not include measures of student quality (see Appendix D, Section 2). The first set of estimates treats the department as the central unit of analysis and reflects the impact for a typical department. These estimates are relevant because the GEI was designed to affect entire departments, not just students who received GEI funding.[5] In the second set, our estimates reflect the impact for a typical student.[6] These *department-weighted* and *student-weighted* estimates will differ to the extent that the GEI had different effects in larger and smaller departments.

The department-weighted estimates are shown in Figure 4.2. The impacts on attrition are shown in the top left panel. There are two lines in this panel; each line indicates the cumulative probability of attrition as of each year in program, as predicted by the model. The gray line shows the probabilities for the case with the GEI. The solid line shows the probabilities for treatment departments for the case without the GEI. Since the gray line is always below the solid line, the figure indicates that the GEI reduced attrition rates. The gap between the lines indicates the magnitude of the GEI's impact. For instance, the probabilities of attrition for year 7 are 0.294 without the GEI and 0.267 with the GEI. The average impact over all years is 0.029 (or 2.9 percentage points), as shown in Table 4.2. A comparison of the "hazard rates" (the probabilities of attrition in a year, for students in the program at the beginning of the year) for the two groups, shown in the top right panel of Figure 4.2, indicates that the primary impact of the GEI on attrition occurred in students' first and eighth years. Although the GEI appears to have reduced attrition between students' first and second years, it was associated with increased attrition between years 3 and 4.

The impacts on completion are shown in the bottom left panel of Figure 4.2. In this case, the gray line is always above the solid line, indicating that the GEI increased cumulative completion rates. For example, the probabilities of completion for year 8 are 0.402 without the GEI and 0.431 with the GEI. The average impact over all years is 0.018 (or 1.8 percentage points), as shown in Table 4.2. This translates into a reduction in mean TTD (as of year 11) of 0.119 years, or 1.4 months. The small impact on TTD is not surprising if the marginal students affected by the GEI, those whose attrition is prevented, are students who will have long degree times.[7] The hazard rates in Figure 4.2 indicate that the primary

---

[5] We obtain these estimates by weighting each observation by the inverse of the size of the student's entering cohort.

[6] We obtain these estimates by giving equal weight to each student in the estimation.

[7] The estimated impact on TTD reflects the combination of two conceptually distinct impacts. The first is the impact of the GEI on TTD for students who would have completed in the absence of the GEI. The second is the impact on measured TTD of changing the set

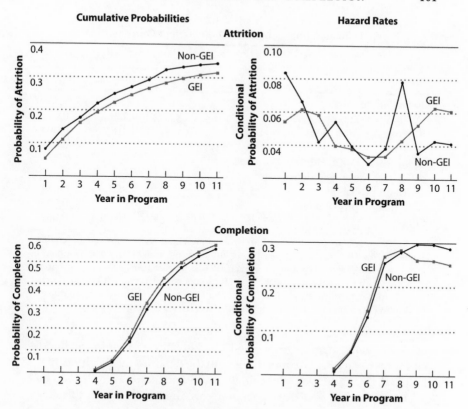

Figure 4.2. Impact of the GEI on Attrition and Completion
Notes: The figures correspond to the department-weighted results in Table 4.2. The hazard rates are the probabilities of attrition or completion in a year, for students in the program at the beginning of the year.

impact of the GEI on completion was in years 6, 7, and 8 (the modal years of completion).

The estimated GEI impacts in the department-weighted version of our baseline model are in the intended direction but modest in magnitude. The student-weighted estimates follow a similar pattern but are smaller in magnitude. The average impacts across years in the student-weighted version are 2.0 percentage points for attrition, 0.5 percentage point for completion, and 0.041 year for TTD (Table 4.2). A comparison of the two

of students who complete. The first impact is likely to be a decrease in TTD. The second impact may be an increase or a decrease in TTD, depending on whether the marginal students affected by the GEI have long or short degree times.

TABLE 4.2

Estimated Impact of the GEI on Student Outcomes

	Weighting	
	Department	Student
Baseline model		
Attrition probability	–0.029	–0.020
Completion probability	0.018	0.005
TTD	–0.119	–0.041
Baseline model with additional controls: Cohort size and student quality		
Attrition probability	–0.026	–0.014
Completion probability	0.015	0.003
TTD	–0.104	–0.062

Notes: Estimates labeled "Student" are from unweighted regressions on student-level data; those labeled "Department" are from regressions on student-level data weighted by the inverse of cohort size. The number in each cell is an average (over years in the program) GEI impact on the cumulative probability of attrition or completion; for TTD, the number is the GEI impact on the average number of years between entry into the PhD program and the awarding of the PhD (for those who finished in 11 years or less).

sets of estimates suggests that the GEI had greater impacts in smaller departments (which receive more weight in the department-weighted analysis than in the student-weighted analysis).[8] Some reasons why the GEI had greater impacts in smaller departments are discussed later in this chapter and in Chapter 6.

Role of Changes in Cohort Size and Student Quality

In addition to measuring the size of the impacts, it is critical to understand the mechanisms by which the GEI influenced outcomes. Although this is a challenge in any evaluation, it is particularly difficult here because, as we have already described, each department implemented the GEI somewhat differently. Furthermore, implementing the GEI was a dynamic process involving extensive experimentation at the departmental level. In this section, we explore the roles of changes in cohort size and student quality in explaining the measured impact of the GEI. (The roles

---

[8] This finding is confirmed by a variation on our model that allows the estimated GEI impacts to vary across subgroups of departments based on department size. We classified departments into three categories based on average cohort size for the 1982–83 through 1990–91 entering cohorts, and the estimated GEI impacts were largest for the small departments (those with an average cohort size of 7.5 or fewer).

of changes in financial-support patterns and changes in program characteristics are discussed in Chapters 5 and 6, respectively.)

We evaluate the role of these potential mechanisms in a two-step process. First, we estimate the impact of student quality and cohort size on student outcomes by including them among the explanatory variables in our estimation model.[9] Second, we estimate the impact of the GEI on student quality and cohort size. The estimated impacts for this step are reported in Table 4.3. The impacts for the first step are reported in Table 4.4 as the effect of each characteristic on the cumulative probabilities of attrition and completion by the end of year 8.

Reducing the size of entering cohorts was often an explicit goal of treatment departments. We find that the GEI did in fact lead to a decrease in cohort size—a reduction of two to three students on average (Table 4.3), with the reductions occurring primarily in the larger departments. The logic was that with smaller cohorts, departments could concentrate their faculty and financial resources on fewer students and thus improve each student's progress. Indeed, smaller cohorts are associated with a lower probability of attrition; however, cohort size is only weakly related to the probability of completion (Table 4.4). Together these findings suggest that reductions in cohort size can explain some of the measured impact of the GEI on attrition.

The reductions in cohort size, together with increases in financial support from the GEI, would be expected to lead to increases in the quality of students who enrolled in treatment departments. We find some evidence of this in GRE scores. We estimate that the GEI increased GRE verbal scores by about 10 points on average; however, we find no impact of the GEI on GRE math scores (Table 4.3). We also find that higher GRE verbal scores are associated with lower attrition (Table 4.4); thus the change in GRE scores can explain some of the measured impact of the GEI on attrition.

Another indicator of student quality, the share of students who held a master's degree at the start of their PhD program, decreased slightly because of the GEI (Table 4.3). In fact, perusal of the departmental reports that were submitted to the Foundation suggests that a reduction in the share of entering students with master's degrees already in hand was an explicit policy change of some departments participating in the GEI; some faculty members in these departments were skeptical of the quality of training that students had received in their master's programs. This change is consistent with the change in GRE verbal scores at treatment

---

[9] For this purpose, we use a simplified version of our model in which the dependent variable represents the cumulative probabilities of attrition, completion, and continuation for year 8.

TABLE 4.3
Changes in Cohort Size and Student Quality

	Sample Mean	GEI Impact
Cohort size	13.2	−2.166
GRE verbal	666.1	10.585
GRE math	632.3	−1.251
Prior master's degree	0.25	−0.141

Notes: Each row comes from a separate regression. The estimates of GEI impacts come from linear models in which the explanatory variables include controls for field and institution and indicators for whether the department is a treatment or control department, whether the GEI was in effect, and the interaction of those indicators. The coefficient of the interaction term is the estimated GEI impact.

TABLE 4.4
Effects of Explanatory Variables on Student Outcomes

	Impact on Attrition Probability	Impact on Completion Probability
Cohort size	0.0023	−0.0010
GRE verbal / 100	−0.0207	0.0104
GRE math / 100	−0.0077	0.0225
Prior master's degree	−0.1262	0.1140
Female	0.0155	−0.0304
Non–U.S. citizen	−0.0632	0.0888
U.S. citizen, minority	0.0242	−0.0362

Notes: Each number is the average marginal effect of the characteristic on the cumulative probability of attrition or completion by the end of year 8. These numbers are based on a regression model that includes controls for field and institution. As of the eighth year in the program, 37 percent had graduated, 37 percent had dropped out, and 26 percent were continuing in their programs.

departments, because students with a prior master's degree tend to have lower GRE scores than other students.

However, having a prior master's degree is a strong predictor of success in a PhD program, presumably because the training that students have received in their master's programs reduces their coursework requirements in the PhD program, and their experience in a master's program likely increases their understanding (relative to people who enter PhD programs directly from undergraduate school) about what PhD study will be like. We estimate that having a master's degree prior to entry to PhD study improves student outcomes as of the eighth year, lowering the probability of attrition by 13 percentage points and increasing the probability of completion by 11 percentage points (Table 4.4). Thus the reduction in the share of students with a prior master's degree actually worked against the goals of the GEI.[10]

One way to summarize the role of changes in student quality and cohort size in the GEI is to include them as control variables in our estimation model and see how this changes the measured impact of the GEI. Doing this decreases the estimated impacts of the GEI somewhat (Table 4.2, bottom panel). This indicates that reductions in cohort size and increases in student quality are responsible for a small part of the impact of the GEI.

The Possibility of Treatment Contamination

Our estimated impacts of the GEI on student outcomes may understate the true impact of the GEI due to treatment contamination. Generically, treatment contamination exists in an intervention when some of the controls are affected by the treatment. To the extent that this occurs, the affected controls are not suitable for use in the evaluation. In this study, the most plausible case of treatment contamination is that control departments in participating institutions (i.e., institutions with treatment departments) were directly influenced by the GEI. Five universities in the study have both treatment and control departments: Cornell, Michigan, Princeton, Stanford, and Yale (see Table 4.1). Control departments at these institutions could have been affected by the GEI through at least two channels. First, institutions could have responded to the increased external support in treatment departments by improving funding in control departments. Second, control departments could have mimicked the structural changes in doctoral programs that were being made by treatment departments.[11]

---

[10] The results reported in Table 4.4 also show that gender, race and ethnicity, and citizenship also influence attrition and completion rates. Women are more likely to have left their PhD programs and less likely to have graduated by the eighth year than men (we discuss these gender differences further in Chapter 7). Non–U.S. citizens are less likely to have left and more likely to have graduated than their citizen counterparts. Finally, minority U.S. citizens (defined here as African Americans, Hispanic Americans, Asian Americans, and Native Americans) are more likely to have left and less likely to have graduated than their white U.S.-citizen counterparts.

[11] It is important for us to stress that because our data cover a period when there was a general nationwide concern for long TTD and low completion rates, and efforts to improve these outcomes, both treatment and control departments in our sample would probably have been taking actions to improve these outcomes independent of the GEI. Our methodology (the difference-in-differences approach) already has controlled for such actions.

We test for contamination by distinguishing between control departments at participating and control departments at nonparticipating institutions. We add variables to our baseline model in order to produce two sets of GEI impacts based on the time pattern of student outcomes in treatment departments relative to either (1) control departments in participating institutions or (2) control departments in nonparticipating institutions. If contamination exists, the introduction of the GEI should be associated with similar changes at treatment departments and at control departments in participating institutions. In this case, the measured impact of the GEI using control departments in participating institutions would be smaller than the measured impact using control departments in nonparticipating institutions.

The results of this test are shown in Appendix Table E.4.1. Using control departments at participating institutions as the comparison group for treatment departments produces estimates of GEI impacts that are larger than (in the case of attrition) or about the same as (in the case of completion) estimates using control departments at nonparticipating institutions. Thus the results provide no evidence for this form of treatment contamination. Of course, changes that may have occurred at treatment departments to improve their graduate programs may have been known to control departments at nonparticipating institutions as well. This in turn may have caused these departments to make similar changes in their programs for competitive reasons. If this were true, all control departments would be somewhat affected by the GEI, and our estimates would understate the true effects of the GEI on student outcomes.

Another reason that our estimates may understate the true impact of the GEI is that the changes made by treatment departments took place gradually over time (see Chapter 3). As such, students in the initial cohorts that were exposed to the GEI may not have been affected very much, but students in later cohorts may have been affected to a greater extent. We test for this by redefining the timing of GEI introduction from the simple pre-post definition to one involving three time periods. In treatment departments, the 1982–83 through 1985–86 entering cohorts had essentially no exposure to the GEI, the 1986–87 through 1990–91 cohorts had some exposure, and the 1991–92 through 2002–03 cohorts were fully exposed to the GEI. Estimated GEI impacts for the fully exposed cohorts are much larger than those for the transition cohorts (Appendix Table E.4.1). This supports the presumption that structural change was a gradual process in treatment departments and the impact of this

---

When we talk about the possibility of treatment contamination, we are referring only to changes in their programs that control departments made in response to the GEI.

change (as well as the direct impact of financial aid) increased with exposure. Relative to the impacts from the baseline model, the estimated GEI impacts for the fully exposed cohorts are about one-third larger.

ADDITIONAL FINDINGS

The estimates provided thus far in this chapter reflect the average impact of the GEI over all departments that participated in the GEI. We know, however, that treatment departments varied in the type of changes made and the degree to which they embraced the goals of the GEI (see Chapter 3). As such, it is of interest whether the GEI was more effective in some departments than in others. We address that issue in this section by providing estimates of GEI impacts by field and by department size. We also provide estimates separately for the coursework and dissertation stages of doctoral programs. Finally, we estimate the impact of the GEI in terms of changes in the student-year cost of producing a PhD.

Estimates of GEI Impacts by Field and Department Size

Estimates of the impacts of the GEI on attrition rates and completion rates by field and department size appear in Appendix Table E.4.2. These estimates are based on a somewhat simpler model than we used in previous sections of the chapter: rather than modeling transition probabilities, we model the cumulative probabilities of attrition, completion, or continuation as of the end of each year.[12] Given the limited number of departments in the study, we analyze impacts by field separately from impacts by department size. This decision, though necessary, complicates the interpretation of these estimates because the distribution of departments by size varies across the fields in our sample (Appendix Table E.4.3). Hence variation in the effects of the GEI across fields may partially reflect

---

[12] We do this for years 1–11 and for students in entering cohorts 1982–83 through 2002–03. We implement this approach using a multinomial logit model for each year, with the dependent variable reflecting whether the student has left, has completed, or is still pursuing the PhD (for years 1–3 we do not include the completion option). We produce estimates of the impacts of the GEI on student outcomes using simulations that are similar to the ones described previously for the competing-risk model. To estimate the impacts separately by field, we allow the coefficients of the intercept terms in our models—whether the department is a treatment or a control department, whether or not the year is one in which the GEI was in effect—and the interaction of the latter two variables to all vary across fields. An analogous procedure is followed when we analyze impacts separately by department size.

differences in department size across fields, and variation in the effects across size groups may partially reflect differences in the distribution of departments across fields by cohort size.

Appendix Figures E.4.1 and E.4.2 present the cumulative probabilities of attrition and completion in each year in program and separately for the cases with and without the GEI.[13] The estimates reported in Appendix Table E.4.2, are the averages of the individual year-in-program differences shown in the figures. The first row of the table shows our estimate of the effects of the GEI on outcomes when one does not estimate separate effects by field or department size. The estimated reduction in attrition probabilities of 0.05 and increase in completion probabilities of 0.03 are each somewhat larger than the baseline estimates that we reported in Table 4.2.

Separate estimates by field of the effect of the GEI appear in the next 10 rows. The largest impacts of the GEI, on both attrition and completion probabilities, are estimated to have taken place in art history, classics, comparative literature, and music. In contrast, much smaller impacts (often close to zero or operating in the wrong direction) took place in anthropology, English, history, and political science. Although one might speculate on the differences in the fields that lead to these differences, it is also the case that the English, history, and political science departments in our sample tend to be the ones with large entering cohorts (Appendix Table E.4.3). As a result, the field differences that we observe may reflect differences in department size.

Did the effects of the GEI differ across department by size class (as measured by the size of entering cohorts)? The bottom three rows of Appendix Table E.4.2 present our estimates of the effects of the GEI by size classes of departments. Consistent with the findings discussed earlier in the chapter, the effects of the GEI on attrition and completion are estimated to be largest for the small departments and smallest for the large departments. Put simply, the GEI appears to have worked better in smaller departments than it did in larger departments.

We can only speculate on the reasons for this here, although we will return to this issue in the next two chapters. On the one hand, GEI funding per student was greater in smaller departments. For example, between

---

[13] In a few cases the cumulative probability of completion (or attrition) found in these figures is lower in one year than it was in the previous year. These anomalies can occur because the sample used to estimate the cumulative probabilities differs from year to year. So, for example, if we are estimating the cumulative probability that a student in English completes by year 11, students who entered their PhD programs in 1993 would not be in our sample (because our data end in 2003), but these students would be in the sample for our estimation of whether a student in English completes by year 10.

1991 and 1999 average GEI funding per student per year (in 1991 dollars) was $1,619 in small departments, $1,116 in medium-sized departments, and $858 in large departments. To the extent that money matters (we address this issue in the next two chapters), one should expect the GEI to have had a greater impact on small departments than on large departments.

On the other hand, the GEI involved much more than money. To the extent that it is easier to get faculty in small departments to "buy into" seriously evaluating their graduate programs, coming to consensus on changes that need to be made, implementing these changes, taking responsibility to see that the changes "stick," and monitoring student progress to see if the changes are working, we might expect to see larger effects of the GEI (or any departmental intervention) in the smaller departments. In Chapter 6, we provide evidence that the GEI influenced some program characteristics more in small departments than in large departments.

Estimates of GEI Impacts by Stage

We also estimate the impacts of the GEI on student outcomes separately for the coursework and dissertation stages of doctoral programs. The coursework stage is defined as the time from entry to the PhD program to advancement to candidacy. The dissertation stage is defined as the time from advancement to candidacy to completion of the PhD. The institutional database contains the date of advancement to candidacy for each student.

Estimates of GEI impacts by stage are shown in Appendix Table E.4.4.[14] We estimate that the GEI reduced attrition during the coursework stage and increased the percentage of entering students who reached candidacy. Our estimates suggest that the GEI also reduced attrition at the dissertation stage but did not increase completion rates (over the first seven years since reaching candidacy) for those who attained candidacy. The greater impact of the GEI in the coursework stage might reflect the fact that this stage is the most structured part of a PhD program and that the GEI was focused on structural aspects of programs. Taken together, the pattern of results for the coursework stage and for the dissertation stage (shown graphically in Figure 4.3) suggests that the GEI increased the per-

---

[14] At the coursework stage, the model is estimated using all entering students, and the outcomes each year are continuation, attrition, and advancement to candidacy. At the dissertation stage, the model is estimated using data on all students who are admitted to candidacy, and the outcomes each year are continuation, attrition, and completion of the PhD.

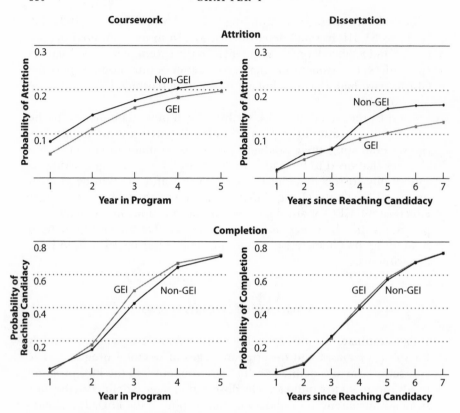

Figure 4.3. Impact of the GEI on Outcomes by Stage

centage of entering students who were still pursuing the PhD many years after entry, the phenomenon we call "languishing."

Estimates of GEI Impacts on Student-Year Cost

In this chapter we have provided separate estimates of the impact of the GEI on attrition rates, completion rates, and TTD. As a way to summarize the combined effect of these different impacts, we use the concept of student-year cost (SYC), which was discussed in Chapters 2 and 3. SYC is the cost of producing a PhD measured in student years. We compute SYC for each treatment and control department separately for a time period before the GEI (the 1982–83 through 1984–85 entering cohorts) and for a time period after the GEI (the 1991–92 through 1993–94 entering cohorts).

TABLE 4.5
Impact of the GEI on Student-Year Cost

SYC and Components	Mean (years)	GEI Impact
SYC	12.4	−0.65
Finishers (by year 11)	7.1	−0.02
Leavers (by year 11)	2.9	−0.73
Continuers (past year 11)	2.4	0.10

Notes: Each row comes from a separate regression. The estimates of GEI impacts come from linear models in which the explanatory variables include controls for field and institution and indicators for whether the department is a treatment or a control department, whether the GEI was in effect, and the interaction of those indicators. The coefficient on the interaction term is the estimated GEI impact.

The measure of SYC used here is based on an 11-year window for measuring completion and attrition. SYC contains three components. The first is the cost related to students who complete the PhD within 11 years of entry. The second is the cost related to students who leave their programs within 11 years. The third is the cost related to students who continued in their programs beyond the 11th year. For this component, we assume that on average these students cost 12 years but do not contribute to the number of PhDs produced by a department.[15]

We use a linear regression model to estimate the impact of the GEI on the average number of student years consumed in the production of a PhD within 11 years. The regression relates SYC to three variables: an indicator for treatment department, an indicator for whether the GEI was in effect, and the interaction between these indicators. The estimated coefficient on the interaction term indicates the change over time in SYC at treatment departments relative to the change at control departments; this is our estimate of the impact of the GEI on SYC. In addition to these three variables, we also include indicators for fields and institutions among the explanatory variables to control for differences in SYC across fields and institutions.

On average across departments and time periods, SYC is 12.4 years. We estimate that the GEI caused a small reduction in SYC of 0.65 year (Table 4.5). Among the three components of SYC, the GEI had the largest estimated impact on the cost related to students who leave their programs within 11 years; our estimate corresponds to a 25 percent reduction in

[15] For the third component, we ignore the possibility that students still pursuing the PhD after 11 years eventually earn the PhD in order to achieve comparability in the measure of SYC between the cohorts before and after the GEI was introduced. See Appendix C for more details on the computation of SYC.

this cost. This reflects the impact of the GEI on reducing attrition, particularly early in programs. The only component for which the GEI is associated with an increase in cost is students who continue to pursue the PhD after 11 years. This again reflects the possibility that the GEI may have contributed to "languishing."

CONCLUSION

The estimates presented in this chapter reveal that the GEI reduced attrition rates, reduced TTD, and increased completion rates. Although these impacts were in the directions intended by its framers, the magnitude of these impacts is modest. However, it is possible that our estimates understate the true effects of the GEI because many of the structural changes inspired by the GEI took place gradually over time and because control departments may have been indirectly influenced by the GEI.

The overall impacts of the GEI appear to have been driven in part by reductions in cohort size and increases in student quality. The next two chapters present evidence that changes in financial-support patterns (Chapter 5) and changes in doctoral-program characteristics (Chapter 6) were important components of the overall impacts of the GEI. In addition, the effects of the GEI on attrition and completion are larger in smaller departments. In Chapter 6 we examine whether the GEI influenced program characteristics differently in small and large departments.

The GEI appears to have had a greater impact at the coursework stage than at the dissertation stage. According to our estimates, the GEI reduced attrition during the coursework stage and increased the percentage of entering students reaching candidacy. At the dissertation stage, the GEI reduced attrition but did not increase the rate of completion. Taken together, these findings suggest that the GEI increased the percentage of entering students who were still pursuing the PhD more than 10 years after entry. Future efforts to increase completion rates may well require new strategies at the dissertation stage.

CHAPTER 5

The Influence of Financial Support

> The availability of fellowships with fairly strict requirements for a research timetable was of great help in maintaining self-discipline.
> —History student who entered in 1986 and completed PhD in 1993

MOST DOCTORAL students in the treatment and control departments receive financial support from their departments at some point during their programs.[1] Such support takes a variety of forms, and its absolute level varies across students and departments. As we know, financial support is critical for both doctoral students and their departments. For students, it covers tuition and living expenses (or at least part of these) at a time when most are devoting their full attention to coursework and research.[2] Moreover, the type and amount of financial support that students receive influence the skills in teaching and research they acquire during their doctoral studies and can facilitate productive interactions with faculty members. Departments use financial support to recruit and retain talented students in their doctoral programs, to meet teaching needs in their universities, to provide research assistance to faculty members, and to provide incentives for students to make timely progress.

Since the Graduate Education Initiative (GEI) was a major financial intervention and treatment departments spent the vast majority of the Foundation's grants on support for students, understanding patterns of financial support is closely tied to evaluating the effects of the GEI. One goal of the GEI was to provide funding, particularly at the dissertation stage. Another was to introduce financial incentives that would encourage students to make timely progress through doctoral programs.

---

[1] According to the institutional database, 90 percent of students have some form of financial support during at least one year in their programs.

[2] The GES asked students whether they were ever registered or enrolled part time at three stages of their doctoral programs. Overall, 8.4 percent of students were part time while completing coursework, 8.6 percent were part time after completing coursework but before completing exams, and 11.4 percent were part time after completing exams but before writing the dissertation proposal or prospectus.

The assumptions underlying the GEI were that students who had to compete for support would finish their degrees more quickly than they would if support were guaranteed, and that tying awards to timely progress would serve that end.

This chapter continues with a general discussion of how financial support affects recruitment, students' allocation of time, and students' effort. The next section examines basic patterns in the financial support data collected as part of the GEI—in particular, how support varies according to year in a program, to a variety of student characteristics, and to departmental characteristics. We then estimate how the GEI influenced financial support patterns by comparing time trends in treatment departments with those in control departments.

We close the chapter with an assessment of the impact of the financial support students received on the outcomes of their doctoral careers. We enrich the model of student progress developed in Chapter 4 by adding to it the type of financial support that students received in each year they were in their programs. This exercise allows us to address questions that are potentially relevant to university and departmental policies of financial aid. For instance, does improving financial support improve student outcomes, and if so, by how much? How can departments reallocate their financial-support budgets among different types of aid in order to improve student outcomes? Does serving as a teaching assistant (TA) affect students' progress toward the PhD, and if so, how?

FINANCIAL SUPPORT, RECRUITMENT, AND STUDENT OUTCOMES

To set the stage for the empirical analyses that follow, this section outlines the potential roles that financial support plays in graduate education. We focus on how financial support affects student outcomes and address several channels within which this relationship plays out, including recruitment, students' time allocation, and students' effort.

Financial Support and Recruitment

Financial support might affect student outcomes indirectly by influencing the types of students who choose to enroll in a department's graduate program. The role of financial support in recruiting is most apparent to students who have been admitted to multiple programs. They must choose a program after weighing various offers of financial support and other salient differences between programs, including faculty members, academic reputation, and geographical location.

Some evidence on the relative importance of financial support for enrollment decisions in the humanities is provided by the Graduate Education Survey (GES). The survey asked students to rank five factors in terms of their importance in choice of a doctoral program:

- Opportunity to work with particular faculty members;
- Reputation of the school or department;
- Financial support offered by the school or department;
- Location of the school; and
- Program attributes (e.g., flexibility with courses or scheduling, no language requirements).

The most important factor, according to the responses, is the reputation of the school or department. Financial support is either the second or third most important factor, depending on the metric used to aggregate responses. The other factor among the top three is the opportunity to work with particular faculty members.[3]

About 73 percent of the students in our sample were offered financial support when they were admitted to the PhD program in which they enrolled, according to the GES. A majority of students (58 percent) were offered more than one year of support. Among those offered multiple years of support, 25 percent had offers for two or three years, 43 percent had offers for four years, 26 percent had offers for five years, and 6 percent had offers for six or more years. Multiyear packages have become much more prevalent over the time period covered in our data. Between 1982 and 1996, the percentage of incoming students with multiyear packages increased from 46 percent to 71 percent (Figure 5.1). The percentage of students admitted with packages of at least four years increased from 30 percent to 58 percent over this period. Later in this chapter we examine whether the GEI contributed to the rise in multiyear packages.

Financial Support and Time Allocation

Offers of financial support at admission matter a great deal to students because the level of financial support affects the amount of time they are able to devote to their studies and the nature of their interactions with faculty. Doctoral students without financial support must support themselves by working, taking out loans, or receiving aid from family members. Students usually are unable to borrow enough to completely cover their

---

[3] School or department reputation was listed as the most important factor by 44 percent of students, faculty by 27 percent, and financial support by 18 percent. The percentages listing each factor as the first or second most important factor are 75 percent for school or department reputation, 48 percent for faculty, and 47 percent for financial support.

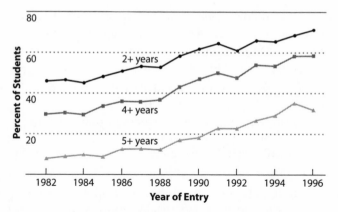

Figure 5.1. Multiyear Packages Offered at Admission, 1982–96
    Note: Years of entry correspond to entering cohorts. For example, figures for
entry year 1982 are based on data for the 1982–83 entering cohort, and figures
for entry year 1983 are based on data for the 1983–84 entering cohort.

educational and living expenses. Thus, some level of financial support is
important to limit the amount of time that students spend working (for
example, waiting tables to pay the rent) rather than studying. This role
of financial support is emphasized by one student: "The Mellon Foundation's financial support . . . was an immense help to all graduate students
and allowed us to focus solely on our studies, rather than juggle library/
restaurant work (or any other paying job) with classes, exams, and the dissertation." Yet not all employment crowds out study time; for instance,
working as a research assistant (RA) or TA may well be part of the professional development process.

    In terms of work activities that may crowd out study time, perhaps the
greatest concern is work other than that as a TA or RA. About 57 percent
of the students in our study were employed for pay at some time during
their doctoral programs, according to the GES. The survey did not in-
quire about what type of work this was, but it did ask students how relevant the work was to their field of study. Among those who were employed
(aside from assistantships), 28 percent said the work was "very" relevant
to their field of study, 30 percent said it was "somewhat" relevant, and 42
percent said it was "not" relevant. That 58 percent of student workers considered their work to be very or somewhat relevant to their studies suggests that at least some of the work differs from the stereotypical jobs of
graduate students (e.g., waiting tables or driving taxicabs). Those who
were employed reported that they worked an average of 10.1 hours per
week while completing coursework, 9.9 hours per week while preparing
for comprehensive exams, and 12.3 hours per week while preparing a dis-

sertation proposal.[4] During the dissertation stage, students worked full time for an average of 9.7 percent of the months and part time for an average of 16.8 percent of the months.

Turning to work that is typically more relevant to professional development, serving as a TA or RA influences the day-to-day environment that graduate students face and therefore may affect their progress toward the degree. RAs usually work closely with professors on their projects, whereas TAs work with professors and fellow graduate students on teaching. (Students on fellowship, by definition, have freedom from work requirements but as a result must structure their time for themselves.)

Based on a concern that extensive teaching was in fact slowing student progress, some treatment departments used the GEI to limit the amount of time their students could spend working as TAs (see Chapter 3). According to the GES, 86 percent of students in the 1982–83 through 1996–97 entering cohorts served as a TA for at least one term during their doctoral studies (Table 5.1). Those who served as TAs did so for an average of 4.8 terms (semesters or semester-equivalents) and worked an average of 14 hours per week. Most students who held TA positions reported that they taught courses in their own departments. However, a modest percentage of students held positions that involved teaching in some other department in their university, or at some other university. The latter positions might be filled by students at universities in urban areas who teach part time at nearby academic institutions. Thus, some departments and universities cannot completely control the total amount of time that their doctoral students spend teaching.

In the humanities, RA positions are not as prevalent as TA positions, but they still represent an important piece of the overall financial support students receive.[5] According to the GES, 40 percent of students served as an RA for at least one term during their doctoral studies. Those who served as RAs did so for an average of 2.6 terms and worked an average of 12 hours per week. In principle, work as an RA may be better than work as a TA in facilitating students' progress in their doctoral programs, if the work RAs do is complementary to their research interests. Consistent with

[4] The GES recorded hours of work using ranges, and we assign a particular number of hours to each range in order to compute averages. The mapping of GES categories into hours is as follows: "did not work" = 0 hours per week; "less than 20 hours per week" = 10 hours per week; "20–34 hours per week" = 27 hours per week; and "35 or more hours per week" = 40 hours per week.

[5] Of those who reported in the GES that they served as either a TA or an RA during their doctoral studies, 55 percent served as a TA only, 3 percent served as an RA only, and 42 percent served as both a TA and an RA. Nettles and Millett (2006) also find that TA positions are much more common than RA positions in the humanities and social sciences.

TABLE 5.1
Teaching Assistant and Research Assistant Experiences

	Teaching Assistant	Research Assistant	Teaching Assistant or Research Assistant
Place of employment (percent "yes")			
Any place	86.0	40.0	88.8
Own department	77.9	31.4	81.2
Other department in same university	16.1	6.7	20.1
Other university	12.3	5.7	14.9
Extent of employment (average)			
Terms during doctoral studies	4.8	2.6	5.7
Hours per week	14.1	12.3	14.7
Task (percent "yes")			
Lead a discussion or review section	89.1	8.9	87.4
Teach a course as a primary lecturer	48.0	4.5	46.9
Prepare course materials or exams	69.3	12.8	69.3
Grade papers or exams	96.6	19.3	94.6
Perform research or other tasks *not* directly relevant to own work	34.9	78.6	53.2
Perform research or other tasks directly relevant to own work	25.5	43.0	32.6

Notes: The GES records terms and place of employment separately for TA and RA positions. We construct terms for the "Teaching Assistant or Research Assistant" column by adding terms as a TA and terms as an RA, for those who were TAs or RAs (thus, we assume that these positions are held in separate terms). The GES records hours and tasks for TA and RA positions combined. We construct separate figures for TA (RA) positions by using only the sample of students who served as a TA (RA) but never served as an RA (TA). Terms, hours, and tasks are for those who served as TAs (RAs). See the notes to Table 5.6 for details on the construction of hours.

this view, a larger percentage of RAs than TAs report in the GES that their primary responsibilities included performing research or other tasks directly relevant to their own work. To be sure, RA positions also appear to involve many tasks that are not directly relevant to students' own work.[6]

In addition to time allocation, another way in which financial support may influence student outcomes is opportunity costs—the financial rewards to being a student compared to other activities. The dollar amount of financial support students receive influences their opportunity costs

---

[6] Unfortunately, the GES data do not allow us to estimate the relative amounts of time spent in these positions on tasks that are directly and not directly relevant to students' own work.

and affects the incentive they have to graduate, leave, or continue in their programs. It is not entirely counterintuitive for more generous aid to discourage completion, especially if the academic labor market is weak and students can expect to receive similar support in subsequent years. On the flip side, the lack of aid in subsequent years can provide an incentive to complete: "My fifth-year Mellon funding was key to my finishing that year, both by allowing me to concentrate and because I knew that by definition, there was NO money after it."

Financial Support and Student Effort

Financial support may influence student outcomes based on the type, amount, and timing of support. Financial support also differs in the conditions under which aid is awarded. In some cases, financial support is awarded by departments on a competitive basis, as for example when a fellowship is awarded to students with top scores on comprehensive examinations. In other cases, financial support is guaranteed—that is, awarded regardless of a student's performance in the program, as for example when incoming students receive multiyear aid packages. This distinction is of particular interest to the GEI because its architects thought that financial support (beyond the first year) that was contingent on the timely completion of requirements, such as comprehensive examinations and dissertation proposals, would be most effective—both as an incentive to meet requirements and as a way of avoiding the granting of support to students less likely to finish.

Although multiyear packages have become more common (see Figure 5.1), it is an open question whether such packages reduce the incentives for students to devote effort to their studies. On the one hand, having a multiyear guarantee of support might free students from worry about finances and lead them to be more focused on their graduate work and able to make better progress. On the other hand, students with multiyear packages may progress in their studies at only a leisurely pace, knowing that their financial support is guaranteed in successive years. The role of financial support in providing incentives for performance is highlighted by one student's remark: "Generally when I was a student multiyear financial aid packages were not offered. So students competed for financial aid every year. You needed to apply every year and I thought this was a great system because it's really based on performance and not on prejudgments."

Multiyear packages may provide some incentives for effort to the extent that the support students receive in successive years is conditional on current performance. The GES addressed this by asking those with multiyear packages whether the support beyond the first year was conditional on satisfactory progress or meeting particular deadlines. A majority of students with packages (about 70 percent) said support was conditional on satisfactory progress. By contrast, only about 23 percent said support was conditional on meeting deadlines. We examined these data over time based on year of entry to doctoral programs from 1982 to 1996. The percentage of students who said support was conditional on satisfactory progress was relatively constant over the period, whereas the percentage who said support was conditional on meeting deadlines increased somewhat over the period, from 18 percent to 34 percent.

PATTERNS OF FINANCIAL SUPPORT

We now examine financial support patterns along a variety of dimensions. The institutional database is the primary source for the evidence presented in this section. For each year students were in their programs, the database indicates whether they received each of four types of financial support: a fellowship, an assistantship, a tuition grant, and summer support. These data in principle represent awards from all sources, internal and external, but we know in some cases that information on external fellowships was incomplete. The dollar amount of awards is also available in most cases. The data used in this section cover both treatment departments and control departments.[7]

Variation by Year in a Program

The type of support that students receive varies greatly across years in a program. Figure 5.2 shows the percentage of students in each year who received each type of financial support. In the first year, 77 percent received a tuition grant, 62 percent received a fellowship, 21 percent held an assistantship, and 18 percent received summer support. (These types

---

[7] The data on financial support in the institutional database are not reported evenly across departments and years. Therefore, we use some simple rules to define the sample of departments and years that are included in the analysis. Department years are included in the sample if at least 75 percent of their students have information on the indicators for fellowship, assistantship, and tuition grant (44 department years for treatment departments and 33 department years for control departments). Analysis of summer support is produced for the subsample of these department years for which the indicator for summer support is available for at least 50 percent of their students (42 department years for treatment departments and 32 department years for control departments).

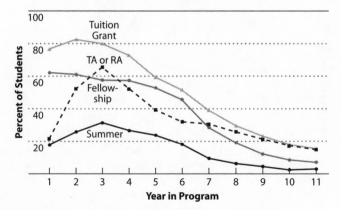

Figure 5.2. Type of Financial Support by Year in Program

are not mutually exclusive; students can and do receive multiple types of support in a given year. Indeed, tuition grants are typically awarded in combination with fellowships and assistantships.)

After the first year, the extent to which each type of support is awarded varies in its own way. Fellowships remain common for the first four or five years (53 percent of fifth-year students have one), but after the fifth year fewer than half of the students have a fellowship, and that share declines in succeeding years. Assistantships increase after the first year; they are most common in years 2–5, peak in the third year, and steadily decline after the third year. Summer support shows a similar pattern over years in a program.[8] When most students are working on their dissertations (years 6–8, the modal years of completion), roughly 30 percent have assistantships and 20–50 percent have fellowships.

An alternative way of viewing these indicators of financial support is to consider tuition grants in combination with assistantships and fellowships, which is often the way those making awards think of aid packages. Figure 5.3 shows the percentage of students in each year who received both a fellowship and a tuition grant, both an assistantship and a tuition grant, or only a tuition grant. Comparing this figure to Figure 5.2 reveals that most fellowships and assistantships are combined with tuition grants; however, a small percentage of students receive only a tuition grant in a given year.

Summary data on the dollar amounts of stipends and tuition grants are presented in Figure 5.4. The amounts shown in the figure are average

[8] Years in a program are defined such that summer follows the academic year. For example, summer support for year 1 refers to the summer after the first academic year.

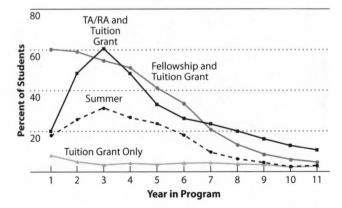

Figure 5.3. Type of Financial Support by Year in Program (Alternative Definition)

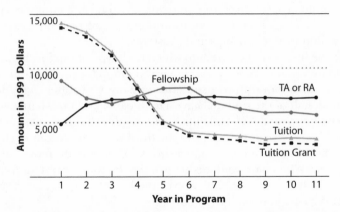

Figure 5.4. Amount of Financial Support by Year in Program and Type of Support

dollar amounts for those with the indicated type of support, expressed in constant (1991) dollars.[9] Stipends for fellowships are similar to those for assistantships and do not vary greatly across years in a program.[10] The size of tuition grants exceeds stipend amounts (for fellowships and assistantships) in the first four years. In later years, the pattern is reversed as the

---

[9] All dollar amounts reported in this chapter are expressed in this way.

[10] An exception is the first year in a program, when the average stipend for fellowships is nearly double the average stipend for assistants. This could mean that those with fellowships have larger stipends (over the same period, such as a semester) than those with assistantships.

size of tuition grants declines, reflecting lower tuition charges for students who have advanced to candidacy. The average amount of tuition grants closely tracks average tuition charges, with the ratio of average grants to average tuition varying from 97 percent in the first year to 83 percent in the 11th year.

Variation by Personal Characteristics

Table 5.2 examines how financial support varies by personal characteristics that reflect students' demographic characteristics and their abilities. The table shows the percentage of students with fellowships and the percentage with assistantships separately for three time periods: the first year in a program, years 2–5 combined, and years 6–11 combined.[11] Appendix Table E.5.1 presents data for these time periods for all types of aid (including tuition grants and summer support) along with average fellowship stipends for the first year. (Throughout the chapter, the figures on average stipends that we report are based on students who received stipends and for whom a positive stipend amount is reported in the database.)

To examine differences in students' aid awards according to their abilities, we use students' GRE scores, which are typically used to determine admission and offers of financial aid for incoming students. We split the sample of scores into three groups of roughly equal size, for both the math and verbal scores on the GRE. Not surprisingly, students in the group with the highest scores are more likely to have fellowships and tuition grants. Higher math scores are associated with larger fellowship stipends, but average fellowship stipends are relatively similar across groups defined by verbal scores. Generally, such differences in financial support across test-score groups are greatest in the first year and lessen with experience in the program as departments witness the performance of students in coursework and research. By the sixth year, there are almost no differences in financial support across test-score groups.

Alternatively, it could reflect patterns of support across terms within the first year. To understand the latter possibility, suppose that stipends for fellowships and assistantships are the same for each semester, say $5,000. Suppose in addition that half of the students have fellowships for both semesters and the other half have a fellowship for the first semester and an assistantship for the second semester. Then fellowship stipends would average $7,500 on an annual basis and assistantship stipends would average $5,000.

[11] The samples used to compute these percentages for years 2–5 and years 6–11 contain multiple observations per student. Each student contributes an observation for each year that she is in the program. For instance, if a student drops out at the end of her fourth year, she contributes three observations to the averages for years 2–5 in the table.

TABLE 5.2
Financial Support and Personal Characteristics (percent)

Characteristic	Year 1 Fellowship	Year 1 TA/RA	Years 2–5 Fellowship	Years 2–5 TA/RA	Years 6–11 Fellowship	Years 6–11 TA/RA
Gender						
Men	61.9	21.3	56.5	52.1	27.3	28.3
Women	62.1	21.6	58.4	53.8	29.4	26.6
U.S. citizenship						
Noncitizen	68.0	19.8	59.1	47.8	26.7	21.8
Citizen	60.8	21.6	57.1	53.8	28.6	28.3
Race/ethnicity[a]						
White	58.9	19.8	57.8	53.6	28.6	28.2
Black	89.0	15.6	71.2	48.0	30.4	21.4
Asian	76.5	18.3	65.0	53.0	35.2	31.0
Hispanic	83.6	18.6	66.5	50.2	30.0	26.3
Prior master's						
No	62.4	18.5	59.5	53.5	29.7	27.1
Yes	62.2	26.2	55.4	50.3	23.6	25.1
Math GRE						
High	71.9	20.1	62.8	54.6	30.0	29.3
Medium	62.1	22.3	58.0	55.1	30.3	28.1
Low	55.9	22.8	55.1	52.3	26.5	25.8
Verbal GRE						
High	69.6	19.7	60.7	54.7	28.2	29.5
Medium	62.6	22.4	59.3	55.7	29.5	28.7
Low	59.3	22.6	56.2	50.9	28.8	24.1

[a]For U.S. citizens only.

Financial support patterns are strikingly similar for men and women. Women comprise nearly half (48 percent) of our sample. The differences between U.S. citizens and non–U.S. citizens, who make up 17 percent of the sample, are modest.[12] U.S. citizens are somewhat more likely to have assistantships; this might reflect differences in language skills that are im-

---

[12] In science and engineering doctoral programs, by contrast, differences in support patterns by citizenship are greater. According to data from the Survey of Earned Doctorates, the percentage of doctorate recipients in science and engineering who reported that fellowships were their primary source of support was greater among U.S. citizens and the percentage with RA positions (or traineeships) as their primary source was greater among non–U.S. citizens. In the social sciences and humanities, the magnitude of these differences was much smaller; Thomas B. Hoffer, Vincent Welch Jr., Kristy Webber, Kimberly Williams, Brian Lisek, Mary Hess, Daniel Loew, and Isabel Guzman-Barron, *Doctorate Recipients from United States Universities: Summary Report 2005* (Chicago: National Opinion Research Center, 2006), Table 20.

portant in teaching. In the first year, non–U.S. citizens are more likely to have fellowships and their fellowship stipends are larger; these differences might reflect differences in external sources of support (in a number of cases, such students arrive with aid from their home countries or families).

Among U.S. citizens, financial support varies across racial and ethnic groups. These differences are evident primarily over the first five years in a program. Black, Asian, and Hispanic students are each more likely than white students to have fellowships, tuition grants, and summer support.[13] Furthermore, their fellowship stipends are larger on average than those for whites. Among these minority groups, black students have the most generous financial support, perhaps due in part to competition among institutions for qualified black candidates.[14]

About a quarter of the students in our sample entered their PhD programs with a master's degree. In the first year, these students are more likely to hold assistantships. This might indicate that students with master's degrees have greater knowledge in advanced subjects, greater teaching experience, or greater willingness to teach while taking courses because of their experience in similar courses at the master's level. However, over the first five years combined, students with master's degrees are no more likely to hold assistantships than are other students.

Variation by Departmental Characteristics

Table 5.3 and Appendix Table E.5.2 examine how financial support varies by the characteristics of the departments at which students were enrolled. We consider variation along three dimensions: field, department size, and institution. Financial support varies considerably by field in our data. For instance, the percentage of students with fellowships in their first year varies from 55 percent in English and history to 80 percent in religion. In addition, the percentage of students with assistantships in years 6–11 varies from 17 percent in art history to 41 percent in classics.

In order to look at differences in financial support awarded by departments of varying size, we divide departments into three groups based on the average size of entering cohorts between 1982–83 and 2002–03. Quite clearly, the larger departments have lower financial support than the small and medium-sized departments. (There are only small differences in support given by small and medium-sized departments.) This

---

[13] Nettles and Millett (2006) found similar results for a broader set of fields.

[14] In Chapters 9 and 10, we provide evidence that publications and job outcomes vary by race and ethnicity.

TABLE 5.3

Financial Support and Departmental Characteristics (percent)

Characteristic	Year 1		Years 2–5		Years 6–11	
	Fellowship	*TA/RA*	*Fellowship*	*TA/RA*	*Fellowship*	*TA/RA*
Field						
Anthropology	68.8	25.6	59.6	46.2	30.5	26.2
Art history	74.6	18.7	67.1	48.4	33.7	16.8
Classics	62.9	25.4	54.7	61.0	39.5	41.1
Comparative literature	64.4	21.7	49.6	56.9	26.6	39.0
English	55.4	17.5	57.7	60.2	26.7	35.3
History	55.2	24.3	55.9	49.1	30.4	22.8
Music	68.1	27.8	57.8	63.9	26.2	25.5
Philosophy	66.9	27.6	56.9	60.5	22.2	32.5
Political science	67.9	16.6	54.9	45.1	24.6	24.9
Religion	79.5	13.0	64.7	47.4	25.8	18.4
Max–min	24.3	14.8	17.5	18.8	17.3	24.3
Department size[a]						
Small	75.6	22.2	62.1	56.5	32.0	30.3
Medium	74.0	25.6	59.2	53.4	28.4	25.0
Large	54.0	19.4	55.6	51.8	27.7	28.1
Small–large	21.6	6.2	6.5	4.7	4.3	5.3
Institution[b]						
Max–min	71.1	70.9	61.3	51.6	42.2	40.7

[a]Based on the average size of entering cohorts from 1982 to 2002. Small: <7.5 (N = 25 departments); medium: 7.5–14 (N = 26); large: ≥14.1 (N = 26).

[b]Institutional figures are not reported to protect the confidentiality of the institutions that provided data.

pattern is particularly evident in the percentage of students with fellowships and the percentage with summer support (the differences in TA/RA are much smaller). For instance, 76 percent of students in small departments have a fellowship in the first year, compared with 54 percent of students in large departments. In later years, there is still a gap in financial support, but the magnitude of that gap is much smaller. Thus, it appears that financial support in large departments is relatively scarce at the coursework stage, but at the dissertation stage it is similar to that available in smaller departments.

The variation in financial support across institutions in our database is quite large. For instance, there is a difference of 71 percentage points between the institution with the highest percentage with fellowships in the first year and the institution with the lowest. In fact, the range from minimum to maximum for the 13 institutions is greater than that for the 10 fields or for the three department size groups for every measure of financial support in the table.

The patterns in Table 5.3 suggest that field, department size, and institution matter for explaining variation in financial support. However, the simple tabulations do not isolate the role of each characteristic, because when a given characteristic is varied, the other characteristics are not held constant. For instance, patterns by field might represent true differences across disciplines, but they could also simply represent the role of average department size in determining the amount of money available. This is because English and history are the largest two fields (with average cohort sizes over 20) and religion is one of the smallest fields (with an average cohort size of 6.6) in our data.

In order to isolate the role of each characteristic, we estimate a series of linear regressions at the departmental level in which the dependent variable is the percentage with a particular type of aid and the explanatory variables are field indicators, institution indicators, and department-size indicators. For nearly all of the financial-support measures (by type of aid and year of award, as shown in Appendix Table E.5.2), the results indicate that variation by institution is what matters most; after accounting for institution differences, variation by field or department size accounts for very little of the variation in financial support. The only exception to this general pattern is for the percentage of students with assistantships; in this case, field matters in addition to institution. Field may matter in the case of TAs because demand for undergraduate courses (particularly large lecture courses that use TAs) varies by field (e.g., most undergraduates take an English course, but few undergraduates take a course in religion).

THE IMPACT OF THE GEI ON FINANCIAL SUPPORT

Treatment departments allocated the vast majority of their GEI grant funds to individual graduate students.[15] The Foundation intended the grants to supplement, rather than supplant, internal funds for the support of graduate students in the treatment departments. As such, participating institutions were required to maintain the real value of their levels of such internal support over the life of the GEI.[16] Thus, we anticipate

[15] Some of the material presented in this section and the next is based on research first presented in Groen et al. (2008).

[16] Our analysis of data from department financial reports submitted to the Foundation suggests that participating institutions did in fact meet this requirement. In treatment de-

that the GEI would lead to an increase in financial support for graduate students.

Foundation support was designed to focus on the times in students' careers when their progress is delayed or comes to a halt. Most departments identified three periods when such delays were likely to occur: the transition from coursework to the beginning of dissertation research; the "finishing up" (final year) of the dissertation; and summers, when students often lost momentum. Once the GEI began, departments reported to the Foundation annually on how they spent the GEI grant funds. On average across departments and over time, approximately 15 percent of the GEI funds were used for predissertation fellowships, 49 percent for dissertation fellowships, 8 percent for tuition remission, and 24 percent for summer support of students, with the remaining 4 percent of the funds used for other purposes (Table 5.4).

In order to estimate the impact of the GEI, we need to examine time trends separately in treatment and control departments. Figure 5.5 captures the spirit of our approach with four panels that examine financial support by year in the program for treatment and control departments before and during the GEI. Each panel is similar to Figure 5.3 and shows the percentage of students in each year with fellowships (and tuition grants), assistantships (and tuition grants), and summer support. The top panels show the change in financial support over time for treatment departments, and the bottom panels show the change for control departments. The figure reveals a general increase in financial support in both treatment and control departments. However, in some cases (such as fellowship support over years 1–6) the amount of the increase was greater in treatment departments than in control departments. Comparisons such as these suggest that the GEI did in fact affect financial support; however, to be sure of this we need to account for the role of institutions and fields.

Therefore, we turn to a regression approach that is similar in spirit to our approach to estimating the impact of the GEI on student outcomes (see Chapter 4). First, we construct measures of financial support using student-level data from the institutional and survey databases. Second, we estimate linear regressions in which a given measure of financial support is the dependent variable and the explanatory variables are indicator variables for institutions and fields and three additional variables that identify the effects of the GEI. The first of these is an indicator that equals 1 for students in treatment departments and 0 for students in control de-

---

partments, the real value of internal support per student increased by an average of about 2 percent per year over the life of the GEI. Treatment departments received an average of $113,000 per year from the Foundation. On average, GEI funding represented about 8 percent of departments' overall budgets for student support.

TABLE 5.4
Allocation of GEI Funding (percent)

Type of Support	Timing of Support			
	Entering Students	Predissertation	Dissertation	Total
Fellowship	0.0	15.3	49.1	64.5
Tuition grant	0.0	3.6	4.4	8.0
Summer support	0.5	9.9	13.6	23.9
Other[a]	1.4	1.3	0.9	3.6
Total	1.9	30.1	68.0	100.0

[a]Money not directly paid to students (e.g., payments to faculty for teaching dissertation-related workshops during the summer).

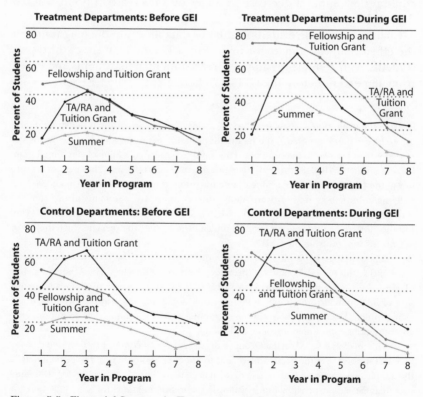

Figure 5.5. Financial Support in Treatment and Control Departments before and during the GEI

partments. The second is an indicator that identifies when the GEI is in effect; it equals 1 for observations in the treatment period and 0 for observations in the pretreatment period.[17] The third variable is the interaction between the other two variables. This variable identifies the impact of the GEI and reflects the time trend of the particular measure of financial support in treatment departments relative to the time trend in control departments.[18]

We find that the GEI did in fact lead to an increase in financial support in the treatment departments.[19] The share of student-year observations with fellowships and the share with tuition grants increased by a greater amount in treatment departments than in control departments (Table 5.5). These impacts were stronger in the first five years in the program than in years 6–11. The GEI had no measurable impact on the share of student years with assistantships; however, the GEI led not to an increase but to a decrease in average income from assistantships. Since the measure of income reflects money received over the academic year, this change could reflect either a decrease in wages or a decrease in hours worked during the year.

Changes over time evident in the raw data illustrate the magnitude of the effect that we estimate for fellowships. The percentage of third-year students with fellowship support in treatment departments increased from 43 percent before the GEI to 70 percent after the GEI, and in con-

---

[17] In the institutional database (which contains multiple observations per student, one for each year in the program), the treatment period depends on a student's entering cohort as well as the year in the program. This variable is assigned a value of zero for all years for students in the 1982–83 through 1985–86 entering cohorts because they were never subject to the GEI. It is assigned a value of one for students in the 1991–92 through 2002–03 entering cohorts because they were always subject to the GEI. Students in the 1986–87 through 1990–91 entering cohorts are assigned a value of zero for this variable for years prior to 1991 and a value of one for 1991 and later years (i.e., the years in which they were eligible for support from the GEI).

[18] A potential problem with this approach is that the wealth levels of institutions grew apart during this period; Ronald G. Ehrenberg, "Studying Ourselves: The Academic Labor Market," *Journal of Labor Economics* 21 (April 2003): 267–87. However, when we add a measure of institutional revenue per student to the model, the relevant coefficients do not change much. The measure of institutional revenue is based on annual data on tuition, state appropriations, endowment income, and giving.

[19] This analysis is based on data from 54 departments that consistently provided data on financial support over the pretreatment and treatment periods. In order to be included in the sample, a department had to have data on each of the indicator variables for academic-year financial support (fellowship, assistantship, and tuition grant) for at least 50 percent of its students in 19 of the 21 years covered by the database. The 54 departments include 37 treatment departments and 17 control departments.

TABLE 5.5
Impact of the GEI on Financial Support (Institutional Data)

	Mean	GEI Impact		
		Years 1–5	Years 6–11	Years 3–7
Share with aid				
Fellowship	0.50	**0.149**	0.057	**0.141**
TA/RA	0.39	0.041	0.013	0.003
Tuition grant	0.65	**0.113**	0.072	**0.101**
Summer support	0.20	0.056	–0.008	0.041
Dollar amount				
Fellowship income	7,645	296	**1,501**	771
TA/RA income	6,471	**–1,365**	**–1,573**	**–1,151**
Tuition grant amount	10,280	–97	**–2,011**	**–958**

Note: Entries in bold type are statistically significant at the 5 percent level.

trol departments it increased from 41 percent to 51 percent. Thus the difference over time was 27 percentage points in treatment departments, compared to 10 percentage points in control departments. In other words, the increase over time was 17 percentage points greater in treatment departments compared to control departments.

In Chapter 4 we report that the GEI increased GRE verbal scores by about 10 points on average. In this chapter we estimate that the GEI increased fellowship support. Taken together, these findings provide indirect evidence that financial support affects the selection of prospective students for doctoral programs. In other words, the improved financial support associated with the GEI provided treatment departments with a competitive advantage in their recruitment of top students.

Our analysis of the GES data indicates that the GEI increased the prevalence of multiyear packages awarded to incoming students.[20] In particular, we estimate that the GEI caused an increase of roughly 9 percentage points in the percentage of incoming students with multiyear packages (Table 5.6). Thus, the GEI is responsible (contrary to its original intent) for much of the upward trend in multiyear packages noted earlier in this

[20] In our analysis of the survey database (which contains only one observation per student), the definition of the indicator variable for the treatment period is somewhat different from the definition in the institutional database. The indicator equals one for students in the 1991–92 through 1996–97 entering cohorts and zero for students in the 1982–83 through 1990–91 entering cohorts. The estimation sample for the regressions covers the 1982–83 through 1996–97 entering cohorts for the analysis of multiyear packages and the 1982–83 through 1986–87 and 1990–91 through 1996–97 entering cohorts for the analysis of TA/RA terms and hours.

132 CHAPTER 5

TABLE 5.6
Impact of the GEI on Financial Support (Survey Data)

	Mean	GEI Impact
Multiyear offer at entry	0.58	**0.085**
TA terms during PhD program	4.84	**−0.492**
TA hours per week	14.14	−0.472
RA terms during PhD program	2.58	−0.153

Notes: Entries in bold type are statistically significant at the 5 percent level. The regression for TA hours per week is estimated on the subsample of students who were TAs but were never RAs. The GES recorded hours per week using three categories, and we constructed a continuous variable by assigning a value to each category: "fewer than 10 hours" = 5 hours; "10–20 hours" = 15 hours; and "more than 20 hours" = 25 hours.

chapter. The GES also asked respondents about the number of terms during their doctoral studies during which they served as TAs or RAs. We find that the GEI decreased the number of terms that students served as TAs but had no impact on the number of terms they served as RAs.

Underlying the change in the average number of TA terms are shifts throughout the distribution of such terms. In treatment departments, the percentage of students with one to five terms increased by 11 percentage points from the pre-GEI period to the GEI period (Table 5.7). By contrast, the percentage of students with zero terms fell by 8 percentage points and the percentage with six or more terms fell by 3 percentage points. The distribution of TA terms in control departments changed in a similar way, but the magnitudes of change were much less pronounced than in treatment departments. Thus, it appears that the GEI may have "leveled" the distribution of teaching responsibilities, with more students doing some

TABLE 5.7
The GEI and the Distribution of TA Terms (percent)

		TA Terms during PhD Program			
		0	1–5	≥6	Total
Treatment	Pre[a]	21.1	47.2	31.7	100.0
	Post[b]	13.3	58.3	28.4	100.0
	Difference	−7.8	11.1	−3.3	0.0
Control	Pre[a]	12.1	55.8	32.2	100.0
	Post[b]	10.7	59.1	30.2	100.0
	Difference	−1.4	3.3	−2.0	0.0

[a]Students in the 1982–83 through 1986–87 entering cohorts.
[b]Students in the 1990–91 through 1996–97 entering cohorts.

teaching but fewer students doing a large amount of teaching. Such a change is consistent with the goal (expressed by many departments) of reducing heavy teaching responsibilities and the goal (expressed by other departments) of providing some teaching experience. Those goals taken together reflected the view that some teaching is a good thing for students but that here, as in other aspects of life, there can be too much of a good thing.

THE IMPACT OF FINANCIAL SUPPORT
ON STUDENT OUTCOMES

[Having a Mellon summer grant] meant that I spent the summer before my qualifying exams not having to hold a job: I could concentrate on exam prep and writing my dissertation prospectus. As a result my 3rd year was efficient and I moved quickly to writing the dissertation. This plus a writing dissertation fellowship freed me to write and complete all requirements by the end of my 6th year.

In this section, we estimate the impact on student outcomes of financial support (where financial support is broadly conceived to include support from all sources, not just the GEI). These estimates are relevant not only for our evaluation of the GEI's increased support but also more generally for documenting relationships that can inform policy. We provide evidence earlier in this chapter that the GEI increased available financial support. Whether these increases can "explain" the overall impact of the GEI on student outcomes (see Chapter 4) depends on whether such increased financial support reduces attrition and increases completion rates. More generally, we provide evidence on questions potentially relevant to the setting of university and department financial-aid policies. For example, can a department expect to improve its completion rate by increasing financial support to its doctoral students? Which forms of aid are most effective at reducing attrition and encouraging timely completion? How does service as a TA affect progress toward the PhD?

As described in more detail in Chapter 4, our model of student outcomes is based on student transitions from one year to the next. The estimation sample for each year in the program is students who have "survived" to the start of that year. The focus of the model is the probabilities of each of three outcomes in that year, given that students started the year: leaving during the year, graduating during the year, or continuing in the program throughout the year. The explanatory variables differ somewhat from the version used in Chapter 4. We continue to include variables for student gender, race and ethnicity, and citizenship as well as indicator variables for institutions and fields. Additionally, we include indicators for the type of financial support received in the current year: indicators for fellowship, assistantship, tuition grant, and summer support.[21] The explanatory variables also include measures of student ability (GRE scores and an indicator for having a prior master's degree) because students with higher measured ability may be more likely to receive certain types of support (see Table 5.2) and have better outcomes than other students. Finally, because our interest in this section is not in the impacts of the GEI, we drop from the model the set of three variables that identify the effects of the GEI (see Chapter 4).

The estimated coefficients on the financial-support indicators in the model capture differences in transition probabilities across types of support, controlling for the other variables in the model. We use simulations to translate the estimated coefficients from the model into estimates of the impact of aid on cumulative probabilities of attrition and completion. We follow the basic structure of our earlier simulations (in Chapter 4) but make some changes to reflect our interest in the impacts of aid rather than the impacts of the GEI. In the present simulations, the sample of students used is all students who appear in the estimation sample, which includes students from all entering cohorts and students from treatment and control departments. We simulate the impacts of aid by predicting cumulative probabilities of attrition and completion (for each year in the program) for students in the simulation sample based on the model coefficients, financial-support profiles that we assign, and students' actual values for the other explanatory variables. The profiles indicate the type of support received in each year. We assign each profile to all students in the simulation sample and then take averages of the cumulative probabilities across students to produce a path of probabilities by year in the program for each profile.

Simulation results are given in Table 5.8. The first three profiles in the table are deliberately unrealistic and are intended to represent the extremes of more and less generous financial support. The first profile contains no support at all, the second profile contains an assistantship in each of the first six years in the program and no support thereafter, and the third profile contains a fellowship in each of the first six years and no support thereafter. Comparing the first and third profiles, for instance, indicates that having a fellowship over the first six years lowers attrition by year 2 by 25.7 percentage points and lowers attrition by year 4 by 37.2 per-

---

[21] We include two fellowship indicators in order to distinguish between small fellowships and other fellowships. Small fellowships are defined as those with an annual stipend of less than $6,000 (in 1991 dollars). In the simulations that follow, fellowships are defined to be large fellowships (with stipends of $6,000 or more).

centage points. In terms of completion, having a fellowship over the first six years increases the probability of completion by year 7 by 15.7 percentage points. More generally, the pattern of these profiles is that more generous financial support is associated with better outcomes. There is a large difference in outcomes between no support and either type of support (assistantship or fellowship); the difference between assistantship and fellowship is smaller, with fellowships associated with better outcomes.

The remaining profiles are more realistic in terms of the support patterns in the raw data. Profiles 4–7 suggest that summer support reduces attrition and increases completion rates. The measured impacts of summer support are greater if the support is provided in years 1 and 2 than in years 3 and 4. Profiles 8–11 isolate variation in the type of support at the dissertation stage. Having a fellowship rather than an assistantship in years 5 and 6 increases the completion rate by 4.1 percentage points by the end of the sixth year and by a smaller amount in later years.

Of all the profiles reported (which are far from exhaustive of all possible combinations), the highest completion rates and lowest attrition rates are associated with having a fellowship for the first six years combined with summer support in the first two years (profile 4). An attractive alternative involves reduced costs for academic-year support by combining a mix of fellowship and TA in the first six years with summer support in the first two years (profile 6). This package is associated with somewhat higher completion rates in years 7 and 9 and considerably lower attrition rates in all time periods than a package involving a fellowship in the first six years but no summer support (profile 3).

A general finding from Table 5.8 is that more generous financial support is associated with better outcomes. This finding, together with the evidence that the GEI led to an increase in financial support, suggests that financial support is an important mechanism in accounting for the estimated impacts of the GEI on student outcomes. The analysis also reveals some impacts on attrition and completion of the nature and timing of financial support provided. First, although more generous aid reduces attrition, even the most generous financial-support packages are associated with considerable attrition (e.g., profile 3, which has fellowships in each of the first six years, has an attrition rate of 22 percent by the end of the sixth year). This finding suggests that factors other than inadequate financial support account for attrition from doctoral programs. Second, more generous support has a greater impact on reducing attrition than on encouraging completion. This result points to differences in the effectiveness of financial incentives at the coursework stage compared to the dissertation stage. And third, reallocating some funds from academic-year fellowship support to summer support may reduce attrition and increase completion. This finding is consistent with the experience of the

TABLE 5.8

Impact of Financial Support on Attrition and Completion

	Profiles						
		Attrition Probability by Year			*Completion Probability by Year*		
Number	*Profile*	*2*	*4*	*7*	*6*	*7*	*9*
1	No aid	36.1	55.0	61.7	12.0	20.1	29.0
2	TA/RA 1–6	13.7	20.5	28.6	13.3	31.2	50.8
3	Fellowship 1–6	10.4	17.8	24.6	18.5	35.8	55.1
4	Fellowship 1–6, Summer 1–2	2.6	10.7	18.2	20.0	38.6	59.6
5	Fellowship 1–6, Summer 3–4	10.4	13.6	21.0	18.3	36.8	57.4
6	Fellowship/TA 1–6, Summer 1–2	3.3	10.6	18.6	18.4	37.5	58.8
7	Fellowship/TA 1–6, Summer 3–4	12.7	15.5	23.1	16.3	34.9	55.4
8	Fellowship/TA 1–4, TA 5–6	12.7	19.2	27.4	14.1	32.1	51.9
9	Fellowship/TA 1–4, TA 5, Fellowship 6	12.7	19.2	27.0	15.7	33.2	52.6
10	Fellowship/TA 1–4, Fellowship 5, TA 6	12.7	19.2	26.3	16.7	34.1	53.4
11	Fellowship/TA 1–4, Fellowship 5–6	12.7	19.2	26.0	18.2	35.2	54.1

Comparisons of Profiles

Number	Comparison	Difference in Attrition Probability, by Year			Difference in Completion Probability, by Year		
		2	4	7	6	7	9
2–1	TA/RA 1–6—No aid	−22.4	−34.5	−33.1	1.3	11.1	21.8
3–1	Fellowship 1–6—No aid	−25.7	−37.2	−37.1	6.5	15.7	26.1
3–2	Fellowship 1–6—TA/RA 1–6	−3.3	−2.7	−4.0	5.2	4.6	4.3
4–3	Fellowship 1–6, Summer 1–2—Fellowship 1–6	−7.8	−7.1	−6.4	1.5	2.8	4.5
5–3	Fellowship 1–6, Summer 3–4—Fellowship 1–6	0.0	−4.2	−3.6	−0.2	1.0	2.3
5–4	Fellowship 1–6: Summer 3–4—Summer 1–2	7.8	2.9	2.8	−1.7	−1.8	−2.2
6–10	Fellowship/TA 1–6, Summer 1–2—Fellowship/TA 1–6	−9.4	−8.6	−7.7	1.7	3.4	5.4
7–10	Fellowship/TA 1–6, Summer 3–4—Fellowship/TA 1–6	0.0	−3.7	−3.2	−0.4	0.8	2.0
7–6	Fellowship/TA 1–6: Summer 3–4—Summer 1–2	9.4	4.9	4.5	−2.1	−2.6	−3.4
9–8	Fellowship/TA 1–4: TA 5 / Fellowship 6—TA 5–6	0.0	0.0	−0.4	1.6	1.1	0.7
10–8	Fellowship/TA 1–4: Fellowship 5 / TA 6—TA 5–6	0.0	0.0	−1.1	2.6	2.0	1.5
11–8	Fellowship/TA 1–4: Fellowship 5–6—TA 5–6	0.0	0.0	−1.4	4.1	3.1	2.2

Notes: TA/RA = teaching assistantship or research assistantship. Profiles for TA/RA and fellowship are defined to include tuition grants. All profiles have no support for years 7–9. Fellowship/TA 1–6 = fellowship for years 1, 4, and 5 and TA/RA for years 2, 3, and 6. Fellowship/TA 1–4 = fellowship for years 1 and 4 and TA/RA for years 2 and 3. The numbers in the table are cumulative probabilities (or differences in probabilities) of attrition or completion by the end of particular years in a program, multiplied by 100.

many departments that reported receiving more "bang for their buck" from summer funding than academic-year funding.

It is possible that our results overstate the pure (causal) impact of financial support on student outcomes because, like nearly all previous research on this topic, ours does not account for a host of factors that explain the type of financial support students receive and that are potentially correlated with students' outcomes.[22] Financial support is allocated based on several factors that are unobservable to us (in addition to the factors we can observe, such as GRE scores), including letters of recommendation, student essays, interviews, and coursework during the PhD program. It is plausible that these factors are positively correlated with student outcomes, that is, that financial support is awarded systematically to students who have lower expected probabilities of attrition, higher probabilities of completion, or both, even after accounting for factors we can observe.

We must provide further caution against overinterpretation of these results. The model underlying the estimates accounts for the impact of aid in the current year on the transition to the next year, but it does not account for the impact of aid received in earlier years or for expectations of aid in future years. The model also does not account for the rules under which aid is awarded by departments, for example, as part of packages awarded at admission or through competition during the doctoral program. Finally, our analysis controls for differences in financial support patterns across institutions and fields, and therefore our estimates reflect impacts for the typical department in our sample. For these reasons it is not possible for the model to determine the optimal package of financial support for individual departments. Instead, we hope that those who direct doctoral programs can draw general lessons from our results.

An important question for future research in this area is how fellowships and TA positions can be combined to best encourage completion of doctoral programs. Suppose, for instance, that a department wants to construct a package of funding over the first five years involving one year of teaching and four years of fellowship. Would it be better to provide the assistantship early (in the second or third year) or late (in the fourth or fifth year)? The answer might depend on the timing of other aspects of doctoral programs, such as coursework, qualifying exams, and field work.

CONCLUSION

The impact of the GEI on financial support is a story of intended and unintended consequences. The intended consequence was an increase in

---

[22] See, for example, Ehrenberg and Mavros (1995) and Bowen and Rudenstine (1992).

financial support. The improved financial support provided treatment departments a competitive advantage in their recruitment of top students. However, the GEI also appears to be associated with an increase in multiyear packages of financial support, a consequence that was not intended. Multiyear packages were becoming more common before the GEI started, but the GEI appears to have accelerated their growth. This impact was probably tied to the overall increase in financial support brought about by the GEI because it fueled competition for students at the admissions stage. Although we provide some evidence in this chapter that multiyear packages facilitate recruitment, it is still an open question whether such packages reduce the incentives for students to devote effort to their studies.

The increase in financial support brought about by the GEI explains part of the overall impact of the GEI on student outcomes. This is because more generous financial support typically reduces attrition and increases completion rates. However, even the most generous financial-support packages are associated with considerable attrition; this finding points to the importance of other factors in accounting for attrition from doctoral programs.

Specifically, we find that fellowships are somewhat better than assistantships at encouraging completion and limiting attrition. At the dissertation stage in particular, having a fellowship rather than an assistantship improves completion rates in the sixth year and beyond. We also find that summer support reduces attrition and improves completion rates.

CHAPTER 6

The Influence of Doctoral Program Designs

> Expectations for the dissertation are extremely high—it's treated less as a learning document than the first draft of a book—one that should revolutionize one's field, no less!—and for me this has been somewhat paralyzing. It does seem something that could be remedied to some extent with some sort of post-proposal workshop or mini-course. I find it all too easy to lose track of the horizon and purpose of this project.
>
> —Student in English who entered in
> 1993 and left the program in 2004

THE ANALYSES we presented in the previous two chapters estimated the impact of the Graduate Education Initiative (GEI) on doctoral students' attrition probabilities, completion probabilities, and time-to-degree (TTD). Although we discussed the important influence of financial support methods on these outcomes in Chapter 5, all other aspects of doctoral education in the humanities were treated as a black box. In this chapter, we use the Graduate Education Survey (GES) to go inside that black box to understand how the characteristics of doctoral programs, including the expectations that doctoral students confronted, were influenced by the GEI and how these changes in turn affected doctoral students' attrition and completion probabilities.[1] In the process, we demonstrate the general relationship between doctoral program characteristics and doctoral student outcomes, and we suggest that our findings may have important implications beyond the evaluation of the GEI.[2]

---

[1] The material presented in this chapter draws heavily on Ronald G. Ehrenberg, George H. Jakubson, Jeffrey A. Groen, Eric So, and Joseph Price, "Inside the Black Box of Doctoral Education: What Program Characteristics Influence Doctoral Students' Attrition and Graduation Probabilities?" *Educational Evaluation and Policy Analysis* 29 (June 2007): 134–50. We are grateful to our co-authors for permitting us to include this chapter in the book. Readers interested in the technical details of our analyses should refer to that paper.

[2] The 44 treatment and 41 control departments whose data are included in our analyses in this chapter are the ones listed in Table 4.1.

At the outset of the discussion, it is important to note two things. First, departments often have little incentive to engage in systematic reform of their doctoral programs. The benefit to any given faculty member of investing time to reform a department's doctoral program is likely to be very small. Absent pressure from outside forces, such as an external review or the provision of financial incentives to undertake reform, such as that which the GEI provided, it is unlikely that reforms will occur.

Second, as we have noted in earlier chapters, departments reported to the Mellon Foundation annually the program changes that they first planned and then made, and how well they perceived these changes were working. However, the departments may have engaged in purely symbolic reform, restructuring programs in a way that was consistent with the goals of the Foundation, but then not putting much effort into implementing that reform. Our analyses in this chapter—which make use of data collected from students in both treatment and control departments about their perceptions of the characteristics of their doctoral programs—allow us to evaluate whether the reforms that departments reported they had implemented were actually perceived by the students to have occurred.

The next section outlines our approach to measuring characteristics of graduate programs and defines the characteristics used in our analysis. Later sections present estimates of the impact that the GEI had on each of these characteristics and of the impact of these characteristics on student outcomes. We then discuss the implications of these findings. Our focus is on evaluating the effects of the GEI, yet the methodological approach we use could be profitably employed in a wide range of program-evaluation studies. This chapter is necessarily somewhat more technical than the rest of the book; but the results of the analysis should be clear even to readers without technical backgrounds.

MEASURING CHARACTERISTICS OF GRADUATE PROGRAMS

Coupled with the data previously reported to the Mellon Foundation by the departments, the GES data provide an opportunity to analyze how the GEI affected selected characteristics of doctoral programs and how these characteristics in turn influenced students' probabilities of attrition from, and completion of, their graduate programs. That is, the data permit us to ascertain the routes by which the GEI influenced PhD students' attrition and completion probabilities.

Although respondents answered numerous questions in the GES about the characteristics of their PhD programs, it was impossible to treat each characteristic as a separate explanatory variable in an analysis of the students' transition probabilities for two reasons. First, it would have been impossible to precisely estimate the effects of each program characteristic because many of them are highly correlated with each other. Second, even though the response rate to the GES was high (74 percent), response rates on individual questions were often much lower. Many survey respondents failed to respond to a number of questions about the characteristics of their programs, at least in part because some questions pertained to the dissertation phase and were therefore irrelevant for respondents who had dropped out of the programs prior to the dissertation stage. If we had tried to use the values of the individual characteristics for each student in our analyses, we would have been plagued by missing-value problems that would again have prevented us from obtaining precise estimates of the impact of the program characteristics on the outcomes of interest to us.

The strategy that we pursue to circumvent these problems is to compute the average value of each program characteristic, for individuals who responded to the relevant question, for each entering cohort and department (for example, students entering PhD study in English at Cornell University in 1988–89) and to use these averages and a statistical technique called *factor analysis* to combine these characteristics into a smaller number of program-characteristic indexes. We then estimate how the GEI influenced each of these indexes and in turn how the indexes influenced PhD students' attrition and completion probabilities. From these two sets of relationships, we can identify and estimate the routes through which the GEI influenced the students' attrition and completion probabilities.

Table 6.1 reports the seven program-characteristic indexes that we have chosen to summarize some of the characteristics of humanities doctoral programs: financial support, seminar requirements, summer expectations, exam requirements, department culture, advising, and clarity of timetables. Under each is the set of specific variables that we use to construct the index, based on responses to questions from the GES. The questions on the GES were chosen to illuminate aspects of graduate program design that the framers of the GEI believed were important in determining students' progress through their PhD programs; as we discuss in Appendix A, many of these questions were based on the initial proposals and the annual reports that treatment departments submitted to the Foundation, which described how their programs were evolving. The specific variables used to construct each index were recoded in such a way that higher values of a variable represent an improvement in the sense that lower rates of attrition and higher completion rates were expected to be associated with it.

For example, the "financial support" index is based on respondents' answers to questions about the number of years of support offered to students at their time of program entry, the type of financial support that

TABLE 6.1
Program-Characteristic Indexes and Their Components

Financial support: Higher values imply more financial support
  1 = Offered at least one year of support, 0 = otherwise
  1 = Offered at least two years of support, 0 = otherwise
  1 = Offered at least three years of support, 0 = otherwise
  1 = Offered at least four years of support, 0 = otherwise
  1 = Fellowship or stipend was primary support during dissertation stage,
    0 = otherwise
  1 = Did not fear losing funding during dissertation phase, 0 = otherwise
  Progress toward PhD was slowed by being employed outside the department
    (1–5: 5 = not at all, 1 = a great deal)

Seminar requirements: Higher values imply more course and seminar
    requirements
  1 = Department expected student to attend a course on research methods,
    0 = otherwise
  1 = Department expected student to attend a course to prepare the
    dissertation proposal, 0 = otherwise
  1 = Department expected student to attend a course on the dissertation
    process after completing the proposal, 0 = otherwise
  1 = Department expected student to complete dissertation proposal as part
    of comprehensive exams, 0 = otherwise
  1 = Department expected student to present dissertation work-in-progress to
    other students, 0 = otherwise
  **1 = Students were required to attend special workshops on dissertation
    writing and related topics, 0 = otherwise**
  **1 = Students were required to present their work at the dissertation
    workshops, 0 = otherwise**
  1 = Financial support was conditional on attending the dissertation
    workshops, 0 = otherwise

Summer expectations: Higher values imply greater number of summer
    expectations set by the department
  **1 = Expected to attend a summer course for comprehensive exams,
    0 = otherwise**
  **1 = Expected to attend a summer workshop on dissertation proposal,
    0 = otherwise**
  **1 = Expected to do field work, travel, or archival research prior to
    dissertation stage during summer, 0 = otherwise**
  1 = Expected to prepare for language exams during summer, 0 = otherwise

Exam requirements: Higher values imply greater effort to modify exam stage to
    facilitate transition from coursework to research stage
  **1 = Students were expected to have their exams tailored, at least in part, to
    their specific dissertation research interests, 0 = otherwise**

(*continued*)

TABLE 6.1 (*Continued*)

1 = Students were expected to complete dissertation proposal or prospectus as part of comprehensive exams, 0 = otherwise

Number of language exams required by department

Department culture: Higher values imply better department culture

1 = Someone took special interest in their work, 0 = otherwise

1 = A faculty member took interest in their work, 0 = otherwise

1 = Met socially with faculty at departmental functions, 0 = otherwise

There was a sense of solidarity among students within the department (1–5: 5 = strongly agree, 1 = strongly disagree)

The department did not foster competitiveness among students (1–5: 5 = strongly agree, 1 = strongly disagree)

Faculty facilitated student involvement in the intellectual life of the department (1–5: 5 = strongly agree, 1 = strongly disagree)

There was a sense of personal involvement and support among faculty, students, and the department (1–5: 5 = strongly agree, 1 = strongly disagree)

Progress was slowed by political struggles or frictions within the department (1–5: 5 = not at all, 1 = a great deal)

Advising: Higher values imply more desirable and higher-quality advising

Program prepared them to teach at the collegiate level (1–5: 5 = strongly agree, 1 = strongly disagree)

Program prepared them to conduct research (1–5: 5 = strongly agree, 1 = strongly disagree)

1 = Someone took special interest in their work, 0 = otherwise

1 = A faculty member took interest in their work, 0 = otherwise

Advising was useful in developing their dissertation prospectus or proposal (1–4: 1 = not advised, 4 = very useful)

Advising was useful in researching and writing their dissertation (1–4: 1 = not advised, 4 = very useful)

Advising was useful in obtaining dissertation grants (1–4: 1 = not advised, 4 = very useful)

Advising was useful in obtaining an academic job (1–4: 1 = not advised, 4 = very useful)

Advising was useful in obtaining a nonacademic job (1–4: 1 = not advised, 4 = very useful)

Progress was slowed by poor academic advising (1–5: 5 = not at all, 1 = a great deal)

Progress was slowed by dissertation supervisor's lack of availability (1–5: 5 = not at all, 1 = a great deal)

Clarity of timetables: Higher values imply greater departmental clarity with regard to rules and better efforts to monitor progress

1 = Informed in writing about course requirements, 0 = otherwise

1 = Informed in writing about policies regarding incompleteness, 0 = otherwise

TABLE 6.1 (*Continued*)

---

1 = **Informed in writing about definition of satisfactory progress, 0 = otherwise**

1 = **Informed in writing about deadlines for completing coursework and exams, 0 = otherwise**

1 = Informed in writing about department or university goals to increase PhD completion rates, 0 = otherwise

1 = **Informed in writing about departmental expectations concerning length of time to complete PhD, 0 = otherwise**

1 = Notified that there is a maximum time to complete the degree, 0 = otherwise

Progress was slowed by poor academic advising (1–5: 5 = not at all, 1 = a great deal)

1 = Letter grades were used to evaluate progress, 0 = otherwise

1 = Written assignments were used to evaluate progress, 0 = otherwise

1 = A formal review with advisor was used to evaluate progress, 0 = otherwise

1 = A formal faculty committee was used to evaluate progress, 0 = otherwise

---

Note: Variables in bold type are the ones that proved to be the most important in each index.

they had during their dissertation year, whether they had fears of losing funding during the writing of their dissertation, and whether their progress toward the PhD was slowed by their being employed outside the department. Improved financial support is expected to reduce attrition and increase completion probabilities.

The "seminar requirements" index is based on requirements to attend courses or seminars during the academic year, which were designed to move students more quickly through the program. Some departments, for example, instituted seminars on research methods or dissertation writing, and some of the latter required students to make presentations on their dissertations in the seminars. The "exam requirements" index was based on efforts to modify examinations to facilitate students' transitions through the program. For example, some departments focused part of the comprehensive examination on the specific area in which each student planned to specialize and write a dissertation.

The "summer expectations" index was based on summer expectations set by the department to facilitate students' progress through the program. Some departments established summer seminars on the dissertation-writing process to aid students in making the transition to research after their comprehensive examinations; others provided funding to allow students to study for language exams or to conduct field research during the summer.

The "department culture" index was based on variables reflecting the interest faculty took in students' work, faculty involvement in the intellectual life of the department, and whether there was a sense of competitiveness or cooperation in the department. One department, for example, in response to students' concerns that they were teaching without having had any training, assigned a number of faculty members to serve as teaching mentors to the students.

The "advising" index was based on variables that reflected more desirable and higher-quality advising. Departments sought to improve advising in a number of ways; some scheduled periodic individual mandatory meetings with individual advisors or the single graduate faculty member in charge of the PhD program, whereas others scheduled more group advising sessions. Still others instituted training for job interviews.

Finally, the "clarity of timetables" index was based on variables that related to departmental clarity with respect to requirements and efforts to monitor student performance. Many departments clarified expectations about the expected timetable for student progress and made these more explicit to students in written form. Others encouraged faculty members to spend more time with students early in the students' graduate careers, discussing the nature of dissertations and the dissertation process.

The variables in bold type in Table 6.1 are the ones that proved to be the most important in each index.[3] For example, the most important variable in the "financial support" index is whether the students were offered at least two years of support when first admitted to the program, and the most important variable in the "exam requirements" index is whether the exams students faced were tailored at least partially to their individual research interests. Similarly, the two most important variables in the "seminar requirements" index are whether the students were required to attend a dissertation-writing seminar and whether they were required to present their dissertation research at such a seminar.

IMPACT OF THE GEI ON PROGRAM CHARACTERISTICS

Table 6.2 presents our estimates of the impact of the GEI on each of the indexes, as well as on two other variables we constructed from the survey data that summarize students' beliefs regarding their departments' expectations about dissertations. The first variable, "Publish prior to PhD," denotes the fraction of respondents in the entering cohort and department who said that the department stressed the importance to them of polishing their dissertations prior to submission, even if this delayed com-

---

[3] See Ehrenberg et al. (2007) for the factor scores that precisely represent the contribution of each variable to a given characteristic.

TABLE 6.2
Impacts of the GEI on Program Characteristics

Characteristic	Impact of GEI (not weighted by cell count)	Impact of GEI (weighted by cell count)
Financial support	0.112	0.202
Seminar requirements	**0.454**	**0.288**
Summer expectations	**0.411**	**0.243**
Exam requirements	−0.056	0.043
Department culture	0.016	−0.150
Advising	0.226	0.059
Clarity of timetables	**0.322**	**0.245**
Publish prior to PhD	−0.013	−0.015
Quick completion	**0.073**	0.007

Notes: Coefficients in bold type are statistically significant at the 5 percent level. Definitions of dissertation variables: "Publish prior to PhD" = proportion of respondents in a cohort who said that the department's attitude toward finishing the dissertation was to publish or polish, even if it delayed completing the degree. "Quick completion" = proportion of respondents in a cohort who said that the department's attitude toward finishing the dissertation was to finish as quickly as possible.

pletion of their degree, or of publishing while in graduate school, even if this delayed completion of their degree. The second variable, "Quick completion," denotes the fraction of respondents in the entering cohort and department who said that the department stressed to them the importance of finishing dissertations as quickly as possible. These two variables do not add up to one (indeed, typically their sum is less than one-half) because students were given the option of responding that their department did not indicate its attitude toward finishing the dissertation or that the attitudes of different members of the department were inconsistent on this issue.[4]

The underlying model used in the second column of Table 6.2 groups the data by entry cohort and department and weights each observation equally. The coefficients found in this column are estimates of the difference between treatment and control departments in the change in each index between the period during which the GEI was in effect and the period before it was in effect.[5] Those coefficients in bold type are those that are statistically significant and the ones on which we focus.

---

[4] We included these dissertation variables separately because of our strong prior assumption that faculty attitudes about the nature of the dissertation were important determinants of attrition and completion rates.

[5] Methodologically, we estimate linear regressions in which the dependent variable is a given characteristic and the explanatory variables are dichotomous variables for department

These estimates provide strong evidence that the GEI really did affect transparency and, to some extent, accountability in the graduate departments included in the sample. They suggest that the GEI's primary effect on doctoral programs in these fields was felt through the "seminar requirements," "summer expectations," and "clarity of timetables" indexes and through increased encouragement to finish dissertations as quickly as possible; these were the only four variables for which the estimated effects were statistically significant.

Sizes of entering cohorts, as well as the fraction of the individuals who responded to the GES, differed substantially across entering cohorts and departments in the sample. Redoing the analyses, weighting each observation by size of entering cohort (giving more weight to large cohorts), allows us to see how program effects differed, on average, between larger and smaller departments. The results of these analyses are found in the third column of Table 6.2.

The weighted results differ somewhat from the unweighted results. In particular, although the GEI still appears to have led to a statistically significant improvement in the "seminar requirements," "summer expectations," and "clarity of timetables" indexes, it is no longer seen to be associated with a statistically significant improvement in the expectation that dissertations would be completed as quickly as possible. This suggests that the improvements in the latter variable that were attributed to the GEI in the unweighted analyses occurred primarily in the smaller programs that took part in the GEI. On the flip side, the weighted results show a greater estimated impact of the GEI on the "financial support" index, which suggests that these improvements occurred primarily in larger programs.[6]

IMPACT OF PROGRAM CHARACTERISTICS ON STUDENT OUTCOMES

To estimate the impact of the different PhD program characteristics on attrition and completion probabilities, we use the individual-level data

---

and institutions, a dichotomous variable for whether the department is a treatment or control department, a dichotomous variable for whether the entering cohort is a pre-GEI cohort or a cohort entering after the GEI was instituted, and the interaction of the latter two variables. The coefficients of the latter variable provide our difference-in-differences estimates. (See Chapter 2 for a discussion of the difference-in-differences approach.) In order to measure longer-run changes, students who began their PhD study between 1986–87 and 1990–91 are excluded from the analysis, because although they entered graduate school before the GEI began (in 1991), they were eligible for financial support from the GEI starting in 1991.

[6] Additional analyses of how sensitive the findings are to the precise statistical models used are found in Ehrenberg et al. (2007).

collected by the treatment and control departments and estimate multi-nomial logit models of the probability that an individual leaves a PhD program or graduates by the end of each year in the program. The explanatory variables included in these models are those in the models of Chapter 4. Here, however, rather than including a variable indicating whether an individual was enrolled in a treatment or a control department, we instead include the estimated values of the seven program-characteristic indexes and the two variables representing departmental dissertation expectations for the individual's entering cohort and department. The estimated coefficients of these variables that we obtain allow us to estimate the effects of changes in the variables on cumulative attrition and completion probabilities.

Estimates of the marginal effects of the program characteristics appear in Table 6.3. The impacts on the cumulative probability of attrition for years 1–11 and on the cumulative probability of completion for years 4–11 are shown in the upper and lower panels, respectively. These marginal effects are estimates of the impact of a one-unit change in each variable on the probability of attrition or completion by each year. (The meaning of a "one-unit change in each variable" may not be intuitive at this point. In the next section, its meaning is clarified as we summarize the distribution of each variable across departments.)

Turning first to attrition, improvements in the "financial support" index reduce the cumulative probability of attrition in almost all years. The effect on the cumulative probability is largest in the first three years, implying that the largest effect is on early attrition. This is not surprising, because the primary variable that was important in the "financial support" index was guaranteeing entering students at least two years of financial support (see Table 6.1). Having a program with better advising or having a program whose timetables are clearer also reduces attrition probabilities in many years, and departmental expectations about the dissertation influence attrition rates in the expected direction.

Departments that emphasize the importance to students of polishing their dissertations and publishing their work while in graduate school (even if this delays completion of the degree) have higher cumulative attrition rates than departments that do not convey clear expectations about the dissertation to students. In contrast, departments that stress to students the importance of finishing dissertations quickly have lower cumulative attrition rates, starting in the early years of the program, than departments that do not convey such clear expectations. Both of these "dissertation advice" variables begin to influence attrition probabilities by year 2, suggesting that students' views of departmental expectations about dissertations affect early attrition. The growing magnitude of the "Publish prior to PhD" variable's effect in the later years implies that this variable increases attrition during the dissertation stage of programs.

TABLE 6.3

Impact of Program Characteristics on Cumulative Attrition and Completion Probabilities

Impact on Attrition Probabilities

Characteristic	Year in Program										
	1	*2*	*3*	*4*	*5*	*6*	*7*	*8*	*9*	*10*	*11*
Financial support	**-0.029**	**-0.026**	**-0.022**	-0.007	-0.012	**-0.021**	**-0.023**	**-0.019**	**-0.014**	-0.013	-0.011
Seminar requirements	0.002	0.005	0.005	0.014	0.009	0.008	0.006	0.006	0.005	0.005	0.001
Summer expectations	0.004	0.009	**0.016**	0.000	0.018	0.008	0.006	0.008	0.010	0.012	0.005
Exam requirements	0.001	-0.003	0.000	0.011	-0.001	-0.001	-0.001	-0.003	-0.006	-0.005	-0.002
Department culture	-0.005	-0.001	-0.003	-0.009	-0.006	-0.005	-0.006	-0.010	-0.008	-0.003	-0.004
Advising	**-0.012**	**-0.021**	**-0.033**	**-0.050**	**-0.058**	**-0.055**	**-0.051**	**-0.046**	**-0.047**	**-0.048**	**-0.049**
Clarity of timetables	**-0.009**	**-0.009**	**-0.012**	-0.003	-0.001	-0.008	**-0.013**	**-0.013**	-0.008	-0.010	-0.006
Publish prior to PhD	-0.006	**0.065**	**0.069**	**0.095**	**0.086**	**0.108**	**0.120**	**0.106**	**0.090**	**0.106**	**0.109**
Quick completion	-0.045	-0.057	-0.051	**-0.127**	**-0.113**	**-0.106**	**-0.074**	-0.053	-0.063	-0.044	**-0.074**

Impact on Completion Probabilities

Characteristic	Year in Program							
	4	*5*	*6*	*7*	*8*	*9*	*10*	*11*
Financial support	-0.001	0.000	**0.011**	**0.022**	**0.027**	**0.026**	**0.031**	**0.044**
Seminar requirements	-0.002	-0.004	**-0.008**	**-0.008**	-0.006	-0.005	-0.005	-0.003
Summer expectations	0.002	-0.005	0.000	0.007	0.008	**0.023**	0.014	0.011
Exam requirements	-0.002	-0.001	-0.001	-0.002	-0.004	-0.006	-0.007	-0.003
Department culture	0.001	0.002	0.003	0.009	0.010	0.005	0.015	0.009
Advising	**0.004**	**0.017**	**0.034**	**0.037**	**0.041**	**0.045**	**0.040**	**0.042**
Clarity of timetables	-0.001	-0.002	0.000	0.008	0.009	0.004	0.001	-0.003
Publish prior to PhD	-0.008	-0.023	**-0.063**	**-0.112**	**-0.107**	**-0.080**	-0.080	-0.078
Quick completion	**0.013**	**0.039**	**0.096**	**0.099**	**0.084**	**0.090**	**0.121**	0.081

Notes: The number in each cell is the marginal effect of a one-unit change in the characteristic on the cumulative probability of attrition (top panel) or completion (bottom panel). Coefficients in bold type are statistically significant at the 5 percent level. For definitions of "Publish prior to PhD" and "Quick completion," see the notes to Table 6.2.

The lower panel of Table 6.3 shows effects on completion probabilities. Increasing the "financial support" index improves cumulative completion probabilities, starting in year 6. However, the "advising" index is perhaps the most important element in the group; when it improves, other characteristics held constant, the cumulative probability of completion increases in all years, and the magnitude of this effect increases with time spent in the program, thus highlighting the importance of improved advising for this central outcome.

The nature of dissertation expectations also proves important in influencing early completion. Relative to the omitted category (not providing clear signals about dissertation expectations), departments whose expectations are that their students will polish their dissertations and that their students will publish while in graduate school (even if this delays completion of their degrees) have significantly lower cumulative probabilities of completion in years 6–8, other variables held constant. Similarly, relative to the omitted category, departments that stress to their students the importance of promptly finishing dissertations have higher cumulative completion probabilities starting in year 4, with the effect substantially higher in years 6–10.

IMPLICATIONS FOR THE GEI AND FUTURE POLICIES

The results we presented in Table 6.2 suggest that effects of the GEI were strongest on the "summer expectations," "seminar requirements," and "clarity of timetables" indexes, and also on the proportion of individuals who said their department encouraged them to complete their dissertations as quickly as possible. Taken together with the results presented in Table 6.3, our findings suggest that the GEI reduced attrition rates and improved completion rates primarily by increasing clarity of timetables and encouraging students to finish their dissertations as quickly as possible.

Measuring the impact of each of these changes on cumulative completion and attrition rates is important. This can be accomplished, for example, by multiplying the estimated impact of the GEI on the "clarity of timetables" index (Table 6.2), 0.322, and the estimated impact of a one-unit change in the "clarity of timetables" on the probability of attrition by the end of year 7 (Table 6.3), −0.013. The estimated effect of the GEI on the probability of attrition by year 7 working through increased program clarity is the product of these two numbers, or −0.004. Similarly, the estimated effect of the GEI on stressing the importance to students of finishing their dissertations promptly was 0.073 (Table 6.2) and the estimated impact of this variable on graduating by year 8 was 0.084 (Table 6.3). Thus the estimated effect of the GEI on the probability of graduating by year 8 working through increased encouragement to students to finish their dissertations promptly is the product of these two numbers, or 0.006.

Although each of these individual effects may seem relatively small, their magnitudes should be interpreted in terms of our analyses of the overall impact of the GEI on attrition and completion probabilities, presented in Chapter 4. There we find that that the GEI reduced attrition rates and increased completion probabilities at treatment departments relative to control departments by about 0.02–0.04. Hence the impact of the GEI on these PhD program characteristics "explains" a substantial share of the overall effect of the GEI. Moreover, our estimates of the effects of the GEI on program characteristics may well be only lower-bound estimates of the true effects of the program. To the extent that control departments in our sample were aware of the changes that the treatment departments were making in their programs and emulated the behavior of the latter, our methodology will understate the GEI's actual effects.

The GEI appears to have had an impact on characteristics of graduate programs, yet there remains substantial room for improvement. Table 6.4 ignores the distinction between treatment and control departments and presents summary statistics for each of the program-characteristic indexes and dissertation-advice variables for cohorts in our sample that entered after the start of the GEI (1991–92 through 1996–97). We use this sample to give the reader a sense of the range of these variables across departments after the GEI had already been instituted.

The mean value of the "clarity of timetables" index was 0.238 across entering cohorts and departments during this period; the 25th percentile value was –0.365 and the 75th percentile was 0.945. The difference between the 25th and 75th percentiles is 1.310, which is more than four times our estimated impact of the GEI on the "clarity of timetables" index. So if the "clarity of timetables" index of departments down at the 25th percentile could be improved to the level of the "clarity of timetables" index for departments at the 75th percentile, the probability of attrition by year 7 in the former departments could be reduced by about 0.02.

Similarly, the mean value of the "Quick completion" variable was 0.248 in this period, but the 25th-to-75th-percentile range in this variable was 0.083–0.357, a difference of 0.274. This is over three times the size of the estimated effect of the GEI on this variable. Again, if departments at the 25th percentile in terms of the "Quick completion" variable could be improved to the level of those at the 75th percentile, the probability of students graduating by year 8 from the former departments could also be increased by about 0.03.

Thus, one important message of this analysis is that the value of the GEI and the study of its effects is greater than just learning how large its influence was on attrition and completion probabilities. Rather, it has pro-

TABLE 6.4
Summary Statistics of Program Characteristics,
1991–92 through 1996–97 Entering Cohorts

| Characteristic | Mean | Percentile | |
		25th	75th
Financial support	0.459	−0.090	1.239
Seminar requirements	0.150	−0.574	0.371
Summer expectations	0.213	−0.316	0.624
Exam requirements	0.308	−0.358	1.570
Department culture	0.167	−0.503	0.913
Advising	0.177	−0.476	0.872
Clarity of timetables	0.238	−0.365	0.945
Publish prior to PhD	0.130	0.000	0.200
Quick completion	0.248	0.083	0.357

Note: For definitions of "Publish prior to PhD" and "Quick completion," see the notes to Table 6.2.

vided evidence that it is possible to identify with some precision those aspects of the intervention that specifically affected the probabilities of certain outcomes, positive and negative. In particular, improving advising, specifying timetables for progress toward the PhD, and clarifying departmental expectations about the nature of dissertations can all significantly reduce attrition and improve completion probabilities.[7] Although there are pitfalls in moving directly from research findings to policy recommendations, these changes are relatively cost-free and pass the test of good sense.

The fact that these changes can be made relatively easily leads us to speculate about why they have not been implemented more widely. One possibility is that the departments did not recognize that these changes matter. Another is that faculty members at selective universities place a lower priority on increasing completion rates and reducing TTD than they do on educating their very top PhDs and preparing them for leadership in their fields. These faculty members may well be the ones who encourage their students to publish while in graduate school and to polish their dissertations prior to submission so that they are nearly suitable for publication.

Faculty members are justifiably concerned about the quality of these students' dissertations, the jobs their PhDs are offered, and their stu-

---

[7] Of course, if the departmental expectation is that the students will polish their dissertations before submitting them or publish their work prior to submitting their dissertations, knowledge of this expectation will lead to higher attrition rates and longer TTD.

dents' subsequent record of publication. We know from departmental reports that some faculty members think that reducing TTD will lead to lower-quality dissertations, and that this in turn may adversely influence their students' job prospects. Although the quality of dissertations (and written work more generally) is difficult to assess, we will address the relationship between TTD, early-career job outcomes, and publishing productivity in Chapters 9 and 10. To preview our findings, longer TTD is not associated with "better" job outcomes or with enhanced early-career publications, even when we hold constant the measures we have of students' competence and the quality of their departments.

We close with one methodological observation and a summary comment on the findings this chapter reports. The methodology on which this chapter is based, the application of factor analysis to a combination of institutional and survey data, should be applicable in other studies of ways to reduce attrition rates and TTD in the humanities. For example, although the 13 universities in the database on which this study draws educate a disproportionately large share of PhDs in the humanities, over four-fifths of doctoral students get degrees from other universities in these fields, and they too confront problems of high attrition and long TTD. The same methodology may also be used in efforts to redesign graduate education in other disciplines altogether, such as the empirical social sciences, mathematics, the physical and biological sciences, and engineering. These disciplines confront problems other than high attrition and long TTD.

Apart from perennial worries about financing graduate education, recent efforts have been focused on how to prepare doctoral students in the sciences for jobs outside the academy, and discussion continues about the need for long periods of postdoctoral training in a number of these fields. These aspects of effectiveness are different from those treated here, but they share a common goal: the best possible use of individual and institutional resources.[8] We think it should be feasible for the National Research Council to survey faculty members, students, administrators, and alumni of a set of graduate programs in sciences and engineering, using an instrument similar to the GES, and then to use factor analysis to identify important program characteristics and link them to completion rates and the later employment of graduates.[9] This would of course require accurate data to be kept on the status of entering students

[8] See Committee on Science, Engineering, and Public Policy, *Reshaping the Graduate Education of Scientists and Engineers* (Washington, DC: National Academies Press, 1995).

[9] In 2005, we suggested that the National Research Council undertake such a survey in departments of science and engineering at a workshop on "STEM Doctoral Students: How Finance Mechanisms Influence the Quality of Their Education," sponsored by the Center for Education of the National Research Council, Washington, DC, June 22.

and their progress toward their degrees as well as on their postgraduate histories. A major initiative such as the GEI would not be needed to collect the necessary data on changes in programs: the natural variation among PhD programs, and within a given program over time, would make the necessary comparisons feasible.

This chapter demonstrates that elements of program redesign can be identified, that the impact of an intervention such as the GEI had on each element can be measured, and that specific effects (or lack of them) on students' progress can be estimated. This methodology takes into account the fact that program redesigns may not have been realized despite their being intended as part of the larger intervention. It also allows for the identification of specific program elements that had significant effects on attrition and completion. For example, better advising is associated with reductions in the cumulative probability of attrition for every one of the 11 years the data cover, whereas better financing has its greatest effects on cumulative attrition rates in the first three years, that is, it reduces early attrition. When it comes to cumulative probabilities of completion of the degree, improved advising once again proves to be the most important element in the GEI interventions. Holding other factors constant, better advising increases the cumulative probability of finishing in all years and the magnitude of the effect grows the longer students remain in graduate school. Improved financing is also associated with the cumulative probability of completing the degree, but its effect is evident in the sixth year, and its importance grows from there onward.

Identifying those aspects of interventions that are most effective and when their effects are strongest should be useful steps forward in redesigning graduate programs. As we noted, the changes in attrition and completion rates associated with particular interventions were small, but their magnitudes should be viewed in light of the GEI's overall effects on completion and attrition. When the magnitudes of the effects of the program elements identified earlier in this chapter are compared to the GEI's overall effects, it is clear that they account for a substantial share of those overall effects. Moreover, since the measured effectiveness of the GEI in treatment departments differed so greatly, it follows that by clarifying expectations or by improving advising or financing in the departments that improved least (i.e., fell within the lowest quartile) to the level of the highest quartile, the probability of completion by the seventh year could be increased. Applying the same exercise for the departments in the highest quartile of late attrition and reducing them to the lowest quartile would decrease late attrition by a nontrivial amount.

The next chapter deals not with changes in programs or departments, but with the important effects of gender and family on graduate students' careers.

CHAPTER 7

The Role of Gender and Family Status

> It seems that the men oftentimes get married
> sometime in the last couple years of the program
> and whether or not they obtain funding continue
> on supported by their spouse. It seems upon re-
> flection, that the women in the program for some
> reason either stop toward the end of the program
> to bear children—then in the end take many
> more years (for ex. 10 years) to graduate or they
> drop out due to lack of funding.
>
> —A 2002 religion PhD who began in 1995

THE ANALYSES we presented in Chapter 4 touched on the association between gender and probabilities of attrition and completion. They showed
that, other factors held constant, women are more likely to have left the program by their eighth year of doctoral study and less likely to have received
a degree than men. Many prior studies have reported similar results.[1]

One of the factors of which we took account in our analyses in Chapter 4 was the field in which a graduate student was enrolled, so differences
across fields in the share of students who are women and in average time-
to-degree (TTD) and completion rates cannot explain our findings.
Moreover, our analyses in Chapter 5 show that there were no differences
in financial support patterns between the men and women in our sam-

---

[1] Previous studies that have addressed gender differences in attrition and completion
probabilities include Bowen and Rudenstine (1992); Belinda Crawford Seagram, Judy
Gould, and Sandra W. Pyke, "An Investigation of Gender and Other Variables on Time to
Completion of Doctoral Degrees," *Research in Higher Education* 39 (June 1998): 319–35; and
Maria Ferreira, "Gender Issues Relating to Graduate Student Attrition in Two Science Departments," *International Journal of Science Education* 25 (August 2003): 969–89. An early study
of the impact of marital status is Saul D. Feldman, "Impediment or Stimulant? Marital
Status and Graduate Education," *American Journal of Sociology* 78 (December 1973): 982–94,
which found that married women, but not married men, face increased pressure to drop out
of their doctoral programs. Finally, Nettles and Millett (2006) report that married PhD students in a variety of fields are less likely to "stop out" of their PhD programs, are more likely
to complete their degrees, and have shorter TTD than students who are single.

ple, so financial support differences are also not responsible for the gender differences we observed.

Neither our study nor most of the previous studies were able to account for the effects of the doctoral student's family status, because most databases on graduate students do not include this information.[2] One of the reasons the Mellon Foundation undertook the Graduate Education Survey (GES) was to obtain information on doctoral students' family status while in graduate school. We use these data, along with the institutional data files, to analyze how gender, marital status, and the presence of children in student families at the time they began doctoral study interact to influence doctoral students' progress toward their degrees.[3] We ask "Do the gender differences in attrition and completion patterns that we have observed reflect differences in family status by gender?"[4]

To preview our findings, we find that there are no gender differences in attrition and completion among students who are single. The overall gender differences in completion rates and attrition rates that we observed in Chapter 5 are driven by the fact that married men are less likely to leave graduate school and more likely to earn degrees than single men, whereas married women and single women do not differ in these respects. Having children at the time of entry to doctoral study is associated with increased chances of completing the degree within 10 years among men (but not significantly so), but this is not the case for women. Furthermore, married men with children at the time of entry to doctoral study have shorter TTD than single men. In short, marriage and fatherhood are beneficial for men when it comes to completing degrees. At the same time, contrary to popular expectation, marriage and motherhood are not detrimental for women.

MARITAL STATUS AND THE GRADUATE EDUCATION SURVEY

As Chapter 2 noted, the GES was administered to students who enrolled in doctoral programs in both treatment and control departments. The GES achieved a response rate of 74 percent, and nearly every respondent answered the survey questions about marital status at the start of doctoral

---

[2] We asked institutions for this information, but some of them could not provide it because they did not routinely collect it.

[3] We should acknowledge one major limitation of our analyses. The GES did not collect any information about the educational or employment activities of a student's spouse or partner. Hence we are unable to analyze how employment of a spouse, or having a spouse who is also a doctoral student, influenced completion probabilities and TTD. These are important questions for future research to address.

[4] The material presented in this chapter summarizes a more detailed analysis conducted by Joseph Price, which first appeared in Joseph Price, *Marriage and Graduate Student Out-*

study. For the analyses in this chapter, we exclude the respondents who did not report information on their age or marital status as well as those students who completed their degrees in 3 years or less or were still pursuing the PhD 11 or more years after starting their degree programs.[5] These restrictions leave a sample of 11,435 individuals.

The GES did not ask respondents for their marital histories or when their current marriage began. Rather it asked for the respondents' marital status at the time of entry and at the time of exit (through attrition or completion) from their doctoral programs. Table 7.1 shows the fraction of students in each of four categories of marital status at the time of both entry and exit from their doctoral programs. A large fraction of these students changed their marital status during their graduate careers; for example, the percentage of men and women in our population who are married when they leave graduate school is twice the percentage who were married when they began.

Ideally one would like to know if students who marry during graduate school are more or less likely to earn degrees than those who remain single. However, students who remain in graduate school longer are more likely to get married while they are enrolled in school simply because they are "exposed" to the possibility of getting married for a longer period of time. The chances of there being a positive association between getting married while in graduate school and long TTD are built into the data. As a result, in the analyses that follow we focus only on marital status at the time of entry to PhD study and compare the outcomes of students who were married or single at that time.

Similarly, one would like to know if students who become parents while enrolled in doctoral programs have a different outcome than students who do not. However, the same analytic problem holds here. The longer one is enrolled in doctoral study the longer one is "exposed" to the possibility of having children; almost by definition, there will be a positive association among completers between having children when they leave doctoral study and their TTD. This association would tell us nothing about the causal effect on TTD of having children while enrolled in doctoral study. Thus, in the analyses that follow we similarly focus only on the presence of children at the time of entry to PhD programs and compare the outcomes of married students with and without children.

Table 7.2 provides summary statistics by gender and marital status. This table shows some of the differences between the single and married stu-

---

comes, Cornell Higher Education Research Institute Working Paper 75 (Ithaca, NY: Cornell Higher Education Research Institute, July 2005).

[5] As noted in Chapter 4, approximately 10 percent of all students who ultimately receive their PhDs do so after year 11.

TABLE 7.1

Marital Status of Students in the GES Sample

	Women				Men			
	At Entry to PhD Study		At Exit from PhD Study		At Entry to PhD Study		At Exit from PhD Study	
	N	Percent	N	Percent	N	Percent	N	Percent
Never married	3,664	66.5	1,857	39.3	4,008	67.6	2,092	40.4
Domestic partner	657	11.9	646	13.7	560	9.5	569	11.0
Divorced or widowed	212	3.8	339	7.2	105	1.8	225	4.3
Married	977	17.7	1,888	39.9	1,252	21.1	2,297	44.3
Total	5,510		4,730		5,925		5,183	

Note: The number of responses at exit from PhD study is smaller than that at entry because some respondents were still enrolled in their programs as of the survey date.

TABLE 7.2

Summary Statistics According to Gender and Marital Status

	Women		Men	
	Single	Married	Single	Married
Demographics				
Age (mean)	**24.8**	**29.8**	**24.8**	**29.3**
Age (median)	**24**	**28**	**24**	**28**
Non–U.S. citizen	0.100	0.104	**0.126**	**0.165**
U.S. citizen, white	0.659	0.670	**0.659**	**0.622**
U.S. citizen, nonwhite	**0.140**	**0.104**	0.106	0.098
GRE scores and prior training				
Prior master's degree	**0.194**	**0.342**	**0.216**	**0.381**
GRE verbal	**676.3**	**660.5**	**680.5**	**660.3**
GRE math	**616.4**	**588.4**	**660.1**	**633.6**
Outcomes				
Completion probability	0.571	0.573	**0.592**	**0.653**
Attrition probability	0.348	0.341	**0.326**	**0.294**
Time-to-degree	6.28	6.35	6.23	6.26
Time-to-attrition	**3.70**	**4.14**	**3.65**	**4.34**
N	4,533	977	4,673	1,252

Note: Entries in bold type indicate that the difference in means between single and married students by gender is statistically significant at the 5 percent level.

dents. (The category "single" in this table and the rest of the chapter includes never-married, cohabiting, and divorced or widowed students.) On
average, students who are married at the start of their doctoral programs
are five years older and have lower GRE verbal scores than those who are
single. Failing to account for these differences in background would dis-
tort comparisons of the outcomes for married and single students.

OUTCOMES BY GENDER AND MARITAL STATUS

We estimated, as we did in Chapter 4, competing-risk duration models.
The explanatory variables in these models were students' gender, martial
status at the time of entry to doctoral study, GRE verbal and math scores,
race, age at entry to the PhD program, whether they had a master's degree prior to enrolling in the doctoral program, and three indicator variables: whether the student was enrolled in a treatment department,
whether the GEI was in effect during the period, and the interaction of
these two variables. The coefficients we estimated from the models were
then used to predict what the probabilities of attrition and completion
would have been each year for the entire sample if all the students had
been members of a certain group (e.g., single men). Predictions were calculated for each of the four combinations of gender and marital status.

   The predictions we obtained are plotted for men and women separately in Figures 7.1 and 7.2. These figures show that there are large differences according to marital status at the time of entry to doctoral study
in the cumulative completion and attrition rates for men, but only small

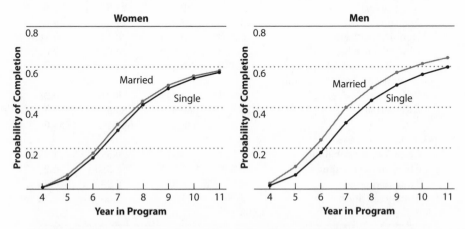

Figure 7.1. Simulated Cumulative Completion Rates by Gender and Marital
Status

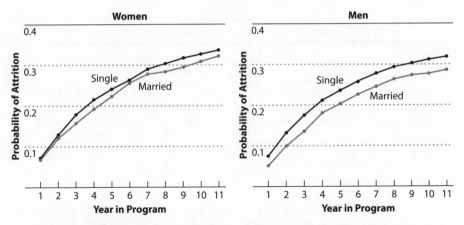

Figure 7.2. Simulated Cumulative Attrition Rates by Gender and Marital Status

differences for women. Married men have higher cumulative completion probabilities and lower cumulative attrition probabilities in each period than single men, other factors held constant. Contrary to popular perceptions, married women similarly have higher cumulative completion probabilities and lower cumulative attrition probabilities in each period than single women, other factors held constant. Differences associated with marital status are much smaller for women than for men.

Table 7.3 summarizes the results presented graphically in Figures 7.1 and 7.2 by averaging the differences in the cumulative completion rate between married and single students among men and among women over years 4–11. The same is done for the cumulative attrition rates for years 1–11. These results indicate that the average difference in the cumulative probability of completing between married and single men is 5.4 percentage points and that this difference is statistically significant. The average difference between married and single women is 1.7 percentage points, which is not statistically significant, and neither is the average difference between single women and single men, –2.2 percentage points.

Similarly, our results indicate that the average difference in the cumulative attrition probabilities between married and single men is –3.0 percentage points, a difference that is statistically significant. The comparable difference between married and single women is –1.4 percentage points, which is not statistically significant. Finally, the average difference in cumulative attrition probabilities between single women and single men in 0.6 percentage point, a difference that is not statistically significant.

Put simply, these results suggest that there are no significant gender differences in completion and attrition probabilities between single men and single women in the GES sample. Similarly, there are no significant

TABLE 7.3
Impact of Gender and Marital Status on Student Outcomes

	Attrition Probability	Completion Probability	TTD
Married women versus single women	−0.014	0.017	**−0.181**
Married men versus single men	**−0.030**	**0.054**	**−0.339**
Single women versus single men	0.006	−0.022	**0.096**

Note: Entries in bold type indicate statistically significant differences (at the 10 percent level) between groups.

differences in completion and attrition probabilities between married women and single women in the GES sample. The gender differences in completion and attrition probabilities that we observed in Chapter 4 are attributable to the fact that married men have higher completion probabilities and lower attrition probabilities than single men and to the absence of such differences among single and married women. Our findings may not generalize to other disciplines or other samples of institutions, but they are strongly at odds with the popular belief that gender per se accounts for the lower completion rates and higher attrition rates of women compared to men.

To estimate differences in the average TTD between married and single students, we estimate the completion rate for each year in the program for single and married students. By taking a weighted average of the completion rates (for which the weights are the years in the program) for each group, the average TTD can be calculated. The final column of Table 7.3 presents our estimates of the differences in average TTD among the various gender and marital status groups. Our estimates suggest that married men complete their degrees on average 0.34 year faster than single men, married women complete their degrees about 0.18 year faster than single women, and single men complete their degrees about 0.10 year faster than single women. Each of these differences is statistically significant, although the absolute values appear to be small.

As with most studies on the impact of marriage, it is possible that these results merely reflect a "selection effect," in which men who are married at the time they enter doctoral programs differ in ways that make them more persistent and help them to complete faster than single men. However, even without clear evidence of a causal interpretation for the estimates, our results show that marital status at the time of program entry can serve as a potential signal of the proclivity of men to do well in graduate school. At the same time, we cannot say whether marrying and having children during graduate study prolongs or shortens TTD for men and women or whether they have significant effects on attrition. Although many continue to believe that married women are less likely to be successful in graduate school because of their family responsibilities, our findings suggest that, once enrolled in humanities PhD programs, women who are married when they begin doctoral study are just as likely to complete their PhDs as single women.

THE IMPACT OF CHILDREN

Concern over the relatively small number of women faculty at major research universities, especially in the sciences, has led many universities to adopt "family-friendly policies" to enhance employment and retention of women faculty.[6] More recently, some major universities have expanded these policies to cover doctoral students; such policies include paid parental leave for new parents, need-based child care grants, subsidized backup care, and child care–related travel funds.[7] These policies have been adopted both in the hope that they will encourage female faculty members to pursue careers at research universities and also to reduce attrition among female doctoral students by making it easier for them to balance academic and family demands while they are enrolled in graduate school.[8] Surprisingly, very little evidence has been presented on whether having children is associated with lower completion probabilities for female doctoral students.

To analyze the impact of the presence of children at the time of doctoral program entry on completion probabilities and TTD for students in the GES sample, we restrict our attention to the subset of respondents who entered their graduate programs prior to 1993 and estimate logit models of the probability that they completed within 10 years. Then for the subset of these respondents who completed within 10 years we ask if their TTD is affected by the presence of children at graduate school entry. The models we estimate contain the same explanatory variables that were used in the models on which Figures 7.1 and 7.2 are based.

Table 7.4 reports our results for men and women by marital status and presence of children. Married men (both with and without children at the time of entry to doctoral study) have about a 4-percentage-point

---

[6] One well-publicized example is the University of California's "UC Faculty Family Friendly Edge," which is described at http://ucfamilyedge.berkeley.edu.

[7] Sierra Millman, "Princeton Expands Family-Friendly Benefits for Graduate Students with Children," *Chronicle of Higher Education,* April 13, 2007, p. A13.

[8] Lisa Harrington, "The Parent Rap: A Conversation with Mary Ann Mason on Why Babies Matter," *The Graduate* 19 (2007): 4–8.

TABLE 7.4

Gender, Marital Status, and Presence of Children at Time of Entry
to Doctoral Study and Completion Probabilities and TTD

	Probability Complete within 10 Years	TTD, Given That Complete within 10 Years
Married men, with children	0.039	**−0.403**
Married men, without children	**0.045**	**−0.368**
Single women	−0.024	**0.141**
Married women, with children	−0.006	0.037
Married women, without children	−0.004	−0.010

Notes: Numbers reported are marginal effects relative to the omitted category, single men. Numbers in bold type indicate that the marginal effect for the group is statistically different (at the 5 percent level) from that for single men.

higher probability of completing within 10 years than single men, although the difference is statistically significant only for married men without children. Conditional on having completed within 10 years, married men (both with and without children at the time of entry to doctoral study) complete in about 0.4 year less time than single men. Married women (both with and without children at the time of entry to doctoral study) do *not* have significantly different completion probabilities or TTD than single men. This is an important finding: the presence of children at the time of doctoral program entry does not appear to have adversely affected 10-year completion probabilities, or TTD, for the women in our sample.

CONCLUSION

We have shown that the gender differences in TTD and completion rates that we observed in our sample in Chapter 4 are *not* due to differences in these outcomes between men and women who are single at the time of entry to doctoral study. Moreover women who are married at the time of entry to doctoral study do about as well as single women. The gender differences that we observe are due solely to the fact that men who are married at the time of entry to doctoral study outperformed single men. Moreover the presence of children in the household at the time of entry to doctoral programs does not adversely affect program success for either men or women.

We stress again that our analyses in this chapter provide evidence of the effects of marital status and the presence of children on completion rates and TTD for men and women *at the time of entry to doctoral study*. They do not tell us how marrying or having children while enrolled in doctoral programs influences these program outcomes, nor do they shed light on why observed gender differences exist. Selection effects are a likely explanation, but the evidence is lacking. Carefully designed evaluations that would permit these questions to be answered and would explore the impact of the "family-friendly" policies that research universities are increasingly adopting for doctoral students are surely in order.

PART III

Transition from Graduate Study to Career

CHAPTER 8

Attrition and Beyond

> I think that it is ironic that this survey is the first
> time anyone has asked me why I didn't complete
> my degree. I never received so much as a postcard
> from the department or my advisor.
>
> —A student in English at University Z
> who entered in 1985 and left in 1993

> I realized I was very unlikely to get a university
> teaching job that would support me so I left. To
> this day no one from [University X] has contacted
> me to ask what I'm doing, whether I intend to re-
> turn, why I went AWOL.
>
> —A student in English at University X
> who entered in 1984 and left in 1992

OVER THE past two decades there has been growing concern about increasing attrition from graduate programs in general and those in the
humanities in particular. Although comprehensive national data are not
collected on attrition rates in PhD programs, studies of individual institutions or sets of institutions often suggest that over 50 percent of students who initially enroll in PhD programs fail to ever receive PhDs.[1]
Such high rates of attrition are thought to be problematic for both universities and the students themselves in terms of wasted resources.[2] Fur-

---

[1] Bowen and Rudenstine (1992); Ronald G. Ehrenberg, "The Flow of New Doctorates,"
Journal of Economic Literature 30 (June 1992): 830–75; Council of Graduate Schools (2004);
Rapoport (1998). More recent data from the Council of Graduate Schools' PhD Completion Project suggest that for a cohort of doctoral students who entered a set of major U.S.
and Canadian universities in the early 1990s, the average completion rate after 10 years was
close to 57 percent; John Gravois, "In Humanities, 10 Years May Not Be Enough to Get a
Ph.D.," *Chronicle of Higher Education,* July 27, 2007, p. A1.

[2] Some argue by contrast that students who leave graduate programs have not "wasted"
their time and that such benefits are rarely considered, much less measured.

thermore, some research suggests that students' decisions to leave may reflect flawed design or operation of their PhD programs.[3]

The preceding chapters have shown how the Graduate Education Initiative (GEI) influenced attrition rates from the PhD programs in the humanities departments that participated in the Initiative (Chapter 4); demonstrated that although the types of financial support that PhD students received influenced their attrition rates, even students with the most generous financial-support profiles still had relatively high rates of attrition (Chapter 5); identified the characteristics of PhD programs in these departments that appear to influence attrition (Chapter 6); and showed that gender and marital status are related to attrition in our sample in ways that are contrary to some popular perceptions (Chapter 7). In this chapter, we turn to a description of the level and timing of attrition as experienced by the departments in our database. Having described who left and when they left, we turn to the pressing questions of why they left and what happens to those students after they leave.

Given the paucity of data available regarding those two topics, Mellon Foundation staff designed the Graduate Education Survey (GES) to gather data to better understand the experiences of the students who leave. The GES is, we believe, the first effort to gather comprehensive data on reasons for attrition and the experiences of the students who leave PhD programs in the humanities. Using responses from the GES participants who did not complete their programs, we analyze their reported reasons for leaving their programs. Then we turn to a detailed discussion of what happens to those students after they leave a given PhD program.

From the perspective of the universities, as we have shown in Chapter 2, other factors held constant, the higher the attrition rate the greater the cost in terms of student years borne by an institution to produce each PhD. Hence reducing attrition rates can reduce the institutional resources devoted to the production of each PhD.

From the perspective of students, the concern is for those who invest large numbers of years trying to obtain a PhD and then leave and wind up in dead-end jobs that make little use of their education. A popular image is that of an ABD (someone who has completed all but a dissertation) from a humanities PhD program who is unemployed or is driving a taxicab to try to make ends meet. The fear is not only that such students' investments have not paid off, but that they have forgone the income and income growth that they would have experienced had they entered the labor force directly after college, or if they had invested in an alternative postgraduate degree.

[3] For a thorough review and bibliography of research on attrition, see Golde (2005).

We show in this chapter that about 40 percent of the students in our study who fail to complete their PhDs leave their programs within the first two years; any losses in income should be relatively small for them.[4] In addition, studies that address the earnings of those who start college but do not graduate find that the payoff to completing each year of college appears to be positive, even if the individual never receives a bachelor's degree.[5] It seems strange to assume that those who fail to complete their PhDs will not receive a similar return for each year they complete in their programs, but the complete absence of data on what happens to students who enroll in, but fail to complete, PhD programs has prevented any direct observations on whether this is true. With the data from GES we can explore these outcomes. Thus the analysis in this chapter is based on students in entering cohorts 1982–83 through 1996–97 who responded to the GES.

Because of the concern that individuals who leave their programs late in their doctoral studies may suffer larger economic losses than individuals who leave early in their programs, we compare early and late leavers in terms of labor force participation, employment, and occupations based on their experiences after leaving.

LEVEL AND TIMING OF ATTRITION
BY DEPARTMENT SIZE AND FIELD

The sizes of the entering cohorts in the humanities PhD programs in our sample vary widely. We divide departments into roughly three equal groups: those with entering cohorts that averaged fewer than 10 students during our sample period, those that averaged 10–16.4 students, and those that averaged 16.5 students or more. For each size class and for the sample as a whole, we compute the average percentage of a cohort that left the program prior to receiving a PhD during their 1st or 2nd year in the program, during the 3rd or 4th years in the program, during the 5th–10th years in the program, and cumulatively by the end of the 10th year in the program.

Figure 8.1 displays these percentages. The right-hand panel indicates that the cumulative attrition rate was 27 percent for the smallest size class

---

[4] This percentage of leavers who leave in the first two years is larger in large departments (47 percent) than in small (37 percent) and medium-sized (36 percent) departments, and it is 42 percent overall.

[5] See, for example, David A. Jaeger and Marianne E. Page, "Degrees Matter: New Evidence on Sheepskin Effects in the Returns to Education," *Review of Economics and Statistics* 78 (November 1996): 733–40, and Thomas J. Kane and Cecilia E. Rouse, "Labor Market Returns to Two- and Four-Year Colleges," *American Economic Review* 85 (June 1995): 600–614.

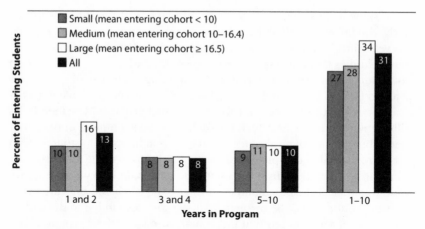

Figure 8.1. Level and Timing of Attrition by Department Size

of programs, 28 percent for the middle size class, and 34 percent for the largest size class. Averaged over all of the programs and years, 31 percent of entering students left their programs prior to receiving their PhDs by the end of their 10th year in the program. Quite strikingly, the remaining panels suggest that virtually all of these differences across size classes occur during the students' first two years in the program, with attrition rates thereafter virtually identical by size class. Whereas 10 percent of the students in the smaller two classes of programs left their programs by the end of the second year, the comparable percentage for the largest class of programs was 16 percent.

Figure 8.2 presents similar data on the level and timing of attrition, this time broken down by field. Because the number of fields is larger than the number of size classes, rather than split the data by year of attrition (which would result in data that would be hard to summarize compactly), we do so by whether those who left did so before or after achieving candidacy. As we discussed in Chapter 4, the distribution of departments by size class varies across fields; hence differences in attrition levels and patterns across fields can at least partially be attributed to differences in department size.

Attrition by the end of students' 10th year in the program varies widely across fields, ranging from a low of about 25 percent in religion and comparative literature to a high of about 35 percent in English and philosophy. Moreover, as when the data were split by size class, much of the variation appears to occur in the early years of students' programs. Whereas 18 percent of the students in religion and comparative literature leave their programs prior to advancing to candidacy, the comparable numbers for English and philosophy are around 26 percent. However, there is also

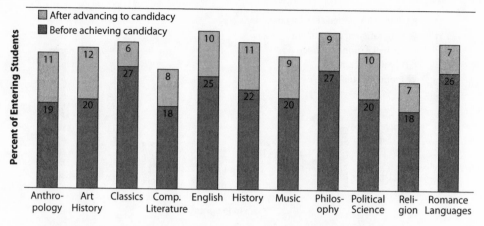

Figure 8.2. Level and Timing of Attrition by Field and before and after Advancement to Candidacy

wide variation among the attrition rates of students who have advanced to candidacy—from 6 percent in classics to 12 percent in art history.

REASONS FOR ATTRITION

Higher completion rates in science and engineering PhD programs (compared to those in the humanities) are often attributed to the fact that PhD students in science and engineering tend to enroll in graduate programs with the aim of working in the laboratory of a particular professor; our findings suggest that the matching of doctoral students and faculty members at the time of program entry is also important in the humanities.[6]

The GES asked students why they had chosen the particular PhD programs they entered. Respondents were asked to rank five reasons, and we focus here on the one that they ranked as the most important. The five reasons were: a desire to study with a particular faculty member in the program, the general reputation of the program, the financial support that the student was offered, the location of the university, and attributes of the program.

Figure 8.3 presents the percentage of respondents who left their programs prior to receiving a degree, according to the most important reason for initially enrolling in their programs. As in Figure 8.1, the analyses are done separately for those who left their programs in the first and

[6] Chris Golde of the Carnegie Foundation as quoted in Scott Smallwood, "Doctor Dropout," *Chronicle of Higher Education,* January 16, 2004, p. A10.

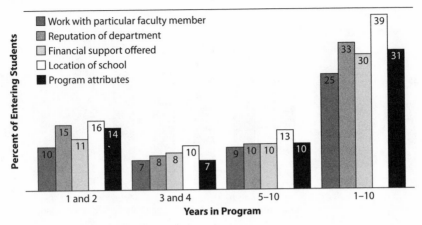

Figure 8.3. Level and Timing of Attrition by Reason for Choosing Program

second years, those who left in the third and fourth years, those who left during years 5–10, and then for those who left at any time during the first 10 years since entry.

Students who left their programs prior to receiving a PhD by the end of their 10th year in the program represent 31 percent of all respondents to the GES but only 25 percent of the GES respondents who chose a given department because they wanted to study with a particular faculty member. We interpret this to mean that choosing a PhD program because there is a particular faculty member with whom a student wants to work reduces the chance that students will leave their program prior to receiving their degree. A lower percentage of women than men in the GES sample (26 percent versus 31 percent) reported that the opportunity to work with a particular faculty member was the most important reason that they chose their doctoral program.

The impact of wanting to study with a particular faculty member is most important in influencing attrition during the first two years in the program. Of the students whose main reason for enrolling in their PhD program was to work with a particular faculty member, 10 percent leave their programs by the end of year 2, whereas 13 percent of all students do so. However, during years 3 and 4 and years 5–10, the rate at which these students leave their programs prior to receiving their PhD is just 1 percentage point lower than that for all students. (See Figure 8.1 for attrition rates for all students.)

During each period shown in the figure, the students with the highest likelihood of leaving their programs prior to receiving their degrees are those whose most important reason for choosing their programs was the location of the university. Almost 40 percent of the students who chose their programs because of geographical location dropped out by the end of their 10th year in the program. Almost 13 percent of the men in the GES sample, but only 8 percent of the women, reported that the location of a program was the most important factor in choosing their program. It seems clear that potential PhD students should be counseled that location per se should not be the most important factor in their choice of a program.

The GES also asked students who left their programs prior to receiving a PhD why they left. Of course, one must be cautious in interpreting their reasons. Departures from PhD programs may be the result of voluntary choices by students or of departments asking students to leave because of lack of progress. Often when students are not progressing satisfactorily, departments may "gently suggest" that they consider other options, but the ultimate decision to leave may be left to the student. Finally, students may report reasons that shift the responsibility for their departure to departmental failures, yet the real reason may simply be their inability to perform satisfactorily. However, in the absence of responses from the departments or faculty advisors, these student reports provide useful insights into why attrition occurs.

Figure 8.4 provides information on the percentage of students who terminated their graduate programs prior to receiving their PhDs according to their reported reason for leaving. The reasons are financial, academic performance, loss of academic interest or drive, family or health considerations, a change in career goals (which included responses indicating that the students realized they could achieve their career goals without a PhD, changed their career plans, or had job opportunities), and dissatisfaction with the department (which included responses indicating that advising was inadequate, that the department lacked expertise in areas in which they were interested, that their advisor had left, or that they were generally dissatisfied with the department). Individuals could list more than one reason, and in general they did so. The percentages reported in the figure make possible a comparison of students who left their programs before achieving candidacy with those who left after advancing to candidacy.

Most strikingly, in keeping with the findings about the role of financial support that we reported in Chapter 5, only 22 percent of the students who left their programs prior to advancing to candidacy and only 17 percent who did so after advancing said that financial factors were an important reason for leaving. Only 11 percent of the leavers prior to achieving candidacy and 26 percent of the leavers after advancing said that their academic performance was an important reason for leaving. The reason cited as important most often was "change of career goals." This could reflect awareness by students in these cohorts of a poor job market for hu-

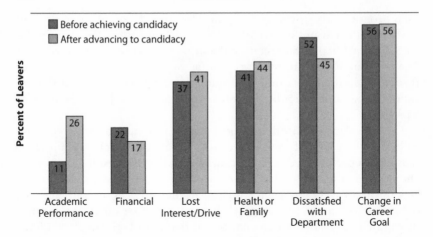

Figure 8.4. Reasons for Leaving a Program by Whether Leaving before or after Advancement to Candidacy

manities PhDs or an advisor's "gentle suggestion" that another career might be a better fit. "Dissatisfaction with the department" (which included the specific response of "inadequate advising") was chosen almost as often as "career change" among pre-candidates but less often by those who had advanced to candidacy. This is consistent with our finding in Chapter 6 that the quality of departmental advising is an important variable influencing attrition behavior.

Figure 8.5 breaks down the reasons for leaving by gender. Financial factors are given as an important reason by roughly 20 percent of both men and women. The factor most frequently cited as important among women is dissatisfaction with the department. Among men the factor most often reported as important is the decision to change careers. Health and family reasons are mentioned more often by women than by men, whereas men are slightly more likely to report poor academic performance as an important reason for their leaving. Whether these gender differences reflect real differences or gender differences in what is perceived to be an appropriate response cannot be determined from the GES data.

EDUCATIONAL OUTCOMES OF THOSE
WHO LEAVE PhD PROGRAMS

There were 12,289 respondents to the GES. Approximately 58 percent of these respondents (7,139 individuals) had completed PhDs at the department in which they initially enrolled. There were also 1,128 respondents who were still pursuing PhDs at their initial department, 21 re-

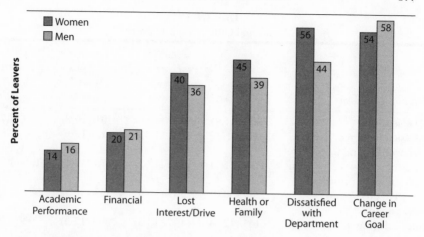

Figure 8.5. Reasons for Leaving a Program by Gender

spondents who were pursuing PhDs or other degrees at a different department in the same institution, and 175 respondents pursuing PhDs or other degrees at a different institution. Because we do not know the ultimate educational outcomes of members of these three groups, we exclude them from our subsequent analyses. We also exclude 459 respondents whose responses to the enrollment-status questions were inconsistent with the status reports from their departments (most often one reporting "still enrolled" and the other reporting "left the program"). This leaves us with a sample of 3,367 leavers from the humanities PhD programs in our sample with data on educational attainment.

The first column in Table 8.1 summarizes their educational outcomes. The largest group (38.0 percent) received academic master's degrees from the department in which they had been enrolled for the PhD; these terminal master's degrees are often awarded to those who leave PhD programs. Another 12.0 percent of the sample received master's degrees from a different department (either at the same institution or from a different institution). A very small percentage (1.7 percent) received professional degrees from the departments in which they had been enrolled for the PhD; in the main these were master of fine arts degrees. A large group (17.7 percent) received professional degrees from other departments at their initial institution or from other institutions; these included law and MBA degrees.[7] Almost 12 percent of the leavers received PhDs

---

[7] Respondents were asked in the GES if they had received a professional degree and, if so, whether it was from an arts and sciences–related department (e.g., master of fine arts in creative writing) or a professional department (e.g., master of business administration). Students who received a law degree would be included among those receiving professional

TABLE 8.1
Educational Outcomes of Leavers

Educational Outcomes	All Leavers	Early Leavers (years 1 and 2)	Midprogram Leavers (years 3 and 4)	Late Leavers (year 5 and later)
PhD elsewhere	400 (11.9)	270 (19.1)	91 (10.2)	39 (3.7)
Professional degree: Same department and institution	57 (1.7)	14 (1.0)	13 (1.5)	30 (2.8)
Professional degree: Different department or institution	595 (17.7)	272 (19.2)	173 (19.4)	150 (14.1)
Master's degree: Same department	1,280 (38.0)	367 (26.0)	329 (36.9)	584 (54.9)
Master's degree: Different department	403 (12.0)	197 (13.9)	111 (12.5)	95 (8.9)
No degree	632 (18.8)	293 (20.7)	174 (19.5)	165 (15.5)
Total	3,367	1,413	891	1,063

Note: Numbers in parentheses are percentages of column totals.

from a different department at the initial institution or from a different institution. Finally, only 18.8 percent of the sample of leavers reported no subsequent degrees.

It has long been known that many individuals who initially enroll as undergraduates at academic institutions transfer and receive their undergraduate degrees from institutions other than the ones at which they started. As a result, data on any undergraduate institution's graduation rate understates the percentage of individuals who start out as freshmen at the institution and ultimately receive undergraduate degrees from some institution. Critics of high attrition rates from PhD programs have ignored the possibility that this may also occur for PhD students. The GES data suggest that, at least for individuals enrolled in humanities PhD programs in the institutions covered by the sample, almost 12 percent of the leavers ultimately receive PhDs at other departments or institutions.[8] In-

---

degrees from a professional department. Almost 80 percent of the leavers who fell into this category had previously been studying for a PhD in English, history, or political science. The proportion of women in our sample who subsequently received professional degrees after leaving their PhD program (16.3 percent) is lower than the comparable proportion among men (22.4 percent). The proportions of this sample who subsequently received professional degrees were about the same for the cohorts of students that entered doctoral study in the 1980s and the 1990s.

[8] We caution that at the time of the GES over 1,000 respondents were still pursuing the PhD in the programs in which they had initially enrolled. Because the survey covered en-

cluding these individuals as PhD recipients raises the percentage of respondents to the GES who received PhDs, as of the survey date, from
about 58 percent to over 61 percent.

How do the educational outcomes of those who leave PhD programs
differ between students who depart from their programs early in their
graduate careers and those who leave after spending a large number of
years in their programs? In the remaining columns of the table we report
similar tabulations for early leavers (those who leave their programs by
the end of year 2), midprogram leavers (those who leave in years 3 and 4),
and late leavers (those who leave in year 5 or later). The percentage of
leavers receiving a PhD elsewhere declines rapidly the longer students
spend in the initial program. In contrast, the percentage receiving a master's degree from their initial department substantially increases as
length of time in the program increases. The percentage receiving no degree decreases the later students leave their PhD programs, but over 15
percent of the late leavers report having received no graduate degree.
Even for late leavers, master's degrees are apparently not handed out automatically as consolation prizes.

Focusing on the leavers who received doctoral degrees, many received
doctoral degrees in fields other than the one in which they initially studied. For those leavers for whom we could identify both the field in which
they initially began doctoral study and the field in which they ultimately
received a PhD, Table 8.2 tabulates the leavers by both of these fields. For
example, of the 25 individuals who began PhD study in anthropology departments in our sample and left those departments without receiving a
PhD but received a PhD elsewhere, 9 received PhDs in anthropology, 15
received PhDs in fields that were not represented in the GEI, and 1 received a PhD in philosophy. Similarly, of the 105 such students who
started PhD study in English, 48 received PhDs in English and the others
earned PhDs in classics (1), comparative literature (3), history (3), music (1), philosophy (1), and other fields (48). What is most striking from
this table is that, save for those in art history and music, the majority of
students in the sample who received PhDs after leaving their initial departments switched fields of study.

Does the shift from one PhD program to another cost students in terms
of departmental prestige? We used information on the 1995 National Research Council (NRC) rankings of doctoral programs to answer this ques-

tering cohorts through the 1996–97 cohort, respondents still pursuing the PhD were in at
least their sixth year in the program as of the survey date. Some would eventually leave their
programs without receiving a PhD and, inasmuch as late leavers are much less likely to go
on for a PhD than early leavers, if we surveyed all leavers about their educational status a
few years later, the proportion of program leavers in the entire sample who would have received PhDs elsewhere would most likely be less than 12 percent.

TABLE 8.2
Initial and Terminal Fields for Program Leavers Who Ultimately Earn a PhD

	Terminal Field											Share Same as Initial Field
Initial Field	Anthropology	Art History	Classics	Comparative Literature	English	History	Music	Other Fields	Philosophy	Political Science	Religion	
Anthropology	**9**							15	1			0.36
Art history		**13**			1			8	1			0.62
Classics			**8**			1		8	1			0.44
Comparative literature				**1**	2			9				0.08
English			1	3	**48**	3	1	48	1			0.46
History	1			2	2	**43**		47	1	2		0.44
Music	1						**22**	5				0.79
Philosophy		1				1		19	**21**		2	0.49
Political science						1		16		**10**		0.37
Religion						1		10	1		**2**	0.14

tion.[9] For the students who received PhDs in the same field as the department in which they were initially enrolled and for whom we can identify both the ranking of the program in which the student was initially enrolled and the ranking of the program from which he or she received the PhD, we computed the difference between the rankings.

We found that although some students may move to more prestigious departments, on balance students who transferred from their initial department to another department in the same field did suffer a loss of departmental prestige when they moved. This result should not be surprising, as the PhD programs participating in the GEI as treatment or control departments were drawn from the nation's best programs. Of the 101 treatment and control programs, 85 were rated by the NRC. Of those 85 programs, 56.5 percent were ranked in the top 10 in their fields, 31.8 percent were ranked 11th–20th, 7.1 percent were ranked 21st–30th, and the rest (less than 5 percent) were ranked 31st or lower in their fields.

LABOR FORCE AND EMPLOYMENT STATUS OF LEAVERS

The GES collected information on the labor market and employment status of survey respondents six months after they had either received a PhD from the department in which they initially enrolled or left that department's PhD program, three years after that date, and as of the survey date. We restrict attention to those who had departed from their initial department at least five years prior to the survey date in order to provide labor force and employment data at three separate points in time.

Economists define an individual as being in the labor force if the individual is either employed or unemployed; an individual is said to be unemployed if he or she is on temporary layoff or searching for a job. The labor force participation rate of a group is then defined as the percentage of the group that is in the labor force.

The top panel of Table 8.3 presents data on the labor force participation rates of those who received a PhD from their initial departments, as well as those who had left their initial PhD programs, six months after departing from their programs, three years after departure, and as of the survey date. Those individuals who received a PhD from the departments in which they were initially enrolled have labor force participation rates in the range of 97 percent at all three points in time. The leavers have lower labor force participation rates, starting at 84 percent six months after departure and rising to 90.3 percent as of the survey date.

[9] Goldberger et al. (1995).

TABLE 8.3
Labor Force Participation and Employment Rates for GES Respondents Who
Left Their Initial PhD Program at Least Five Years before the Survey (percent)

	Six Months	Three Years	Survey Date
Labor force participation rate			
PhD from initial department	97.1	97.5	96.7
All leavers	84.1	86.8	90.3
Early leavers	84.6	88.4	91.7
Midprogram leavers	86.7	85.4	90.2
Late leavers	80.0	86.8	87.5
Employment rate			
PhD from initial department	91.9	97.4	97.8
All leavers	90.5	96.8	95.3
Early leavers	91.7	96.4	95.2
Midprogram leavers	88.2	95.6	95.7
Late leavers	90.8	96.8	94.8

That the leavers' labor force participation rates are lower than those of the PhD completers is not surprising, especially since at the six-month and three-year intervals some of them are enrolled in other educational programs. Labor force participation rates six months after departure from a program are lower for those who leave their PhD programs late in their course of study than for early or midprogram leavers; however, this difference is not observed at the three-year point and is smaller at the survey date.

A multivariate statistical analysis suggests that, even after one controls for demographic factors, individuals in the sample who did not receive a PhD from the department in which they initially enrolled had lower labor force participation rates than those who did receive PhDs from the original department (Appendix Table E.8.1). These analyses also suggest that gender and family status are important determinants of labor force participation; as compared to single men without children, married women with children present at the date they left graduate school are less likely to participate in the labor force at all three points of time, and married women without children are less likely to participate both at three years after program departure and at the survey date.

The employment rate of a group is defined as the percentage of the labor force members of a group who are employed at a point in time; the employment rates for these groups are found in the bottom panel of Table 8.3. For individuals in the labor force who received a PhD from their initial departments, six months after graduation 91.9 percent were employed (which meant that the unemployment rate for the group was

8.1 percent). By the three-year point and as of the survey date, the employment rate for completers exceeded 97 percent (which meant that the unemployment rate was less than 3 percent).

The employment rate for leavers is only slightly lower (by about 1.5–2.5 percentage points) than that for those who received their PhDs from their initial departments. Among leavers, employment rates do not vary systematically by the length of time after initial enrollment at which they dropped out of their PhD programs.

A multivariate analysis of the probability of being employed suggests that differences in employment rates between those who received a PhD from their initial departments and those who left their program persist even after one controls for demographic factors (Appendix Table E.8.2). Gender, marital status, and the presence of children while in graduate school are also related to the probability of being employed.

OCCUPATIONAL DISTRIBUTION OF EMPLOYED LEAVERS

The GES also collected information on the occupations in which leavers were employed, and Table 8.4 summarizes this information at six months after program departure, three years after program departure, and as of the survey date.[10] The data suggest considerable occupational mobility of leavers after departure from their programs.

Six months after departure, 10 percent of the employed program leavers were employed in clerical or administrative support positions. However, three years after departure the share of leavers employed in these roles had fallen to 4.5 percent, and as of the survey date the share had fallen to 2.2 percent. Although some leavers from humanities programs get "trapped" in clerical and administrative support positions, the share of these is very small.

One major occupational employment category for leavers is administrators, executives, and managers. Between 15.6 percent and 17.1 percent of the leavers are employed in this category, with approximately a third of them employed in higher-education administration. A second major employment category is artists, entertainers, writers, public-relations specialists, and broadcasters—positions held by between 12.3 percent and 15.4 percent (depending on the time period) of the employed leavers. Two other major categories are employment as "professors—all ranks" and postsecondary teachers (primarily lecturers and instructors). These categories together represent 15.6 percent of the leavers at the six-month

---

[10] Information on the occupational distributions is presented separately in Appendix Table E.8.3 for early, midprogram, and late leavers.

TABLE 8.4
Occupational Distribution of Leavers (percent)

	Six Months	Three Years	Survey Date
Administrators, executives, managers	16.6	15.6	17.1
Artists, entertainers, writers, public-relations specialists, broadcasters	12.3	15.4	13.5
Clergy and other religious workers	0.5	0.6	1.1
Clerical or administrative support	10.0	4.5	2.2
Computer-related specialists	3.9	5.7	5.6
Counselors	0.5	0.4	0.5
Curators	1.0	0.9	0.6
Education			
Elementary- or secondary-school educators	6.8	8.4	6.5
Postdoctoral appointments	1.5	0.3	0.3
Postsecondary teachers	4.9	3.4	3.1
Professors—all ranks	10.7	8.7	9.6
Research appointments	2.3	1.4	0.9
Other education	3.6	3.0	2.7
Engineers, architects, surveyors	0.5	0.8	1.1
Financial or human resources professionals	2.4	3.4	2.9
Health occupations	1.0	0.9	2.7
Lawyers and judges	2.6	7.4	12.8
Librarians	1.4	2.1	2.2
Sales and marketing	3.2	3.5	2.3
Scientists	0.5	0.5	0.7
Service occupations	2.3	1.7	0.9
Social scientists	1.9	2.2	1.7
Social workers	0.3	0.9	0.5
Other occupations	9.3	8.3	8.7

point and 12.7 percent at the survey date. This percentage is not surprising because (as we have shown) almost 12 percent of leavers ultimately received PhDs. Program leavers were also employed in other education-related occupations, including over 6 percent as elementary- or secondary-school educators.

At six months after departure from their PhD programs, 2.6 percent of the employed leavers were working as lawyers or judges. But by the survey date this percentage rises to 12.8 percent. As should be clear, many of the leavers who pursued professional degrees were pursuing law degrees; the law was an attractive profession for those who left these humanities degree programs. As one might expect, Appendix Table E.8.3 confirms that leavers who became lawyers or judges were more likely to be early leavers than late leavers. However, only about 72 percent of respondents who reported being lawyers or judges at the survey date also reported having received a professional degree; the others reported receiving PhDs (27 percent) or other degrees (3 percent).

Data on individuals' earnings were not collected in the GES. Thus, we can make no summary statement about whether the earnings of the leavers from the PhD programs in our sample are higher (or lower) than they would have been if they had never entered their programs. Nonetheless, the occupations in which these leavers are employed, a large majority of which are professional ones, suggest that the vast majority of them are not trapped in menial, low-level jobs and that they in fact received a payoff from their investment in doctoral education.

Early Careers

> What helped me finish? It was made clear to me
> from the moment I arrived that delays getting the
> degree would not help me on the job market.
>
> —A 1995 history PhD who began in 1990

> Seeing the job-search experience of students just a
> few years ahead of me in graduate school, my an-
> ecdotal impression is that hiring committees be-
> gan paying much more attention to whether or not
> candidates were finished at some point during the
> time that I was in graduate school. Those finding
> jobs in the late '80s and early '90s had a very dif-
> ferent experience and completion was less impor-
> tant than other factors. By the mid '90s completion
> seemed to me to be the first of the criteria, but
> pressure and advice from graduate faculty did not
> recognize this shift.
>
> —A 1995 PhD in English who began in 1988

MANY NEW PhDs in the humanities aspire to tenure-track teaching positions at four-year colleges and universities.[1] How successful were the
PhDs in our sample in obtaining such positions, and what were the factors that influenced their success? Do new PhDs who initially find employment in non-tenure-track positions get locked into these positions or
do they move into tenure-track positions? How does job-market success
vary with new PhDs' gender, marital status, and family status? Do a substantial fraction of new PhDs in these fields wind up as tenured faculty
members within 15 years after they enter their PhD programs? Finally,

---

[1] Maresi Nerad, "Confronting Common Assumptions: Designing Future-Oriented Doctoral Programs," in Ronald G. Ehrenberg and Charlotte Kuh, eds., *Doctoral Education and
the Faculty of the Future* (Ithaca, NY: Cornell University Press, 2008), pp. 80–89, presents data
showing that a number of entering PhD students in several humanities fields are not planning on academic careers when they enter PhD programs. However, the vast majority of entering PhD students in the humanities do aspire to careers in academia.

given that a goal of the Graduate Education Initiative (GEI) was to improve doctoral education, not just to reduce attrition and increase completion rates, did the GEI improve the job-market outcomes of new PhDs in these fields?

JOB-MARKET SUCCESS

Table 9.1 presents information from the Graduate Education Survey (GES) on employment outcomes six months and three years after respondents received their PhDs, broken down by the three-year interval in which they received their PhDs. The first interval shown is 1992–94. Although some GES respondents received their PhDs in earlier years, because the first entry cohort included in the GES was the entering cohort of 1982–83, earlier exit cohorts of GES respondents in our sample (such as the 1986–88 and 1989–91 cohorts) necessarily had to be disproportionately composed of quick completers. To the extent that employment outcomes for completers depend on their time-to-degree (TTD)—and we will show later in the chapter that this is in fact the case—including data for these earlier exit cohorts in the table would confound the effects of changing employment prospects faced by the cohort with the changing time distribution of completers in the cohort.[2]

The top panel of Table 9.1 presents their outcomes six months after receipt of the PhD. The overall percentage that was employed rose from 87.4 percent for the 1992–94 exit cohorts to about 89 percent for later cohorts of graduates. The percentage that was employed in the non-education sector rose steadily from 9.3 percent for the 1992–94 cohorts to 14.0 percent for the 1998–2000 cohorts of graduates. The percentage employed in educational institutions other than four-year colleges and universities—including elementary and secondary schools, two-year colleges, and professional schools—fell from 6.4 percent to 4.5 percent during the period. The vast majority of respondents were employed at four-year colleges and universities.[3] However, the percentage of respondents employed at these institutions fell slightly from 71.7 percent for the graduating cohorts of 1992–94 to 70.3 percent for the graduating cohorts of 1998–2000.

To say that these PhDs were employed at four-year institutions does not mean that they were all employed in tenure-track teaching positions. Indeed, only 34.9 percent of the 1992–94 graduating cohorts were em-

---

[2] Simulations reported in Appendix D, Section 3, suggest that this problem is eliminated if we begin Table 9.1, as we have done, with the 1992–94 exit cohorts.

[3] Subject to rounding error, the sum of columns 2–4 equals column 1 in this table.

TABLE 9.1

Job Outcomes Six Months and Three Years after PhD Receipt (percent employed)

Exit Years	Total	Non-Education	Education Non-Four-Year	Four-Year Institution	Four-Year Tenure-Track	Four-Year Full-Time Non-Tenure-Track	Four-Year Part-Time	Four-Year Postdoctoral	Four-Year Nonfaculty
				Six Months after PhD Receipt					
1992–94	87.4	9.3	6.4	71.7	34.9	18.9	12.8	4.6	5.7
1995–97	89.0	12.3	5.7	70.8	33.0	16.0	14.8	5.4	6.0
1998–2000	89.1	14.0	4.5	70.3	30.2	17.5	12.8	6.1	7.7
				Three Years after PhD Receipt					
1992–94	95.1	12.0	7.0	76.0	57.2	11.5	6.8	1.3	4.4
1995–97	93.8	15.0	6.7	72.1	55.1	10.3	7.0	1.3	3.3
1998–2000	94.3	17.3	5.3	71.3	52.0	11.2	6.6	2.1	3.7

ployed in tenure-track positions at four-year colleges and universities six months after graduation. This percentage fell to 30.2 percent for the 1998–2000 cohorts. The percentage of the graduates employed in full-time non-tenure-track teaching positions actually fell slightly over time (from 18.9 percent to 17.5 percent), whereas the percentage employed part-time as adjunct faculty members remained constant (at 12.8 percent). The percentage employed in postdoctoral positions increased during the period from 4.6 percent to 6.1 percent. Finally, the percentage employed in nonfaculty positions, either as administrators or as researchers, rose from 5.7 percent to 7.7 percent.[4] As Appendix Table E.9.1 indicates, the percentage of new PhDs in the three largest fields in our sample (English, political science, and history) that were employed in four-year institutions and in tenure-track positions at four-year institutions six months after receipt of the PhD declined in a manner similar to the overall sample results during the period.

The bottom panel of Table 9.1 presents similar employment information for the PhDs three years after receipt of their degrees. Greater percentages of the graduates were employed three years after receipt of their degrees than six months after receipt of their degrees, both in total and in the non-education sector. Over 17 percent of the graduates from the 1998–2000 cohorts were employed in the non-education sector. Individuals employed in the non-education sector were employed in a wide variety of occupations. The largest of these categories, in terms of numbers of respondents, were (in order, starting with the largest): artists, entertainers, writers, public-relations specialists, and broadcasters; administrators, executives, and managers; social scientists; computer-related specialists; and lawyers and judges.

The percentage of graduates who have found tenure-track positions in four-year institutions is also much higher three years after receipt of their degrees. For example, 57.2 percent of the 1992–94 cohorts were in such positions, as compared to the 34.9 percent six months after receipt of the degree. The higher percentage in tenure-track positions three years out is associated with lower percentages employed in both full-time and part-time non-tenure-track positions. These data also show that the percentage of graduates in tenure-track positions at four-year institutions three years after receipt of their degrees declines substantially from the early 1990s to the late 1990s, falling to 52 percent for the 1998–2000 cohorts.

The bottom panel of Appendix Table E.9.1 suggests that the decline in this percentage over this period was similar for each of the three large

---

[4] The sum of columns 5–9 sometimes exceeds column 4 in the table because some respondents may have classified themselves in more than one category (e.g., teaching part time while in a postdoctoral fellow position, or while an administrator).

190

CHAPTER 9

fields in our sample (English, political science, and history). The percentages of new PhDs in each of these fields that were employed in tenure-track positions three years after receipt of the PhD fell by between 3.5 and 7.7 percentage points.

ARE NON-TENURE-TRACK POSITIONS DEAD-END JOBS?

The decline in the shares of new PhDs in tenure-track positions three years after receipt of their PhDs may lead to fears that new PhDs in the humanities are increasingly being trapped in dead-end non-tenure-track positions. However, the fact that a much greater share of new PhDs are in tenure-track positions three years after receipt of the PhD than six months after the PhD suggests that there is considerable early-career mobility.

Table 9.2 confirms that this is the case. It shows the percentage of new PhDs employed in various types of academic non-tenure-track positions six months after degree receipt who were in tenure-track positions in four-year colleges and universities three years after degree receipt. The top row of the table indicates that 57.8 percent of the people who were in full-time non-tenure-track teaching positions six months after receipt of their PhDs had moved to tenure-track positions within three years of receipt of the PhD. Moreover, the percentage that successfully moved to tenure-track positions did not change very much over the 15-year sample period.

The remaining rows provide similar data for other groups. New PhDs in part-time non-tenure-track positions at the six-month point had a 43 percent chance of moving to a tenure-track position within three years of

TABLE 9.2
Percentage of Individuals Employed in Non-Tenure-Track Positions at
Four-Year Institutions Six Months after PhD Receipt Who Were in
Tenure-Track Positions Three Years after PhD Receipt, by Exit Years

Position at Six Months	Exit Years					
	1985–2000	1985–88	1989–91	1992–94	1995–97	1998–2000
Full-time non-tenure-track	57.8	59.7	53.0	59.2	59.3	57.1
Part-time non-tenure-track	43.0	[a]	35.8	43.2	46.2	37.2
Postdoctoral positions	66.1	[a]	53.8	68.9	71.6	63.4
Nonfaculty positions	45.2	[a]	31.7	41.3	54.7	44.9

[a]Not reported because cell contained fewer than 20 observations.

receipt of the PhD. The comparable percentages for postdoctoral fellows and PhDs in nonfaculty positions at the six-month point were 66.1 percent and 45.2 percent, respectively. Although there are some fluctuations in these percentages over time, on balance there is no suggestion that mobility out of these positions has systematically declined over time.

Appendix Table E.9.2 presents similar information for the three largest fields in our sample (English, history, and political science). In each of these fields, the percentage of full-time non-tenure-track faculty members moving to tenure-track positions by three years after receipt of their PhDs is greater than 50 percent, and the percentages do not appear to be lower for the most recent cohorts. Although sample sizes are too small to report these figures by three-year cohorts for the other non-tenure-track types of positions, for the entire sample period the transition rates into tenure-track positions for individuals initially in postdoctoral positions, nonfaculty positions, and part-time non-tenure-track positions is always greater than 40 percent.

It is difficult for us to determine from these data whether the glass is half full or half empty. On the one hand, there is considerable mobility from these different types of academic non-tenure-track positions to tenure-track faculty positions. On the other hand, substantial fractions of the new PhDs initially in these positions have not moved into tenure-track positions within three years of receipt of their PhDs.

Given that the goal of many PhDs in the humanities is to obtain tenure-track positions at four-year colleges and universities, at what age do those who attain this goal reach it? More generally, how old are humanities PhDs when they enter the job market and, on average, how long after receiving their PhDs do they reach the goal of attaining a tenure-track position?

Table 9.3 presents information on median and mean age at receipt of PhD for GES respondents who received their degrees from treatment or control departments. Median age at degree varies across these fields from a low of 30 in the classics to a high of 33 in music and religion. For each field, the mean age at degree receipt is roughly a year or two higher than the median age; this reflects the long right tail of the distribution of TTD (which we have described in Chapter 4), with some students taking many years to complete their degrees.[5]

---

[5] These mean and median ages at degree are substantially lower than the comparable figures found nationally in data from the Survey of Earned Doctorates. For example, nationally the median age at degree for people receiving degrees between 1980 and 2002 in the fields we have studied ranged from 33 in classics to 37 in religion. The lower ages at degree for the individuals in our sample are not surprising; they were enrolled at departments with high admission standards, and they received much more generous levels of financial support while doctoral students than did most students in their fields nationally.

TABLE 9.3

Median Age at PhD Receipt and Age at First Tenure-Track
Appointment for PhD Completers

Field	Age at PhD Receipt	Age at First Tenure-Track Appointment
Anthropology	32 (33.9)	37 (37.8)
Art history	32 (33.5)	35 (36.1)
Classics	30 (30.7)	33 (34.0)
Comparative literature	31 (31.9)	33 (34.3)
English	31 (31.9)	33 (34.7)
History	31 (32.8)	34 (35.5)
Music	33 (33.9)	36 (37.7)
Philosophy	30 (31.2)	32 (33.8)
Political science	31 (31.5)	33 (34.1)
Religion	33 (34.2)	35 (36.7)
All	31 (32.5)	34 (35.2)

Notes: Mean age is given in parentheses. All figures are based on GES respondents. Only 41.9 percent of the PhD recipients in the GES reported both ever having a tenure-track appointment at a four-year institution and their age at entry to their PhD program.

The last column of the table presents data on the median and mean ages at which GES respondents first received tenure-track appointments at a four-year institution. Only about 42 percent of respondents to the GES reported both ever having been employed in a tenure-track position at a four-year institution *and* the age at which they first began that position. The median age of first appointment to a tenure-track position for these individuals ranged from 32 in philosophy to 37 in anthropology. The age at first tenure-track appointment varied across fields from three to five years more than the age at receipt of PhD for GES respondents. We must caution that we are comparing apples and oranges here (those who obtain tenure-track appointments are only a subset of the PhD respondents to the GES); nevertheless this difference suggests that it takes time for many new PhDs in the humanities to achieve tenure-track positions.[6]

[6] Nationally, in 2004 the median age of new doctorates in the life sciences was over four years lower than the median age of new doctorates in the humanities; Thomas B. Hoffer, Vincent Welch Jr., Kimberly Williams, Mary Hess, Kristy Webber, Brian Lisek, Daniel Loew, and Isabel Guzman-Barron, *Doctorate Recipients from United States Universities: Summary Report 2004* (Chicago: National Opinion Research Center, 2005). However, many PhDs in the life sciences must fill multiple multiyear postdoctoral positions before they can seriously be considered for tenure-track faculty positions; National Research Council, *Trends in the Early Careers of Life Scientists* (Washington, DC: National Academies Press, 1998). The problems faced by postdoctoral fellows in the life sciences are very similar to the problems faced by young humanists in non-tenure-track positions.

DO TIME-TO-DEGREE AND PUBLICATIONS
DURING GRADUATE SCHOOL MATTER?

Given that an objective of the GEI was to reduce TTD, it is of interest to know if TTD is associated with the types of positions that new PhDs obtain. Are new PhDs like fine red wine, in the sense that they have to age and mature before they are worth having? If so, this would suggest that shortening TTD would adversely affect their job outcomes. In contrast, perhaps after some point a long TTD signals that a new PhD is unlikely to be a major contributor to new knowledge, and this will have an adverse effect on her or his job outcomes.

We saw in Chapter 6 that one of the routes by which the GEI improved completion rates, reduced attrition rates, and reduced TTD was in having more departments encourage their students to finish their dissertations as quickly as possible, rather than encourage them either to publish before submitting their dissertations or to polish their dissertations before submitting them. Shorter TTD may be associated with fewer publications during graduate school, and this may adversely affect the employment experiences of new PhDs.

In the next chapter, we analyze the impact of the GEI on publications, both during graduate school and during individuals' early careers. Here we examine directly the associations between TTD and publications during graduate school and early-career employment outcomes. We define publications as books or articles in refereed journals (the two types of publications given heaviest weight in tenure and promotion decisions in the humanities) that were published or accepted for publication while the PhDs were in graduate school. These publication counts were self-reported by the GES respondents; we discuss in the next chapter how accurate these self-reported data are likely to be.

Table 9.4 tabulates job outcomes for the doctoral recipients in the GES sample, stratified by TTD. The percentages of being employed, of being employed at a four-year institution, and of being employed in a tenure-track position at a four-year institution six months after receipt of the PhD all decline fairly steadily with TTD. Although doctoral recipients who complete their degrees in five years have a 42.6 percent chance of being employed in a tenure-track position six months after graduation, those who complete their degrees in nine years have only a 30.5 percent chance. Three years after completion of the PhD all the employment percentages are higher, but they continue to decline with increases in TTD. For example, 63.6 percent of the individuals who received their degrees in five years are employed in tenure-track positions at that time, but the comparable percentage for individuals who received their degrees in nine years is 48.6 percent. Put simply, once a student takes more than six

TABLE 9.4

Job Outcomes Six Months and Three Years after PhD Receipt,
by TTD (percent employed)

TTD (years)	Six Months after PhD Receipt			Three Years after PhD Receipt		
	Total	Four-Year Institution	Tenure Track	Total	Four-Year Institution	Tenure Track
5 or less	92.3	76.0	42.6	96.5	77.4	63.6
6	89.7	76.6	38.6	93.5	76.5	63.5
7	90.5	76.6	38.0	95.7	78.6	61.9
8	89.5	72.7	35.8	95.8	76.4	57.5
9	85.6	67.6	30.5	93.1	72.5	48.6
10	86.8	67.7	32.8	94.2	73.5	51.3
11 or more	85.1	63.7	23.4	92.5	68.7	39.3

Note: Based on GES respondents who received a PhD between 1985 and 2000.

or seven years to graduate, the probability of him being employed in a tenure-track position declines.

What is true on average in the sample is not necessarily true for each field. Appendix Table E.9.3 presents similar data on the percentages of PhDs employed in a tenure-track position, by TTD, for each of the three largest fields in our sample. At both six months and three years after receipt of the PhD, the percentages of English and political science PhDs employed in tenure-track positions decline steadily with TTD. For example, over 72 percent of the English PhDs who received their degrees in five years or less have such positions three years after receipt of the PhD, but only 53 percent of those who took nine years to complete their degrees are in such positions at the three-year mark. In contrast, the percentage of history PhDs who are in tenure-track positions does not vary with TTD at the six-month point and declines only slightly with TTD three years after the receipt of the degree.

Although on average longer TTD appears to hurt employment prospects, larger numbers of publications enhance them. Table 9.5 presents information on the percentages of PhD recipients in the sample who were employed, employed at four-year institutions, and employed in tenure-track positions at four-year institutions, stratified by the number of publications the PhDs had during graduate school. The percentage employed in a tenure-track position six months after receipt of the PhD increases only moderately with publications, rising from 34.2 percent for people with no publications to 40.2 percent for people who had three or more publications. However, three years after receipt of the PhD, the relationship is much stronger. Although 35.2 percent of the PhDs who had no publications in graduate school are employed in tenure-track posi-

TABLE 9.5

Job Outcomes Six Months and Three Years after PhD Receipt, by Number of
Publications during Graduate School (percent employed)

Number of Publications	Six Months after PhD Receipt			Three Years after PhD Receipt		
	Total	Four-Year Institution	Tenure Track	Total	Four-Year Institution	Tenure Track
0	88.4	71.0	34.2	90.4	57.8	35.2
1	91.2	76.7	38.7	96.4	77.1	58.9
2	91.8	75.6	37.7	96.1	82.3	62.3
3 or more	88.4	71.8	40.2	96.9	84.3	70.4

Note: Based on GES respondents who received a PhD between 1985 and 2000.

tions, this percentage increases to 58.9 percent for people with one publication, 62.3 percent for people with two publications, and 70.4 percent for people with three or more publications. On average, publications during graduate school appear to be an important predictor of early-career success at attaining tenure-track positions.

Appendix Table E.9.4 provides similar data for each of the three largest fields. Again, what is true on average does not hold for each field. Although the percentages of English PhDs with tenure-track appointments at both six months and three years after receipt of the PhD are higher for PhDs with more publications during graduate school, we do not observe similar relationships for history and political science.

Of course, our results for the impact on early-career job outcomes of both TTD and publications during graduate school are simply tabulations that do not control for other variables that reasonably might be expected to influence job outcomes. These include the PhD field of the individual, the university that he or she attended, the balance of demand and supply in the PhD job market during the year that she or he received a PhD, and the quality of the student's PhD program.[7] Personal characteristics of the individual, such as ability (as measured by GRE scores), age, gender, race and ethnicity, marital status, the presence of children in the family (as of the completion of graduate school), and whether the individual is a U.S. citizen surely also influence job outcomes.

---

[7] We measure the quality of the respondent's PhD program by its 1995 National Research Council ranking. Labor-market tightness in the year the respondent received the PhD is measured by the percentage of all doctoral recipients from treatment and control departments in the year who reported that they were employed, or had accepted employment, at four-year colleges and universities at the date they responded to the Survey of Earned Doctorates. This latter measure was computed by us from the survey and includes all doctoral recipients from the sample departments, regardless of whether they responded to the GES.

To ascertain if we still observe the relationship between early-career job outcomes and TTD and publications during graduate school after these other variables are controlled for, we estimated logit models of the probability that the PhDs were employed in tenure-track positions six months and three years after receiving the PhD that included all of the foregoing as explanatory variables. The estimated marginal effects of each of the variables, holding the other variables constant, on the probabilities that a PhD in the sample was employed in a tenure-track position six months and three years after receipt of the PhD are found in Table 9.6. (See Chapter 2 for a description of marginal effects.)

The results in this table are quite striking. Once one controls for characteristics of the individuals, the quality ranking of their graduate programs, the fields of their degrees, their institutions, and the labor market for new PhDs in these fields, longer TTD is significantly adversely associated with lower probabilities of being in a tenure-track position six months after receipt of the PhD. Other factors held constant, individuals who take 10 or more years to complete their degrees are 6.3 percentage points less likely to be in tenure-track positions six months after completing their degrees than individuals who complete their degrees in seven years. Similarly, individuals who complete their degrees in five years are 4.6 percentage points more likely to be in a tenure track position six months after completing their degrees than individuals who completed their degrees in seven years.

Three years after receipt of the PhD, longer TTD significantly reduces the probability of being in a tenure-track position, for individuals who took eight or more years to complete their degrees. As contrasted with those who completed their degrees in seven years, the probability of being in a tenure-track position is 4.5 percentage points lower for those who completed their degrees in 8 years, 10.6 percentage points lower for people who completed in 9 years, and 15.3 percentage points lower for people who completed in 10 or more years. Completing a PhD in less than seven years did not significantly enhance the probability that an individual would be in a tenure-track position three years after receipt of the PhD relative to those who completed their degrees in seven years.[8]

---

[8] We conducted similar analyses of the probability of being in a tenure-track position at the three-year point separately for PhDs in English, history, and political science, our three largest fields. A summary of the marginal effects of TTD on that probability is found in Appendix Table E.9.5. Because the sample sizes are smaller for the field-specific analyses, it is more difficult to identify significant TTD effects for them. However, individuals who took 10 or more years to complete their PhDs in English were about 21 percentage points less likely to be observed in tenure-track positions than their counterparts who completed their degrees in seven years. The comparable percentage-point differences were 16.6 in history and 18.9 in political science. We also tested whether the impact of longer degree lengths on the probability of being in a tenure-track position at the three-year point has worsened

TABLE 9.6

Marginal Effects of Variables on the Probability of Having a Tenure-Track
Position at Six Months and Three Years after PhD Receipt

	Six Months	Three Years
Had master's degree	**0.035**	**0.038**
GRE verbal	−0.001	0.013
GRE math	0.011	0.006
Age	0.013	−0.005
Single male	—	—
Married male, no children	0.033	0.015
Married male, children	**0.078**	**0.051**
Single female	**0.070**	**0.054**
Married female, no children	**0.063**	0.015
Married female, children	0.015	−0.050
Non–U.S. citizen	0.027	**0.062**
U.S. citizen, minority	**0.208**	**0.201**
Volume published	0.016	0.000
Published	0.036	**0.083**
TTD 4 years or less	−0.005	−0.012
TTD 5 years	**0.046**	0.020
TTD 6 years	−0.009	0.012
TTD 7 years	—	—
TTD 8 years	−0.003	**−0.045**
TTD 9 years	−0.025	**−0.106**
TTD 10 years or more	**−0.063**	**−0.153**
Rank of graduate program	**−0.004**	**−0.006**
Share employed at four-year institution	−0.065	−0.370

Notes: Based on GES respondents who received a PhD between 1985 and 2000. These estimated marginal effects are derived from a logit analysis of the probability that an individual was employed in a tenure-track position at a four-year institution at six months (or three years) after PhD receipt. The analysis also controlled for the field and institution from which the PhD was received. Marginal effects in bold type are statistically significant at the 5 percent level. Rank of graduate program is based on 1995 National Research Council rankings. "Share employed at four-year institution" is the share of new PhDs in the individual's field who were employed at four-year institutions after PhD receipt, based on data from the Survey of Earned Doctorates.

Neither having published during graduate school nor the number of such publications is significantly associated with the probability of being in a tenure-track position at the six-month mark. However, having published in graduate school is an important predictor of the probability of being employed in a tenure-track position three years after receipt of the

---

during the period covered by our data. In the main, these analyses did not suggest any systematic worsening of the impact of TTD on job prospects between the 1982–83 through 1985–86 entry cohorts and cohorts that entered between 1989–90 and 1993–94.

PhD. Other factors held constant, those new PhDs who have published have a probability of being employed in a tenure-track position then that is 8.3 percentage points higher than that for new PhDs who did not publish during graduate school.

Taken together, these are very strong findings. They suggest that— although we found in Chapter 6 that departmental policies that encourage PhD students to publish during graduate school lengthen TTD and increase attrition rates—to the extent that these policies are associated with more publications in graduate school, they also enhance the probability that doctoral recipients will obtain tenure-track positions within three years after completion of their degrees. Only long TTD (eight years or more) adversely affects the probability of obtaining a tenure-track position. In the next chapter, we will investigate how publications during graduate school vary with TTD.

Turning to other findings in the table, attending a better PhD program, as measured by a lower National Research Council ranking, is associated with a higher probability of obtaining a tenure-track position. Improving the ranking of the program from which a new PhD graduated by 10 (for example, a movement from the 15th best program in a field to the 5th best program in the field) increases the probability that the PhD is in a tenure-track position three years after graduation by 6 percentage points.

The gender, race and ethnicity, marital and family status, and citizenship status of new doctorates also influence their employment prospects. Three years after receipt of the PhD, non–U.S. citizens are 6.2 percentage points more likely to be employed in tenure-track positions than their nonminority U.S. citizen counterparts.[9] This may reflect the fact that foreign students who do not achieve such positions may return to their home countries; the GES response rate was lower for foreign students than for U.S. citizens. U.S. citizens who are minorities are 20.1 percentage points more likely to be employed in tenure-track positions than their nonminority counterparts; this undoubtedly reflects the efforts of colleges and universities to diversify their faculty by hiring more PhDs of color. Relative to single men, married men with children at the time of graduation and single women both have higher probabilities of being employed in tenure-track positions; three years after receipt of the PhD, married men with children are 5.1 percentage points more likely and single women 5.4 percentage points more likely than single men to achieve tenure-track positions. Married women, both with and without children at the time of graduation, do not have significantly different probabilities of being in a tenure-track position three years after receipt of the PhD than single men.

---

[9] Minority citizens are defined to include African Americans, Hispanic Americans, and Native Americans. Nonminority citizens include whites and Asian Americans.

WHAT TYPE OF TENURE-TRACK POSITIONS?

Reporting that a new PhD was employed in a tenure-track position at a four-year institution three years after degree receipt tells us little about the type of institution in which the individual was employed or the "quality" of that institution. When we tabulated the data by individuals' years of entry to PhD study for those individuals employed in tenure-track positions at four-year institutions three years after receiving their PhDs, we found that for each entry cohort about 50–60 percent of these individuals were employed at doctoral universities, 15–25 percent were employed at master's-level institutions, and another 15–22 percent were employed at liberal arts colleges.[10]

As a crude measure of the quality of the institutions, we make use of the 1995 *U.S. News & World Report* (*USNWR*) rankings of institutions as national universities and national liberal arts colleges. Of those new PhDs employed in tenure-track positions at doctoral universities three years after receipt of their PhDs, over 50 percent of each entering cohort were employed at universities ranked among the top 50 national universities by *USNWR*. Similarly, of those employed in tenure-track positions at bachelor's-level institutions three years after receipt of the PhD, 43–70 percent were employed at colleges ranked among the top 25 national liberal arts colleges. Given that the PhDs in our sample were obtaining their degrees from among the most selective humanities PhD programs, it should not surprise the reader that their initial tenure-track employment was often at our nation's top liberal arts colleges and research universities.

For the sample of individuals who were employed in tenure-track positions at doctoral institutions three years after receipt of the PhD, we estimated equations to see if we could understand the determinants of the probabilities that they would be employed at *USNWR* top-25 or second-25 national universities. Similarly, for those individuals employed in tenure-track positions at bachelor's-level institutions three years after receipt of the PhD, we estimated equations to see if we could understand the determinants of the probability that they would be employed at *USNWR* top-25 national liberal arts colleges. Of key concern to us was whether publications during graduate school and TTD affected these probabilities, as well as whether the GEI led to an improvement in these probabilities. We found no evidence that the GEI or publications had a statistically significant impact on these probabilities. (In these analyses, we take as given whether the individual was in a tenure-track position at a doctoral institution or a liberal arts college.) However, we did find evi-

---

[10] In addition, some of these PhDs were employed in foreign institutions and some were employed in specialized institutions, such as conservatories.

dence that degree times of nine years or more led to a statistically significant reduction in the probability that PhDs employed in tenure-track positions at doctoral institutions three years after receipt of their PhDs were employed in *USNWR* top-25 national universities.

Recently great concern has been expressed about the underrepresentation of women in tenure-track positions in science and engineering fields at major research universities; female PhDs in these fields are much more likely to be found in tenure-track positions at liberal arts colleges than at research universities.[11] For example, in 2004–05, 38.9 percent of assistant professors on tenure tracks in economics departments at liberal arts colleges were women, but only 26.3 percent of the assistant professors on tenure tracks in economics departments at doctorate-granting universities were women.[12]

Various hypotheses have been offered to explain this underrepresentation, including the possibility of gender differences in preferences for teaching versus research; perceptions by female PhDs that research universities are not hospitable environments for them or that there is more gender discrimination against female faculty at research universities; actual gender discrimination against female PhDs in the hiring process and against female faculty in salary, tenure, promotion, and resource allocation decisions at research universities; and the difficulty women face in combining family and career at research universities.[13] Evidence suggests that the latter has been a particularly important factor.[14] Research uni-

---

[11] Committee on Science, Engineering, and Public Policy, *Beyond Bias and Barriers: Fulfilling the Potential of Women in Academic Science and Engineering* (Washington, DC: National Academies Press, April 2007). This underrepresentation was pointed out over 40 years ago by Helen S. Astin, *The Woman Doctorate in America: Origins, Career, and Family* (New York: Russell Sage, 1969).

[12] American Economic Association, *Newsletter of the Committee on the Status of Women in the Economics Profession*, Winter 2000, Tables 2 and 4.

[13] Two decades ago, Jonathan R. Cole and Harriet Zuckerman, "Marriage, Motherhood and Research Performance in Science," *Scientific American* 256 (February 1987): 119–26, summarized literature that showed that male scientists tended to publish more than female scientists, but that the gap had been closing for more recent cohorts. Furthermore, once women scientists elected full-time careers, being married and having children did not affect their publication productivity. Indeed, the evidence suggested that married women publish more than single women, and there was no difference in rates of publication of married women with and without children. We revisit these issues for our more recent sample of young humanities PhDs in the next chapter.

[14] See, for example, Mary Ann Mason and Mark Goulden, "Do Babies Matter (Part II)? Closing the Baby Gap," *Academe* 90 (November–December 2004), and Yu Xie and Kimberlee A. Shauman, *Women in Science: Career Processes and Outcomes* (Cambridge, MA: Harvard University Press, 2003).

versities have taken a number of steps to mitigate these concerns, and recent efforts to make research universities more family friendly have filtered down from the faculty level to the doctoral-student level, as a number of universities have announced programs that provide paid parental leave, subsidized on-campus child care, and child-care-related travel funds for doctoral students.[15]

The difficulty of combining family and career at research universities may be less for women with PhDs in the humanities than for their counterparts in science and engineering fields because assistant professors in the humanities do not have to worry about setting up research laboratories and obtaining grant funding to support their research, graduate students, and postdoctoral fellows. Thus, one might expect the underrepresentation problem at research universities to be much less severe in the humanities.

To test whether this was true, we looked at the individuals in our sample who were employed in tenure-track positions at either research universities or liberal arts colleges three years after receipt of the PhD and asked what percentages of men and women employed in these categories were employed at the research universities. We found that the percentages were almost equal: 77.4 percent for men and 77.5 percent for women. Put simply, in our sample, female PhDs were not underrepresented in tenure-track positions in research universities.

LONGER-RUN CAREER SUCCESS

The career goal for most students entering PhD programs in the humanities is to achieve a tenured faculty position at a four-year college or university.[16] Because of its sampling frame the GES is not well designed to measure how successful PhDs are in achieving this goal. The GES surveyed only the entering cohorts of 1982–83 through 1996–97, and data collection occurred in 2002. At the time the GES was undertaken, it had been 20 years since the "oldest" entering cohorts began their PhD programs.

If we restrict the sample to those respondents who started their doctoral programs in 1987 or earlier, our focus is on those who began their

---

[15] Millman (2007).

[16] Evidence that this is true for PhDs in English is provided in Nerad and Cerny (1999) and for PhDs in art history in Sadrozinski et al. (2003). However, some students expressed frustration that any interest in a different career path was discouraged by their faculty mentors. For example, an anthropology PhD said, "Graduate schools which assume only university employment as an outcome do students serious harm. They neither prepare them for other possibilities, nor do they admit the truth of the current state of the academic job market."

graduate study 15–20 years before they were surveyed. There were 2,738 respondents who received PhDs in this group in the GES, and 65.8 percent had achieved tenure by the survey date. The comparable percentages for the three large fields were 60.2 percent, 63.5 percent, and 65.8 percent for English, history, and political science, respectively.[17]

Of course, a problem with this approach is that for the latest entrance cohorts in this subgroup, the probability of being employed in a tenured position is, by definition, inversely related to the respondent's TTD. For example, individuals in the GES sample who started their programs in 1987 and took nine years to finish would have at most six years of employment after receiving their doctorates, whereas respondents who took seven years to finish would have at most eight years of employment after receiving their doctorates. Tenure decisions are typically not made until the seventh year of employment at an academic institution, and thus only the seven-year completers in this example would have a reasonable chance of having received tenure. More generally, if individuals with shorter TTD are more likely to obtain tenured appointments, our calculation will overstate the percentage of PhDs in the GES who will ultimately get tenure.

With this in mind, it is still interesting to ask what the characteristics of the PhDs and their programs were that led to their achieving tenure by the survey date. Table 9.7 summarizes our estimates of the marginal effect of each explanatory variable on the probability that the PhDs had achieved tenure as of the survey date, holding constant all of the other variables.

As expected, we observe a negative impact of longer TTD on tenure probabilities; this may be at least partially due to the mechanical relationship between TTD and tenure prospects described previously. However, several other more meaningful results stand out. Having published during graduate school appears to be a good predictor of longer-run career success; individuals who had published during graduate school have a probability of attaining tenure within 15 years after entrance to their doctoral programs that is 8.2 percentage points higher than the probability for those who had not published during graduate school. Married men, both those with and those without children, have a higher proba-

---

[17] The 60.2 percent figure for English PhDs can be contrasted with the 53 percent tenure rate that Nerad and Cerny (1999) found for PhDs in English who received their PhDs from 61 doctorate-granting universities in the United States between July 1, 1982, and June 30, 1985, and were surveyed in 1995. Their sample covers a different period than ours and a different set of institutions, and their PhDs were all 10–13 years past receipt of their degrees. In contrast, our sample includes many individuals with shorter times since receiving the PhD.

TABLE 9.7

Marginal Effects of Variables on the Probability of
Having a Tenured Position as of the Survey Date

Had master's degree	0.013
GRE verbal	0.021
GRE math	**–0.024**
Age	**–0.053**
Single male	—
Married male, no children	**0.070**
Married male, children	**0.103**
Single female	0.012
Married female, no children	0.012
Married female, children	–0.010
Non–U.S. citizen	**–0.132**
U.S. citizen, minority	0.028
Volume published	–0.012
Published	**0.082**
TTD 4 years or less	0.023
TTD 5 years	—
TTD 6 years	–0.005
TTD 7 years	–0.052
TTD 8 years	**–0.114**
TTD 9 years	**–0.272**
TTD 10 years or more	**–0.392**
Rank of graduate program	–0.003
Share employed at four-year institution	–0.384

Notes: Based on GES respondents who received a PhD between 1985 and 2000. These estimated marginal effects are derived from a logit analysis of the probability that an individual was employed in a tenured position at a four-year institution as of the survey date. The analyses also controlled for the field and institution from which the PhD was received. Marginal effects in bold type are statistically significant at the 5 percent level. Rank of graduate program is based on 1995 National Research Council rankings. "Share employed at four-year institution" is the share of new PhDs in the individual's field who were employed at four-year institutions after PhD receipt, based on data from the Survey of Earned Doctorates.

bility of attaining tenure than single men or single women. Non–U.S. citizen PhDs have a lower probability of attaining tenure (relative to nonminority U.S. citizens), even though they had a higher probability of having a tenure-track position three years after receipt of their PhDs. Finally, there is no difference between the probability of achieving tenure for minority-citizen and nonminority-citizen PhDs. Although diversity considerations influence initial hiring decisions, the probability of having a tenured appointment as of the survey date does not depend on the race or ethnicity of a U.S. citizen with a PhD.

DID THE GEI AFFECT THE PROBABILITY OF ACHIEVING TENURE-TRACK POSITIONS?

The stated purpose of the GEI was to improve doctoral education in the humanities, not simply to reduce TTD and attrition rates. So it is natural for us to ask if the improvements that the GEI induced (which we described in Chapters 4 and 6) had any impact on the early-career employment prospects of new PhDs. We focus on obtaining a tenure-track teaching position at a four-year college or university as a measure of job-market success.[18]

To answer this question, we use the same difference-in-differences approach that we described in Chapter 2 and used in Chapters 4–6. Using the GES survey data and information provided by the institutional data files, we focus on the probabilities that a PhD is employed in a tenure-track position at a four-year institution six months and three years after receipt of the PhD; we ask if the changes in these probabilities between the period in which the GEI was in effect and the period before it was in effect were different for PhDs who received their degrees from treatment and control departments. If they were, then we attribute the difference in differences to the effects of the GEI. And, as in our prior analyses, we make these comparisons controlling for individuals' race and ethnicity, citizenship status, and field of study. We also test whether our conclusions are influenced by controlling for students' GRE scores (because we have shown that the GEI led to an improvement in scores at treatment departments) or the universities that they attended.

Our findings proved to be robust to whether we included in our estimation models controls for student quality or university attended. Our estimates of the effects of the GEI on the probabilities of being employed in a tenure-track position six months or three years after receipt of the PhD were modest in magnitude, sometimes positive and sometimes negative, and never statistically significant. Put simply, the GEI did not appear to influence the early-career job-market success of students in treatment departments.

---

[18] Our sample period is too short to allow us to analyze whether the GEI affected the probability that the respondents had received tenure 10 or 15 years after receipt of their PhDs. The GEI began in the fall of 1991; when the GES was undertaken in 2002–03, very few PhDs subject to the GEI were 10–15 years beyond *receipt* of the degree at that time.

If the GEI improved the quality of entering graduate students and the quality of education in treatment departments relative to control departments, why wasn't the GEI associated with improvements in the probability that graduates of treatment departments received tenure-track positions? We believe the reason for this finding is that the GEI affected job outcomes in at least two different ways.

On the one hand, it increased the probability that students enrolled in treatment departments received PhDs. If those who would have otherwise left their programs prior to getting their degrees in the absence of the GEI were, on average, of lower quality than other students in their departments, the average quality of the pool of graduates from the departments participating in the GEI may have been of slightly lower quality than would have been the case in the absence of the GEI, even though the GEI caused the average quality of participating departments' entering cohorts to increase. This would cause their graduates to have slightly worse job outcomes.

On the other hand, the GEI shortened average TTD (Chapter 4) and, as we will show in the next chapter, increased the publication rates of PhD students while they were in graduate school. As our findings (summarized in Tables 9.4–9.6) indicate, these latter changes should have improved job-market outcomes. Apparently these two routes by which the GEI affected job-market outcomes—through its effects on the probability of receiving the PhD and its effects on TTD and publication rates—offset each other and led to our finding of no significant impact.

CHAPTER 10

Publications: Patterns and Influences

The biggest factor slowing down progress on my
dissertation was publishing articles.
—A history student who began in 1993
and was still pursuing a PhD in 2003

I got my job based on the quality of my dissertation, and I would have been more competitive if
I'd had publications prior to receiving the PhD. A
good-enough dissertation is not good enough to
get a job, and once you have a job, you don't have
time to write.
—A 1989 anthropology PhD who began in 1982

ONE OF THE primary goals of PhD programs in the humanities is to prepare doctoral students to be contributors to the production of new knowledge. We turn in this chapter to an analysis of the publications experiences of humanities PhD students during graduate school and during
their early careers. Our analyses are based on self-reports of publication
experiences that the respondents to the Graduate Education Survey
(GES) provided. Given the well-known problems with self-reported publications data, we sought to validate the reported publication records by
comparing them with annual records for a sample of individuals; we
found that self-reports and actual counts were quite similar.[1]

---

[1] Because of the confidentiality conditions under which the GES was conducted, only
those Mellon Foundation staff members specifically approved to access the names were permitted to do this checking and only on the condition that the results be kept confidential
regarding any individual findings. Out of a random sample of 100 cases, in 60 cases self-
reports were validated. For 21 other cases, it was possible to confirm that the respondents
had published the reported number of articles, but it was not possible to confirm whether
these articles were accepted for publication within three years of PhD receipt. Finally, there
were only six cases in which it appeared that the self-reports overstated the number of publications. As for the remaining cases, either they were not appropriate for the sample—
claimed zero and had zero publications—or Foundation staff were unable to locate them;
thus they are not counted as either confirmed or unconfirmed.

HOW MUCH DO THEY PUBLISH?

Respondents to the GES were asked to report if they had ever authored or co-authored a publication, the number of such publications, and the types of publications; the choices given for type were book, journal article, other article, and book review. These questions were asked separately for works accepted for publication during respondents' doctoral studies and for those accepted for publication during their first three years after receipt of the PhD. The questions on numbers of publications did not distinguish between sole-authored and co-authored publications, and in the analyses that follow we make no distinction between these types of publications. For the fields in our study, this does not appear to be an issue; of the respondents to the GES who reported publishing during their doctoral studies, over 90 percent had at least one sole-authored publication during this period.

We focus on the types of publications that are given heaviest weight in hiring and tenure decisions in the humanities—journal articles and books. Table 10.1 tabulates, for all respondents to the GES and for the three largest fields in the sample (English, history, and political science), whether or not respondents published any books or journal articles during their doctoral studies or during the first three years after receiving their degrees, as well as the average number of books and articles they published during each of these periods.[2] We make no distinction between books and articles published; our preliminary analyses suggested that giving more weight to books had no impact on the qualitative nature of the results that follow.

The data suggest that about 26 percent of the GES respondents did not publish during either their doctoral studies or their first three years after receipt of the PhD. About 6 percent published during but not after their doctoral studies, 33 percent published after but not during their doctoral studies, and 34 percent published both during and after their doctoral studies. These numbers imply that about 40 percent of the sample published during graduate school and a majority of the sample, about 68 percent, published at least once during their first three years after receipt of the PhD. The pattern of responses is very similar across the three fields.

On average, respondents published 0.8 publication during graduate school and 1.7 publications during their first three years after receipt of the PhD. These averages include those who did not publish anything. If instead one restricts attention to the respondents with publications, those who published at least one publication during their doctoral careers pub-

---

[2] These tabulations do not control for the respondents' employment status during their first three years after receipt of their PhDs; we discuss this issue later.

TABLE 10.1

Early-Career Publications of New Doctorates during Graduate School
and the First Three Years after PhD Receipt, by Field

	Overall	English	History	Political Science
Published (yes/no)				
Never	0.26	0.24	0.28	0.28
During but not after	0.06	0.07	0.07	0.04
After but not during	0.33	0.29	0.34	0.40
Both during and after	0.34	0.40	0.32	0.28
During	0.40	0.36	0.39	0.32
After	0.68	0.69	0.66	0.68
Number of publications[a]				
During	0.80	0.99	0.76	0.67
After	1.71	1.75	1.50	1.94

Note: Publications are defined as the sum of books and refereed articles published.
[a]Based on all respondents, including those reporting zero publications.

lished, on average, 2 publications during graduate school (0.80/0.40).
Similarly, those who published at least one publication during their first
three years after receipt of the PhD published, on average, 2.5 publications during that period (1.71/0.68). Again, results for each of the three
major fields are very similar.

Table 10.2 presents similar data for all respondents, this time broken
down separately for U.S. citizens who are not underrepresented minorities, U.S. citizens who are underrepresented minorities, non–U.S. citizens, men, and women. For the purpose of this table, underrepresented
minorities are defined as African Americans, Hispanic Americans, and
Native Americans; Asian Americans are included with whites in the nonminority category.[3]

Non–U.S. citizens are less likely to never publish than U.S. citizens.
They also publish more, on average, both during their doctoral studies
and during the first three years after their studies, than U.S. citizens. A
previous study by Gregory Attiyeh and Richard Attiyeh suggested that major U.S. PhD programs often discriminate against foreign PhD student
applicants in their admissions process, in the sense that foreign applicants have a lower probability of being admitted than U.S.-citizen applicants with similar GRE scores, all other factors held constant. Yet their
study did not find any evidence that this occurs in the field of English,

---

[3] Less than 0.5 percent of GES respondents (63) were Native Americans.

TABLE 10.2

Early-Career Publications of New Doctorates during Graduate School and the First Three Years after PhD Receipt, by Citizenship, Race and Ethnicity, and Gender

	U.S. Citizen, Nonminority[a]	U.S. Citizen, Minority[a]	Non–U.S. Citizen	Men	Women
Published (yes/no)					
Never	0.28	0.35	0.22	0.25	0.32
During but not after	0.06	0.08	0.04	0.05	0.07
After but not during	0.33	0.38	0.34	0.33	0.34
Both during and after	0.33	0.19	0.39	0.37	0.28
During	0.39	0.27	0.44	0.42	0.34
After	0.66	0.57	0.74	0.70	0.62
Number of publications[b]					
During	0.78	0.49	1.09	0.93	0.66
After	1.63	1.47	2.27	1.95	1.44

Notes: All citizen/race/ethnicity proportions in each row are statistically different from each other (at the 5 percent level) except for those for "During but not after." All gender proportions in a row are statistically different from each other (at the 5 percent level) except for "After but not during."

[a]African Americans, Hispanic Americans, and Native Americans are classified as minorities, and whites and Asian Americans are classified as nonminorities.

[b]Based on all respondents, including those reporting zero publications.

the only field within the humanities that it analyzed.[4] So we doubt that our finding reflects the fact that foreign PhD students in these fields are inherently more talented publishers than U.S.-citizen PhD students. Rather we suspect that only the best foreign PhDs get to stay in the United States, and that these were the foreign PhDs in the treatment and control departments who were most likely to respond to the GES.[5]

The data in the table also suggest that among U.S. citizens, respondents who were minorities were less likely to have ever published (65 versus 72 percent), less likely to have published during their doctoral programs (27 versus 39 percent), and less likely to have published during their first three years after receipt of the PhD (57 versus 66 percent) than nonminorities. Similarly their average number of publications was lower than that for nonminorities during both periods. The average number of

[4] Gregory Attiyeh and Richard Attiyeh, "Testing for Bias in Graduate School Admissions," *Journal of Human Resources* 32 (Summer 1997): 524–48.

[5] The response rate to the GES was 13 percentage points lower for foreign students than U.S. citizens. The difference is primarily due to the inability of those conducting the survey to obtain valid addresses for a number of foreign students; it was not primarily due to a difference in response rates, given that valid address information was obtained.

publications is averaged over both publishers and those who never published. Once we restrict the sample to those who published at least one work during the period, the minority-citizen average number of publications rises to 1.81 (0.49/0.27) during doctoral studies and to 2.58 (1.47/0.57) during the first three years after the PhD, whereas the nonminority numbers rise, respectively, to 2.0 (0.78/0.39) and 2.47 (1.63/0.66). So among U.S. citizens who publish, minority PhDs actually publish slightly more during the first three years after receipt of the PhD than nonminorities.

The last two columns of the table provide publications data stratified by gender. Men are less likely to have never published than women and are more likely to have published during graduate school (42 versus 34 percent) or during the first three years after receipt of the PhD (70 versus 62 percent) than women. Men also average more publications during both periods, either not conditional on having published at all (as reported in the table) or conditional on having published. Men with publications published an average of 2.2 (0.93/0.42) publications during graduate school and 2.8 (1.95/0.70) publications in the first three years after receipt of the PhD; the comparable numbers for women were 1.9 (0.66/0.34) and 2.3 (1.44/0.62), respectively.

Similar data are presented in Appendix Table E.10.1, separately for sample respondents from the fields of English, political science, and history. In the main the pattern of results for each field is similar to the pattern described here for the sample as a whole.

WHAT DETERMINES PhD STUDENTS' EARLY PUBLICATION SUCCESS?

The differences that we observed in publication success by gender, race and ethnicity, and citizenship are gross differences that do not control for other factors that may influence publication success. For example, if noncitizen PhDs were of higher ability than citizen PhDs the citizenship differences that we observed might reflect only ability differences, not differences that were due to citizenship per se. To understand whether gender, race and ethnicity, and citizenship per se really do matter, it is necessary to conduct a multivariate analysis in which the effects of these variables are estimated while holding constant other factors that might be expected to affect publication success.

Previous research on the determinants of publication rates of young scholars and graduate students in the humanities has been limited to the field of English and has focused on reporting trends in the publication rates of faculty and doctoral students.[6] However, a wide body of literature, primarily by economists and sociologists, has addressed the determinants of publication success of academics in a variety of fields and found that individual characteristics (such as GRE scores and demographic variables), characteristics of their PhD advisors (including advisor publication productivity), and characteristics of their PhD departments (including National Research Council rank) all influence early-career publication success.[7]

[6] For example, Jeffery P. Bieber and Robert T. Blackburn, "Faculty Research Productivity 1972–1988: Development and Applications of Constant Units of Measure," *Research in Higher Education* 34 (October 1993): 551–67, and David G. Brown, *The Mobile Professors* (Washington, DC: American Council on Education, 1967), address the publication propensities of faculty members in English, and Wade M. Lee, "Publication Trends of Doctoral Students in Three Fields from 1965–1995," *Journal of the American Society for Information Science* 51 (January 2000): 139–44, addresses publication trends in analytical chemistry, experimental psychology, and American literature.

[7] For example, see Thomas C. Buchmueller, Jeff Dominitz, and W. Lee Hansen, "Graduate Training and the Early Career Productivity of PhD Economists," *Economics of Education Review* 18 (February 1999): 65–77; Frank Clemente, "Early Career Determinants of Research Productivity," *American Journal of Sociology* 79 (September 1973): 409–19; Donna Ginther and Shulamit Kahn, "Women in Economics: Moving Up or Falling Off the Academic Career Ladder?" *Journal of Economic Perspectives* 18 (Summer 2004): 193–214; Thomas H. Goodwin and Raymond D. Sauer, "Life Cycle Productivity in Academic Research: Evidence from Cumulative Publication Histories of Academic Economists," *Southern Economic Journal* 61 (January 1995): 728–43; Wayne A. Grove and Stephen Wu, "The Search for Economics Talent: Doctoral Completion and Research Productivity," *American Economic Review* 97 (May 2007): 506–11; W. Lee Hansen, Burton Weisbrod, and Robert Strauss, "Modeling the Earnings and Research Productivity of Academic Economists," *Journal of Political Economy* 86 (August 1978): 729–41; Timothy Hogan, "Faculty Research Activity and the Quality of Graduate Training," *Journal of Human Resources* 16 (Summer 1981): 400–415; Sharon Levin and Paula Stephan, "Research Productivity over the Life Cycle: Evidence for Academic Scientists," *American Economic Review* 81 (March 1991): 114–32; J. Scott Long, "Productivity and Academic Positions in the Scientific Career," *American Sociological Review* 46 (December 1978): 422–42; J. Scott Long, "Measures of Sex Differences in Scientific Productivity," *Social Forces* 71 (September 1992): 159–78; John McDowell, Larry Singell Jr., and Mark Stateer, "Two to Tango? Gender Differences in the Decision to Publish and Coauthor," *Economic Inquiry* 44 (January 2006): 153–68; Barbara Reskin, "Scientific Productivity, Sex and Location in the Institution of Science," *American Journal of Sociology* 83 (March 1978): 1235–43; Steven Stack, "Gender and Scholarly Productivity: 1970–2000," *Sociological Focus* 35 (August 2002): 285–96; Yu Xie and Kimberlee A. Shauman, "Sex Differences in Research Productivity: New Evidence about an Old Puzzle," *American Sociological Review* 63 (December 1998): 847–70; and Harriet Zuckerman, Jonathan R. Cole, and John T. Bruer, eds., *The Outer Circle: Women in the Scientific Community* (New York: W. W. Norton, 1991).

Although we do not have access to the names of GES respondents' dissertation advisors and hence do not have their advisors' publication records, we do have detailed information from the GES on the types of interactions the respondents reported having with their advisors and the characteristics (as reported by the respondents) of their PhD programs. We have incorporated this information into multivariate models of the probability that the respondents in our sample published during graduate school and of the number of publications they had during graduate school. A summary of the marginal effects of various factors on these outcomes, holding constant each of the other factors included in our analyses, appears in Appendix Table E.10.2.

The estimates in this table suggest that, even while holding other variables constant, single women and U.S. citizens who are minorities both have lower probabilities of publishing and fewer publications during their PhD programs than single men who are nonminorities and U.S. citizens. On average, respondents published 0.8 paper and book during graduate school (Table 10.1); our estimates suggest that single women and U.S.-citizen minorities each published almost 0.3 paper or book fewer than single men who are nonminorities and U.S. citizens. In contrast, other variables held constant, non–U.S. citizens have higher publication probabilities and a greater number of publications (0.2) than U.S. citizens. Marital status at the date of entry to doctoral study does not appear to influence publications during graduate school for either men or women.

Turning to the marginal effects of other variables included in the analysis, our estimates indicate that students who had a master's degree before enrolling in their PhD program and students who reported that they attended seminars regularly during graduate school both had higher probabilities of publishing and published more than other students. In contrast, neither students' verbal or math GRE scores, nor their age when they started their programs, had a significant effect on publication success during graduate school.

Students who said that their advisors expected them to finish their PhDs as quickly as possible had 0.13 fewer publication in graduate school than other PhD students, other variables held constant. Students who said they met with their advisors to discuss their research at least twice a month published more than other students. Students who said that their department prepared them for research were more likely to publish during graduate school and to publish a greater volume of work then, whereas students who said that their departments did not prepare them for research were less likely to publish during graduate school, other variables held constant. However, students' perceptions of specific characteristics of the PhD program—such as expectations for the dissertation and requirements to attend dissertation seminars and to present research in these seminars—did not matter.

Appendix Table E.10.3 presents similar estimated marginal effects on respondents' probabilities of publishing and their volume of publications during their first three years after graduate school. The number of publications that a doctoral student had during graduate school and the presence of children in the student's family as of the date of receipt of the PhD are included in the models underlying this table as additional explanatory variables, to see if they are useful signals for early postdegree publication success.

Publications during graduate school are an important predictor of early-career publications. The average respondent in our sample published 1.71 papers or books during his or her first three years after receipt of the PhD (Table 10.1), and our estimates suggest that each additional publication during graduate school is associated with almost 0.5 more publication during the first three years after receipt of the PhD. Once publications during PhD study are controlled for, having entered PhD study with a prior master's degree does not significantly influence early-career publications, but having often attended seminars during PhD study is a significant positive predictor of early-career publication success.

Other variables held constant, we find that during the first three years after receipt of the PhD, single women and married women without children publish less, and noncitizens publish more than nonminority citizens. These results are invariant to whether or not the initial job outcome (employed in a tenure-track position in a four-year institution, employed in another academic position, employed in a nonacademic position, or not employed) of the PhDs is controlled for in the estimation. In contrast, whether minority-citizen PhDs publish less than nonminority-citizen PhDs depends on whether initial job outcome is controlled for in the model; when it is, minority PhDs publish an average of 0.17 paper or book less, but when it is not, there is no statistically significant difference in publication success. Being employed initially in a tenure-track position at a four-year institution has a large impact on the number of publications during the first three years after the PhD (0.408); this may be due to these respondents' having greater time and support for research. These findings imply that, other factors held constant, minority respondents were more likely than nonminority respondents to attain tenure-track positions at four-year institutions (a finding presented in Chapter 9).

Turning to advisor and department characteristics, respondents who indicated that their departments expected them to publish or to polish their dissertations prior to receipt of the PhD published more than did other respondents. However, conditional on the departmental expecta-

tions, having an advisor who expected the respondent to publish or polish the dissertation prior to receipt of the PhD had an insignificant negative effect in most of the specifications on early-career publication success. As with publications during the doctoral program, having an advisor
who met with the respondent at least twice a month to discuss research
increased early-career publication numbers, but having an advisor who
was not available to meet with the student to discuss dissertation research
had a negative effect on early-career publications. Students who said that
their departments prepared them for research published more, but being required to attend a dissertation seminar actually reduced early-
career publications. Taken together these results suggest that students
who are motivated to attend seminars during their PhD programs publish more during their early careers, but the requirement to attend a dissertation seminar per se does not facilitate early-career publications.

DOES PROLONGING DOCTORAL STUDY
TO ENHANCE PUBLICATIONS MAKE SENSE?

Publications during doctoral study increase both the likelihood and the
number of early-career publications. Does it make sense, then, for doctoral students to prolong their doctoral studies to enhance their publications prior to completion? We saw in Chapter 9 that, while holding
other variables constant, the probability of obtaining a tenure-track position at a four-year institution after receipt of the PhD is significantly
lower for individuals who take eight years or more to complete their degrees than for individuals with shorter time-to-degree (TTD). There were
no significant differences in the probabilities of being employed in a
tenure-track position three years after receipt of the PhD for degree
lengths of five to seven years. Hence, if the data suggest that students can
enhance their publications during graduate school by delaying receipt of
their degrees by a year within this interval, a longer TTD might enhance
their chances of receiving a tenure-track position.

To understand the relationship between publications and the time respondents spent pursuing their PhDs, we re-estimated the models that
underlie Appendix Tables E.10.2 and E.10.3, adding in as additional explanatory variables the number of years that it took respondents to receive their PhDs. The estimated marginal effects of TTD on publications
during graduate school and on early-career publications that we obtained
are presented in Table 10.3. The numbers in the table are the marginal
effects of receiving a PhD in the indicated number of years, relative to the
omitted category, which is receiving a PhD in six years.

TABLE 10.3
Estimated Marginal Effects of TTD on Publications during
Graduate School and Early-Career Publications

TTD (years)	Number in Graduate School[a]	Probability of Publishing in Graduate School[a]	Number during First Three Years[b]	Probability of Publishing during First Three Years[b]
4 or less	0.120	0.010	**0.331**	0.026
5	**0.420**	**0.065**	**0.530**	**0.054**
6	—	—	—	—
7	–0.029	–0.015	**–0.336**	**–0.052**
8	**–0.127**	**–0.037**	**–0.559**	**–0.108**
9 or 10	–0.109	**–0.071**	**–0.729**	**–0.158**
11 or 12	–0.014	–0.033	**–0.971**	**–0.218**
13 or more	0.028	–0.061	**–1.011**	**–0.243**

Notes: All marginal effects are relative to a six-year TTD. Marginal effects in bold type are statistically significant at the 5 percent level.

[a]Estimates come from a generalization of the models underlying Appendix Table E.10.3 that include variables for TTD.

[b]Estimates come from a generalization of the models underlying columns 1a and 2a in Appendix Table E.10.3 that include variables for TTD. When generalizations of the models underlying columns 1b and 2b were estimated, the estimated marginal effects of TTD were virtually identical to those reported here.

Quite dramatically, the probability of publishing during graduate school and the number of publications that respondents have during graduate school are maximized among GES respondents at a degree length of five years. Students who take longer to complete their programs have significantly lower numbers of publications during graduate school. Respondents who completed their degrees in five years were 6.5 percentage points more likely to publish during graduate school than those who finished in six years, whereas respondents who finished in eight years were 3.7 percentage points less likely, and those who finished in nine or ten years, 7.1 percentage points less likely, to have published than those who finished in six years. Similarly, respondents who finished in five years had 0.42 more publication during graduate school, and those who finished in eight years had 0.127 fewer publication than those who finished in six years.

Early-career publications also vary systematically with TTD. Respondents who finished in five years were 5.4 percentage points more likely to publish and had 0.53 more publication during the first three years after completing the PhD than those who finished in six years. In contrast, both publication numbers and the probability of publishing early in the career declined monotonically with TTD for degree times greater than six years.

These findings cannot unambiguously answer the question "Should doctoral students delay receipt of the PhD to enhance their publications during graduate school to, in turn, enhance their early-career publications?" What they do show is that, on average, students who received their degrees in five years were the ones who published the most, both in graduate school and during their early careers, other factors held constant. To the extent that TTD serves, on average, as a signal to potential employers about the likely publishing productivity of PhD students in the humanities, delaying receipt of the PhD to enhance publications during graduate school may prove to be a very risky strategy for an individual doctoral student in these fields.

DID THE GEI ENHANCE PUBLICATION SUCCESS?

The stated purpose of the Graduate Education Initiative (GEI) was to improve doctoral education in the humanities. Given that one important role of PhD programs is to prepare students to be contributors to the body of knowledge in their fields, it is important for us to analyze the impact of the GEI on the publication success of PhD students in these fields, both during their doctoral study and early in their careers after receipt of the PhD.

To answer this question, we use the same difference-in-differences approach that we have used throughout the book to analyze the impact of the GEI on doctoral students' attrition and completion probabilities and on early-career job-market outcomes. Using the GES survey data and information provided by the institutional data files, we ask if the change in publication probabilities or numbers of publications between the period in which the GEI was in effect and the period before it was in effect were different for the PhDs who received their degrees from treatment and control departments. If they are, then we attribute the difference in the differences to the effects of the GEI. For these analyses, we define entering cohorts starting with 1991 (1991–92 through 1996–97) as being in the postprogram period and entering cohorts before 1991 (1982–83 through 1990–91) as being in the preprogram period.

Of course (as we have shown), publications differ across individuals by gender, race and ethnicity, and citizenship status, and since the composition of students along these lines in treatment and control departments may systematically have changed between the two periods, we control for these variables in our analyses. Because publication rates may differ across fields of study, we also control for each individual's field of study. In conducting these analyses we also investigate whether our findings about the impact of the GEI on publication rates are sensitive to whether our analyses control for changes in student quality or the specific institution at which a student received the PhD.

A summary of our findings is presented in Table 10.4. Our findings are robust to whether we include in our estimation models controls for student quality or the institution the student attended. We estimate that the GEI increased the probability of students publishing by roughly 7.5 percentage points and their number of publications by about 0.16 during their graduate studies. These numbers should be contrasted with a mean publication rate during graduate study for the sample of under 0.4 and a mean number of publications in the sample during graduate study of 0.8 (Table 10.1). Hence these estimated effects of the GEI should be considered large—each is on the order of 20–25 percent of the mean.

Similarly, we estimate that the GEI increased the probability of respondents publishing during the first three years of their careers by about 5–6 percentage points; this is less than a tenth of the mean publication rate in the sample during the first three years of respondents' careers (Table 10.1). Although we estimate that the early-career publication numbers of respondents also increased by between 0.16 and 0.20, which is slightly larger than one-tenth of the mean number of publications in the sample during this early-career period, we cannot conclude that this effect is statistically significant. A fair assessment is that the GEI increased doctoral students' publications during doctoral study by a greater percentage than it increased their early-career publications.[8]

We must caution readers that the difference-in-differences approach that we have employed attributes changes in publication rates between treatment and control departments to the effects of the GEI. Although we have controlled in these analyses for some other variables that may be responsible for these changes (such as differential changes in measures of student quality), we cannot control for unobserved (by us) changes that were correlated with the GEI. For example, suppose it were the case that, for reasons other than the GEI, the quality of faculty at treatment departments increased after the GEI was instituted by more than the quality of faculty at control departments, and higher-quality faculty led to more student publications. Then the improvement in the publication records of students in treatment departments that we attribute to the effects of the GEI may in fact be due to the unobserved (by us) differences in the change in faculty quality. However, absent evidence that this situation applies, it seems reasonable to adopt the simpler explanation that the GEI did affect publication rates.

[8] We also redid these analyses using departmental weights rather than individual weights and found quite similar results. So it does not appear that the impact of the GEI on publication rates and numbers of publications varied between large and small departments.

TABLE 10.4

Estimated Marginal Effects of the GEI on Publications
during and after Graduate School

Include Student Quality	Include Institution Indicators	Probability of Publishing during	Probability of Publishing after	Number of Publications during	Number of Publications after
No	Yes	**0.075**	**0.060**	**0.167**	0.196
No	No	**0.072**	**0.059**	0.153	0.191
Yes	Yes	**0.076**	**0.051**	**0.158**	0.165
Yes	No	**0.076**	**0.056**	0.152	0.181

Notes: All models include gender, race and ethnicity, citizenship, field variables, and in-dicator variables for whether the department was a treatment department, whether the stu-dent entered before or after the start of the GEI, and the interaction of being a treatment department and entering after the start of the GEI. The models with student quality also include whether the student had a prior master's degree and the student's verbal and math GRE scores. Coefficients in bold type are statistically significant at the 5 percent level.

SOME KEY FINDINGS

We have found that publishing was the norm for the PhDs who responded to the GES: two-thirds of them published at least one article or book during the first three years after receipt of the PhD. Men were more likely to pub-lish than women; among U.S. citizens, minorities were less likely to publish than nonminorities.

The interaction of students with their advisors and their departments clearly influences their publication success during graduate school. Re-spondents whose advisors expected them to finish their degrees quickly published less in graduate school, whereas those who met with their ad-visors regularly to discuss research published more. Similarly respon-dents who said that their departments prepared them to do research were more likely to publish during graduate school.

Respondents' publications during graduate school were important pre-dictors of their publications during their first three years after receipt of the PhD, even after we controlled for whether they were employed in tenure-track positions at four-year institutions after receipt of the degree. And, as we indicated in Chapter 9, publications during graduate school also enhanced the probability that our respondents would be employed in tenure-track positions after receipt of their degrees. Faculty who urge their students to publish during graduate school clearly understand the importance of publishing for their students' future careers. However, we cannot say whether the publication success of students with such advisors was due to the advisors per se or rather to the students with the greatest aptitude for publishing having associated themselves with such advisors.

Enhancing publications was never a stated objective of the GEI, but improving the quality of PhD programs was. If it is true that the quality of a PhD program correlates directly with the publishing success of its students, it is reassuring to have found that the GEI was associated with an increased level of publication by GES respondents—both during graduate school and during their first three years after program completion. However, the increases were much larger during graduate school than during their early careers.

PART IV

Lessons and Findings

CHAPTER 11

Redesigning Doctoral Programs:
Lessons Learned

We have begun to analyze some of the data on our
participating departments and their students
which we are required to compile and forward to
the Foundation as part of the GEI. Those analyses
. . . have already started to bear fruit. . . . It has
helped to generate a local interest in self-examination through sophisticated social research, an
interest that we are currently striving to satisfy.
                    —Provost at University X, 1993

THIS CHAPTER describes lessons provided by the Graduate Education Initiative (GEI) for future efforts to redesign graduate programs in the humanities. The chapter that follows reviews the study's principal findings.
Here we focus on challenges encountered in implementing the GEI and
in its assessment, which may beset other efforts to introduce change into
this corner of the academy. In some cases these lessons might help those
who face challenges in implementing change in other contexts.

The GEI began, as we have noted, with the premise that scholars could
be educated more effectively, even in the strongest universities. The Mellon Foundation provided considerable funds over a long period of time
to underwrite changes that university administrators and department faculty members considered important, within broad outlines set by the
Foundation. Since administrators and department members played a major role in designing the programs that were introduced in each university, the GEI would have seemed uncontroversial. Indeed by some measures it was. Some faculty members remained enthusiasts to the end, and
the changes some departments introduced proved exceptionally successful in accomplishing the twin objectives of reorganizing and improving
graduate education. However, this was not the case in all departments, nor
was it so throughout the 10 years during which the GEI was in place.

Should others decide to introduce GEI-like initiatives, they may wish
to pay attention to lessons we drew from overseeing it and assessing its
outcomes:

- It is necessary to define the objectives of the intervention clearly and repeatedly. Objectives blur as time passes. Veteran participants leave and new ones become involved. Even when objectives are clear, faculty members, administrators, and students cannot be counted on to agree with them, or on the right ways to measure their achievement, or that achievement should be measured at all. Indeed, the main parties involved may not agree that an intervention is even occurring.
- Faculty and departments are central to making decisions about graduate programs. Provosts and deans may sometimes exercise more influence in shaping programs than is helpful. At the same time, their influence in keeping interventions on track and in enabling departments to maintain or to improve their accomplishments cannot be underestimated.
- Having systematic procedures in place for learning how well the intervention is proceeding while it is in process, rather than waiting until after it is completed, is key if midcourse corrections are contemplated. If data are to be collected and to be useful, commitment to maintaining their quality must be unswerving.
- Efforts to link specific interventions with specific outcomes and to identify the mechanisms in play often produce vexing logical and methodological problems for those charged with overseeing the intervention as a whole. This is especially the case when a classic experimental research design is unfeasible or undesirable, or both. But such efforts to identify "what works" are needed if others seeking to introduce change are to benefit from prior experience.

Beyond these four lessons, our experiences suggest that other innovators need to be alert to potential outside forces. The outcomes of the GEI were influenced by three powerful forces well beyond its confines: first, like all interventions, it had unanticipated consequences, some of which countered the intended objectives; second, uncontrollable events occurred in the world beyond the intervention, which undermined its success; and third, long time horizons are characteristic of the academy, and these have independent consequences for assessing the GEI. Change is often slow, and it takes time for results, beneficial and otherwise, to become visible, even when appropriate measures of accomplishment are in place.

IDENTIFYING GOALS AND THE INEVITABLE DISAGREEMENTS ABOUT THEM

It is axiomatic that the goals of an intervention should be clear and that straightforward means should be available to determine whether goals are being achieved. This said, goals may initially be misunderstood, and commitment to them tends to erode with the passage of time. For example, reducing attrition was a stated objective of the GEI. More specifically, it was believed that if attrition is to occur, it should occur early rather than late in graduate students' careers. The message that attrition should be reduced was clearly heard. Early attrition dropped significantly in the majority of treatment departments. However, the more precise objective of reducing late attrition evidently was not clearly communicated, or at least it did not register. Reports from departments whose early attrition rates increased as they instituted rigorous reviews of students were apologetic, taking the increase as a measure of failure rather than success, despite reassurances from Foundation staff that they were on target. Moreover, emphasizing reduction in attrition rates diverted attention from the growing numbers of students who had begun to "languish" later on in their graduate careers. Thus concern about high rates of attrition and the drive to reduce them trumped the GEI's stated and better-targeted objective of reducing late attrition. We now know that although early attrition (in years 1–4) was significantly reduced, late attrition and late completion increased in those same cohorts.

Even when objectives are clear, faculty members, some administrators, and indeed students themselves cannot be counted on to agree on them. When the Foundation called attention to the pervasiveness of low completion rates in doctoral programs in the humanities and to the long time it took to earn the PhD, faculty members' views differed about the importance of these outcomes, what had brought them about, and how they might be improved. How long is "too long" for the PhD? Was the lack of money for graduate students the real problem? Could changes in curriculum and program structure be made that would satisfy the faculty while increasing students' chances of completing their degrees in a timely fashion? Did faculty members and students need to change their thinking about how long a program would and should take to complete?

Most particularly, there was disagreement about the putative benefits of reducing time-to-degree (TTD). Some faculty members were unconvinced that reducing expected TTD to six years was educationally defensible. They argued that students cannot master the relevant material, acquire the relevant skills, and do the research and writing required for acceptable dissertations in so brief a time.[1] This view surfaced at the outset and continued to be expressed throughout the decade during which the GEI was in place.

The difficult job market in the humanities that prevailed in the 1990s and through the early years of the next decade reinforced faculty resist-

---

[1] A typical debate on the various goals for graduate education and the trade-offs among them was held at the 2008 annual meeting of the American Political Science Association; Jaschik (2008).

ance to reducing TTD. Insisting that students finish as quickly as they could seemed, to some faculty members, to be at odds with the important objective of getting good jobs. That such jobs were rare led those faculty members to counsel students not to rush, to stay in graduate school even if dissertations were complete, to polish them for publication, to continue to teach, and perhaps to write some papers. This advice—combined with students' own anxieties about getting jobs and their concerns about losing health insurance, subsidized housing, and library access upon completing their degrees—led a number to conclude that it was better to stay than to finish. One student wrote in the Graduate Education Survey (GES): "I could certainly have finished my dissertation up to a year sooner, if I had had a job in prospect. I chose to delay my defense and graduation by one year in order to continue qualifying for a TA-ship, which in turn enabled me to retain my health insurance and to defer my undergrad loan repayment." Postponing the actual award of the degree and securing employment are consistent with the data presented in Chapter 9, that is, if "staying" lasted no longer than seven years from entry. As we noted, those who stayed in graduate school more than eight years did not do better in the job market.[2] Those seeking academic jobs in a competitive market found that having the degree in hand had far more value than being close to but not yet finished.

Students too had mixed opinions about the benefits of shortening TTD. One student acknowledged the competing goals and argued for shorter TTD:

> The one exceptional advantage that all [University X] graduate students had is that we weren't forced to teach and lead classes ourselves. Did this make us less prepared to teach? Perhaps. On the other hand, it was possible to graduate in a reasonable amount of time ($6\frac{1}{2}$ years) and have a dissertation in good enough shape to publish relatively quickly. Folks I know from other schools were not so lucky. I never realized how important finishing "quickly" was until after I did it. I have served on many search committees as a faculty member both at [University X] and now here at [College Y]. We were usually faced with 60+ applicants. The first thing the committee usually did was to strike folks in graduate school for more than 8 years. People who can't finish a dissertation in a reasonable amount of time are not going to be able to publish while teaching and fulfilling the burden of service obligations that tenure-track faculty face.

But another student saw the relative merits of the competing goals quite differently:

---

[2] We do not know to what extent staying longer confers additional intellectual benefits, but these would have to be compared with the opportunity forgone (the benefits of being out and on one's own) to be fairly assessed.

One becomes a scholar in graduate school and that is not a process that can be squeezed into a set schedule. Every project, and every scholar, is different. Working as an assistant professor is enormously time-consuming and demanding. It is not possible under those circumstances to do research and analysis for one's first book-length project in the same way that can be done while in graduate school. So the rush to complete PhDs and to get professional appointments hurts scholarship and makes a scholar's path to tenure that much more difficult and uncertain.

Even among those who thought that reducing TTD was desirable, a number of faculty members were unsure about reducing attrition. They held that attrition was to be expected and even encouraged (a view not inconsistent with the GEI's objective, even if, as we noted, it was sometimes assumed to be so). The argument was made that once in graduate school, some students find that the academic life is not what they thought it would be, and they should leave. Furthermore, making judgments about admitting students to graduate school is a necessarily imperfect process. Indeed, some universities accepted some students for graduate work in the humanities whose records were promising but not top-flight, so as to give them a chance to prove their merits in very rigorous competition. In these circumstances, a kind of "selective attrition" was official policy; it was assumed that it would correct for the inevitable imperfections in the admissions process, since it was believed that surviving the first years of study was the ultimate test.

The presence of competing views is endemic to the academic culture, or nearly so. There is evidence from the GES and the department reports that not all faculty members or students "signed on" to the GEI, with predictable unwanted effects on its outcomes. However skillfully interventions are designed and introduced, disagreement can be expected about larger objectives, about those that are more narrowly defined, and about how they are to be achieved and assessed. Indeed, the presence of disagreement was anticipated by the framers of the GEI, who described it in print as "avowedly interventionist" and asserted that its insistence on establishing norms for the length of the PhD; on monitoring, reporting, and accountability; and on the establishment of timetables "may seem unduly regimental and insensitive to the problems of individual students and their programs."[3] It would appear that merely foreseeing resistance will not forestall it.

---

[3] The framers go on to add, however, that "We would regret any such interpretations and would be unhappy if our intentions were misread. We start from the proposition that quality of accomplishment matters more than anything else. But we have come to recognize that graduate education is costly in human terms—in years and years of study, which result too often in dashed hopes and deep resentments"; Bowen and Rudenstine (1992), pp. 280, 288, and 289.

The example of the GEI suggests that focusing on several well-chosen measures rather than relying on just one can shed light on the complex nature of the outcomes being sought and the interactions among them, and their relative merits in accomplishing the overriding goal.[4] If, for example, increasing completion rates is deemed most critical in improving doctoral education, then it may be necessary to reduce expectations for briefer TTD. This trade-off has in fact been suggested by Daniel Denecke, director of the Council of Graduate Schools (CGS) PhD Completion Project. CGS's general findings, drawn mainly from institutions other than those that participated in the GEI, are consistent with our own: a nontrivial share of doctoral students in the humanities take more than 10 years to finish. Denecke concludes that "Those findings may call into question the wisdom of setting time limits on doctoral study, as some universities do."[5]

However, if a measure of the use of institutional resources in doctoral production, such as student-year cost (SYC), is also available, it becomes possible to make a decision based on a third criterion: the extent to which the time and resources of students, faculty members, and institutions are consumed when 10 years are spent on producing an average PhD in the humanities. Choosing to measure the outcome of the GEI using these measures (TTD, attrition rates, and SYC) draws attention to the possible conflict between these objectives and permits more informed evaluation of interventions to be made.[6]

And, of course, unanticipated changes occurred in the larger system that affected the outcomes and the evaluation of the GEI. One unanticipated event was the rapid diffusion of GEI-like programs into departments unconnected to the Initiative. One reason for instituting the GEI, of course, was the hope that innovations the participating departments found useful would spread to other departments in the humanities. And spread they did. Enthusiastic graduate deans at GEI institutions made GEI-like support available to other departments willing to review and change their programs. More or less simultaneously, other universities made changes in their doctoral programs, and in 2002–03 the CGS began its seven-year-long PhD Completion Project, in which 29 research universities were given support for intervention projects aimed at increasing completion of the doctorate. Thus the GEI's objectives, and in

---

[4] This is all apart from the value of having multiple indicators of the same phenomenon.

[5] Gravois (2007).

[6] In earlier chapters, we noted that these competing goals point to the need for a comprehensive measure of outcome, which, following David Brenneman, William Bowen, and Neil Rudenstine, we call SYC. A version of this measure is being used at Harvard as a means of assessing the success of departments; Jaschik (2008).

some respects the changes it supported, spread through the academy far more quickly and pervasively than had initially been anticipated. The adoption of such changes has had the decidedly positive effect of amplifying the influence of the GEI's objectives while undermining efforts to assess its outcomes by comparing control and treatment departments. We cannot be sure whether the widespread diffusion of these efforts is traceable to the GEI or to the acknowledgment that long TTD and high attrition rates in the humanities were truly serious problems. We know that limited efforts to deal with them were already in place in 2 of the 10 participating universities before the GEI started, but these were small in number and in scale. It cannot be all bad that evaluation of the GEI's effects was undermined by its unanticipated replication.

The rapid spread of guaranteed multiyear packages of support offered by major private universities, and some public ones, is a second event external to the GEI that affected its implementation and its outcomes. In the early 1990s competition among institutions and departments for students deemed "most promising" became acute. In order to recruit the students they most wanted, universities made offers of admission that included richer stipends and guarantees of support for multiple years.[7] The introduction of multiyear packages also led major research universities with large graduate programs to reduce the number of students they admitted so as to provide higher levels of financial aid. In doing so, they also raised their expectations of students' academic qualifications, a change that affected student outcomes independent of the GEI. Despite considerable variation among universities in the share of students covered, size of stipends offered, years of support promised, amount of teaching required, summer support granted, and travel funds provided, it was the predictability of multiyear packages that changed the basic character of financial aid in these institutions. Those students fortunate enough to have such packages no longer had to worry at the end of each year about whether they would be funded for the next.

Multiyear packages were fundamentally at odds with a basic principle of the GEI—that the provision of funding was to be conditional on students meeting specified timetables. This stipulation stemmed from the less-than-satisfactory TTD and completion histories of holders of the major national fellowships studied by Bowen and Rudenstine.[8] As it turned

---

[7] Multiyear packages were not new. Major national portable fellowship programs such as those sponsored by the Danforth Foundation, the Mellon Foundation, and the Woodrow Wilson National Fellowship Foundation covered students' funding over a period of several years. However, these were portable and not subject to institutional control, nor were they designed to affect institutional competition for students.

[8] Bowen and Rudenstine (1992), Chapter 11.

out, market pressures on universities and departments proved irresistible, and these forces overcame the GEI's stipulations concerning conditional support.[9] Funding in most institutions continued to be conditional on students meeting standards of academic performance, but other restrictions on allocation of support were softened or disappeared altogether. Only one aspect of GEI funding remained conditional—the limitation of dissertation-year fellowship awards to students who were in their sixth year of study or earlier. In order for funds to be given to students who were beyond year 6, the universities had to petition the Foundation. For the most part, the universities petitioned prudently, and those rare petitions were granted, as was appropriate, for students in fields requiring long periods of field work or the mastery of many languages.[10]

The spread of guaranteed multiyear funding has no doubt been successful in enabling universities to recruit the students they want. However, many leading public universities and some less well-endowed private ones could not (and cannot) afford to assist all or even most of their students in this way. Even when they do, their packages often do not compete with those offered by private universities in the extent and variety of benefits they offer. This situation has had the effect of stratifying financial aid, and it could possibly have other consequences that are not yet clear. It has also made it impossible to assess the effects of funding that is awarded on the condition that students meet specified timetables. Our analysis indicates that in combination with efforts to reduce attrition, the increasing use of multiyear support packages is associated with later attrition and increased languishing.

WHO MAKES THE CHANGES?
THE CENTRALITY OF DEPARTMENTS

Many features of graduate programs that influence the progress students make are controlled by the graduate deans and provosts. Yet it would be an understatement to say that faculty members and departments not only shape graduate programs at the outset but are also responsible for their continuing character. This said, the GEI experience in general contains several not altogether consistent lessons about intervening in the cultures

[9] Several graduate deans were unenthusiastic about the introduction of multiyear packages, not only because they reduced incentives for students to progress rapidly but also because they required commitments on financial aid at the time of admission that were of a longer term than the deans thought appropriate.

[10] This is not to say that the universities always sought the Foundation's approval or did not insist on the merits of the claims of particular students.

and practices of departments and about the role of university administrators. An obvious point worth reiterating is that interventions are not
likely to be successful unless they come from and have the support of faculty members. Our analyses suggest that innovations that were initiated
by the departments were much more likely to be successful than those
that were initiated "top down."[11] The difficulty of changing the cultures
of departments and getting faculty agreement and commitment to interventions should not be underestimated. Faculty members, especially
those who are tenured, take as a matter of course that graduate education is their business; they insist on their independence, and they resist
following policies they do not endorse.

However, the importance of graduate deans and provosts cannot be
discounted. Their command over financial resources and rewards and
their capacity to monitor departmental performance make them powerful indeed. As the vignettes in Chapter 3 suggest, assistance from central
administrators can be critical in making departmental efforts work.

The GEI experience also suggests that changes in department programs require sufficient time for their elements to be established as custom and thereby become part of departmental culture. Maintaining commitment to an intervention is a central problem (as social scientists who
study change know well)—one that only becomes more pronounced
when leadership turns over and participants regularly come and go. A
major test the GEI faced in every department was identifying successive
leaders who accepted its goals and were willing to work on its behalf.

THE ROLE OF DATA AND INFORMATION

The designers of the GEI understood the need for and the potential
power of data in determining whether its intended outcomes were being
realized. As we noted, they required the participating universities to collect their own data in order to receive funding and to be involved in the
Initiative. This requirement ultimately had the second-order effect of encouraging these institutions to reform their own data-collection procedures. The GEI became an opportunity for collecting data where no previous process had existed, and it permitted these institutions—many for
the first time—to undertake inquiries about their own operations.

---

[11] Top-down interventions were often easy to identify when the goals for attrition and
TTD, plans for department design, and plans for distributing financial aid were uniform
across all departments in a particular institution. In such instances we surmised that the
dean or provost was the principal designer. Such a high level of agreement among individual faculty members across departments seemed most unlikely.

During the design phase of the GEI, when baseline data were being collected, a number of departments reported that this exercise taught them more about their students' progress than they had known before and, as a consequence, increased their willingness to consider making changes in their programs. As the GEI continued, the departmental reports often cited the data that had been gathered as an effective tool in monitoring student progress and in evaluating both student progress and departmental practices. We also know that most graduate deans have now standardized the collection of basic information about students and departments and use it as a matter of course in making decisions about departmental performance and in allocating resources. If due caution is exercised in interpreting the data, it is hard to imagine that others would not also benefit from undertaking similar studies.

This view is becoming increasingly widely shared as the CGS continues to report the findings of its PhD Completion Project. And it will surely be reinforced when the National Research Council (NRC) releases its evaluation of doctoral programs in 2009. That study—which has broader coverage of doctoral programs than any other and is based on methods of data collection and analysis vetted by the National Academy of Sciences —will include information on many aspects of the effectiveness and quality of doctoral programs, rather than relying in large part, as its antecedents did, on "reputational" measures. The NRC's evaluation is very likely to reveal departmental attributes on which information was heretofore limited or unavailable. As a result, even potential graduate students will be able to gauge the effectiveness of departments to which they are considering applying. Daniel Denecke of the CGS sums up the value of this trend:

> Traditional measures of research productivity were largely faculty-centric, referring to such things as publications, citations and research grants. Although such measures still play an important role in ratings, rankings and program review, doctoral program assessment tends to focus more on what might be called student-focused measures of research productivity: "on what students know and can do as a result of their graduate education." Objective indicators such as completion rates, attrition patterns and career outcomes are among the best overarching measures of doctoral education quality, for they reflect or refract virtually everything else that a program does to select, retain and ensure the success of its students.[12]

The larger effect of these multiple efforts in data collection and analysis is that institutions can no longer define their own outcome measures

[12] Peggy L. Maki and Nancy A. Borkowski, eds., *The Assessment of Doctoral Education* (Sterling, VA: Stylus, 2006), p. xii.

and base them on the data they happen to have at hand. In order to calculate the outcome measures that are used in this study and elsewhere, institutions must keep data on all students in each entering cohort and, at a minimum, they must record each student's entry date, date of advancement to candidacy, and date of completion or attrition. The commitment to gather such data must be long term and unswerving. Saving on collection costs by removing some students from databases or by skipping years of data collection reduces the value of the database as a whole for the purposes of measuring completion and attrition rates and comparing them at different time periods or to those of other institutions. Eventually, these data will be most useful if cooperation among institutions continues, as attempts are made to define attrition and to measure accurately and uniformly advancement to candidacy and other milestones in the graduate career.[13]

Even if the right data are collected and they are properly maintained, making use of them, especially in the humanities, offers special problems, as we noted in Chapter 2. The long TTD prevalent in many of the disciplines means that 10–12 years must elapse before 90 percent or more of the students in an entry cohort will complete their degrees or leave graduate school. As a consequence, calculating accurate completion or attrition rates requires not simply 6–7 years of data but 10–12 years of data from the time a given cohort begins graduate school. Not only does this call for committed and faithful data-collection teams, it also means that the departmental faculty or senior administrators who review the data are not likely to have been in place when a given set of students began or an intervention was introduced.[14] Although universities have long time horizons, the tenures of individual department leaders and administrators are often short.

Identifying and interpreting outcome measures in interventions like the GEI are complicated by the slow pace of change that is typical in the academy. It takes time not only for interventions to take hold but also for their consequences to become visible. Immediate evaluation of the effectiveness of interventions can be misleading or impossible. In the case of attrition, annual feedback on the post-GEI cohorts suggested that the GEI had been successful. It was not until these cohorts moved past their fifth years that it become apparent that the reductions in early attrition

[13] See Appendix C for a discussion of some of the data requirements and pitfalls associated with these outcome measures.

[14] At only three institutions was the same person responsible for data collection over the entire 17 years of the GEI. At the other 10 institutions, a total of 40 people were directly involved in providing data reports over the span of the Initiative. With so many personnel changes, constant re-education regarding definitions and formats was required.

were not being matched by equivalent increases in timely completion. Moreover, the length of time it took for the languishing effect to be uncovered and understood meant that feedback was delayed and counterproductive policies continued to be in place over an extended period.

It follows that those in charge of interventions have to think hard not only about how outcomes are measured but also about how long it takes for them to become measurable. Hard thinking is also in order about whether midcourse corrections are needed and, if they are, when and at what costs. As the GEI progressed, some departments concluded that the initial changes they had made were not having the intended effects. As one might expect, they modified the innovations they had made earlier.[15] Since the Foundation's goal was to improve doctoral education, and not to run a controlled experiment, staff encouraged departments to tinker with their program designs as they saw fit. This had the effect of curtailing the life spans of innovations whose effectiveness over the longer term could not be determined. Further problems in assessing the effectiveness of changes made by departments are traceable to turnover in the faculty and administrative leadership responsible for the GEI and a waning commitment among some faculty members to particular innovations or the program as a whole.

We have already commented on the most common and most vexing problem in calculating attrition and completion rates for entering cohorts: the ambiguity in determining when students who leave have actually left.[16] Unless institutions are diligent in defining attrition, students may remain in a database as continuing students long after they have moved to another institution or taken another career path altogether. This results in understated attrition rates or cases of attrition being recorded as occurring much later than they actually did. Thus calculations of recent attrition are more likely to be inaccurate than those for prior years.[17] For further commentary on calculating these outcome measures, see Chapter 2 and Appendix C.

[15] See Chapter 3 for several specific examples.

[16] One complication not addressed in the GEI data until the GES was conducted was cases of students transferring to other PhD programs. Individual institutions cannot hope to follow these students to determine if they eventually complete a degree, but national studies might (assuming away issues of anonymity and confidentiality). The GES found that approximately 12 percent of the cases of attrition among the GEI population resulted in the student earning a PhD at another institution (see Chapter 8).

[17] In our experience the nature of attrition reporting leads to problems when comparing earlier cohorts to more recent cohorts. For example, as of 2008 the end-of-fourth-year attrition rates for entering cohorts 1985–86 through 1990–91 will be more accurate than the attrition rates for entering cohorts 1998–99 through 2004–05, since the four-year cumulative attrition rates for the 2003–04 and 2004–05 cohorts are very likely to be underreported.

Notwithstanding these difficulties, efforts in collecting standard outcome measures have become increasingly vigorous, and great progress has been made in calculating and reporting national statistics. Although the gathering and standardization of data collection have been an ongoing challenge both for the GEI and for the doctoral education community as a whole, the benefits accruing from having comprehensive and reliable data are likely to justify the effort required, as they contribute to better-informed decisionmaking and increased accountability.

MECHANISMS OF CHANGE: WHAT WORKED?

Never intended as a tightly controlled experiment with the usual apparatus of randomly assigned treatments, the GEI presents special and vexing problems in linking changes in departmental practices with changes in students' outcomes. Even establishing whether a practice has actually been introduced is itself problematic, entirely apart from identifying its effects and how they came about. Such a detailed inquiry into presumed causes and effects would seem to be important if effective interventions are to be identified and replicated. Although it may seem that associating changed practices with desirable outcomes would have been simple, it was not. Because it proved so surprisingly difficult to make such connections, we describe some of those difficulties, so that others may avoid our missteps.

Let us begin with the assumption that an intervention of interest (for example, clarifying students' expectations about how long it should take them to get the doctoral degree) has been identified. The first step is to determine which departments implemented the intervention and maintained it for a significant period of time. The second step is to ascertain whether changes in outcomes are associated with those departments that implemented the specific intervention. In this way, it is possible to establish whether there is a connection between the intervention and the outcome.

Chapter 3, which is focused on the departments and their responses to the GEI, takes note of the problems of identifying interventions ("innovations") and classifying them so that particular departments can be characterized as having adopted a certain class of innovation while others did not. It also touches on the separate problem of how long departments kept specific innovations in place and on the difficulty of controlling for attributes of the larger contexts or environments within which departments operate, which could themselves affect the outcomes of interest. Such attributes could include practices specific to universities and to graduate schools (rules, for example, concerning the length of time students may receive financial support) as well as to the broader milieu: strength of the job market, pressure on institutions to reduce costs, and aspects of cultures in specific fields, such as the significance accorded to publishing before graduation. All of these variables need to be taken into account in efforts to identify "what worked." Their importance must be acknowledged if efforts to redesign graduate programs are to improve.

In Chapter 6, the association of specific programmatic practices in departments and changes in students' outcomes was probed at length. There a decision was made on how to determine whether the practices of interest were actually in place, that is, whether department reports were reliable indicators. We decided that what students said in their responses to the GES about departmental policies, requirements, and cultures was preferable to accepting without question what departments said they did. This decision was based on the lack of clarity in department reports about what departments actually did (see Chapter 3). It did not derive from doubts about the veracity or reliability of those reports.

The decision to use survey responses was based on the assumption that if a department had been successful in implementing a particular practice, the students would recognize it and report it as part of their experience. This assumption may be faulty in that students need not have been aware of a practice in order to have been influenced by it. At the same time, the GEI had strongly emphasized clarifying students' awareness of departmental expectations, program rationales, and financial incentives. It seemed reasonable, therefore, to rely on students' awareness that a policy was in place instead of relying exclusively on departmental reports that a policy had been instituted. This also seemed to be a way of dealing with the related issue of how long a policy remained in place when the department reports did not cover this question.

In order to explore further which mechanisms—that is, which specific actions or practices—produced a given outcome, we did a detailed analysis of both departmental reports and students' responses to the GES (which, it will be recalled, was conducted in part to determine whether and how students experienced the changes their departments had made). Table 11.1 examines student responses to selected survey questions about classes of innovations; responses of students in "innovating" departments are compared to responses of those in "non-innovating" departments. This comparison would permit us to determine whether what the departments said they did was mirrored in students' own experiences.[18] In depart-

[18] Innovations are described in column 1, and their classification is listed in column 2. The number of departments that reported having made the innovation (innovating departments) is listed in column 3. The specific survey question relevant to each innovation is indicated in column 4. Column 5 reports the difference (from the pre- to the post-GEI period) in the percentage of students from innovating departments whose responses were

ments that reported having made a given change, we expected that the share of students testifying to its presence would be larger than the share in departments that did not report making the same change.

In preparing Table 11.1 and the analysis underlying it, we originally assumed that very few students in both sets of departments during the period before the GEI was instituted would say that any of the innovations existed in their departments, since the new ways of doing things were not yet in place. However, this assumption was proved faulty by a complication that was specific to the design of the GEI and that we hope would not pose a problem for other efforts. Since the GEI and its data collection had focused on *change,* the departments were classified as having made changes or not. The classification scheme ignored the fact that some departments had already put a particular program element into place before the GEI and thus did not report it as part of the GEI. Thus some number of non-innovating departments in fact had certain innovating practices already in place, thereby confusing (or at least blurring) the analysis of outcomes achieved in innovating and non-innovating departments.

For example, instead of asking "Is the prospectus required for advancement to candidacy?" we asked "Has the department changed/added the requirement of prospectus for advancement to candidacy?" By contrast, students' reports in the GES described practices that were present, not those that had changed. The obvious lesson to be drawn here is that collecting data on the *status ante quo* needs as much careful attention as collecting data on the extent and nature of change once an intervention has been made.

Given this feature of the data collection, in Table 11.1 we compare innovating and non-innovating departments in terms of the change over time in student perceptions, from the period before the GEI was in place to the period during which the GEI was in place.[19] Table 11.1 presents

---

consistent with the characterization of the innovation. Similarly, column 6 reports the difference (from the pre- to the post-GEI period) in the percentage of students from non-innovating departments who described their department as having the characteristic of interest. The more dissimilar are the differences reported by the students in innovating and non-innovating departments (comparing columns 5 and 6 in any given row), the more students were aware of the innovations the departments said they had made, whereas the more similar are the differences reported, the less students were aware of their departments having introduced such innovations.

[19] Thus the difference shown in Table 11.1 is not a percent change, but rather the percentage-point difference between the percents reported in the two time periods. For example, if 10 percent of the students in the pre-GEI time period reported that they expected to complete their degree in eight years and 40 percent of the students in the post-GEI cohorts reported that they expected to complete their degree in eight years, the difference would be 30 percentage points.

TABLE 11.1

Differences between Pre-GEI and Post-GEI Student Perceptions of Intended Innovations in Innovating and Non-Innovating Departments

Intended Innovation Reported by Department (1)	Broad Category of Innovation (2)	Number of Innovating Departments (3)	Survey Question Asked (4)	Difference in Percent of Affirming Responses from Pre- to Post-GEI Period (percentage points)	
				Innovating Departments (5)	Non-Innovating Departments (6)
1 Clarify TTD expectations	Expectations	17	When you began how long did you expect to take? (8 years or less) [A4]	8.1	7.7
2 Clarify TTD expectations	Expectations	13	Were you informed in writing regarding expectations concerning TTD? [A11f]	17.3	13.3
3 Offer workshops to prepare prospectus	Groups and workshops	15	Did the department expect you to attend a course to help prepare the prospectus? [A9b]	17.2	–6.1
4 Offer workshops to reduce isolation	Groups and workshops	12	How often did you attend seminars or brown bags? [B4a]	–3.2	–3.5
5 Change prelim structure to lead into research	Curricular changes	28	Did the department expect you to have portions of your prelims tailored to your specific dissertation research interest? [A9d]	8.8	11.7

6	Modify policy regarding incompletes	Curricular changes	12	Were you informed in writing of the policy regarding incompletes? [A11b]	3.8	3.9
7	Improve advising	Advising	19	Poor academic advising slowed me a great deal. [B9d]	0.5	-4.0
8	Require schedule of advising	Advising	24	During coursework did you have formal review with your advisor or other faculty member? [A14c]	11.2	2.1
9	Add placement advisor	Advising	13	How useful was advising for finding a job? (percent very useful) [B3d]	11.9	6.3
10	Require summer prospectus-writing workshop	Summer tasks	20	Did your department expect you to take a summer course or workshop to prepare a dissertation proposal? [A10.1b]	22.6	0.3

some interesting and somewhat unexpected findings. We found that students recognized some innovations reported by the departments but did not recognize others. The first row in Table 11.1 lists the clarification of expectations about TTD, a class of changes that (as we know from the analysis in Chapter 6) is highly correlated with increased completion rates. Did programmatic changes associated with the GEI and aimed at this objective lead to clearer expectations? Comparison of columns 5 and 6 shows virtually no difference between the change over time in students' responses in departments that said they had introduced innovations to clarify expectations about TTD and the corresponding change in departments that had not made this a priority. The percentage of students in innovating departments who said that they expected it would take them eight years or fewer increased by 8.1 percentage points, whereas in non-innovating departments it increased 7.7 percentage points. Since this question might not reflect the nature of the innovation departments introduced, we turned to responses to the more precise question, "Were you informed in writing about expectations concerning TTD?" (see row 2). However, even this more precise question does not elicit much greater change in awareness on the part of students who were studying in innovating departments (17.3 percentage points) as compared to the change in non-innovating departments (13.3 percentage points).

Departments' reports that they undertook a broadly defined effort to clarify expectations had only modest correlation to the change in students' perceptions once the GEI was in place. Several explanations might account for this finding: the innovating departments might have intended to clarify expectations but failed to do so; the departments that did not report having made this innovation might have actually changed their programs in ways that clarified expectations; the rising concern about long TTD was experienced by students in all departments, and they adjusted their expectations consistent with that concern; or the survey questions still did not really capture the pervasiveness of concern, since they dealt with more specific matters and not the broad innovation.

By way of contrast, row 3 shows just the kind of dissimilarity we expected to find. In this instance, the share of students who said that they were required to attend a course that would help them prepare their prospectuses moved in opposite directions over time in innovating compared to non-innovating departments. In innovating departments that reported having workshops with the specific purpose of helping students in writing the prospectus, this percentage increased by 17 percentage points, which suggests that these departments were in fact requiring such courses and that students were aware of this. In non-innovating departments, by contrast, this percentage decreased by 6 percentage points. However, students' responses to the introduction of workshops in general, with the less-specific objective of "reducing isolation" (row 4), are consistent with a hypothesis that innovations must attain a level of specificity and precision to be noticed. Reductions over time in the percentage of students in innovating and non-innovating departments who reported having attended department seminars or brown bags were similar not only in extent but also in direction.

Responses to the cluster of questions regarding student advising further support the idea that it is those innovations which involve specific practices, objectives, and even timing that capture students' attention, whereas those innovations that are defined broadly, such as clarifying students' expectations about TTD, are less likely to be recognized and noted. It would appear that when the departments report putting a specific practice or mechanism into place, students are more likely to be aware of it and to respond to inquiries about it.

With respect to improving advising, students who studied in departments that reported having improved advising were no more likely to say that advising in general had improved after the GEI than students in departments that had not explicitly mentioned improving advising (see row 7). However, when asked specific questions about whether they had regularly scheduled advising (row 8) or asked to rank the usefulness of the advising for finding a job (row 9), students in innovating departments (those that listed the specific innovations of implementing a formal schedule for advising or adding a placement advisor) showed a much greater change in pre-post perceptions than those in non-innovating departments.

As a final example of the benefit to narrowly defining departmental innovations, we look at an innovation that elicited the largest differences between students' responses in innovating and non-innovating departments among all of our comparisons. Introducing the expectation that students participate in a summer workshop to prepare their prospectuses (see row 10) is a very specific innovation, one indicating both purpose and timing. The change over time in student responses was much greater in innovating departments (an increase of 22.6 percentage points) than in non-innovating departments (an increase of just 0.3 percentage points).

Thus, the use of specific questions and narrowly defined innovations makes it easier to connect an innovation to students' perceptions that it had been made. The point here is that one must be as precise as possible in research on the usefulness of particular interventions. We do not claim that precise innovations are more likely to achieve a given end. Rather, if it is necessary in order to determine whether an innovation "worked" that the individuals (here, students) who are the subjects of that innovation are aware of it so as to be able to answer questions about it, then questions and the innovation itself have to be quite precise for this to occur.

Viewing the survey data through the lens of Table 11.1 has another disconcerting effect: in many cases what departments said they intended to do is not highly correlated with students' reports of their experiences. This raises intriguing questions about why the correlations between the two are not higher. Without taking on questions of social perception, we can say that analysis of the findings in Table 11.1 points to the need to revise methods of research in the future to enable interventions and outcomes to be linked more precisely.[20] Methods to improve such linkages might include defining the innovations so that they state some specific mechanism by which change is to be produced; identifying innovating and non-innovating departments according to whether practices are actually in place rather than their being newly introduced; and taking great care in the phrasing of survey questions so that they closely describe the nature of the intended changes and thereby evoke a relevant response.

Had we anticipated having to determine whether a change had occurred, and when and in what form, by comparing what the departments said they had done and what the students said had happened, the survey

[20] Getting a good fit between innovations departments said they had made and the relevant survey question can be a challenge. A good example is the innovation classified as a "change in the nature of the advancement to candidacy." Departments reported making a wide range of changes, including altering the format of exams, changing coverage of material, combining preparation with papers, and offering preparation seminars. One of the changes often cited was an attempt to have the topics of the prelim reflect and lead into the dissertation research. Departments that made any of these types of changes were all categorized as having made a "change in the nature of advancement to candidacy." The survey question reported in row 5 of Table 11.1 (A9d) asks "Have portions of your qualifying exam been tailored, at least in part, to your specific dissertation research interests?" We expected students in departments that had made this particular change to say "yes" whereas students in that department prior to 1991 would say "no." But since we do not see the expected dissimilarity in columns 5 and 6 of row 5, it may be useful to look at how changes were measured. First, many departments were included in this category of innovation because they made some other change, say from a written to an oral format, in their requirements for advancement to candidacy, but did not make an effort to tailor the exam. Second, some students who began their PhD programs before 1991 (perhaps in 1989 or 1990) might be affected by the new format or tailoring of the prelim exam that would take place in their second or third year in the program (1991 or 1992). They would probably say "yes" even though they officially entered during the pre-GEI period.

Another example of a question that did not match the intended innovation appears in row 6. It asks if the student had been informed in writing about the policy regarding incompletes. The innovation itself usually included better enforcement of an existing policy or a change in that policy, but not necessarily in how the student was informed—thus the phrase "informed in writing" was unlikely to capture the student's experience of the change. We also note that adding a placement advisor is not the same thing as finding an advisor who is very useful in the job search.

questions could have been crafted so that answers to them were more precise. Such are the problems of identifying the mechanisms by which outcomes occur and using sample surveys, however assiduously they are pretested. They are part and parcel of doing research that was not—and indeed could not have been—carried out according to the rules of strictly controlled experiments, in which "treatments" are part of the design and thus are not only clearly identified but also known to have occurred.

RECOMMENDATIONS
Identifying and Measuring Objectives

Redesigns of programs require objectives to be defined and operational objectives to be specified. Ideally, the objectives should reflect the views of the relevant participants, though this may not always prove to be feasible. They should also be unambiguous and sufficiently realistic with regard to the participants' circumstances that there is a real possibility that they can be achieved. Lest this point seem obvious, it was quite clear that departments that began the GEI with a majority of students taking 10 or more years to earn their degrees and that stated that they intended to reach within a few years a mean TTD of 6 years did not consider how many students would have to finish very, very quickly to reduce their current mean TTD. Failure and disappointment are inevitable in these cases. Care should be exercised in selecting outcome measures so that they accurately reflect the real objectives of an enterprise. It is well known that instituting measures of performance has a way of shaping what actors do in response to them.

Faculty Members and Departments Are Central

In retrospect, understanding the outcomes of the GEI and how they came about would have benefited greatly from knowing more about the views of the faculty members charged with its implementation. This is the case despite the annual reports to the Foundation from department chairs and directors of graduate study. They generously answered questions, often in some detail, about how the GEI was proceeding, met with Foundation staff on site visits, and attended three conferences focused on the GEI.

When the decision was made to survey the students, some consideration was given to surveying faculty members as well. This proposal was put aside based on its likely cost, the time it would require, and the fact that the funds a major survey would have consumed could be better used, for

example, in endowing graduate fellowships and other program enhance-
ments. We know that some faculty members were deeply committed to
the objectives of the GEI, and they were convinced that their students
would fare better if programs were reorganized and if financial support
were increased. We do not know whether this was true of the majority or
whether they had other views about how to educate scholars. One central
question concerning faculty members is how firmly they supported the
objective of reducing TTD, and whether that support varied among disciplines and universities. Knowing more than we do would have added
much to understanding the outcomes of the redesigns.

There are a set of concrete questions about the behavior of faculty
members that might affect attrition and TTD, and in turn the outcomes
of the GEI. Knowing whether departments had instituted annual assessments of the work and prospects of each student would have added to an
understanding of rates of early and late attrition. Knowing more than we
did about dissertation advising and how often it occurred (and about vari-
ations among faculty members in their approach to it), how vigorously
departments and deans monitored advising, and whether attention was
paid to the time it took for the advisees of particular faculty members to
earn their degrees would have made the analysis of "mechanisms" more
productive.

And finally, our understanding of practices influencing TTD would
have been improved by getting a better fix on faculty involvement in
placement. In the period during which the GEI ran, departments and faculty members in many universities became far more active in placing students in jobs than they had been (in part because of the difficult job market students were confronting, but also because administrators were now
paying attention). But we do not know how much departments and faculty advisors actually did in practical terms in placing students and how
this affected completion rates and TTD.

Answers to some, but not all, of these questions could be inferred from
analyzing students' responses to the GES. However, direct and first-order
information from faculty members would have been preferable and
would have illuminated those instances in which students' responses and
reports from departmental chairs or directors of graduate study did not
mesh.

Keeping Track of Basic Information on Students and Departments

Even in the absence of an intervention, departments need reliable,
timely, and reasonably comprehensive information in order to monitor
their students' progress rather than depending on the often incomplete

impressions of faculty members. This includes information on students long gone and out of sight as well as those currently at hand. Similarly, senior administrators have their own needs for systematically collected data on students, faculty members, and departments; they too must rely on regular data-collection efforts. Such efforts are not cost-free, and they require a degree of expertise and (as we noted) commitment on the part of those charged with them. The GEI experience demonstrates that highly competent institutional researchers exist at a number of institutions and can provide timely standardized reports for all students of whatever entry cohort. In addition to the kinds of data the GEI collected on students' progress, detailed information on the demands of the teaching and research assistantships each student holds (how many hours per week, courses per term, and number of preparations required) should be part of students' records.[21] The staffs of individual departments do not usually have the wherewithal or time to take on this important chore.

The GES proved invaluable in providing detailed information about how doctoral programs looked from the perspective of graduate students. It showed that retrospective surveys of current and former students could be done, could achieve sufficiently high response rates, and could provide a useful corrective to the rosy pictures of graduate education maintained by some faculty members. Our analyses persuade us that survey data such as those the GES collected can be used to identify aspects of programs that influence probabilities of attrition and completion. At the same time, surveys of students—and faculty—are very expensive to do well; their costs would have to be carefully estimated and balanced against other investments graduate schools might make. Even so, it might make sense for universities or their representative groups, such as the CGS, to identify basic data that would be useful, how they are to be collected, and the basic measures to be used, so that these tasks do not have to be reinvented each time a department or university decides to collect information.

In retrospect, the GEI would have benefited from having included descriptive statistics regarding faculty behavior, incentives, and attributes. Senior administrators have access to several pieces of information on faculty, including the number of faculty members assigned to departments, turnover rates, data on department leadership and its continuity, the number of dissertations each faculty member has directed each year, and whether incentives are in place for faculty members to encourage timely completion by their students.[22] New policies at Harvard University suggest

[21] The maximum demands of assistantships are usually subject to university regulation but do not generally appear in individual students' or departmental records.

[22] Having attempted to collect data on the size of the participating GEI departments, we know that departmental membership is a far-from-precise indicator of departmental

that incentives may be needed for faculty as well as for students: "A series of new policies in the humanities and the social sciences at Harvard University are premised on the idea that professors need the ticking clock, too. For the last two years, the university has announced that for every five graduate students in years eight or higher of a PhD program, the department would lose one admissions slot for a new doctoral student."[23]

Information on students is increasingly more plentiful, but as we have repeatedly observed, it would be highly desirable to have complete information on students' financial support, including awards won from extramural sources. Ideally, better information about all sources of support on which students could draw would clarify the effects of financial aid on their progress. However, seeking information on students' earnings and the funds they receive from their families and others may be considered a violation of privacy and thus should be avoided. Information on the fellowships and other awards they have won is less sensitive, especially if these awards are in any way public knowledge. It may be that universities are well along in assembling complete information of this kind. It was not available when the GEI was put into place.

Finally, this study on educating scholars, rich as it is in information about the progress of graduate students though their studies, lacks direct evidence on the fundamentally important but mostly ineffable essentials of graduate education: the quality and breadth of the curricula students are offered, the stimulation their peers provide, their exposure to the scholarship and teaching of first-rate faculty members, the intellectual resources research universities provide, and the level of scholarship demanded of them from the time of their arrival until they get their degrees. These aspects of graduate education call for perceptive and nuanced qualitative inquiry by expert observers—an avenue of investigation that, given the scale of the GEI and its long duration, would have strained even its ample resources.[24]

---

responsibility. The growing interest in multidisciplinary activities makes such counts ever more difficult.

[23] Scott Jaschik, "How to Cut Ph.D. Time to Degree," *Inside Higher Ed*, December 17, 2007.

[24] One effort along this line is the exploration of graduate education as a means of developing students to serve as "stewards of the discipline." Golde and Walker (2006) contains essays by a group of distinguished scholars in the humanities on the substance of graduate education as they would like to it to be. These scholars include Joyce Appleby, Thomas Bender, and William Cronon on history; Gerald Graff and Andrea Lunsford on English; and Catherine Stimson on the humanities generally. The volume also contains papers on the sciences (by Yehuda Elkana), neuroscience (Steven E. Hyman), chemistry (Ronald Breslow), and mathematics (Hyman Bass).

Unforeseen Events and Unintended Consequences

Unforeseen developments and unintended consequences must be anticipated in general even if their details cannot be known. They are endemic to all efforts to change social arrangements and often interfere with their realization—and the GEI was no exception. Consider one example of an unforeseen development and another of an unanticipated consequence. The framers of the GEI did not foresee how strongly the behavior of students and their advisors would be influenced by their readings of the job market, or that they would conclude that the costs of completion were higher than those of delaying the degree.

The probable role played by guaranteed financial-aid packages in delaying attrition is a classic example of the unanticipated consequences of purposive action.[25] Largely intended to attract students to study at particular universities, guaranteed financial aid was not introduced to reduce attrition, although it was certainly not at odds with that goal. Improved aid, after all, would help students remain in school more effectively than year-by-year assistance. However, there is no evidence that anyone guessed that guaranteed packages would not prevent attrition but only delay it. Knowing that outcomes will likely not accord with intent may be salutary, but it is unlikely that much can be done to forestall them. By definition, unforeseen developments and unanticipated consequences are most often identified in hindsight.

The Long Time Horizon in the Academy: Outcomes Develop Slowly

In graduate education, it takes time for outcomes to develop and to become tangible. This is due in part to long time lags between interventions and their effects. Indeed, time lags in doctoral education in the humanities can run a decade or longer. Reports from various institutions that began participation in the GEI in 1991 suggest that changes that were planned initially began in fits and starts and took time to take hold. The GEI's records contain proud reports from several institutions that the "new" policies are now—16 years later—fully implemented. Others were implemented only briefly and then dropped. It follows that, like change itself, its measurement is a multistep process and needs to be of long duration, lest failures and successes remain unidentified.

[25] Robert K. Merton, "The Unanticipated Consequences of Purposive Social Action," *American Sociological Review* 1 (December 1936): 894–904.

CONCLUSION: MUCH HAS BEEN ACCOMPLISHED
AND MUCH REMAINS TO BE DONE

All told, redesigning doctoral education in the humanities has proved harder than imagined at the outset. But recognition of the need to do better has spread and expectations are changing. Most noticeably, large-scale efforts such as the evaluation of doctoral programs by the NRC and the CGS's PhD Completion Project are under way and rely substantially on major data collections, while most universities have institutionalized their own systems of data-based monitoring of students. Now that more and better data are becoming available, doctoral programs are more often being evaluated, and the capacity to share information has been greatly expanded as standardized outcome measures come into wide use. No longer is mean TTD the only measure used to evaluate the effectiveness of programs. Understanding of attrition and attrition rates and their measurement are much improved, and it is likely that administrators and faculty members (and perhaps students) will increasingly want to know the costs in time and resources associated with various programs in producing the PhD. Faculty already have more and more varied information with which they can monitor students and programs.

Students are beginning to expect departments and universities to provide them with information about the length of time it takes to get a doctorate—and also about historical completion rates, financial aid, faculty research accomplishments, and university resources—as they weigh which programs are best for them. Improved data collection and new outcome measures will make efforts to identify program characteristics that are significantly associated with improvement in doctoral education more widespread and will increase the possibility that these will be considered in future redesigns of programs. At the same time, as resources become available to accurately compare programs, competition among them, already intense, will only intensify. It is not yet clear whether further competition will, on balance, improve graduate education or work to its detriment.

CHAPTER 12

Principal Findings and Implications

AT THE END of the day—or, more precisely, after more than a decade of the Graduate Education Initiative (GEI) and the research it generated—what have we learned about graduate education in the humanities? This chapter reviews our principal findings and spells out some of their main implications.

First we review the GEI's effects on the progress students made in graduate school and the unanticipated consequences of major changes in graduate funding. These findings inevitably raise questions about the likely success of future efforts to improve graduate education and its effectiveness. Since departments were central to the GEI effort, we then sketch out significant changes they experienced as participants in the Initiative—first, in how they supported graduate students and in reducing the size of entering cohorts and, second, in the efficacy of their graduate programs. We then touch briefly on received wisdom on a number of matters pertinent to our study: for example, the role that underfunding of graduate students plays in high attrition and lengthy degree times; the degree to which teaching interferes with graduate students' academic careers; whether women fare as well in graduate school as men; whether better jobs go to students who publish while still in graduate school; whether leaving graduate school presages career failure; and finally, what effects the difficult job market had on the subsequent careers of new PhDs. In the process, we note that received wisdom with respect to these matters is at best partially true. Then we emphasize observations that—regardless of the source of the data, type of analysis, or section of the book—we think have major implications for future efforts to improve the education of scholars. We conclude with comments on the fundamental questions: Did the GEI benefit graduate education in the humanities? Was the Initiative worth the considerable effort that went into it?

THE EFFECTS OF THE GEI
ON STUDENT PROGRESS

The GEI was a complicated, evolving intervention that affected students, faculty members, administrators, departments, and graduate education in the humanities well beyond the 10 universities initially involved. Its influence was also complicated, evolving, and varied. Here we summarize its effects on students' progress toward their degrees—completion rates, attrition, and time-to-degree (TTD)—while taking account of the implications of the multiyear financial aid packages that became increasingly pervasive as the GEI proceeded.

Changes in Time-to-Degree, Attrition, and Completion Rates

The GEI was a prototype; it was intended to demonstrate that, with judicious planning and the expenditure of considerable amounts of money, it would be possible to educate a larger number of scholars in briefer periods of time while not jeopardizing the quality of the education they received. The data on hand reveal little directly about the quality of graduate education the departments provided, but the annual reports from faculty members make it clear that quality was a matter of continuing concern, that the departments were intent on maintaining the excellence of their programs, and that they served as persistent guardians of educational value.

Completion rates and TTD, though not indicators of quality, nonetheless tell much about the functioning of departments. Based on statistical analyses, we found that both metrics improved in GEI departments, but their records were only modestly better, on average, on these two main indicators of effectiveness than those of control departments. We also found that the modest average changes in outcomes concealed considerable variation among departments. Like the use of means more generally, averages can distract attention from high points and low ones. Some GEI departments improved markedly (27 departments increased their 8-year cumulative completion rates by more than 5 percentage points, and 10 departments increased them by more than 20 percentage points), whereas others did no better than they had before the GEI, and some departments even retrogressed.

Although completion rates generally improved, the average time students spent earning their PhDs fell; but the observed changes were small. Yet in a number of departments, average TTD dropped substantially. But only six departments managed to reach the hoped-for six-year norm. The variation in outcomes that we observed among departments leads us to conclude that intensive case studies of the exemplary departments and of those that did particularly poorly should be the first order of business for any further studies of the GEI and the Graduate Education Survey (GES).

Reductions in TTD were principally the result of contraction in the time students spent taking courses and passing their exams. The time students spent on dissertation research and writing barely changed after the introduction of the GEI. It appears that departments can more readily make changes that reduce the time students spend on coursework and in meeting requirements than make changes that reduce the length of the difficult and often solitary phase of the dissertation.

Attrition rates also declined on average; relatively fewer graduate students left school, especially in the early years of graduate study; but the extent of these changes was modest. However, attrition also fell among students in the early years of study in control departments, suggesting that some forces affecting attrition were at work generally, for example, that attrition had become a matter of broad concern. But this seems unlikely, since departmental reports to the Foundation suggested that reducing attrition was by no means as high a priority as reducing TTD, and it was often viewed as the consequence of problems faced by individual students rather than the overall conditions of graduate study or the departments in which those students studied.[1]

Reductions in early attrition were not matched by comparable increases in completion, as one might have assumed they would be. Instead, attrition rates increased among those remaining in graduate school five years or more. This occurred despite the GEI being explicitly aimed at "front-loading" attrition, that is, at concentrating attrition in the early years of graduate study by encouraging departments to advise students who were likely not to complete degrees to leave early, for their own benefit and for the benefit of the institution.

The modest changes we reported in TTD and the uneven impacts on completion rates, combined with the mixed effects on the timing of attrition, would seem to suggest that the GEI had little influence on the effectiveness of graduate education. This is not the case. These modest changes, when added together and adjusted for PhD production, resulted in large decreases in student-year cost (SYC), the measure we used to capture the investments departments or universities make in producing a completed PhD. SYC calculations show that thousands of student years were saved by the changes that occurred within the 11-year limit on which the computation was based.

The experience of the GEI leads us to think that increasing completion rates and reducing TTD simultaneously may be very difficult indeed. In the future, it may be necessary to think in terms of making trade-offs between the two. From the perspective of the institution, reducing the expenditure of departmental or university resources per PhD by reducing time-to-attrition and by raising completion rates may be as helpful, or more so, than focusing exclusively on shrinking TTD. We are reluctant

[1] This result is consistent with the findings of a study by the American Historical Association's Committee on Graduate Education; Bender et al. (2004), pp. 95–96.

to offer particular policy recommendations on how long a degree should take, although the 11-year time frame adopted for the SYC calculation does seem to be too long. Our data on the GEI population show that degree times briefer than eight years were associated with better academic job placement as well as reduced resource costs. There are good reasons for universities to impose deadlines beyond which doctorates will not be awarded without careful review. A doctoral degree is assumed to signify that degree recipients have mastered knowledge that is current, not 10 years old. Equally important, deadlines put a cap on the investments institutions make in any particular student, and they encourage students who find that the academic life is not what they had supposed to leave and get on with their lives.

Packages of Guaranteed Financial Aid

The reductions we observed in early attrition following the GEI coincided with increases in the number of institutions providing guaranteed multi-year packages of financial aid and in the number of students benefiting from them. Guaranteed packages were introduced by universities for two reasons: to provide students with assurances of continuing support over the course of their graduate study, and to increase departments' success in the increasingly heated competition to recruit those students deemed most promising. The funds the GEI contributed to the 10 universities may have fueled the spread of multiyear packages among other institutions, but we do not know whether this actually occurred. We are sure that the two funding regimes, guaranteed and conditional, are at odds with each other, and we have no evidence that the departments gave thought to how the two might be meshed. It appears that achieving success in the competitive market for student recruitment was accorded top priority in shaping departmental and institutional financial-aid policies, and the perceived power of guaranteed support in recruiting proved irresistible. By the end of the GEI, every one of the 10 universities had adopted multiyear packages in some form.

Judging from the testimony of many students and some faculty members, guaranteed support reduced students' anxieties about their finances, although it would not be justified to conclude that students who had such packages were well off. They were not. But freedom from worry about how next year's bills will be paid is one of the outcomes of multiyear packages. They also reduced the annual competition among students for departmental funds, thereby contributing, we were told, to more collegial relationships among them. These benefits are not unimportant, but they are unlikely to provide the incentives associated with conditional awards.

The packages appear to have three unwelcome consequences, which are worth underscoring. We do not know definitively whether the introduction of guaranteed multiyear financial aid was the cause of changes in the timing of attrition. Nor do we know whether it led to increased "languishing" (that is, remaining in graduate school while neither earning the degree nor leaving). But all three trends coincided and may have been intertwined. A plausible scenario is that students with guaranteed funding stay longer and drop out later than they would have done had they not had the promise of funds or teaching appointments to pay their keep. Some might argue that languishing is a choice students make and thus is not the business of the institution. But languishing consumes institutional and departmental resources that might be applied to achieving more constructive ends.

A second outcome of the spread of guaranteed multiyear packages is less a matter of conjecture. They require departments and institutions to place very large bets on individual students well before they arrive in graduate school, thereby making the quality of students' work in graduate school far less relevant than their earlier college records to their receiving financial aid. Moreover, the practice of awarding guaranteed multiyear packages raises the cost of selection errors and is likely to discourage taking risks in making awards to interesting applicants whose credentials may in some respects be wanting. The packages also reduce the leeway departments have in providing for students who failed to qualify for a package on admission but nonetheless do well subsequently. It is unwise to predict in advance whether the current level of competition for excellent graduate students will prevail in the future, but now that some version of guaranteed multiyear financial aid is in place in the humanities in leading institutions, it seems unlikely that it will disappear, at least in the short run.

Last, the widespread adoption of guaranteed packages has made it more difficult to determine whether targeted conditional funding is more effective than guaranteed support, much less whether some combination of guaranteed funding (for example, for the first year and for dissertation writing) and targeted conditional funding (for example, for summers and predissertation work) might prove most effective of all.

CHANGES THE GEI BROUGHT TO DEPARTMENTS

Increases in Financial Aid

Chapter 5 outlined in some detail the effects on financial aid produced by the grants associated with the GEI. Overall, it led to increases in fel-

lowship support available to students in GEI departments during the first
five years of graduate school, but a similar pattern of increases also occurred in control departments, raising questions about contamination
effects and probably moderating differences in outcomes between treatment and control departments. Important differences in funding between treatment and control departments occurred later in students'
careers. Once the GEI was instituted, larger shares of students in the treatment departments had fellowship support and tuition grants in their
fifth, sixth, and seventh years—the dissertation-writing years—than in the
control departments, just as the GEI intended. Slightly more than half
(51 percent) of students in their fifth year who studied in treatment departments had fellowships and tuition grants, and another 33 percent
held assistantships that paid a stipend and tuition. When combined, this
brought the total of students receiving support in this period of their
studies up to almost 85 percent. The proportion of students having fellowships and assistantships dropped off in the sixth year, yet a majority of
those in treatment departments continued to have one of the two most
common forms of support. Students who reached their seventh years and
thereafter were far less likely to be supported, and those who did were
more likely to have assistantships than fellowships. The same is true in the
control departments.

   As levels of financial aid increased, student outcomes improved. The
quantitative measures accord with students' testimony. Having both time
and support facilitates completion of the degree. We also know that targeted awards, such as summer support, reduced TTD and increased completion rates. (Summer support helps students fulfill program requirements, gives them the chance to assess the feasibility of dissertation
topics, and obviates the need for employment unrelated to their work.)
At the dissertation stage, having a fellowship is correlated with an increased probability of degree completion, and having a fellowship instead of an assistantship is associated with improved completion rates in
the sixth year and beyond. This finding should not be surprising, not only
because dissertation fellowships free students to work on their research
but also because such fellowships were to be awarded specifically to students who the faculty judged were likely to finish. Therefore, due to the
impossibility of controlling for all the relevant variables, we cannot say
that dissertation support is unequivocally related to dissertation completion in the following two years. The caution expressed here is a reflection
of the statistical difficulties involved in the analysis and is not intended to
suggest that dissertation fellowships do not facilitate degree completion.

   At the same time, the data also indicate that even the most generous
support (holding a fellowship for six years plus having summer support)
is associated with considerable attrition. This striking finding suggests

that financial need is not the exclusive cause of attrition and that more attention needs to be paid to attrition among students who are likely to have been considered promising and in whom major investments have been made.

Decreases in Cohort Size

As a consequence of the GEI, differences in the size of departments (measured by the size of entering cohorts) that existed among them initially were considerably reduced. This was accomplished by small reductions in average cohort size, which were driven by large-scale cutbacks by the big departments in the numbers they admitted for graduate study. These reductions permitted the departments to spread both their existing funds and those from the GEI among fewer students, as Chapter 3 indicated.

Reductions in size also made it possible for the larger departments to become more selective in recruitment and thus to raise the quality of the students they admitted, at least as quality is crudely measured by GRE scores. Having students with higher GRE verbal scores was associated with reduced attrition and higher rates of completion; thus the increase in GRE scores may in turn have contributed to observed improvements in attrition and completion.[2] Still another outcome of reductions in cohort size was (in at least six departments) the graduation of more, not fewer, PhD recipients during the GEI period—an indicator of greatly improved effectiveness.

Program Redesigns

Complicated as it is to demonstrate the effects on students' progress of better financial assistance, estimating the effects (positive and negative) of new and revised programs proved to be even more so. In Chapters 6 and 11, we described the difficulties of determining the nature, timing, and duration of program changes the departments made, whether students were aware they had occurred, and whether they responded to them.

Chapter 6 describes the use we made of factor analysis of students' responses to the GES in identifying changes that had significant effects on the probabilities of completion and attrition. Factor analysis addressed eight kinds of program changes (in addition to increasing financial aid) that were part of the GEI. None individually had large effects on proba-

[2] Higher GRE math scores were associated with higher completion rates but not lower attrition rates.

bilities of completion or attrition, but the effects of four were significant and merit reiteration: the quality of advising students received and having someone interested in their work; whether departments emphasized the importance of finishing the degree quickly; whether rules and time-tables concerning degree completion were clear; and whether students were expected to publish during graduate school.

It says much that faculty advising, including the specific advice given and students' views about its usefulness, was a significant factor in influencing the probabilities of whether students stayed and finished or left without degrees. The effect on the probability that students would complete their degrees of having a faculty member (or some other person at the university) interested in their work or of having an advisor students considered helpful before and during the dissertation was significantly positive in each and every year of study (starting in the fourth year). Conversely, the probability of leaving before completing the degree was greater among students who said their progress had been slowed by poor advising; the effect of advising on probabilities of attrition increased each year from students' first through fifth years and remained significant afterward. These are key findings. They highlight how important faculty advisors are in students' careers, for good and for ill. A skeptical observer might respond that students who leave graduate school are more likely to blame their advisors than themselves. This is no doubt true in a number of instances. But faculty members are not entirely blameless, as observers of faculty behavior know full well.

Expectations departments hold out for students about expeditious completion of the dissertation are also significantly associated with improved probabilities of finishing the degree. However, studying in a department emphasizing polishing the dissertation and publishing while in graduate school, even if both mean that graduation must be delayed, is associated with significantly higher probabilities of attrition. Apparently, the prospects of long-term polishing and publishing are daunting enough to increase probabilities of attrition even among students who were nowhere near beginning the dissertation.

Last, the clarity of departmental rules concerning requirements, incompletes, timetables, and TTD significantly affected the probabilities that students would complete their degrees. More specifically, probabilities of attrition increased when students reported that departmental rules were not clearly stated, but probabilities of completion were not significantly affected. Ambiguity apparently takes a quite specific toll.

The relatively small effects of these programmatic changes need to be assessed in light of the overall effects of the GEI. Taken together, they account for a significant share of the effects of the changes we were able to identify. Moreover, as in so many of the findings we report, the measured effects of the particular programmatic elements varied a great deal among departments. As we noted, if improvements, for example in advising, could be introduced into departments ranked in the lowest 25th percentile in terms of advising, so that they would come to resemble departments in the 75th percentile, their rates of completion should improve and their rates of attrition should decline.

Improving advising; increasing the attention students receive; clarifying expectations, rules, and regulations; and emphasizing the importance of finishing expeditiously appear to be relatively inexpensive changes to introduce, but they do consume faculty time and require departmental will to make sure they are sustained. Here the burden of improvement falls on the faculty. Making changes along these lines requires a high degree of faculty commitment.

Why the Measured Effects of the GEI Were Modest

One might ask why the average effects of the GEI on completion rates, attrition, and TTD were no stronger than those we observed. We have already called attention to the very considerable variation in these indicators among departments—variation that is concealed in the calculation of averages. In some departments, the GEI had quite strong effects of the kind that were originally contemplated.

A number of circumstances exogenous to the GEI, along with those originating in the GEI itself, muted its outcomes. The poor job market prevailing at the time the GEI began, which continued throughout its term, worked against rapid completion of the PhD. Graduate students close to finishing weighed the benefits and costs of getting the degree and were reluctant to give up assistantships that provided some income (small as it was), library access, health insurance, and (in some instances) university housing for academic jobs with what seemed to them to be poor prospects, or for no job at all. Job-market prospects may well have led students not close to finishing to be somewhat more leisurely than they might have been if good jobs had been abundant.

Another exogenous development that was likely to have dampened the impact of the GEI was its introduction at a time when the issues it addressed were becoming important in graduate education in general, not only in the participating departments. As we saw, a number of departments had already begun to introduce changes consonant with the GEI's goals when it was first put into place. Moreover, in some GEI universities, deans wanted to improve all their departments and deliberately leveled the playing field. Control departments received more financial aid, and in some instances they were encouraged to make specified programmatic changes. Furthermore, control universities reflected a growing nation-wide concern about long TTD and high attrition, and put measures into place to reduce them. These changes made the control departments more similar to the treatment departments than we assumed, potentially muted measured differences between them, and thus reduced the size of the estimated GEI effects. It would have been neither appropriate nor feasible for the Foundation to discourage these efforts. Yet it is a bit ironic that the GEI's success in focusing broader attention on high attrition and long TTD in the humanities may have undermined the prospect of gauging the true extent of its more specifically targeted effects on the participants.

There are also reasons to think that the effects of programmatic changes associated with the GEI were weakened owing to the very large number of changes that were made, that new changes were introduced midcourse and later, and that some, considered unfeasible, were quickly eliminated. It would have been helpful to have direct evidence on the duration of particular programmatic interventions. Some that were short lived might have had more decisive effects had they been in place longer.

Finally, we do not underestimate the importance of faculty ambivalence toward the goals of the GEI in moderating its effects. Some faculty members strongly questioned the importance of reducing TTD and attrition; some questioned the means by which such reductions were to be achieved (the institution of tighter timetables, for example). Skepticism about goals and means among some faculty members very likely militated against the GEI having more robust results. From the faculty's perspective, maintaining the standards of graduate training they considered important, ensuring the high quality of their students' work, and helping prepare them for the kinds of jobs after the degree that they judged desirable were paramount. Improving effectiveness was, in their view, a less pressing matter. There is also reason to think that support for the GEI was more vigorous and longer lasting in some departments than in others, and that those differences contributed to the variation we observed in the effectiveness of the GEI.

COMPLICATED OUTCOMES, PARTIAL TRUTHS, AND PARTIAL ERRORS IN RECEIVED WISDOM

Throughout this book, we have emphasized findings that bear on what might be described as received wisdom about graduate education in the humanities, graduate students, and their fates on leaving school. In this section, we highlight a sample of those that are partial truths, partial errors, and often more complicated than they first appear. These include, for example, the view that if only graduate students were better funded, low completion rates and long TTD would disappear. Similarly, do students teach so much that their progress is slowed or they decide to leave school altogether? Do women finish their degrees less often than men? Are students who fail to finish in a decade likely not to finish at all? Do students who finish their degrees quickly get better jobs than their slower classmates? Does publication while still in graduate school help new PhDs get jobs? Does failure to find a tenure-track appointment upon completing the PhD mean that securing such jobs is forever foreclosed? Do those who leave graduate school without degrees ultimately settle for low-level jobs? And finally, how bad was the job market in the humanities and what kinds of jobs did degree recipients actually get?

Insufficient Financial Aid—Was It the Prime Problem?

Graduate students in the humanities *are* poorly supported, and they are supported less well than their counterparts in the physical and biological sciences and the "hard" social sciences.[3] As we have seen, those having more generous financial aid are less likely to drop out and to finish their degrees more quickly. Improved financial aid associated with the advent of the GEI contributed importantly to the better outcomes we observed. Those who had fellowships were more likely to complete their degrees and less likely to leave school. However, since fellowships are more likely to go to students who faculty members believe are "good bets," we cannot rule out the contribution of selection effects to the better performance of fellowship recipients.[4] Summer support also matters; it enhances students' progress toward the degree. It helps them to use their summers productively, by fulfilling program requirements (such as studying for language examinations or preparing the dissertation prospectus), and to begin research more promptly. But money is evidently not the only thing that matters. Generous financial aid does not prevent attrition, nor does it necessarily preclude long TTD. Increasing both the share of students

[3] For recent evidence, see Audrey Williams Dare, "Graduate Students' Pay and Benefits Vary Widely, Survey Shows," *Chronicle of Higher Education*, December 5, 2008, p. A1. These differences derive in part from graduate students in the sciences being supported for the full year. However, the principal differences between graduate students in the humanities and those in the sciences and empirical social sciences reside in the much larger shares of those in the humanities not receiving any support at all or receiving modest support in the form of tuition remission.

[4] Such selection effects clearly operated in the selection of recipients of dissertation fellowships. GEI-supported fellowships were supposed to go to students close to finishing.

who receive financial aid and the amounts they are given is desirable, but such changes will not, by themselves, solve the problems of either attrition or long TTD.

Do Graduate Students in the Humanities Teach Too Much?

Some students in GEI departments did teach quite a bit, that is, they served as assistants for multiple semesters.[5] But, as Chapter 5 indicated, the effects of holding an assistantship are not straightforwardly negative; assisting is not detrimental for graduate students. In fact, those students who never held an assistantship were less likely to graduate than those who did.[6] In comparison with having no support, holding an assistantship is beneficial; holding one for as long as six years is associated with higher probabilities of completion and lower probabilities of attrition, although holding a fellowship is unsurprisingly more beneficial than either when it comes to reducing probabilities of attrition and increasing probabilities of completion. But holding an assistantship confers benefits that fellowship recipients do not necessarily enjoy—including the opportunities to confer with faculty members and other graduate students and relevant preparation for later teaching careers, both of which are useful for graduate students' education.

However, the majority of students do not serve as assistants for extended periods of time. Most students do their stints as assistants in their third years, and the share that do so declines steadily thereafter. However, 30 percent serve as assistants while they are doing their dissertations (years 6–8 being the modal years of completion). If holding assistantships diverts students from completing their degrees, it is likely that students are at greater risk during this period, although the chances that assistants will leave after having been in graduate school for so long are very small.

In short, the effect of holding an assistantship depends not only on how long students serve, when in their careers they do so, and in what sequence they are supported by fellowships and assistantships or receive no support at all. This account treats the bare-bones effects on students of serving as assistants. It does not address the intense engagement many teaching assistants have with their students and the effort they devote to their classes. It is not clear at this time whether such intense engagement

---

[5] As we have said, the data do not discriminate between teaching and research assistantships, but research assistantships are far less common in the humanities than teaching assistantships. Therefore, we infer that those who served as assistants were teaching assistants.

[6] This could be the result of a selection effect, that is, of assistantships being awarded preferentially to better students than to those who received no support at all.

over a number of years diverts assistants from their graduate studies. If it does, it does not register in the data at hand.

Are Women Less Likely to Complete Degrees Than Men?

An increasing share of the entering PhD cohorts in virtually all fields are women, and this is decidedly the case in the humanities—so much so that these fields are thought to be in the throes of being "feminized."[7] This demographic fact would be particularly significant if women were more likely to leave graduate school than men, if those who finish do so later than men, and especially so if some faculty members are reluctant to give women financial aid as a consequence. The evidence, as usual, is not uncomplicated. It requires some disaggregation for its meaning to be properly understood.

First, the data we report in Chapter 5 on gender-specific patterns in financial aid show that women are just as well supported as men. Furthermore, in all the fields represented in this study, attrition rates for single women are the same as those for single men. Attrition rates for women who are married at the time of entry to doctoral study do not differ substantially from those for single women. Furthermore, women who were married at the time they began graduate school, whether they had children or not, completed their degrees and did so as quickly as single men. However, men who were married when they began graduate school were less likely to leave, more likely to graduate, and graduated more quickly than single men. In short, being married at the time of beginning graduate school benefited men but provided no such benefit for women.[8] But this important finding should not detract attention from the fact that neither the probabilities of completion nor the TTD of women in our sample were adversely affected by their having children when they began graduate school.

---

[7] See Lynn Hunt, "Democratization and Decline? The Consequences of Demographic Changes in the Humanities," in Alvin B. Kernan, ed., *What's Happened to the Humanities?* (Princeton, NJ: Princeton University Press, 1997), pp. 17–31. Although the feminization of fields is thought to depress their prestige and their wages, recent data suggest that men continue to choose fields on the same grounds they always have. See Paula England, Paul Allison, Su Li, Noah Mark, Jennifer Thompson, Michelle J. Budig, and Han Sun, "Why Are Some Academic Fields Tipping toward Female? The Sex Composition of U.S. Fields of Doctoral Receipt, 1971–2002," *Sociology of Education* 80 (January 2007): 23–42.

[8] Among PhDs in the sciences, marriage confers benefits on both men and women. Contrary to intuition, married women and married men are more productive scientists than single women and single men; Cole and Zuckerman (1987). These findings have been reproduced in dozens of studies of U.S., European, and Israeli scientists, but they may not apply to graduate students.

However, we were unable to answer the critical question of whether becoming parents during graduate school slows down students' progress.
To have done so would have required far more detailed longitudinal information than we had on when children were born and who took responsibility for their care. Our data do indicate that very few graduate
students (men or women) begin graduate school with children, but, as
one would expect, the longer students remained in school, the more
likely they were to have children. Untangling the causal order of the relationship between duration of study and probabilities of childbearing
among graduate students in the humanities (that is, concluding either
that having children lengthens the time graduate students remain in
school or that remaining in school longer gives them more time to have
children) is beyond the limits of our evidence. This question deserves an
answer.[9] Our data show that married men who begin graduate school
with children have a slight edge in completing their degrees quickly over
comparable women, that is, those who were married and parents when
they began school. However, since women who are married do just as well
as men who are not, our data provide little support for thinking that gender alone is a good predictor of student outcomes.

How Likely Are Long-Term Graduate
Students to Finish Their Degrees?

How long does it take for late finishers to finish? About 25 percent of
those in our sample who completed their degrees took 10 years or more
to do so. The humanities in this sense, as in others, march not simply to
a different drummer but to a slower one as well.

That a nonnegligible fraction of graduate students take so long to finish degrees in the humanities raises real questions about the efficacy of
the system, including, for example, the numbers admitted to graduate
school, the extent and timing of financial support, and the standards
of advising that prevail (especially long past the time that students begin

[9] Mary Ann Mason, "Graduate Student Parents: The Underserved Minority," presentation to the 2006 annual meeting of the Council of Graduate Schools, December 9, 2006,
http://www.cgsnet.org/portals/0/pdf/mtg_am06Mason.pdf. Mason's data on graduate
student histories derive from a survey of University of California matriculants. She does not
report on completion rates or TTD for this group. Her studies of the effects of childbearing are for doctoral recipients in the sciences and social sciences who received tenure. In a
more comprehensive study using technically demanding methods, Xie and Shauman
(2003) report that "it is not being married per se, but being married *and* having children
that hampers women's careers" (p. 203). (However, graduate students are not included in
their analysis.) See also Xie and Shauman (1998).

their dissertations). Even though some students both in our study and in the one sponsored by the Council of Graduate Schools (CGS) complete their degrees a decade or more after beginning graduate school, these findings provide little basis for concluding that such extended degrees are desirable. Given the individual, intellectual, and institutional costs of such long periods of graduate study, adopting an "anything goes" policy does not seem justified. Rather, instituting incentives and deadlines for satisfactory progress does seem the better choice.

Do Those Who Finish Quickly Get Better Jobs?

Reducing TTD is not unambiguously consistent with graduate students' succeeding in the job market, nor is it consistent with the aspirations their faculty advisors have for them. Obtaining tenure-track jobs upon graduation, unlikely as that is in the current economic climate, remains the gold standard that faculty members in highly ranked PhD programs hold out for their students and to which many students continue to aspire. Whether the best jobs go to the fast finishers depends on the definition of "fast." Although new PhDs were more likely to receive tenure-track appointments if they finished their degrees within seven years, those who finished more quickly than that did no better in the job market. Put more precisely, more rapid degree completion (reducing it to five or six years from seven) seems not to have any noticeable effect on students' chances of obtaining tenure-track positions within three years of receiving their degrees.[10] However, those who took eight years or longer to complete their degrees (about half of the sample) were less likely to find jobs on the tenure track than their counterparts who finished more quickly.

Judging from the reports the Foundation received on the GEI and from the student questionnaires, faculty members are greatly concerned about their students' postgraduate placement as well as about maintaining the quality of dissertations. If placement of their students has high priority for faculty members, those in fields in which students generally complete their PhDs within seven years have little reason to push them to finish more quickly. Very rapid completion can lead, as one faculty member said, to "undercooked dissertations." Even so, it does not follow that staying in graduate school for more than seven years produces improved job-market outcomes.

---

[10] These findings are at odds with those reported for new PhDs in the social sciences by Maresi Nerad. See Scott Jashick, "The Impact of 'Time to Degree'," *Inside Higher Ed*, January 30, 2009. Nerad's calculations are based on the average TTD of those holding tenure-track jobs and those holding other academic jobs.

Does Publishing during Graduate School
Improve Students' Career Prospects?

Our data do not allow us to gauge the quality of contributions made by graduate students' publications—if only they did. We do know whether they published, and how much. These data indicate that having published during graduate school increases the chances that new PhDs will get tenure-track jobs. This seems obvious. However, remaining longer in school is not associated with increased probabilities of publishing. After controlling for other individual and departmental characteristics, those who completed their degrees in six years or fewer were actually more likely to have published more than those whose degrees took longer (see Table 10.3). And, as we have shown, remaining in graduate school for more than seven years is negatively related to the chance of getting a tenure-track job. Inasmuch as publication while still in graduate school is correlated with better employment prospects later on, the conclusion to draw from these data is not that degree completion should be drawn out. Rather, those faculty members and departments seeking to improve their students' chances on the job market should encourage them to get their research into print if prevailing TTD in their disciplines is reasonably brief, whereas faculty members and departments whose students take longer than seven years to earn the degree should encourage their students both to finish faster *and* to publish during graduate school—no mean feat.

Must Those Who Drop Out of Graduate
School Settle for Low-Level Jobs?

There is little disagreement that attrition rates are high in doctoral programs in the humanities. According to the institutional data the GEI collected, about half of all students earned degrees within 10 years from the departments at which they first matriculated, whereas just under a third of those who began graduate school at the same time were officially counted as having left—that is, they neither earned degrees nor were still in graduate school.[11] The CGS PhD Completion Project reports about the same attrition rates among those in graduate school for 10 years.[12]

---

[11] This leaves about a fifth still matriculated but not having earned degrees.

[12] Council of Graduate Schools, *Ph.D. Completion and Attrition: Analysis of Baseline Program Data from the Ph.D. Completion Project* (Washington, DC: Council of Graduate Schools, December 2007), Tables 4-3 (p. 17) and 4-24 (p. 40).

However, the true rate of attrition is not as high as these data indicate. The GES shows that approximately 12 percent of those reported by their institutions as having left said they had earned PhDs from a different department at the same university or from another university.[13] Thus, because attrition data are kept by institutions according to the departments in which students first matriculated, they do not show how many earned PhDs after changing departments or by transferring to another institution. Moreover, attrition data do not take into account the fact that an additional 18 percent of graduate school leavers earned postgraduate degrees in other fields, such as in law and business, and that the vast majority of the rest left with master's degrees. Only 19 percent of those who left earned no postgraduate degree at all. Attrition rates in the humanities are high, but conventional means of measuring them overstate their extent.

Many of those who left graduate school did well later on. The GES showed that 17 percent of those who left graduate school held managerial jobs, and 13 percent were judges or lawyers; the majority of the rest found jobs in education, mostly in colleges and universities. These findings may fly in the face of the stereotype of the taxi-driving all-but-dissertation graduate student. But given the talents of former graduate students in leading departments, their having achieved considerable success is not implausible. We also know from the GES that school leavers most often cited a "need for a career change" or that their "career plans had changed" as the main reasons for their having left. Few attributed their having left to financial need or to academic failure. Retrospective rationalization is bound to occur. But what former students say cannot be rejected entirely out of hand. A certain fraction of them did not find the academic life to their taste.

High attrition rates that continue to prevail are unlikely to result entirely from unrelated individual decisions and have nothing to do with the experiences students have in graduate school. High attrition should not be discounted and should concern students considering graduate school, faculty members, and institutions—all of whom have to consider how to devote their resources to greater effect. Attrition is not cost-free.

How Bad Was the Job Market and What Effects Did It Have?

Judging from the job histories of former graduate students who responded to the GES, the job market in the humanities in the 1990s and

[13] Put precisely, a larger share of students entering PhD programs ultimately receives the degree than of those who receive PhDs from the department in which they first started graduate school.

early 2000s was difficult, and the proportion of graduates who received tenure-track appointments right out of graduate school fell year by year. However, chances for tenure-track jobs were not foreclosed altogether. The probability of moving from a non-tenure-track position (held six months after the degree) to a tenure-track position in the three years that followed remained roughly constant during the period covered by our data. Almost 60 percent of the PhDs who reported being employed in full-time non-tenure-track positions six months after graduation had moved to tenure-track positions within three years.[14]

These data are encouraging insofar as they indicate that a majority of those who begin in non-tenure-track jobs eventually get tenure-track jobs; most PhDs from GEI departments did not get "locked" into non-tenure-track positions or into holding a succession of them. Yet the data are discouraging in that 40 percent remained in non-tenure-track jobs for more than three years after receipt of their PhDs. Moreover, since the PhDs in the GEI database come from leading departments, it would be unwise to generalize from their employment histories to those of PhDs in the humanities overall: they may be worse, better, or entirely different owing to the considerable segmentation of the academic job market. Patience and continuing publication would seem to be in order if a new PhD desires an academic job with tenure prospects. This no doubt seems cold comfort to new degree recipients eager to get on with their lives.

IMPLICATIONS FOR EFFORTS TO
REDESIGN THE EDUCATION OF SCHOLARS

The following observations—drawn from the preceding statistical and descriptive analyses, the institutional and survey data, and various discussions in previous chapters—are germane to redesigning graduate education in the humanities:

- Unanticipated (and often immeasurable) external forces, such as job markets and broad national trends in higher education, can undermine the success of interventions while also making it difficult to assess their outcomes.
- The apparently correct equation "Total outcomes in graduate education = Completion + Attrition" is wrong. Languishing is a significant third component—one that calls for further understanding and analysis.

[14] This is consistent with data that indicate that new graduates compete with more experienced ones for tenure-track positions and that the latter are more likely to have the publications and teaching qualifications that employers seek.

- Increasing funding does not necessarily raise rates of completion or encourage earlier completion. The motivation to finish the PhD is complicated and, in the humanities at least, is not necessarily greatly influenced by financial incentives.
- All increases in funding do not have the same impact. Targeted funding during the summer has great potential to improve both the efficiency and the quality of the education of scholars—it requires modest resources and permits students to focus on graduate study.
- The effects of the timing of funding on students' progress are not yet clear. Research is needed to identify effective sequences of funding.
- Setting overly simplistic goals for shorter or longer TTD may not be useful. Doubts persist among faculty members about the quality of doctorates in many fields of the humanities that are completed in less than five to six years. Insisting on "fast" degrees is likely to evoke resistance from faculty members, whose role in graduate education is central. The educational requirements of particular fields obviously differ, but in general our study suggests that seven years or fewer is a reasonable objective—one that is likely to maintain quality and improve effectiveness.
- Front-loading of attrition is a goal that is generally accepted but rarely accomplished. Students and institutions pay a high price for late attrition. Leavers are not failures. They often succeed in careers better suited to their interests. More often than is generally assumed, they earn PhDs elsewhere or transfer to and complete other degree programs.
- Comparing the educational outcomes of men and women is misleading. Single men and single women finish in similar times and at similar rates; single women and married women finish in similar times and at similar rates. Marriage benefits men in these respects but not women.
- Faculty and departments are central in graduate education and thus central in making improvements in the education of scholars. They determine the curriculum, do the teaching, set the standards, and administer changes. Thus, faculty agreement is an essential component of all successful interventions. Our findings on the characteristics of successful departments as well as the comments of students in the GES support this point.

THE BENEFITS OF THE GEI

Viewed with the perspective provided by the passing of almost 10 years since the conclusion of the Initiative, what long-lasting benefits accrued from the GEI? We know this: the GEI encouraged university administrators and faculty members in the treatment departments and universities to think concretely and critically about their doctoral programs in the humanities. To our minds, the greater attentiveness of departments to the organization of graduate study in the humanities is a major benefit of the Initiative. Just as important or more so are the long-term improvements in financial support the GEI brought to excellent graduate students. Both are significant and positive outcomes.

The GEI also emphasized the importance of standardizing data-collection practices across departments and universities and of using empirical data to track the progress of students and program success. It stimulated the improvement of data-collection practices across universities, with the consequence that programs are now evaluated on more uniform and perhaps more objective criteria.[15] Furthermore, TTD is no longer the only measure used to determine the effectiveness of programs, since measures of attrition and completion are better understood and more accurately gauged.

The GEI called particular attention to the sprawling nature of doctoral programs in the humanities and their often tangled requirements. It also highlighted the costs that long TTD and high rates of attrition imposed on institutions and individuals. These concerns about doctoral education in the humanities were not new when the GEI began, but the GEI accentuated them and brought them wider attention. What was new in the GEI was its insistent focus on graduate departments as the principal locus of graduate education and its emphasis on changing departmental practices as well as on increasing student support. Combining more extensive and uniform data collection with the adoption of newer outcome measures, efforts will continue to identify program changes that are likely to benefit the enterprise.

Some specific changes that the GEI instituted remain in place in the universities that benefited from it. Reductions in the numbers admitted to the largest departments remain, and vigorous efforts continue to be made to improve student funding, in part with the help of endowment support the Foundation provided when GEI funding ceased. Other changes did not stick—and for good reason. Some depended too much on individual faculty members' efforts (for example, offering dissertation seminars every summer), whereas others proved too complicated to administer over the long term. The intensification of interest in the effectiveness of graduate education in the humanities well beyond the 10 treatment universities is itself a measure of the GEI's influence. And there are

---

[15] For one recent example, see David Glenn, "Ohio State Gets Jump on Doctoral Evaluations," *Chronicle of Higher Education*, November 7, 2008, p. A1.

no signs that such interest is flagging, although the widespread pressures on universities imposed by hard economic times and shrinking endowments are likely to raise the priority of issues other than graduate education in the humanities.

Given the hard times the humanities and kindred social science fields were experiencing at the time the GEI began, and the difficulties students confronted in graduate school and afterward, the GEI's efforts to improve graduate education proved immensely encouraging. It energized many of those involved and conferred a degree of legitimacy on thinking about improving doctoral education and making changes to that end. These outcomes seem as worthwhile now as they did at the outset of the Initiative. And if the intensive critical attention doctoral programs received resulted in better and more effective graduate education, this would be the ultimate measure of success—not least because such improvements are intrinsically long-lived and have ramifying effects. The education scholars receive stays with them; its influence flows into their teaching and research and finally to the successive generations of their students. These after all are the ultimate outcomes of the educating of scholars.

Appendixes

Data Collection

INSTITUTIONAL DATABASES: INDIVIDUAL-LEVEL DATA

THE STUDENT-LEVEL DATA provided by the 13 universities consist of two parts: data collected upon students' entry into graduate school, and yearly reports of their progress. Aware at the outset that the quality of the data would depend on having clear rules for data collection and reporting, the Mellon Foundation established standardized formats for both. Each university was tasked with reporting raw data on every student registered in the relevant departments.[1] The Foundation took responsibility for making all statistical calculations to ensure that they were uniform and that reliable comparisons could be made. Each year, the Foundation transformed the data it received and provided summary tables to the universities and departments for their own use.

To preserve confidentiality, the records were provided anonymously to the Foundation. The universities assigned identification numbers to the students for the purpose of connecting their records year by year. The Foundation agreed that any publication of the data or analyses would be presented in such a way that neither individual students nor individual departments could be identified.[2]

---

[1] Additional student data were added from the records kept by the Woodrow Wilson National Fellowship Foundation on all students to whom portable Mellon Fellowships in the Humanities had been awarded. Since many of these students studied in treatment and comparison departments in the GEI and had been deemed especially promising, having such information would permit controls to be introduced for assessed student quality. However, this particular analysis has not been undertaken to date.

[2] The Foundation's requests for data were reviewed by one university's institutional review board, and the other universities subsequently accepted this agreement as binding. A separate file—which, by agreement, was accessible only to one of the authors and her assistant, as well as several staff members at Mathematica Policy Research, all of whom had completed human subjects protocol training—was later constructed that contained the names of the students and their identification numbers. This file was used to locate addresses for individuals for whom the institutions were unable to provide current addresses, so that these individuals could be included in the Graduate Education Survey (described later in this appendix).

Static Data Report: Information on Characteristics
of All Graduate Students at Time of Entry

Information on students' characteristics at the time of entering PhD programs (referred to as the Static Data Report because, presumably, this information did not change over the time while students were in graduate
school) included demographic data, information on educational backgrounds, and GRE scores, when available, as follows:

Year of entry
Date of entry
Department
University
Gender
U.S. citizenship
Race and ethnicity
Marital status upon entry (when available)
GRE verbal score
GRE math score
Undergraduate grade point average
Departmental ranking of student at admission (when available)
Bachelor's degree year
Bachelor's degree institution
Bachelor's degree field of study
Master's degree earned prior to entry (yes or no)

Status Data Report: Information on the Academic Progress and Financial
Support of Graduate Students Provided Annually by Institutions

The institutions also provided information on each student's progress
through the doctoral program and on the extent and forms of financial
support awarded each year (referred to as the Status Data Report because
it varied year by year). Students' progress was recorded by placing them
in one of four categories at the end of each year: coursework, advanced to
candidacy, completed PhD, or terminated study. If students had advanced
to candidacy or graduated, the dates for these events were reported.[3]

Data on annual financial support included the forms of support (tuition,
stipends, and compensation from teaching and research assistantships)

---

[3] We attempted to identify and collect data on an earlier milestone in a student's progress
through the program. However, the institutions did not have uniform data on any milestone
prior to advancement to candidacy. For example, most institutions did not record the date
that students completed their coursework.

allocated to each student during the academic year and the dollar amount of each form.[4] These dollar amounts were to include funds from all sources, internal and external, but in more than a few instances information on external fellowships was incomplete. In addition, treatment departments were asked to report which students received academic-year or summer fellowships from the Foundation under the GEI program and the dollar amounts of each of these awards.[5] The following elements were reported annually by the institutions:

Reporting year
Progress during the year (achieve candidacy or earn PhD)
Attrition during year (yes or no)
    Date of attrition
    Reason for attrition (if known)
Date of achieving candidacy
Date PhD granted
Fellowship support (not associated with work effort)
    Yes or no
    Dollar amount
Guaranteed multiyear package of support (yes or no)
Tuition grant (paid to student or waiver)
    Yes or no
    Dollar amount of grant
    Dollar amount of tuition due
Summer support (yes or no)
Teaching or research assistantship (yes or no)
    Number of terms (values: 1 term, more than 1 term)[6]
    Dollar amount of income from assistantship

---

[4] However, these amounts were not reported for the early years in some departments. Treatment departments were more likely to provide dollar amounts than were control departments.

[5] Treatment departments were also asked to provide placement information for the students six months and three years after they had received their PhDs. For the years prior to the start of the GEI, their responses were uneven; some institutions provided such information for over 90 percent of their graduates, whereas others were able to report on only 65–70 percent in some years. Once the GEI was under way, response rates tended to be even lower, and the comparison departments were never asked to provide this information. We have not used these data in the analyses reported here, focusing instead on the placement information that students reported in response to the Graduate Education Survey (described later in this appendix).

[6] Unfortunately, we did not collect information on the number of courses in a term or the tasks undertaken.

Primary source of support
  Internal fellowship
  External fellowship
  Teaching assistantship
  Research assistantship
  Student's own funds[7]
Mellon GEI award
  Type (summer, predissertation, or dissertation)
  Dollar amount

The Foundation assigned a central staff person, one of the co-authors of this book, to coordinate, manage, and oversee the data collection by designated data providers at each university, and to make sure that the data were submitted to the Foundation each year. In 1993, a two-day conference with Mellon staff and all of the institutional data providers was held with the objective of ensuring that the data from the institutions would be comparable. Each datum was discussed, and if its definition or reporting procedure differed among institutions, standard definitions were established and nonconforming information was adjusted. This meeting enabled Mellon staff to understand the sources of the few cases of incompatible reporting in need of modification.

As new data were uploaded into the institutional database each year, several consistency checks were done to ensure that the data were congruent with information submitted in earlier years.[8] This required cooperation from the data providers at each institution and vigilance on the part of Mellon staff.[9] That the same Mellon staff member was in charge of the database throughout the entire period of the GEI was invaluable in maintaining the consistency and quality of the data. So, too, were the efforts of the data providers. As a by-product of their efforts, many im-

---

[7] It was not possible to determine the sources of these "own funds"—some or all may have been loans or external employment.

[8] For example, if a student had been reported as completing or leaving a program in year $t-1$, no new data should have been reported for the student in year t. If a new record was reported in year t, Mellon staff contacted the data provider at the university and requested that a check be made on which year's data were accurate. Often this resulted in a revision of a prior year's record; a student who had been reported as having left the program may actually have been "on leave" and was enrolled in the program in the current year. Sometimes students who had been reported as continuing in the program in a prior year would retrospectively be reported as having left the program that year, based on the more up-to-date report.

[9] We know that the data providers spent long hours with staff at the individual departments to clarify students' actual status when the official records did not square with prior data reported.

provements in data collection and maintenance at participating graduate schools have been introduced. This consistency-checking process improved the accuracy of the database considerably.

DEPARTMENT-LEVEL DATA ON DEPARTMENTS OR PROGRAMS

The departments (or programs) provided reports on the GEI each year as well as information on financial support they received. These reports consisted of responses to questions Mellon staff posed each year in an effort to learn more about the GEI, about the departments' assessments of the descriptive data they were given, and about the general circumstances that affected their graduate students, especially the job market they confronted. In particular, Mellon staff went to considerable effort to identify all programmatic changes ("innovations") that were made and to summarize how they differed across departments. Examples of the types of innovations made in six departments that span four fields—English, history, political science, and "other humanities"—are given in Table 3.7.[10]

Financial reports on each department, usually prepared by the university administration, were made each year to show how all funds for graduate education, including the money received from the Foundation, were spent. These reports were required because the Foundation made the grants conditional on their being supplemental rather than substitutional, that is, the Foundation did not want its support to "crowd out" funds that the departments would otherwise have to spend on graduate education. These reports were also helpful in identifying the mix of financial support for which the Mellon grant funds were used.

GRADUATE EDUCATION SURVEY

The Graduate Education Survey (GES) was designed by the Foundation and conducted by Mathematica Policy Research. Between November 2002 and October 2003, 18,320 individuals who had matriculated in the treatment and control departments were surveyed. The 13,552 who responded produced a response rate of 74 percent—exceptionally high for a retrospective survey. As might be expected, the response rate was greater for individuals who had completed their PhDs (81.3 percent) than for students still enrolled in their programs (75.8 percent), which in turn was higher than the response rate for those who had left their pro-

---

[10] Per agreement with the participating departments and universities, the university names have been suppressed.

grams (62.8 percent). The low response rate for the last group was partially due to the fact that 20 percent of program leavers, many of whom had left their programs 15–20 years earlier, could not be located. For the same reason, response rates differed by entry cohort, with response rates declining the further back in time the recipients had been graduate students. The 1991–92 through 1997–98, 1986–87 through 1990–91, and 1982–83 through 1985–86 response rates were 77 percent, 74 percent, and 70 percent, respectively.

The first section of the questionnaire (see Appendix B) asked students about entering graduate school and the departments in which they studied. It included questions on the form of financial aid they were offered, their views of their department's academic expectations and requirements, and the means by which these expectations and requirements were conveyed to them. The second section asked about their interactions with faculty and fellow students (both during coursework and while working on the dissertation), the overall learning environment, and departmental culture. It also sought information about the time it took the students to complete different phases of their programs, their source of financial support during their final year in their programs, and their publications, if any, while in graduate school and during their early careers. This section provided an opportunity for students to identify the factors they believed had influenced their progress toward degree completion.

The third section asked about work experiences, including work as a teaching or research assistant as well as full- and part-time work outside of the department. The fourth section solicited information about attrition or degree completion (which permitted validation of institutional data on attrition and completion). If students had left their programs, they were asked to identify the reasons why they had left and to describe their subsequent educational experiences. A fifth section solicited demographic information, including the students' marital status and the number of children in their families during their years of graduate study. The sixth and final section focused on the respondents' employment status six months after degree completion or departure from their programs, three years afterward, and as of the survey date.

The survey data were checked by Foundation staff, as were the other databases, to ensure their accuracy. The respondents' replies about their status (whether they had received the PhD, had left graduate school, or were continuing in the program) were compared to the most recent institutional data and, in the instances in which they proved to be different, Mellon staff and the institutional representatives worked to resolve these discrepancies, in most cases satisfactorily.

Concern about the accuracy of the self-reported publications data led the sole Foundation staff member who had access to the names of survey respondents to check publications data for a sample of respondents against independent publications information obtained from Web pages and bibliographic indexes. In almost all cases the self-reported publications data were consistent with the independent information. The publications data collected in the GES were used for the entire sample in Chapters 9 and 10. This is the first effort to validate self-reported publication information we know of, and it is reassuring that it proves to be reliable.

Questionnaire for the
Graduate Education Survey

GRADUATE
EDUCATION
STUDY

(ID number, Department and School)

Sponsored by: **Conducted by:**
Andrew W. Mellon Foundation   **Mathematica Policy Research, Inc.**

IMPORTANT: PLEASE READ

This survey focuses on graduate education. Because some of you will have completed your doctoral degrees, some are still in the process of doing so, and some have left a doctoral program, not all questions pertain to everyone. We are aware that you may have enrolled in more than one doctoral program.

- **For this survey, we want you to respond to the questions based only on your experience as a student in the department indicated on the label on the front cover.**

- Since we only have the name of your PhD department and not your specific program, most references are to "your department." If applicable, in your answers, please consider your program within the department listed.

- If you were in an interdepartmental program, please answer the questions about departments referring to that interdepartmental program.

- The questions are written in the past tense. If you are still registered in the department noted on the front cover, please answer based on your experience to date.

Because not all questions will apply to everyone, you may be asked to skip certain questions.

- Follow all "SKIP" and "GO TO" instructions AFTER marking a box. If no "SKIP" or "GO TO" instructions are provided, continue to the NEXT question.

- If you are unsure about an answer, please make your best estimate.

- Participation in this survey is completely voluntary and you may skip over any questions that you do not wish to answer.

Thank you for taking the time to complete this questionnaire.

Prepared by Mathematica Policy Research, Inc.

SECTION A: ACADEMIC EXPERIENCES

A1. Thinking about the doctoral department at which you most wanted to study (your first choice), which of the following statements **best** describes your experience?

MARK ONE ONLY

1 ☐ You were accepted by and studied at your first choice

2 ☐ You applied and were accepted by your first choice, but decided to study elsewhere

3 ☐ You applied, but were not accepted by your first choice

4 ☐ You didn't apply to your first choice department

A2. At the time you were applying to graduate school, how important were each of the following factors in your choice of a doctoral program?

- *Please put a "1" next to the most important factor, a "2" next to the 2nd most important, and so on until each factor is ranked*

_____ Opportunity to work with particular faculty members

_____ Reputation of the school or department

_____ Financial support offered by the school or department

_____ Location of the school

_____ Program attributes (e.g., flexibility with courses or scheduling, no language requirements)

A3. When you **first** enrolled as a graduate student in the department indicated on the front cover, did you . . .

MARK YES OR NO FOR EACH

	Yes	No
a. Already have a Master's degree?	1 ☐	0 ☐
b. Transfer to this department from some other PhD program?	1 ☐	0 ☐
c. Receive course credit or advanced standing from this department as a result of earlier graduate work?	1 ☐	0 ☐

A4. When you **first** enrolled in the PhD department listed on the front cover, how many years did you think it would take you to complete your PhD?

MARK ONE ONLY

1 ☐ Fewer than 5 years

2 ☐ 5 to 6 years

3 ☐ 7 to 8 years

4 ☐ 9 or more years

5 ☐ Had no specific expectation

A5. When you were admitted to the PhD program in the department listed on the front cover, were you offered financial support?

- *Do not count the financial support awarded either after or outside the initial offer*

1 ☐ Yes

0 ☐ No → **SKIP TO A9 (PAGE 2)**

A6. Was the initial offer of financial support for one year or for multiple years?

1 ☐ One year → **SKIP TO A9 (PAGE 2)**

0 ☐ Multiple years

A7. Was the financial support beyond the first year **conditional** on any of the following factors . . .

MARK YES OR NO FOR EACH

	Yes	No
a. Satisfactory progress?	1 ☐	0 ☐
b. Meeting particular deadlines?	1 ☐	0 ☐
c. Something else? *(Specify)*	1 ☐	0 ☐

_____

A8. Assuming satisfactory progress, how many years of financial support were you promised in that initial offer?

NUMBER OF YEARS: |____|

A9. As part of your PhD program, did your <u>department</u> expect you to:

- *Please include informal expectations as well as formal requirements.*

	MARK YES OR NO FOR EACH		
	Yes	No	Don't Know/ Not Applicable
a. Take a course or practicum on research methods in preparation for the dissertation?	1 ☐	0 ☐	-1 ☐
b. Attend a course or seminar to help prepare the dissertation proposal?	1 ☐	0 ☐	-1 ☐
c. Attend a course or seminar on the dissertation process <u>after</u> completing the proposal?	1 ☐	0 ☐	-1 ☐
d. Have portions of your qualifying or comprehensive exam(s) tailored, at least in part, to your specific dissertation research interest?	1 ☐	0 ☐	-1 ☐
e. Complete your dissertation proposal or prospectus as part of the qualifying or comprehensive exam?	1 ☐	0 ☐	-1 ☐
f. Present your dissertation work-in-progress to other students?	1 ☐	0 ☐	-1 ☐

A10. Listed below are some tasks that departments may expect students to accomplish during the summer. Indicate in column A10.1 if each of the following were expected of you. In column A10.2 (regardless of department expectations), please indicate if you did this. In column A10.3, indicate whether you received summer funding for this activity.

	A10.1 Summer Expectation?			A10.2 Did you do this?			A10.3 Did you get summer funding for this?	
	Yes	No	Don't Know	Yes	No	Not At This Stage Yet	Yes	No
a. Attend a summer course or seminar on preparing for qualifying or comprehensive exams	1 ☐	0 ☐	-1 ☐	1 ☐	0 ☐	-4 ☐	1 ☐	0 ☐
b. Take a summer workshop or course to prepare a dissertation proposal	1 ☐	0 ☐	-1 ☐	1 ☐	0 ☐	-4 ☐	1 ☐	0 ☐
c. Do field work, travel, or archival research prior to dissertation stage	1 ☐	0 ☐	-1 ☐	1 ☐	0 ☐	-4 ☐	1 ☐	0 ☐
d. Prepare for language exams	1 ☐	0 ☐	-1 ☐	1 ☐	0 ☐	-4 ☐	1 ☐	0 ☐

A11. Please indicate if you were informed <u>in writing</u> about each of the following, and if so, by whom.

	A11.1 Informed In Writing		A11.2 By Whom		
	No	Yes	Department	University	Don't Know
a. Course requirements	0 ☐	1 ☐ →	1 ☐	2 ☐	-1 ☐
b. Policies regarding incompletes	0 ☐	1 ☐ →	1 ☐	2 ☐	-1 ☐
c. Definition of satisfactory progress	0 ☐	1 ☐ →	1 ☐	2 ☐	-1 ☐
d. Deadlines for completing coursework and exams (e.g., advancement to candidacy)	0 ☐	1 ☐ →	1 ☐	2 ☐	-1 ☐
e. Department or university goals to increase PhD completion rates	0 ☐	1 ☐ →	1 ☐	2 ☐	-1 ☐
f. Departmental expectations concerning length of time to complete the PhD	0 ☐	1 ☐ →	1 ☐	2 ☐	-1 ☐

A12. When you <u>first</u> began your doctoral program at the department listed on the cover, was there a university or graduate school policy regarding the <u>maximum amount of time</u>, without any extensions, in which students were expected to complete the PhD?

MARK ONE ONLY

- 1 ☐ Yes
- 0 ☐ No
- -1 ☐ Don't know → SKIP TO A14

A13. What was the maximum number of years the university allowed for completing a PhD?

- • *Do not include any extensions*

MARK ONE ONLY

- 1 ☐ Less than 5 years
- 2 ☐ 5 to 6 years
- 3 ☐ 7 to 8 years
- 4 ☐ 9 or more years
- -1 ☐ Don't know

A14. Please indicate <u>how</u> your department evaluated your progress during the following stages.

- • *If you have reached or completed the dissertation stage: Mark "yes" or "no" for each item in both the "Coursework and Exams" column and the "Dissertation" column*
- • *If you have not reached the dissertation stage:* ☐ *Mark here, then ONLY mark "yes" or "no" to each item in the "Coursework and Exams" column. After completing "Coursework and Exams" column,* SKIP to A16
- • *If you don't know if an item was used to evaluate progress, mark the don't know (DK) column*

	Coursework and Exams			Dissertation		
	Yes	No	DK	Yes	No	DK
a. Letter grades	1☐	0☐	-1☐	1☐	0☐	-1☐
b. Written assessments (other than letter grades)	1☐	0☐	-1☐	1☐	0☐	-1☐
c. Formal review with advisor or other faculty member	1☐	0☐	-1☐	1☐	0☐	-1☐
d. Formal faculty committee review to determine progress	1☐	0☐	-1☐	1☐	0☐	-1☐
e. Other *(Specify)*	1☐	0☐	-1☐	1☐	0☐	-1☐

A15. Which of the following statements best characterized your <u>dissertation advisor's</u> attitude towards finishing the dissertation?

MARK ONE ONLY

- 1 ☐ Finish as quickly as possible
- 2 ☐ Polish the dissertation, even if it delayed completing the degree
- 3 ☐ Publish, even if it delayed completing the degree
- 4 ☐ Advisor didn't indicate a preference
- 5 ☐ Did not have advisor

A16. Which of the following statements best characterized your <u>department's</u> attitude towards finishing the dissertation?

MARK ONE ONLY

- 1 ☐ Finish as quickly as possible
- 2 ☐ Polish the dissertation, even if it delayed completing the degree
- 3 ☐ Publish, even if it delayed completing the degree
- 4 ☐ Department didn't have a preference or preferences were inconsistent

A17. How <u>well</u> did your doctoral program prepare you for each of the following:

- • *A "5" means the program prepared you very well and a "1" means the program did not prepare you well at all. You may use any number from 5 to 1*
- • *If you are unable to rate or if an item doesn't apply to you or your program, please mark the don't know, not applicable (DK/NA) column*

	Very Well				Not at All Well	DK/NA
	5	4	3	2	1	
a. Teaching at the collegiate level	5☐	4☐	3☐	2☐	1☐	-1☐
b. Conducting research	5☐	4☐	3☐	2☐	1☐	-1☐
c. Publishing research in academic books or peer-reviewed journals	5☐	4☐	3☐	2☐	1☐	-1☐
d. Applying for research grants	5☐	4☐	3☐	2☐	1☐	-1☐
e. Presenting papers at professional conferences	5☐	4☐	3☐	2☐	1☐	-1☐

SECTION B: ADVISING AND DEPARTMENTAL CULTURE

In this section, please think only about the department listed on the front cover.

B1. While you were completing your coursework and exam requirements, did any faculty members or department administrators take a <u>special interest</u> in your work—that is, was there someone you could turn to for academic advice, support or encouragement?

- ₁ ☐ Yes
- ₀ ☐ No → **SKIP TO B3**

B2. Who took a special interest in your work while you were completing your coursework and exam requirements?

MARK ALL THAT APPLY

- ₁ ☐ Eventual dissertation advisor or sponsor
- ₂ ☐ Assigned faculty member other than dissertation advisor
- ₃ ☐ Other faculty member
- ₄ ☐ Department administrator/secretary
- ₅ ☐ Someone else

B3. In general, how useful was the advising you received in each of the following areas?

	MARK ONE FOR EACH				
	Very Useful	Some-what Useful	Not Useful	Not Advised	Have Not Reached This Stage/ Not Applicable
a. Developing your dissertation prospectus/ proposal	₁ ☐	₂ ☐	₃ ☐	₄ ☐	-4 ☐
b. Researching and writing your dissertation	₁ ☐	₂ ☐	₃ ☐	₄ ☐	-4 ☐
c. Obtaining dissertation grants	₁ ☐	₂ ☐	₃ ☐	₄ ☐	-4 ☐
d. Obtaining an academic job	₁ ☐	₂ ☐	₃ ☐	₄ ☐	-4 ☐
e. Obtaining a non-academic job	₁ ☐	₂ ☐	₃ ☐	₄ ☐	-4 ☐

B4. While you were enrolled in the department listed on the front cover, how often did you . . .

	MARK ONE FOR EACH				
	Often	Some-times	Rarely	Never	Not Available
a. Attend optional seminars, workshops or brown bags for students and faculty?	₁ ☐	₂ ☐	₃ ☐	₄ ☐	₅ ☐
b. Make use of department space for work (e.g., office space or lab space)?	₁ ☐	₂ ☐	₃ ☐	₄ ☐	₅ ☐
c. Meet socially with faculty members at department functions?	₁ ☐	₂ ☐	₃ ☐	₄ ☐	₅ ☐

B5. After a dissertation proposal was approved, did your department offer special workshops, seminars, or brown bags on dissertation writing or related topics?

- ₁ ☐ Yes
- ₀ ☐ No ┐
- -1 ☐ Don't know ┘ → **SKIP TO B8 (PAGE 5)**

B6. Were students <u>required</u> to . . .

	MARK YES OR NO FOR EACH		
	Yes	No	Don't Know
a. Attend such workshops?	₁ ☐	₀ ☐	-1 ☐
b. Present their work at these workshops?	₁ ☐	₀ ☐	-1 ☐

B7. Was financial support conditional on attending these workshops?

- ₁ ☐ Yes
- ₀ ☐ No
- -1 ☐ Don't know

B8. To what extent do you agree or disagree with the following statements?

	MARK ONE FOR EACH				
	Strongly Agree	Somewhat Agree	Neither Agree Nor Disagree	Somewhat Disagree	Strongly Disagree
a. There was a sense of solidarity among students within the department......................	1 ☐	2 ☐	3 ☐	4 ☐	5 ☐
b. The department fostered competitiveness among students	1 ☐	2 ☐	3 ☐	4 ☐	5 ☐
c. Faculty facilitated student involvement in the intellectual life of the department	1 ☐	2 ☐	3 ☐	4 ☐	5 ☐
d. There was a lack of personal involvement and support among faculty, students and the department...	1 ☐	2 ☐	3 ☐	4 ☐	5 ☐

B9. Thinking about the doctoral program at the department listed on the front cover, how much, if at all, did each of the following factors <u>slow</u> your progress towards completing your PhD?

- *A "5" means the factor slowed your progress a great deal and a "1" means it did not slow your progress at all. You may use any number from 5 to 1*

- *Please mark "Not Applicable" if an item does not pertain to your situation or department*

	SLOWED YOUR PROGRESS					
	A Great Deal				Not At All	Not Applicable
	5	4	3	2	1	
a. The number of required courses	5 ☐	4 ☐	3 ☐	2 ☐	1 ☐	-4 ☐
b. Holding a TA or RA position	5 ☐	4 ☐	3 ☐	2 ☐	1 ☐	-4 ☐
c. Being employed outside the department.......................................	5 ☐	4 ☐	3 ☐	2 ☐	1 ☐	-4 ☐
d. Poor academic advising	5 ☐	4 ☐	3 ☐	2 ☐	1 ☐	-4 ☐
e. Dissertation supervisor's lack of availability (e.g., being on leave, infrequent meetings or scheduling problems)	5 ☐	4 ☐	3 ☐	2 ☐	1 ☐	-4 ☐
f. The time required for research or field work.................................	5 ☐	4 ☐	3 ☐	2 ☐	1 ☐	-4 ☐
g. Language requirements...	5 ☐	4 ☐	3 ☐	2 ☐	1 ☐	-4 ☐
h. Job search activities (e.g., taking time away from writing dissertation)	5 ☐	4 ☐	3 ☐	2 ☐	1 ☐	-4 ☐
i. Time needed to find an acceptable job (delaying official completion of your dissertation)...	5 ☐	4 ☐	3 ☐	2 ☐	1 ☐	-4 ☐
j. Political struggles or friction within the department	5 ☐	4 ☐	3 ☐	2 ☐	1 ☐	-4 ☐
k. Personal reasons (e.g., personal, family or health reasons)	5 ☐	4 ☐	3 ☐	2 ☐	1 ☐	-4 ☐
l. Other *(Specify)* ↘	5 ☐	4 ☐	3 ☐	2 ☐	1 ☐	-4 ☐

_____

B10. How many language exams were you required to pass (excluding any English as a Second Language requirements)?

NUMBER OF REQUIRED
LANGUAGE EXAMS: _____   OR   0 ☐ NONE

B11. While you were completing coursework and exam requirements at the department on the front cover, were you ever registered or enrolled part-time . . .

MARK YES OR NO FOR EACH

	Yes	No
a. While completing your coursework?...........	1 ☐	0 ☐
b. After completing your coursework, but before completing exams?	1 ☐	0 ☐
c. After completing your exams but before writing your dissertation proposal or prospectus?...	1 ☐	0 ☐

B12. In total, for how many terms were you registered or enrolled part-time?

NUMBER OF TERMS
REGISTERED/ENROLLED PART-TIME: _____

0 ☐ NONE

B13. Before completing your comprehensive exams, (sometimes called comps or quals or orals), did you ever take time off officially or unofficially?

- Do *not* include any leaves for academic research

		Number of Terms
a. Official leave	1 ☐ Yes →	_____
	0 ☐ No	
b. Unofficial leave (time off)	1 ☐ Yes →	_____
	0 ☐ No	

B14. For which of the following reasons did you take a leave?

☐ Did not take any leave → GO TO B15

MARK YES OR NO FOR EACH

	Yes	No
a. Financial reasons	1 ☐	0 ☐
b. Medical reasons	1 ☐	0 ☐
c. Employment obligations	1 ☐	0 ☐
d. Personal or family obligations	1 ☐	0 ☐
e. Other *(Specify)* ⟩	1 ☐	0 ☐

_____

B15. Did you complete all of your <u>course</u> requirements?

0 ☐ No, course requirements not completed → SKIP TO B17

1 ☐ Yes, at department listed on front cover

2 ☐ Yes, at some other department

B16. When did you complete all of your PhD <u>course</u> requirements?

MARK ONE ONLY

1 ☐ By the end of the first academic year

2 ☐ By the end of the second academic year

3 ☐ By the end of the third academic year

4 ☐ By the end of the fourth academic year

5 ☐ After the fourth academic year

B17. Did you complete your <u>exam requirements</u> which lead to advancement to PhD candidacy?

0 ☐ No, exam requirements not completed

1 ☐ No exam requirements
→ SKIP TO B19 (PAGE 7)

2 ☐ Yes, completed at department listed on cover

3 ☐ Yes, completed at some other department

B18. Did you complete your last exam requirements . . .

MARK ONE ONLY

1 ☐ <u>Before</u> finishing coursework

2 ☐ <u>Concurrently</u> with finishing coursework

3 ☐ <u>Within 3 months</u> of finishing coursework

4 ☐ <u>3 to 6 months</u> after finishing coursework

5 ☐ <u>6 months to a year</u> after finishing coursework

6 ☐ <u>More than a year</u> after finishing coursework

The next series of questions is about the Dissertation Stage.

B19. Did you complete your dissertation proposal?

- 1 ☐ Yes
- 0 ☐ No → **SKIP TO B22**

B20. Was it completed in the department listed on the front cover?

- 1 ☐ Yes
- 0 ☐ No → **SKIP TO B36 (PAGE 8)**

B21. When was your dissertation proposal or prospectus approved?

MARK ONE ONLY

- 0 ☐ Not Applicable—proposal approval not required
- 1 ☐ Not Applicable—have not had my dissertation proposal approved
- 2 ☐ <u>Before</u> completing exam requirements
- 3 ☐ <u>Concurrently</u> with completing exam requirements
- 4 ☐ <u>Within 3 months</u> of completing exam requirements
- 5 ☐ <u>3 to 6 months</u> after completing exam requirements
- 6 ☐ <u>6 months to a year</u> after completing exam requirements
- 7 ☐ <u>More than a year</u> after completing exam requirements

B22. Have you begun work on your dissertation?

- 1 ☐ Yes, started but not yet completed
- 2 ☐ Yes, completed dissertation → **SKIP TO B25**
- 0 ☐ No → **SKIP TO B36 (PAGE 8)**

B23. When do you expect to finish your PhD?

MARK ONE ONLY

- 1 ☐ Within the next year
- 2 ☐ Within the next 2 years
- 3 ☐ Within the next 3 years
- 4 ☐ More than 3 years from now
- 5 ☐ Do not expect to finish the degree
- -1 ☐ Don't know/No specific plans

B24. Are you in contact with your dissertation advisor?

- 1 ☐ Yes
- 0 ☐ No

B25. While enrolled in the department listed on the front cover, was your dissertation advisor in this department or in a different department or school?

- If you had more than one advisor or supervisor in this department, please answer for the one with whom you worked most closely

- 1 ☐ This department
- 2 ☐ Different department or school

B26. Was your dissertation advisor:

- 1 ☐ Female
- 2 ☐ Male

B27. Was your dissertation advisor:

MARK ONE ONLY

- 1 ☐ Tenured?
- 2 ☐ Not tenured, but became tenured during the time you worked on your dissertation?
- 3 ☐ Not tenured?
- -1 ☐ Don't know

B28. Did you ever change your dissertation advisor?

- 1 ☐ Yes
- 0 ☐ No → **SKIP TO B30 (PAGE 8)**

B29. Why did you change your advisor?

MARK YES OR NO FOR EACH

	Yes	No
a. Changed dissertation topics	1 ☐	0 ☐
b. Changed departments	1 ☐	0 ☐
c. Bad working relationship	1 ☐	0 ☐
d. Advisor left or became unavailable (e.g., retired, over-committed, became ill, or moved)	1 ☐	0 ☐
e. Wanted advisor with more expertise or relevant experience	1 ☐	0 ☐

B30. How often did you communicate with your dissertation advisor at each of the following stages?

- *Your best estimate is fine*

	Weekly or More Often	2-3 Times a Month	Once a Month	Once Every 2 to 3 Months	Less Than Once Every 3 Months	Does Not Apply/Not to This Stage
a. While preparing your dissertation proposal or prospectus..........	1 ☐	2 ☐	3 ☐	4 ☐	5 ☐	-4 ☐
b. While researching and writing your dissertation.........	1 ☐	2 ☐	3 ☐	4 ☐	5 ☐	-4 ☐
c. At the end-stage of your dissertation writing................	1 ☐	2 ☐	3 ☐	4 ☐	5 ☐	-4 ☐

B31. Did you complete and defend your dissertation?

MARK ONE ONLY

- 1 ☐ Yes, completed and defended
- 2 ☐ Completed dissertation, not yet defended
- 3 ☐ Completed dissertation, but defense not required
- 4 ☐ Dissertation not completed → SKIP TO B36

B32. Which of the following factors, if any, kept you focused on finishing your dissertation during your final months of writing?

MARK YES OR NO FOR EACH

	Yes	No
a. Had a job offer?......................................	1 ☐	0 ☐
b. Knew your department would hire you as a post-doc or instructor if you graduated within a certain time period? .	1 ☐	0 ☐
c. Wanted to limit student loans?	1 ☐	0 ☐
d. Feared losing health care privileges?......	1 ☐	0 ☐
e. Feared losing housing privileges?..........	1 ☐	0 ☐
f. Feared losing library privileges?.............	1 ☐	0 ☐
g. Feared losing funding?...........................	1 ☐	0 ☐
h. Wanted to avoid tuition increase?	1 ☐	0 ☐
i. Had a dissertation fellowship that allowed you to work exclusively on writing?...	1 ☐	0 ☐
j. Personal or family issues?	1 ☐	0 ☐
k. Other? *(Specify)*	1 ☐	0 ☐

B33. After defending your dissertation, were you required to make:

MARK ONE ONLY

- 1 ☐ Major revisions
- 2 ☐ Minor revisions
- 3 ☐ No revisions
- 4 ☐ Not yet defended or no defense required → SKIP TO B36

B34. Approximately how many months elapsed between your dissertation defense and the date your degree was conferred?

- *Consider the date on your diploma or transcripts as the date conferred*
- *If less than one month elapsed, please enter a "1"*

NUMBER OF MONTHS: _____

- -1 ☐ Don't know/Don't remember

B35. During the year in which you completed the dissertation, what was your primary source of financial support?

MARK ONE ONLY

- 1 ☐ Fellowship income
- 2 ☐ Stipend from teaching or research assistantship
- 3 ☐ Other part-time employment
- 4 ☐ Full-time employment
- 5 ☐ Support from spouse, family, or savings
- 6 ☐ Other *(Specify)*

The next section asks about publications, regardless of where you were studying at the time.

B36. Have you ever published or had accepted for publication any papers, reviews, or books?

- 1 ☐ Yes
- 0 ☐ No → SKIP TO C1 (PAGE 9)

B37. While you were still a PhD candidate, did you ever coauthor a publication with . . .

MARK YES OR NO FOR EACH

	Yes	No
a. Your dissertation advisor?......................	1 ☐	0 ☐
b. Other faculty members (including those from other departments or institutions)?	1 ☐	0 ☐

B38. <u>After completing your PhD</u>, did you ever coauthor a publication with . . .

☐ Have not completed PhD ➙ **SKIP TO B40**

MARK YES OR NO FOR EACH

	Yes	No
a. Your dissertation advisor?	₁☐	₀☐
b. Other faculty members (including those from other departments or institutions)?	₁☐	₀☐

B39. Are you <u>sole or first author</u> on any papers, reviews or books published or accepted for publication . . .

☐ MARK HERE IF NOT A SOLE OR FIRST AUTHOR ON ANY PUBLICATIONS ➙ **SKIP TO C1**

	Yes	No
a. While you were a PhD candidate?	₁☐	₀☐
b. Within 3 years of completing your PhD or leaving the program? *(If less than 3 years have elapsed since completing PhD or leaving program, consider publications accepted to date)*	₁☐	₀☐

B40. On how many publications or works accepted for publication are you the sole or first author?

- *If less than 3 years have elapsed since completing PhD or leaving program, consider publications accepted to date*

	As PhD Candidate	Within 3 Years of Leaving or Completing PhD
a. Books (including edited collections)	₀☐ None	₀☐ None
b. Refereed journal articles	₀☐ None	₀☐ None
c. Other article length publications (e.g., chapters in books or proceedings)	₀☐ None	₀☐ None
d. Book reviews	₀☐ None	₀☐ None

SECTION C: TEACHING AND RESEARCH ASSISTANTSHIPS

C1. Did you ever hold a teaching assistantship (TA) or graduate student instructor position?

MARK ALL THAT APPLY

₁☐ Yes, in the department and university listed on label

₂☐ Yes, but in some other department within that university ➤ **SKIP TO C3**

₃☐ Yes, at some other university

₄☐ No, never held TA

C2. Do you believe that not having teaching experience as a TA or instructor limited your ability to secure a faculty position after earning your PhD?

MARK ONE ONLY

₋₄☐ NOT APPLICABLE—NOT INTERESTED IN FACULTY POSITION

₋₆☐ NOT APPLICABLE—HAVEN'T EARNED PhD

₁☐ Yes, limited my ability

₀☐ No, did not limit my ability

₋₁☐ Don't know

C3. Did you ever hold a research assistantship (RA)?

MARK ALL THAT APPLY

₁☐ Yes, in the department and university listed on label

₂☐ Yes, but in some other department within that university

₃☐ Yes, at some other university

₄☐ No, never held RA

C4. Did you answer "yes" to <u>either</u> C1 or C3—held TA, graduate student instructorship, or research assistantship anywhere?

₁☐ Yes

₀☐ No ➙ **SKIP TO C8 (PAGE 10)**

C5. Regardless of where you held these positions, for how many terms during your doctoral studies did you serve as a . . .

		Number of Terms
a. Teaching Assistant (TA) or graduate student instructor?	_____	₀☐ None
b. Research Assistant (RA)?	_____	₀☐ None

C6. While working as a TA, graduate student instructor, or RA, did your primary responsibilities include . . .

MARK YES OR NO FOR EACH

	Yes	No
a. Leading a discussion or review section?......	₁ ☐	₀ ☐
b. Preparing course materials or exams?	₁ ☐	₀ ☐
c. Grading papers or exams?...........................	₁ ☐	₀ ☐
d. Performing research or other tasks <u>not</u> directly relevant to your own work?..............	₁ ☐	₀ ☐
e. Performing research or other tasks <u>directly</u> relevant to your own work?	₁ ☐	₀ ☐
f. Teaching a course as a primary lecturer?....	₁ ☐	₀ ☐

C7. In an <u>average</u> week, how many hours did you work as a TA, graduate student instructor, or RA?

MARK ONE ONLY

₁ ☐ Fewer than 10 hours

₂ ☐ 10 to 20 hours

₃ ☐ More than 20 hours

C8. Other than the assistantships (TA/RA) described above, were you employed for pay at any time during the period you were enrolled in the PhD program listed on the front cover?

₁ ☐ Yes

₀ ☐ No → SKIP TO SECTION D (PAGE 11)

C9. Excluding TA or RA positions, how much did you work, on average, during each of the following stages of your PhD program?

- *Exclude summer months if appropriate*

	Did Not Work	Less than 20 Hrs/ Wk	20-34 Hrs/Wk	35 or More Hrs/Wk	Not to This Stage
a. While completing coursework.............	₁ ☐	₂ ☐	₃ ☐	₄ ☐	-₄ ☐
b. While preparing for comprehensive exams	₁ ☐	₂ ☐	₃ ☐	₄ ☐	-₄ ☐
c. While preparing my dissertation proposal	₁ ☐	₂ ☐	₃ ☐	₄ ☐	-₄ ☐

C10. Approximately how many months elapsed between the time you passed your exams and your dissertation defense or your decision to leave the program?

- *Your best estimate is fine*

☐ MARK HERE IF STILL WORKING ON DISSERTATION AND **SKIP TO C12**

NUMBER OF MONTHS: _____

C11. For how many of those months were you working full-time and how many part-time?

- *Do not consider any TA or RA appointments you might have held*

NUMBER OF MONTHS FULL-TIME: _____ or ₀ ☐ None

NUMBER OF MONTHS PART-TIME: _____ or ₀ ☐ None

C12. In general, how relevant was your employment to your field of study?

- *Do not consider any TA or RA appointments you might have held*

MARK ONE ONLY

₁ ☐ Very relevant

₂ ☐ Somewhat relevant

₃ ☐ Not relevant

SECTION D: OUTCOMES OF GRADUATE STUDY

D1. Referring to the department on the front cover, did you terminate your graduate study at this department?

    ₁ ☐ Yes

    ₀ ☐ No → **SKIP TO D14 (PAGE 12)**

D2. In what month and year did you terminate your graduate study at the department listed on the front cover?

    |__|__| / |__|__|__|__|
    MONTH   YEAR

D3. When you left the department listed on the cover, did you think you would eventually complete your PhD?

    ₁ ☐ Yes

    ₀ ☐ No

D4. Students leave PhD programs for many reasons. How important were each of the following in your decision to leave the department listed on the front cover?

	MARK ONE FOR EACH		
	Very Important	Somewhat Important	Not at All Important
a. I could achieve my career goals without a PhD	₁ ☐	₂ ☐	₃ ☐
b. I had family or personal reasons	₁ ☐	₂ ☐	₃ ☐
c. I changed career plans (e.g., chose non-academic career)	₁ ☐	₂ ☐	₃ ☐
d. I had health problems	₁ ☐	₂ ☐	₃ ☐
e. I lost the interest or drive to complete it	₁ ☐	₂ ☐	₃ ☐
f. I had a good job opportunity elsewhere	₁ ☐	₂ ☐	₃ ☐
g. My department or university did not provide me with adequate financial support	₁ ☐	₂ ☐	₃ ☐
h. My advisor or dissertation supervisor left	₁ ☐	₂ ☐	₃ ☐
i. I received inadequate advising (e.g., poor advice, not enough attention)	₁ ☐	₂ ☐	₃ ☐
j. My department lacked expertise in my specific area of interest	₁ ☐	₂ ☐	₃ ☐
k. I was generally dissatisfied with my department or program	₁ ☐	₂ ☐	₃ ☐
l. I exceeded my department's time limit for enrollment	₁ ☐	₂ ☐	₃ ☐
m. My academic performance was unsatisfactory (e.g., low course grades, too many incompletes, did not pass qualifying exams)	₁ ☐	₂ ☐	₃ ☐
n. I was not making satisfactory progress on my dissertation	₁ ☐	₂ ☐	₃ ☐
o. Other (Specify) ⟩	₁ ☐	₂ ☐	₃ ☐

D5. Did your department or university ask you to leave the PhD program?

    ₁ ☐ Yes

    ₀ ☐ No → **SKIP TO D9 (PAGE 12)**

D6. Was unsatisfactory academic performance your main reason for leaving?

    ₁ ☐ Yes → **GO TO D7 (PAGE 12)**

    ₂ ☐ No → **SKIP TO D8 (PAGE 12)**

D7. Were you given adequate notice that unsatisfactory academic performance could lead to dismissal?

₁ ☐ Yes

₀ ☐ No

D8. Were the student dismissal procedures clearly described in official handbooks or orientation materials?

MARK ONE ONLY

₁ ☐ Yes, clearly described

₀ ☐ No, not clearly described

₂ ☐ Not aware of written dismissal procedures

D9. Did you receive a Master's degree from your department before you left?

₁ ☐ Yes

₀ ☐ No

D10. What was your <u>primary</u> source of financial support during the year in which you left the department listed on the front cover?

MARK ONE ONLY

₁ ☐ Fellowship income

₂ ☐ Stipend from teaching assistantship

₃ ☐ Stipend from research assistantship

₄ ☐ Part-time employment

₅ ☐ Full-time employment

₆ ☐ Support from spouse, family, or savings

₇ ☐ Other *(Specify)* ❯

_____

D11. Since leaving the department listed on the front cover, have you re-enrolled in this program?

₁ ☐ Yes

₀ ☐ No → SKIP TO D13

D12. In what month and year did you return to the department?

|__|__| / |__|__|__|__| → SKIP TO D14
MONTH   YEAR

D13. Do you intend to re-enroll in the PhD program listed on the front cover?

₁ ☐ Yes

₀ ☐ No

Question D14 is to be answered by everyone.

D14. Which one of the following best describes you?

MARK ONE ONLY

Have completed degree . . .

₁ ☐ PhD in department listed on cover → SKIP TO D17

₂ ☐ PhD in different department but at same school → SKIP TO D16

₃ ☐ PhD at a different school

₄ ☐ Professional Degree (e.g., JD, MD, etc.)

₅ ☐ Other degree (e.g., BA, MA, certificate etc.)

→ GO TO D15

Am still pursuing PhD . . .

₆ ☐ In department listed on cover

₇ ☐ In different department but at same school

₈ ☐ At a different school

Am not pursuing PhD . . .

₉ ☐ Left department and no longer pursuing PhD

→ SKIP TO SECTION E (PAGE 13)

D15. Granting Institution:

_____

D16. Department in which degree was completed:

_____

D17. Date Conferred:

- *For date conferred, please use the date on your diploma or transcripts*

|__|__| / |__|__|__|__|
MONTH   YEAR

SECTION E: BACKGROUND INFORMATION

E1. Overall, how satisfied are you with the graduate education you received from the department listed on the front cover?

MARK ONE ONLY
1 ☐ Very satisfied
2 ☐ Somewhat satisfied
3 ☐ Neither satisfied nor dissatisfied
4 ☐ Somewhat dissatisfied
5 ☐ Very dissatisfied

E2. Did the department listed on the front cover receive financial support for its doctoral program from the Andrew W. Mellon Foundation?

1 ☐ Yes
0 ☐ No
-1 ☐ Don't know ⟶ SKIP TO E5

E3. Were you aware of this Andrew W. Mellon Foundation support when you first entered the program?

1 ☐ Yes
0 ☐ No ⟶ SKIP TO E5

E4. Did knowing about your department's participation in the Andrew W. Mellon Graduate Education Program encourage you to apply to that department's PhD program?

1 ☐ Yes
0 ☐ No

E5. How old were you when you **first enrolled** in the program listed on the front cover?

AGE: _____

E6. When you **first enrolled** in the department listed on the front cover, were you:

MARK ONE ONLY
1 ☐ Married
2 ☐ Living with a domestic partner
3 ☐ Widowed
4 ☐ Divorced
5 ☐ Separated
6 ☐ Never married

E7. When you first enrolled in the department listed on the front cover, were there any children under the age of 18 in your household?

1 ☐ Yes
0 ☐ No ⟶ SKIP TO E9

E8. What were your caregiver responsibilities? Did you have . . .

1 ☐ Primary responsibility for caregiving
2 ☐ Shared responsibilities for caregiving
0 ☐ No responsibilities for caregiving

E9. When you **completed or left** that PhD program, were you . . .

☐ STILL PURSUING PhD ⟶ GO TO E12

MARK ONE ONLY
1 ☐ Married
2 ☐ Living with a domestic partner
3 ☐ Widowed
4 ☐ Divorced
5 ☐ Separated
6 ☐ Never married

E10. When you completed or left that PhD program, were there any children in your household?

1 ☐ Yes
0 ☐ No ⟶ SKIP TO E12

E11. What were your caregiver responsibilities? Did you have . . .

1 ☐ Primary responsibility for caregiving
2 ☐ Shared responsibilities for caregiving
0 ☐ No responsibilities for caregiving

E12. When you **first enrolled** in the department indicated on the front cover, what was the highest level of education your mother and father had attained?

	Mother	Father
Less than a high school graduate	1 ☐	1 ☐
High school graduate	2 ☐	2 ☐
Some college/vocational school	3 ☐	3 ☐
Bachelor's degree	4 ☐	4 ☐
Some graduate school	5 ☐	5 ☐
Master's or professional degree (e.g., MA, MBA, MD, JD)	6 ☐	6 ☐
Doctoral degree	7 ☐	7 ☐
Other *(Specify)*	8 ☐	8 ☐
Don't know	-1 ☐	-1 ☐

SECTION F: EMPLOYMENT INFORMATION

Please indicate your current PhD status.

MARK ONE ONLY

- 1 ☐ Completed PhD (from any school)
- 2 ☐ Not completed, not pursuing PhD
- 3 ☐ Not completed, still pursuing PhD → SKIP TO F29 (PAGE 17)

The next questions are about jobs you might have held at three points in time:

1) 6 months after completing a PhD, or if you haven't completed your degree at any school, 6 months after leaving the department on the front cover;

2) 3 years after completing a PhD or leaving the department; or

3) currently.

What columns do I answer?

- If you completed a PhD or left the department more than 3 years ago, complete all 3 columns
- If you completed a PhD or left the department less than 3 years ago, complete "at 6 months after" and "current job" columns
- If you completed a PhD or left the department less than 6 months ago, complete only the "current job" column

Please answer all questions (F1-F12) in a single column before moving on to the next column.

	AT 6 MONTHS AFTER	AT 3 YEARS AFTER	CURRENT JOB
F1. Please indicate your employment status at each time period listed in column headings.			
Employed	1 ☐	1 ☐	1 ☐
Not employed (looked or looking)	2 ☐ → SKIP TO F1 NEXT COLUMN	2 ☐ → SKIP TO F1 NEXT COLUMN	2 ☐ → GO TO F13 (PAGE 16)
Not in job market (not employed, not looking)	3 ☐	3 ☐	3 ☐
F2. Who (is/was) your principal employer?			
• Please record the full name of your principal employer, e.g., university, company or institution name (no abbreviation).		☐ MARK HERE IF SAME AS 6 MONTH → SKIP TO F6 THIS COLUMN	☐ MARK HERE IF SAME AS 3 YEAR → SKIP TO F6 THIS COLUMN
F3. Which of the following BEST describes your principal employer?	MARK ONE ONLY	MARK ONE ONLY	MARK ONE ONLY
An educational institution	1 ☐	1 ☐	1 ☐
A for-profit company, business or individual, paying wages, salary or commissions (excluding educational institutions)	2 ☐	2 ☐	2 ☐
A not-for-profit, tax-exempt, or charitable organization (excluding educational institutions)	3 ☐	3 ☐	3 ☐
Local, state, or federal government (excluding educational institutions)	4 ☐	4 ☐	4 ☐
Self-employed	5 ☐	5 ☐	5 ☐
Other	6 ☐ (Specify) ➤	6 ☐ (Specify) ➤	6 ☐ (Specify) ➤
F4. What kind of work did you do for this employer; that is, what is your occupation? *Please be as specific as possible including area of specialization—e.g., High school teacher—English*			

	At 6 Months After	At 3 Years After	Current Job
F5. Turn to back cover and choose the code that BEST describes the work you did for this employer. (Enter code in boxes)	☐☐ OCCUPATION CODE	☐☐ OCCUPATION CODE	☐☐ OCCUPATION CODE
F6. Was your principal employer an educational institution? Yes..................... No.......................	1 ☐ 0 ☐ → GO BACK TO F1, NEXT JOB COLUMN	1 ☐ 0 ☐ → GO BACK TO F1, NEXT JOB COLUMN	1 ☐ 0 ☐ → GO TO F13 (PAGE 16)
F7. Was this educational institution a:	MARK ONE ONLY	MARK ONE ONLY	MARK ONE ONLY
Four-year college or university, other than a professional school	1 ☐	1 ☐	1 ☐
Two-year college, community college, or technical institute	2 ☐	2 ☐	2 ☐
Professional school (including university-affiliated hospital or medical center, law school, or business school)	3 ☐	3 ☐	3 ☐
Preschool, elementary, middle school, secondary school or system	4 ☐ → GO BACK TO F1, NEXT JOB COLUMN	4 ☐ → GO BACK TO F1, NEXT JOB COLUMN	4 ☐ → GO TO F13 (PAGE 16)
F8. Was this a faculty position? In addition to teaching and research, include deanships, provostships, and post-doctoral appointments.			
Yes, full-time faculty position	1 ☐	1 ☐	1 ☐
Yes, part-time faculty position	2 ☐	2 ☐	2 ☐
No, not a faculty position	3 ☐ → GO BACK TO F1 NEXT JOB COLUMN	3 ☐ → GO BACK TO F1 NEXT JOB COLUMN	3 ☐ → GO TO F13 (PAGE 16)
F9. When did you start work in this position?	___/___ MONTH YEAR	___/___ MONTH YEAR ☐ MARK HERE IF SAME AS 6 MONTH → SKIP TO F11	___/___ MONTH YEAR ☐ MARK HERE IF SAME AS 3 YEAR → SKIP TO F11
F10. In which department were you employed?	_____ DEPARTMENT	_____ DEPARTMENT	_____ DEPARTMENT
F11. At each of the time periods listed in column headings, which of the following BEST describes this faculty position?	MARK ONE ONLY	MARK ONE ONLY	MARK ONE ONLY
Post-Doctoral Fellow (1)	1 ☐	1 ☐	1 ☐
Instructor or Lecturer (2)	2 ☐	2 ☐	2 ☐
Adjunct faculty (3)	3 ☐	3 ☐	3 ☐
Assistant Professor—Non-tenure-track (4)	4 ☐	4 ☐	4 ☐
Assistant Professor—Tenure-track (5)	5 ☐	5 ☐	5 ☐
Associate/Full Professor—Non-tenure-track (6)	6 ☐	6 ☐	6 ☐
Associate/Full Professor—Tenure-track (7)	7 ☐	7 ☐	7 ☐
Other faculty position (8)	8 ☐ (Specify) _____	8 ☐ (Specify) _____	8 ☐ (Specify) _____
F12. What was your PRIMARY work activity for this faculty position?	MARK ONE ONLY	MARK ONE ONLY	MARK ONE ONLY
Mainly teaching	1 ☐	1 ☐	1 ☐
Mainly research	2 ☐	2 ☐	2 ☐
Teaching and research equally	3 ☐	3 ☐	3 ☐
Teaching, research and administration	4 ☐	4 ☐	4 ☐
Mainly administration such as budgeting, committee work, or advising	5 ☐	5 ☐	5 ☐
	GO BACK TO F1, NEXT JOB COLUMN	GO BACK TO F1, NEXT JOB COLUMN	CONTINUE TO F13 (PAGE 16)

F13. Which category applies to you?

- *Please include deanships, provostships, and post-doctoral appointments*

1 ☐ Have held a faculty position

0 ☐ Never held faculty position → **SKIP TO F27 (PAGE 17)**

F14. Was your first faculty position:

MARK ONE ONLY

1 ☐ The 6 month job described above

2 ☐ The 3 year job described above → **SKIP TO F20**

3 ☐ Your current job

4 ☐ A position held at some other time

F15. Within how many months or years of completing your PhD or leaving the program, did you accept your first faculty position?

MARK ONE ONLY

1 ☐ Prior to or while completing PhD

2 ☐ Within six months

3 ☐ Within 1 year

4 ☐ Within 2 years

5 ☐ Within 3 years

6 ☐ More than 3 years after completing PhD or leaving the program

F16. Who was your employer for that first faculty position?

- *Please write out the entire name of the department and institution, including a specific campus if applicable*

Department:_____

Institution:_____

F17. Which of the following best describes your first faculty position when you were hired?

MARK ONE ONLY

1 ☐ Post-Doctoral Fellow

2 ☐ Instructor or Lecturer

3 ☐ Adjunct faculty

4 ☐ Assistant Professor—Non-tenure-track

5 ☐ Assistant Professor—Tenure-track

6 ☐ Associate/Full Professor—Non-tenure-track

7 ☐ Associate/Full Professor—Tenure-track

8 ☐ Other faculty position *(Specify)* ➤

_____

F18. Was your first faculty position after leaving graduate school:

1 ☐ A full-time position

2 ☐ A part-time position

F19. What was your primary work activity for this position?

MARK ONE ONLY

1 ☐ Mainly teaching

2 ☐ Mainly research

3 ☐ Teaching and research equally

4 ☐ Teaching, research, and administration

5 ☐ Mainly administration such as budgeting, committee work, or advising

F20. Have you ever held a tenure-track position?

1 ☐ Yes

0 ☐ No → **SKIP TO F27 (PAGE 17)**

F21. Was your first tenure-track position:

MARK ONE ONLY

1 ☐ The 6 month job described above

2 ☐ The 3 year job described above

3 ☐ Your current job → **SKIP TO F24 (PAGE 17)**

4 ☐ The first faculty position described above

5 ☐ Some other position

F22. Where was your first tenure-track position?

- *Please write out entire name of department and institution including a specific campus if applicable*

Department:_____

Institution:_____

F23. When did you assume this tenure-track position?

DATE POSITION
WAS ASSUMED: |___|___| / |___|___|___|___|
　　　　　　　　Month　　　Year

F24. Have you ever been <u>granted tenure</u> at a U.S. college or university?

MARK ONE ONLY

0 ☐ No ⟶ **SKIP TO F27**

1 ☐ Yes, at school where <u>first</u> tenure-track position was held ⟶ **SKIP TO F26**

2 ☐ Yes, at a different U.S. college or university

F25. Where was your <u>first</u> tenured position?

- *Please write out entire name of department and institution including a specific campus if applicable*

Department:_____

Institution:_____

F26. When was your tenure granted?

DATE TENURE
GRANTED: |___|___| / |___|___|___|___|
      Month   Year

F27. Altogether, within the first 3 years of completing your PhD or leaving the program, how many different full- and part-time paid jobs did you hold that lasted at least six months?

- *Consider a <u>full-time</u> job to average 35 or more hours per week*

- *Consider a <u>part-time</u> job to average less than 35 hours per week*

Number of full-time jobs held in first three years .... ☐☐

Number of part-time jobs held in first three years .... ☐☐

F28. How many of the jobs included in F27 above were full-time or part-time faculty positions?

- *In addition to teaching and research please include deanships, provostships, post-doctoral appointments.*

a. Full-time faculty positions: _____

  0 ☐ NONE

b. Part-time faculty positions: _____

  0 ☐ NONE

F29. Questionnaires often don't allow respondents to report their experiences in their own words. Please use this space to tell us about the experiences you had in graduate school that bore the most heavily on your progress towards your degree. Any other thoughts or comments about graduate school will be welcomed and appreciated. Attach another sheet if necessary.

OCCUPATION CODES

The following broad occupation codes are listed in ALPHABETICAL order.

Administrators, Executives, Managers (e.g., administrators, executives, top and mid-level managers, self employed in the following fields) *(Codes listed below)*

10	Post-secondary educational institutions
11	Other educational institutions
12	Sales, marketing, retail businesses
13	Health organizations
14	Other areas
15	**Artists, Entertainers, Writers, Public Relations Specialists, & Broadcasters** (e.g., authors, musicians, editors, reporters, translators)
16	**Clerical/Administrative Support** (e.g., accounting clerks, bookkeepers, secretaries, receptionists, telephone operators)
17	**Clergy and Other Religious Workers**
18	**Computer Occupations** (e.g., computer programmers, computer system analysts, computer engineers)
**	**Consultants** *(select the code that comes closest to your usual area of consulting)*
19	**Counselors**—Educational and Vocational
20	**Curators** (e.g., museums, galleries, historical societies)

Education Occupations

**	Administrators—use codes 10 or 11, see above
**	Counselors—use code 19, see above
**	Librarians—use code 31, see below
21	Post-Doctoral appointments
22	Professors—postsecondary, all ranks
23	Research appointments
	Teachers
24	Elementary/Secondary including special education
25	Post-secondary
26	Other Education Occupations
27	**Engineers, Architects, Surveyors**
28	**Financial, Human Resource Professionals** (e.g., accountants, auditors, other financial specialists, personnel training, human resources, labor relations specialists)
29	**Health Occupations** (e.g., doctors, nurses, health practitioners, health technologists and aides)
30	**Lawyers, Judges**
31	**Librarians** (including archivists, corporate and academic librarians)
32	**Sales and Marketing** (e.g., insurance, securities, real estate, retail and commodities sales)
33	**Scientists** (e.g., natural, biological, physical, mathematical—non-faculty position)
34	**Service Occupations, Except Health** (e.g., food preparation and service, firefighters, police, security)
35	**Social Science Occupations** (e.g., anthropology, economy, political science, psychology, sociology—non-faculty)
36	**Social Workers**
37	**Other Occupations**

Outcome Measures

TIME-TO-DEGREE (TTD)

THROUGHOUT THIS BOOK, we measure TTD as elapsed time-to-degree, which is the number of years that have elapsed between entering a PhD program and the time the PhD is awarded.

Drawbacks. TTD can be calculated only for those students who earn the PhD. Furthermore, the mean TTD for a group of students is greatly affected by the years since the group began graduate study. The mean TTD for students who began 8 years ago must, by definition, be 8 years or fewer, whereas the mean TTD for those who began 10 years ago can include some degree times that are longer than 8 years. Thus when comparisons are made between two time periods, the means must be truncated to include only those students whose potential years in the program are the same.

Calculation. $TTD^{mean} = [\Sigma(PhD\ date - Entry\ date)/365]/C$, where C is the absolute number of students earning the PhD.

Alternative versions.

- Total time-to-degree: Elapsed time from bachelor's degree to completion of the PhD degree. This measure is used when dates of PhD entry are not available.
- Registered time-to-degree: Omits terms when student has not been enrolled.
- Half-life: The time in years necessary for half of an entering cohort to earn the PhD. This measure was created by C. Anthony Broh, while he served as registrar at Princeton University, to facilitate comparisons that capture both the pace and the extent of completion. It can be compared for groups entering in different years.

CUMULATIVE COMPLETION RATE (CCR)

The completion rate is the percent of an entering cohort who have earned the PhD degree. Greatly affected by time elapsed since entry, it should be standardized by the number of years since entry. The CCR is the completion rate of a given entry cohort as of a given number of years since entry. When the CCRs for all years are depicted graphically, they show both the overall completion rate and its marginal increase as students' years since entry increase (i.e., the years when large shares of students graduate, the years when additional students graduate, and the time at which the rate of increase in completions levels off).

Drawbacks. Requires that data be maintained for all entering students until they either leave a program or graduate from it.

Calculation. $CCR_T = C_T/N$, where T is the number of years since entry, C_T is the number of students with TTD less than T.17, and N is the number of entering students.[1]

Alternative versions.

- Minimum completion rate: Any completion rate calculated before all entering students have either left or completed. It is always possible that the continuing students might complete and thus increase the total completion rate.
- Truncated cumulative completion rate (*T*-year cumulative completion rate): The percent of entering students who have completed by the end of any given year (T). For example, the 8-year cumulative completion rate is the percent of entering students who have finished before the end of the eighth year since entry.

TIME-TO-ATTRITION (TTA)

TTA is the number of years elapsed between date of entry and date of attrition, as defined by the institution.

Drawbacks. As with all attrition calculations, identifying the exact date of attrition is difficult. Often the date is not known until long after students have elected not to continue. Students often make this decision without notifying the department or the university, and it is only after they have not registered for some number of quarters or semesters that they are declared to have discontinued their studies.

Calculation. $TTA^{mean} = [\Sigma(\text{Attrition date} - \text{Entry date})/365]/A$, where A is the absolute number of students leaving a program.

---

[1] T.17 (i.e., $T + 0.17$) is used in this study to allow for students who completed in T years and one or two months (e.g., a student who enters on August 15 and completes on October 15; 2/12 is about 0.167) to be counted along with those who completed in T years or fewer.

CUMULATIVE ATTRITION RATE (CAR)

The CAR is the percent of an entering cohort that leaves a program by the end of a given number of years since entry. When the CARs for all years are depicted graphically, they show both the overall attrition rate and its marginal increase as students' years since entry increase.

Drawbacks. Requires that data be maintained for all entering students until they either leave a program or graduate. Although calculation of the CAR requires only the year that attrition occurred rather than the specific date, it is often difficult to identify students who have left until several years after they have done so. Thus the attrition rate is often understated for any recent year, especially the most recent year.

Calculation. $CAR_T = A_T/N$, where T is the number of years since entry, A_T is the number of students with TTA less than T.17, and N is the number of entering students.

Alternative versions.

- Minimum attrition rate: Any attrition rate calculated before all entering students have either left or completed. It is always possible that the continuing students may have been incorrectly identified as such and thus that updated information will increase the total attrition rate.
- Truncated cumulative attrition rate (*T*-year cumulative attrition rate): The percent of entering students who have left the program by the end of any given year (*T*). For example, the 4-year cumulative attrition rate is the percent of entering students who have left the program before the end of the fourth year since entry.

STUDENT-YEAR COST (SYC)

SYC estimates the number of years spent by all students in an entering cohort in order to produce one PhD from that cohort. It is a measure that captures investments by students and by institutions.

Drawbacks. Heavy data requirements—data must be maintained on all entering students and on dates of completion and attrition. SYC is most meaningful if 10 or more years of data are available on cohorts since they entered graduate school. This cost-benefit measure assumes that all costs in time are comparable in assessing investments in obtaining a PhD. It does not allow for benefits that accrue to those who leave with master's degrees or for benefits from the educational experiences of those who leave before earning degrees.[2]

[2] For a more complete discussion of this measure, its strengths and weaknesses, as well as the details of the computations, see Bowen and Rudenstine (1992), Chapter 9.

Calculation.

Step 1: Count the number of students who completed the PhD by the end of the Tth year (C_T).

Step 2: Calculate the mean TTD (TTD^{mean}) for those who completed and multiply by C_T.

Step 3: Count the number of students who left the program without finishing by the end of the Tth year (A_T).

Step 4: Calculate the mean number of years spent in the program before leaving for those who left (TTA^{mean}) and multiply by A_T.

Step 5: Count the number of students who have neither left nor finished by the end of the Tth year (called languishers, L_T). Multiply by the number of years in the program (T).

Step 6: Add all of the years spent by completers, leavers, and languishers (i.e., the results of steps 2, 4, and 5) and then divide the sum by the number of PhDs produced by the end of the Tth year (C_T). The result is the SYC.

To identify the three components of total SYC (from completion, attrition, and languishing), as an alternative to step 6, simply divide the contribution of each element of SYC by C_T before combining: SYC = TTD^{mean} + (TTA^{mean} × A_T/C_T) + (T × L_T/C_T).

Methodology

THIS APPENDIX provides additional detail on particular aspects of our methodology. The first two sections of the appendix relate to the model of student outcomes that is introduced in Chapter 4 and also used in Chapters 5–7. The third section relates to the sample of completion cohorts used for one of the tables in Chapter 9.

1. THE COMPETING-RISK DURATION MODEL

This section describes the empirical model of student outcomes that is introduced in Chapter 4.[1] In the model, time is discrete and measured in years. We directly model student transitions from one year to the next. Given that a student is in a PhD program in a particular year, he or she may continue on in the program the following year, leave the program without completing it, or complete the program and receive the PhD before the start of the following year. Thus given that the student is in the program in year $t-1$, the three transition probabilities that we are interested in are the probability that the student will still be in the program in year t, the probability that the student will have dropped out of the program by year t, and the probability that the student will have received the PhD by year t.

We specify these transition probabilities as functions of explanatory variables using a multinomial logit form. We allow the parameters of the model to vary freely across years. The sample of students used to estimate the model for a given year is the subsample of students in the program at the beginning of that year. (For years 1–3 we do not allow the completion option, so we simply have a binary logit model for continuation versus attrition.)

---

[1] For a more technical discussion of competing-risk duration models, see Aaron Han and Jerry A. Hausman, "Flexible Parametric Estimation of Duration and Competing Risk Models," *Journal of Applied Econometrics* 5 (January–March 1990): 1–28.

This model includes both time-varying and fixed explanatory variables. Our baseline model includes explanatory variables for student gender, race and ethnicity, and citizenship. It also includes indicator variables for institutions and fields, in order to capture the effects of institution-wide factors and field-specific factors such as differences in curriculum. A subsequent model includes measures of student quality (test scores, prior master's degree) and cohort size to see how sensitive our findings are to the inclusion of these variables. The forms of financial aid received by students each year are not included in the models underlying the findings in Chapter 4; they are analyzed in detail in Chapter 5.

Three other explanatory variables are included in the model to identify the effects of the Graduate Education Initiative (GEI). The first is an indicator variable that equals one for students in treatment departments and zero for students in control departments. This variable allows us to control for differences in transition probabilities that existed, on average, between treatment and control departments during the period prior to the GEI. The second is an indicator variable that identifies when the GEI is in effect; it equals one for observations in the treatment period and zero for observations in the pretreatment period. The definition of this variable depends on a student's entering cohort as well as his year in the program. This variable is assigned a value of zero for all years for students in the 1982–83 through 1985–86 entering cohorts because they were never subject to the GEI. It is assigned a value of one for students in the 1991–92 through 2002–03 entering cohorts because they were always subject to the GEI. Students in the 1986–87 through 1990–91 entering cohorts are assigned a value of zero for this variable for years prior to 1991 and a value of one for 1991 and later years (i.e., the years in which they were eligible for support from the GEI). The third variable is the interaction between the other two variables.

Holding other variables included in the model constant, the coefficient of the first variable for a given probability (for example, attrition between years 1 and 2 in a PhD program) tells us, on average, the difference in the probability between treatment and control departments in the years prior to the institution of the GEI. Similarly, holding the other variables included in the model constant, the coefficient of the second variable tells us, on average, how much the probability changed in control departments after the GEI was instituted. These changes are not attributed to the GEI but are due to other factors that we have not captured in our model. Finally, holding other variables in the model constant, the coefficient of the third variable tells us, on average, how much (more or less) the probability changed for treatment departments than for control departments after the GEI was instituted.

2. COMPUTING TIME-TO-DEGREE FROM COMPLETION RATES

In Chapter 4 we estimate the impact of the GEI on average elapsed time-to-degree (TTD) using the pattern of cumulative completion rates shown in Figure 4.2 and similar figures. The figures involve cumulative completion rates for students in treatment departments under two scenarios, with and without the GEI. We compute an average TTD of completers within 11 years separately under each scenario, and the difference between these numbers is the impact of the GEI on TTD. This section explains how we compute average TTD from the pattern of cumulative completion rates by year.

We explain our method by presenting our formula and showing how it relates to the typical way of computing TTD. The input to the formula is a pattern of cumulative completion rates by year: G_t, $t = 4\text{–}11$, which is the percent of a cohort that completes in t years or fewer. Note that for simplicity our models record TTD in discrete years (e.g., 6 or 7 but not 6.5). Let N_t be the number of students in the cohort that completes in t years. Let N be the number of entering students in the cohort, including students who complete the PhD and those who do not. Then the percent of the cohort that completes in t years is $g_t = G_t - G_{t-1}$ if $t = 5\text{–}11$ and $g_4 = G_4$. Our measure of average elapsed TTD for this cohort is

$$\frac{\sum_{t=4}^{11} t \cdot g_t}{G_{11}}.$$

The numerator is the sum of products in which the product for a given year t involves t and the percent of the cohort that graduates in t years. The denominator is the percent of the cohort that completes in 11 years or fewer. Using $g_t = N_t/N$ and the definition of G_{11}, the ratio becomes

$$\frac{4 \cdot \dfrac{N_4}{N} + 5 \cdot \dfrac{N_5}{N} + \ldots + 11 \cdot \dfrac{N_{11}}{N}}{\dfrac{1}{N} \sum_{t=4}^{11} N_t}.$$

Multiplying the numerator and denominator by N and expanding the denominator gives

$$\frac{4 \cdot N_4 + 5 \cdot N_5 + \ldots + 11 \cdot N_{11}}{N_4 + N_5 + \ldots + N_{11}} = \frac{\sum_{t=4}^{11} t \cdot N_t}{\sum_{t=4}^{11} N_t}.$$

This is simply the average number of years to degree for students who completed the PhD within 11 years, which is the familiar way to compute average TTD (see Appendix C).

3. CHANGING TTD BY EXIT COHORT
IN THE GRADUATE EDUCATION SURVEY

This section provides a numerical example to explain why we eliminate early cohorts of completers from the analysis presented in Table 9.1. For simplicity, suppose that the number of new entrants to PhD programs was 100 in every year between 1982 and 1996, the entry years covered by the Graduate Education Survey (GES). Suppose also that every entrant to these PhD programs completes his or her degree and that the distribution of TTD is the same for every entering cohort. In particular, suppose that 15 percent finish in 5 years, 50 percent finish in 7 years, 25 percent finish in 9 years, and 10 percent finish in 11 years. In this case, the average TTD for each entry cohort would be 7.6 years, and this average would be constant over time.

If we focus on exit cohorts, there would be 15 completers in 1987; these would be the 15 individuals who began their programs in 1982 and who finished their degrees in 5 years. Similarly, there would be 15 completers in 1988; these would be the 15 students who began their programs in 1983 and who finished their degrees in 5 years. So the average TTD would be 5 years for both the 1987 and the 1988 completers.

The 1989 exit cohort would consist of 65 people; these would be the 15 people who started in 1984 and finished their programs in 5 years and the 65 people who began their programs in 1982 and finished in 7 years. So the average TTD for the 1989 exit cohort would be $(15/65) \times 5 + (50/65) \times 7$, or 6.54 years. Continuing this type of reasoning, one would find the following distribution of mean TTD and number of new PhDs by exit year:

Exit Year	Number of PhDs	Mean TTD (years)
1987	15	5.00
1988	15	5.00
1989	65	6.54
1990	65	6.54
1991	90	7.22
1992	90	7.22
1993	100	7.60
1994	100	7.60

(*continued*)

Exit Year	Number of PhDs	Mean TTD (years)
1995	100	7.60
1996	100	7.60
1997	100	7.60
1998	100	7.60
1999	100	7.60
2000	100	7.60
2001	100	7.60
2002	85	8.06

In this simple numerical example, exit cohorts prior to 1993 would disproportionately consist of early finishers, and the 2002 exit cohort would disproportionately consist of late finishers. If job outcomes vary with TTD, a comparison of the experiences of the 1987 exit cohort with those of the 1993 exit cohort would confound the effect of changing job-market conditions and the effect of changing shares of early finishers.

This example is only meant to be illustrative. The size of entering cohorts in the GES varied across years, as did the average TTD for those in each cohort who completed. Attrition from PhD programs, which we have assumed away in the example, also took place. However, the example should make clear why we have eliminated early cohorts of completers from the analyses presented in Table 9.1.

Additional Tables and Figures

TABLE E.3.1
Range of Outcomes in Pre-GEI and Post-GEI Time Periods, by Department Size

	Small		Medium		Large		All	
	Min	Max	Min	Max	Min	Max	Min	Max
7-year cumulative completion rate (%)								
Pre-GEI cohorts	0	68	8	48	7	47	0	68
Post-GEI cohorts	13	59	13	57	13	54	13	59
8-year cumulative completion rate (%)								
Pre-GEI cohorts	22	77	13	57	9	54	9	77
Post-GEI cohorts	26	63	21	63	21	62	21	63
11-year cumulative completion rate (%)								
Pre-GEI cohorts	30	88	22	72	17	70	17	88
Post-GEI cohorts	42	85	39	68	26	70	26	85
Mean years from entry to advancement to candidacy								
Pre-GEI cohorts	1.78	5.21	1.47	4.77	1.56	4.52	1.47	5.21
Post-GEI cohorts	1.73	4.50	1.58	4.09	1.25	4.33	1.25	4.50
Mean years from advancement to candidacy to PhD								
Pre-GEI cohorts	1.57	5.22	2.98	5.79	2.83	5.62	1.57	5.79
Post-GEI cohorts	0.65	5.52	2.87	5.50	3.01	6.73	0.65	6.73
Mean time-to-degree								
Pre-GEI cohorts	5.80	8.58	6.54	8.38	6.01	8.22	5.80	8.58
Post-GEI cohorts	5.15	7.78	6.05	8.09	5.22	8.06	5.15	8.09
Mean time-to-attrition								
Pre-GEI cohorts	1.76	5.51	2.79	5.25	1.49	6.35	1.49	6.35
Post-GEI cohorts	1.85	5.86	2.54	4.54	1.97	5.64	1.85	5.86

Notes: Pre-GEI: 1982–83 through 1984–85 entering cohorts; post-GEI: 1991–92 through 1993–94 entering cohorts. Size categories are based on the average size of pre-GEI entering cohorts. Small: <10; medium: 10–16.4; large: ≥16.5. Mean times are computed using times of 11 years or less.

TABLE E.3.2
Departmental and Institutional Environment and Change in
Cumulative Completion Rates and Student-Year Cost

	Dependent Variable: Change in Cumulative Completion Rate as of:			Dependent Variable: Change in Student-Year Cost
	7th Year	8th Year	11th Year	
Baseline variables				
Pre-GEI cumulative completion rate	**–0.405**	**–0.595**	**–0.650**	**0.138**
Cohort size	**–0.411**	**–0.401**	**–0.451**	**0.115**
Pre-GEI mean verbal GRE score	0.007	0.047	0.016	0.001
Pre-GEI mean math GRE score	0.031	0.022	0.022	0.003
Student-faculty ratio	0.764	0.466	1.131	0.228
Environment variables				
Enthusiasm for GEI goals	7.187	**9.228**	**9.057**	**–1.639**
Appetite for change and prior experience	**13.790**	**14.541**	**14.413**	**–3.563**
Top-down institutional influence	–3.645	–2.729	–5.108	1.091
Supportive enforcement from administration	–7.750	–6.791	–10.228	1.987
Observations	43	43	43	43
R^2	0.413	0.719	0.569	0.629
Adjusted R^2	0.258	0.644	0.455	0.530
Mean of dependent variable	7.793	8.294	7.361	–1.650

Notes: Coefficients in bold type are statistically significant at the 5 percent level. Student-faculty ratios are based on 1993 data.

DEPARTMENTAL AND INSTITUTIONAL
ENVIRONMENT VARIABLES IN TABLE E.3.2

Enthusiasm for GEI goals. Departments were coded as "yes" if the faculty had a positive attitude toward the goals of the GEI, reviewed their programs, and made agreed-upon changes. A "no" was assigned to departments whose reports indicated that faculty members were convinced that the "quality" of scholars and scholarly research they produced was related to their spending more time on the dissertation. Departments were also assigned a "no" if the faculty registered indifference to the process. A "no" indicated the faculty had not "bought into" or adopted the GEI goals.

Appetite for change and prior experience. Did the department have prior experience with introducing GEI-like changes? Had departments begun to examine their programs and to reform them before the GEI began? This variable was coded as "yes" for departments that had already begun to redesign their programs to reduce attrition or time-to-degree before the GEI began. It also identifies those departments that wanted to make changes even without the encouragement of the GEI and the funds it provided.

Top-down institutional influence. Did the dean or provost impose program changes? This attribute refers to an institutional structure in which control was centralized and the design of the GEI was uniform across departments. If this variable is negatively correlated with improved completion rates, it suggests that departments should have influence on changes if their efforts are to be effective.

Supportive enforcement from administration. Were departmental efforts supported by the university? Were departmental policies and deadlines enforced? Were official decisions made to assist the departments? A "yes" indicates that administrators facilitated a department's efforts. A "yes" also indicates that incentives were provided by the administration to encourage students to move expeditiously through their programs, and that the graduate school played an independent role in helping departments achieve the objectives of the GEI. Conceptually, this variable should be associated positively with better completion rates when the departments have accepted the GEI goals.

TABLE E.4.1

Impact of the GEI on Student Outcomes: Robustness Checks

	Attrition Probability	Completion Probability	TTD
Baseline (Table 4.2)	−0.029	0.018	−0.119
Baseline without institutional indicators	−0.026	0.019	−0.136
Contamination model[a]			
Treatment versus controls in participating institutions	−0.041	0.014	−0.091
Treatment versus controls in nonparticipating institutions	−0.011	0.019	−0.086
Timing of GEI introduction			
Post-GEI cohorts (1991–92 through 2002–03) versus pre-GEI cohorts[b]	−0.039	0.024	−0.111
Transition cohorts (1986–87 through 1990–91) versus pre-GEI cohorts[b]	−0.007	0.009	−0.145

Note: Weighting is by department (see notes to Table 4.2).

[a]The contamination model does not include institutional indicators because in some fields there is only a single department of a given type of control.

[b]1982–83 through 1985–86 entering cohorts.

TABLE E.4.2

Impact of the GEI on Student Outcomes by Field and Department Size

	Attrition Probability	Completion Probability
Baseline	−0.050	0.033
Field		
Anthropology	−0.003	−0.034
Art history	−0.142	0.095
Classics	−0.151	0.153
Comparative literature	−0.175	0.127
English	−0.018	−0.003
History	−0.005	−0.065
Music	−0.091	0.137
Philosophy	−0.045	0.064
Political science	0.028	−0.036
Religion	−0.048	−0.007
Department size		
Small	−0.062	0.092
Medium	−0.047	0.033
Large	−0.018	−0.036

Notes: Weighting is by department (see notes to Table 4.2). Size categories are based on the average size of entering cohorts from 1982–83 to 1990–91. Small: <7.5; medium: 7.5–14.4; large: ≥14.5.

TABLE E.4.3
Distribution of Departments by Field and Size

	Small	Medium	Large	Total
Anthropology	3	4	2	9
Art history	3	5	0	8
Classics	7	1	0	8
Comparative literature	4	1	1	6
English	0	2	10	12
History	0	3	8	11
Music	4	3	2	9
Philosophy	4	4	0	8
Political science	1	2	6	9
Religion	2	3	0	5
Total	28	28	29	85

Note: Size categories are based on the average size of entering cohorts from 1982–83 to 1990–91. Small: <7.5; medium: 7.5–14.4; large: ≥14.5.

TABLE E.4.4
Impact of the GEI on Student Outcomes by Stage

	Both Stages (entry to PhD)	Coursework (entry to candidacy)	Dissertation (candidacy to PhD)
Attrition probability	−0.029	−0.024	−0.027
Completion probability	0.018	0.023	0.004
Elapsed time (years)	−0.119	−0.131	−0.025

Notes: Weighting is by department (see notes to Table 4.2). The numbers for elapsed time represent the impact of the GEI on the mean number of years taken to complete the stage, for those who complete the stage in *x* years or less, where *x* is 11 for both stages, 5 for the coursework stage, and 7 for the dissertation stage.

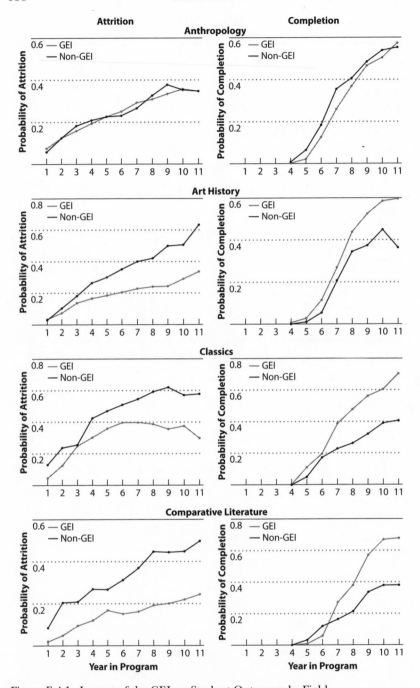

Figure E.4.1. Impact of the GEI on Student Outcomes by Field

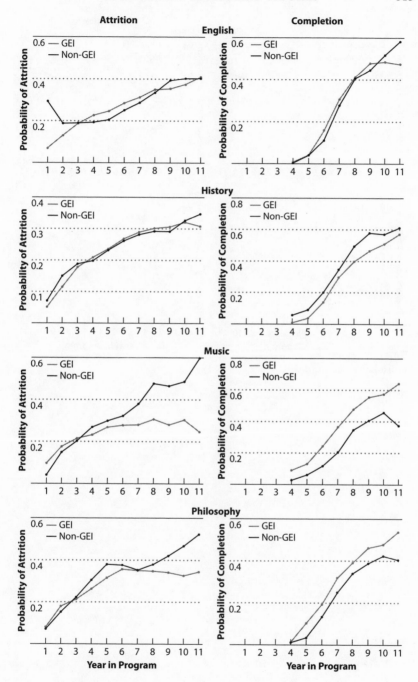

Figure E.4.1. *Continued*

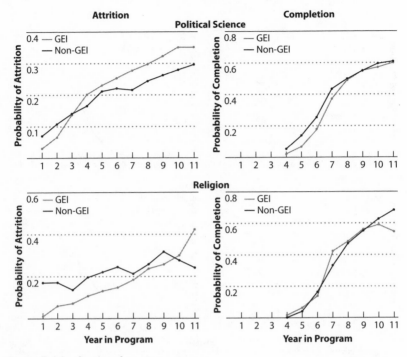

Figure E.4.1. *Continued*

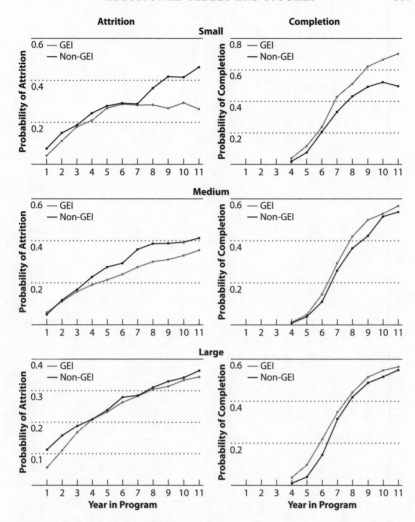

Figure E.4.2. Impact of the GEI on Student Outcomes by Department Size

TABLE E.5.1

Financial Support and Personal Characteristics

Characteristic	Percent of Students	Fellowship Amount	Year 1				Years 2–5				Years 6–11			
			Fellowship	TA/RA	Tuition	Summer	Fellowship	TA/RA	Tuition	Summer	Fellowship	TA/RA	Tuition	Summer
Gender														
Men	51.7	$8,906	61.9	21.3	77.1	17.7	56.5	52.1	74.2	26.4	27.3	28.3	36.4	10.5
Women	48.3	$8,881	62.1	21.6	76.0	17.5	58.4	53.8	74.9	27.6	29.4	26.6	38.1	10.4
U.S. citizenship														
Non-citizen	16.5	$9,400	68.0	19.8	80.2	21.0	59.1	47.8	75.6	27.8	26.7	21.8	32.2	10.3
Citizen	83.5	$8,783	60.8	21.6	75.8	17.0	57.1	53.8	74.4	26.8	28.6	28.3	38.0	10.5
Race and ethnicity[a]														
White	82.2	$8,558	58.9	19.8	73.9	15.2	57.8	53.6	74.2	26.4	28.6	28.2	38.2	10.6
Black	6.1	$9,808	89.0	15.6	93.6	30.6	71.2	48.0	82.1	39.1	30.4	21.4	41.9	13.6
Asian	6.5	$9,379	76.5	18.3	83.8	20.9	65.0	53.0	77.6	31.8	35.2	31.0	44.4	13.4
Hispanic	5.1	$9,510	83.6	18.6	87.5	28.7	66.5	50.2	79.6	37.1	30.0	26.3	41.8	11.4
Prior master's														
No	73.6	$8,889	62.4	18.5	76.3	17.4	59.5	53.5	77.2	27.7	29.7	27.1	37.6	10.5
Yes	26.4	$8,849	62.2	26.2	77.6	19.1	55.4	50.3	69.5	26.4	23.6	25.1	35.5	8.0
Math GRE														
High	37.2	$9,253	71.9	20.1	84.3	19.2	62.8	54.6	78.2	29.5	30.0	29.3	38.4	11.6
Medium	30.4	$8,816	62.1	22.3	77.2	17.6	58.0	55.1	76.6	27.9	30.3	28.1	38.8	10.1
Low	32.3	$8,518	55.9	22.8	71.7	18.1	55.1	52.3	73.7	26.0	26.5	25.8	37.2	9.3
Verbal GRE														
High	29.7	$8,931	69.6	19.7	83.4	17.8	60.7	54.7	76.8	27.8	28.2	29.5	38.4	10.0
Medium	40.6	$8,946	62.6	22.4	77.9	18.4	59.3	55.7	76.9	28.4	29.5	28.7	39.3	10.7
Low	29.7	$8,849	59.3	22.6	72.8	18.8	56.2	50.9	74.7	27.2	28.8	24.1	36.0	10.1

Note: The figures in columns labeled Fellowship, TA/RA, Tuition, and Summer are percentages of students who have the given type of support for the given year(s) in the program.

[a]For U.S. citizens only.

TABLE E.5.2

Financial Support and Departmental Characteristics

Characteristic	Year 1						Years 2–5				Years 6–11			
	Cohort Size	Fellowship Amount	Fellowship	TA/RA	Tuition	Summer	Fellowship	TA/RA	Tuition	Summer	Fellowship	TA/RA	Tuition	Summer
Field														
Anthropology	9.6	$9,302	68.8	25.6	84.8	22.2	59.6	46.2	75.2	25.5	30.5	26.2	36.3	10.3
Art history	8.4	$8,374	74.6	18.7	82.4	19.4	67.1	48.4	70.5	30.9	33.7	16.8	28.3	10.8
Classics	5.0	$9,861	62.9	25.4	80.0	13.0	54.7	61.0	76.1	26.5	39.5	41.1	47.7	13.5
Comparative literature	8.2	$8,809	64.4	21.7	80.0	13.3	49.6	56.9	69.5	20.8	26.6	39.0	44.8	8.6
English	21.0	$8,802	55.4	17.5	68.2	15.0	57.7	60.2	78.6	27.1	26.7	35.3	45.1	9.4
History	25.2	$8,690	55.2	24.3	73.5	17.8	55.9	49.1	71.0	26.5	30.4	22.8	34.7	10.8
Music	8.9	$7,965	68.1	27.8	79.8	20.8	57.8	63.9	77.8	22.1	26.2	25.5	31.0	5.3
Philosophy	7.9	$8,949	66.9	27.6	78.1	22.1	56.9	60.5	78.9	31.9	22.2	32.5	36.3	12.6
Political science	18.3	$9,433	67.9	16.6	84.2	17.2	54.9	45.1	74.2	29.0	24.6	24.9	32.6	13.2
Religion	6.6	$9,541	79.5	13.0	84.7	18.2	64.7	47.4	76.3	24.9	25.8	18.4	35.5	8.1
Max–min	20.2	$1,896	24.3	14.8	16.6	9.2	17.5	18.8	9.4	11.1	17.3	24.3	19.4	8.2
Institution[a]														
Max–min	22.5	$2,638	71.1	70.9	41.2	57.0	61.3	51.6	25.5	54.8	42.2	40.7	50.2	25.4
Department size[b]														
Small	5.2	$9,312	75.6	22.2	86.0	25.6	62.1	56.5	79.0	34.6	32.0	30.3	40.8	14.7
Medium	10.6	$8,828	74.0	25.6	85.7	27.5	59.2	53.4	75.7	32.4	28.4	25.0	31.6	12.9
Large	23.5	$8,817	54.0	19.4	70.6	11.7	55.6	51.8	73.1	22.7	27.7	28.1	39.0	8.8
Small–large	–18.3	$495	21.6	2.8	15.4	13.9	6.5	4.7	5.9	11.9	4.3	2.2	1.8	5.9

Note: The figures in columns labeled Fellowship, TA/RA, Tuition, and Summer are percentages of students who have the given type of support for the given year(s) in the program.

[a]Institutional figures are not reported to protect the confidentiality of the institutions that provided data.

[b]Based on the average size of entering cohorts from 1982–83 to 2002–03. Small: <7.5 (*N* = 25 departments); medium: 7.5–14 (*N* = 26); large: ≥14.1 (*N* = 26).

TABLE E.8.1
Marginal Effects on Labor Force Participation

	Six Months	Three Years	Survey Date
PhD, same department and institution	**0.141**	**0.107**	**0.068**
Married female without children	−0.008	**−0.036**	**−0.113**
Married male without children	**0.020**	0.004	0.005
Married female with children	−0.118	−0.086	−0.141
Married male with children	**0.024**	**0.039**	−0.014
Single female without children	**0.018**	0.007	**−0.091**
Single (male or female) with children	−0.006	**0.037**	**−0.092**
U.S. citizen	**0.034**	−0.009	**−0.018**
Urban location of institution	−0.004	−0.002	0.002
Potential experience since college	0.000	0.001	**−0.002**
N	6,730	6,608	6,828

Notes: Additional controls include indicators for missing family composition and missing experience and year fixed effects for last year in the initial department. The omitted group for family composition is single men without children. Marginal effects in bold type are statistically significant at the 5 percent level.

TABLE E.8.2
Marginal Effects on Being Employed (among Those in the Labor Force)

	Six Months	Three Years	Survey Date
PhD, same department and institution	**0.031**	0.006	**0.029**
Married female without children	**0.030**	**0.022**	0.005
Married male without children	0.014	**0.014**	**0.014**
Married female with children	−0.016	0.008	**−0.027**
Married male with children	0.007	**0.017**	−0.001
Single female without children	**0.034**	**0.015**	−0.001
Single (male or female) with children	0.037	0.000	0.020
U.S. citizen	**0.057**	0.002	**−0.014**
Urban location of institution	−0.006	0.000	0.003
Potential experience since college	−0.001	**−0.001**	0.000
N	6,183	6,096	6,373

Notes: Additional controls include indicators for missing family composition and missing experience and year fixed effects for last year in the initial department. The omitted group for family composition is single men without children. Marginal effects in bold type are statistically significant at the 5 percent level.

SUMMARY OF TABLES E.8.1 AND E.8.2

Table E.8.1 presents estimates of the marginal effects of each explanatory variable on the probability the survey respondent is in the labor force six months after departure from graduate study, three years after departure from graduate study, and as of the survey date, holding all other explanatory variables constant. The labor force includes respondents who report being employed as well as those who are not employed but who are seeking work; those who are not employed and not seeking work are not in the labor force. The explanatory variables included in the models are degree status, family composition, citizenship, institutional location in an urban area, potential experience since college graduation, and year fixed effects for the year that the student left graduate school (to control for labor-market conditions).

Individuals who received a PhD from their initial department are more likely to be in the labor force at all three points in time, but this effect diminishes over time from 14.1 to 6.8 percentage points. Family composition explains much of the variation in labor force participation. Relative to single men without children, married women without children while in graduate school are just as likely to be in the labor force six months after they leave graduate school, but they are less likely to be in the labor force at the three-year mark and at the survey date. Married women with children are less likely to be in the labor force relative to single men without children. Single women without children are more likely to be in the labor force at six months but less likely to be in the labor force at the survey date. Finally, U.S. citizens are more likely to be in the labor force at six months but less likely to be in the labor force at the survey date.

Table E.8.2 presents similar estimates of the marginal effects of each explanatory variable on the probability of being employed (conditional on being in the labor force) six months after departure from the doctoral program in which the individual was initially enrolled, three years after departure from the program, and as of the survey date, holding constant all other explanatory variables. These estimates were obtained from models that included the same set of explanatory variables as the models in Table E.8.1.

Individuals who received a PhD from their initial departments are 3.1 percentage points more likely to be employed than individuals who left their programs without receiving a doctoral degree from their initial departments six months after departure from the program and 2.9 percentage points more likely to be employed as of the survey date. Family composition variables are again important predictors of employment status. Conditional on being in the labor force, married women without children are more likely to be employed six months and three years after departure from their programs than are single men without children. Married men without children are 1.4 percentage points more likely to be employed than single men without children three years after departure from their PhD programs and as of the survey date. Finally, single women without children are also more likely than single men without children to be employed six months after PhD program departure and three years after departure.

TABLE E.8.3

Occupational Distribution of Leavers, by Timing of Leaving (percent)

	Six Months			Three Years			Survey Date		
	Early	*Midprogram*	*Late*	*Early*	*Midprogram*	*Late*	*Early*	*Midprogram*	*Late*
Administrators, executives, managers	15.5	17.2	18.5	15.8	17.2	13.0	15.8	18.8	17.9
Artists, entertainers, writers, public-relations specialists, broadcasters	12.4	12.0	12.3	16.3	13.9	15.3	14.4	12.7	12.4
Clergy and other religious workers	0.2	0.4	1.3	0.4	0.8	0.7	1.0	1.0	1.4
Clerical or administrative support	11.2	10.2	6.8	5.1	4.4	3.0	1.6	1.9	3.8
Computer-related specialists	3.3	3.9	5.3	5.5	4.6	7.3	5.6	5.7	5.7
Counselors	0.4	0.7	0.4	0.3	0.8	0.0	0.5	0.4	0.5
Curators	0.4	1.6	1.8	0.7	1.4	1.0	0.3	0.8	1.2
Education									
Elementary- or secondary-school educators	7.2	6.3	6.6	9.2	7.4	7.7	6.0	6.1	8.1
Postdoctoral appointments	2.1	1.3	0.7	0.4	0.3	0.0	0.4	0.0	0.2
Postsecondary teachers	4.0	4.0	7.9	2.8	3.8	4.3	3.4	2.1	3.6
Professors—all ranks	12.4	9.3	8.8	9.4	7.4	8.7	10.3	10.8	6.7
Research appointments	2.4	0.9	4.0	0.8	2.2	2.0	0.5	0.8	2.1
Other education	3.3	4.0	3.7	3.3	2.4	3.0	2.4	3.0	3.1
Engineers, architects, surveyors	0.4	0.5	0.7	0.4	1.7	1.0	0.9	1.3	1.1
Financial or human resources professionals	2.7	2.2	2.2	3.9	2.7	3.3	3.0	4.0	1.2
Health occupations	1.0	1.6	0.4	0.6	1.4	1.0	3.0	2.5	1.9
Lawyers and judges	2.3	2.9	2.9	6.2	10.1	7.0	13.8	12.7	10.5
Librarians	0.7	1.8	2.4	2.2	1.9	2.0	1.8	2.5	3.1
Sales and marketing	3.2	4.5	1.5	3.3	3.0	4.7	2.1	2.5	2.6
Scientists	0.3	0.7	0.7	0.3	1.0	0.3	0.2	1.3	1.1
Service occupations	2.6	2.7	1.3	1.8	1.0	2.3	1.0	1.1	0.2
Social scientists	1.9	2.0	1.8	1.9	3.0	1.7	1.5	1.7	2.1
Social workers	0.3	0.2	0.7	0.7	0.8	1.7	0.5	0.2	0.7
Other occupations	10.2	9.3	7.3	8.8	6.8	9.0	10.0	6.4	8.6

TABLE E.9.1
Job Outcomes Six Months and Three Years after PhD Receipt,
by Field (percent employed)

	English		History		Political Science	
Exit Years	Four-Year Institution	Tenure-Track	Four-Year Institution	Tenure-Track	Four-Year Institution	Tenure-Track
Six Months after PhD Receipt						
1992–94	75.4	35.9	71.1	35.6	76.3	48.7
1995–97	74.9	36.9	77.5	36.2	67.8	32.6
1998–2000	72.2	33.9	74.7	33.5	72.2	36.8
Three Years after PhD Receipt						
1992–94	76.0	58.6	80.6	64.1	75.9	63.4
1995–97	74.9	57.0	77.7	60.1	64.4	58.4
1998–2000	72.1	52.5	76.4	56.4	69.3	59.9

TABLE E.9.2
Percentage of Individuals Employed at Four-Year Institutions Six Months after PhD
Receipt in Positions Other Than Tenure-Track Positions Who Moved to Tenure-Track
Positions by Three Years after PhD Receipt, by Field and Exit Years

	Exit Years					
Position at Six Months	1985–2000	1985–88	1989–91	1992–94	1995–97	1998–2000
English						
Full-time non-tenure-track	51.2	55.0	46.2	50.0	56.0	50.0
Part-time non-tenure-track	49.7		54.2	48.0	44.9	57.1
Postdoctoral positions	76.3					
Nonfaculty positions	48.1					
History						
Full-time non-tenure-track	60.6	53.3	48.7	63.6	64.7	63.3
Part-time non-tenure-track	45.0		33.3	48.8	50.8	25.0
Postdoctoral positions	73.2					
Nonfaculty positions	42.6					
Political science						
Full-time non-tenure-track	68.9	66.7	64.3	60.7	80.6	66.7
Part-time non-tenure-track	55.7					
Postdoctoral positions	63.9					
Nonfaculty positions	78.8					

Note: Blank cells had fewer than 20 observations.

TABLE E.9.3

Percentage of New PhDs Employed in a Tenure-Track Position at a Four-Year Institution Six Months and Three Years after PhD Receipt, by TTD and Field

	Six Months			Three Years		
TTD (years)	English	History	Political Science	English	History	Political Science
5 or less	48.1	36.4	56.3	72.4	62.8	74.7
6	44.8	36.3	43.5	68.0	64.9	68.0
7	40.8	35.5	45.5	64.1	66.6	69.4
8	40.9	37.1	39.3	59.9	61.0	62.8
9	34.4	39.5	35.4	53.2	59.8	50.0
10 or more	34.3	33.2	28.1	48.2	53.2	45.3

Note: Based on GES respondents who received a PhD between 1985 and 2000.

TABLE E.9.4

Percentage of New PhDs Employed in a Tenure-Track Position at a Four-Year Institution Six Months and Three Years after PhD Receipt, by Number of Publications during Graduate School and Field

	Six Months			Three Years		
Number of Publications	English	History	Political Science	English	History	Political Science
0	35.9	34.2	39.0	54.9	59.3	60.5
1	43.7	38.8	47.8	66.3	64.8	69.0
2	48.7	40.6	45.9	70.5	69.4	62.7
3 or more	50.8	35.3	34.4	71.2	58.9	67.3

Note: Based on GES respondents who received a PhD between 1985 and 2000.

TABLE E.9.5

Impact of TTD on the Probability of Having a Tenure-Track Position at a Four-Year Institution Three Years after PhD Receipt, by Field

TTD (years)	English	History	Political Science
4 or less	0.077	0.031	−0.088
5	0.071	0.001	0.091
6	0.047	0.010	−0.011
7	—	—	—
8	−0.049	−0.043	−0.073
9	−0.098	−0.059	**−0.146**
10 or more	**−0.210**	**−0.166**	**−0.189**

Notes: Based on GES respondents who received a PhD between 1985 and 2000. Numbers reported are the marginal effects of TTD on the probability of having a tenure-track position, based on field-specific models similar to the one underlying the estimates in Table 9.6. Marginal effects in bold type are statistically significant at the 5 percent level.

TABLE E.10.1

Early-Career Publications of New Doctorates during Graduate School and the First
Three Years after PhD Receipt, by Citizenship, Race and Ethnicity, Gender, and Field

	U.S. Citizen, Nonminority	U.S. Citizen, Minority	Non–U.S. Citizen	Men	Women
English					
Published (yes/no)					
Never	0.24	0.36	0.15	0.19	0.28
During but not after	0.06	0.09	0.06	0.05	0.08
After but not during	0.29	0.35	0.31	0.27	0.30
Both during and after	0.42	0.20	0.48	0.48	0.35
Number of publications[a]					
During	0.99	0.54	1.47	1.22	0.84
After	1.74	1.27	2.42	2.11	1.50
Political science					
Published (yes/no)					
Never	0.28	0.34	0.22	0.25	0.32
During but not after	0.05	0.02	0.04	0.04	0.05
After but not during	0.39	0.49	0.38	0.38	0.44
Both during and after	0.28	0.15	0.35	0.33	0.18
Number of publications[a]					
During	0.66	0.26	0.98	0.78	0.44
After	1.88	2.00	2.37	2.17	1.48
History					
Published (yes/no)					
Never	0.28	0.35	0.22	0.24	0.32
During but not after	0.07	0.10	0.07	0.06	0.08
After but not during	0.34	0.34	0.31	0.33	0.35
Both during and after	0.31	0.22	0.41	0.37	0.25
Number of publications[a]					
During	0.73	0.52	1.13	0.89	0.60
After	1.43	1.16	2.06	1.71	1.23

Note: Publications are the sum of books and refereed articles published.
[a]Based on all respondents, including those reporting zero publications.

TABLE E.10.2
Marginal Effects of Variables on Publications during Graduate School

	Number of Publications (1)	Probability of Publishing (2)
Student characteristics		
Had a master's degree	0.079	**0.031**
GRE verbal	−0.015	0.014
GRE math	−0.018	0.004
Married male	0.065	0.014
Single female	**−0.299**	**−0.095**
Married female	−0.117	−0.027
Non–U.S. citizen	**0.212**	**0.049**
U.S. citizen, minority	**−0.267**	**−0.084**
Age at start of program	0.037	0.026
Age squared	−0.002	0.019
Attends seminars often	**0.130**	**0.048**
Advisor characteristics		
Expected you to finished quickly	**−0.131**	−0.020
Expected you to publish or polish	−0.003	0.023
Good advice on research	0.059	0.015
Not available to meet often	−0.018	−0.029
Met 2+ times per month during dissertation research	**0.178**	0.043
Met 2+ times per month during dissertation writing	−0.020	−0.010
Department characteristics		
Expected you to finish quickly	0.019	0.007
Expected you to publish	0.031	−0.019
Provided course on research process	0.004	0.012
Expected you to present research	−0.022	0.005
Program prepared you for research	**0.159**	**0.047**
Did not prepare you for research	−0.062	**−0.066**
Students are involved in academic life	−0.035	−0.006
Students are not involved in academic life	−0.045	−0.014
Required to attend dissertation seminar	−0.010	−0.001
Worked as a research assistant	−0.021	0.011

Notes: These models also include controls for the student's field and the institution at which the student received the PhD. The numbers in column 1 are the estimated marginal effects on the number of publications a student had during graduate school of changing each explanatory variable by one unit, holding constant all other variables. The numbers in column 2 are the estimated marginal effects on the probability of having at least one publication during graduate school of each explanatory variable, holding constant all other variables. Marginal effects in bold type are statistically significant at the 5 percent level.

TABLE E.10.3

Marginal Effects of Variables on Publications during the First Three Years after PhD Receipt

	Number of Publications (1a)	Number of Publications (1b)	Probability of Publishing (2a)	Probability of Publishing (2b)
Student characteristics				
Had a master's degree	0.001	0.009	0.003	0.004
GRE verbal	-0.061	**-0.072**	0.002	0.001
GRE math	**-0.070**	**-0.073**	**-0.016**	**-0.015**
Married male without children	0.090	0.065	0.032	0.027
Married male with children	0.110	0.069	**0.050**	0.038
Single female	**-0.278**	**-0.330**	-0.024	**-0.042**
Married female without children	**-0.233**	**-0.262**	**-0.048**	**-0.060**
Married female with children	**-0.173**	**-0.216**	-0.029	-0.045
Non–U.S. citizen	**0.305**	**0.296**	**0.056**	**0.046**
U.S. citizen, minority	-0.093	**-0.171**	**-0.069**	**-0.096**
Age at start of program	-0.118	-0.120	-0.021	-0.022
Age squared	0.002	0.002	0.000	0.000
Attends seminars often	**0.195**	**0.149**	**0.044**	**0.030**
Publications during graduate school	**0.473**	**0.464**	**0.264**	**0.241**
Advisor characteristics				
Expected you to finish quickly	**-0.119**	**-0.125**	-0.017	-0.022
Expected you to publish or polish	-0.059	-0.054	**-0.033**	**-0.030**
Good advice on research	-0.012	-0.022	0.005	0.003

	(1a)	(1b)	(2a)	(2b)
Not available to meet often	**-0.162**	-0.111	**-0.041**	-0.027
Met 2+ times per month during dissertation research	**0.285**	**0.295**	-0.018	-0.020
Met 2+ times per month during dissertation writing	-0.089	-0.071	-0.015	-0.004
Department characteristics				
Expected you to finish quickly	-0.033	-0.064	0.001	-0.013
Expected you to publish or polish	**0.219**	**0.185**	**0.061**	**0.051**
Provided course on research process	0.111	0.149	0.013	0.026
Expected to present research	0.071	0.072	0.019	0.017
Program prepared you for research	**0.318**	**0.306**	**0.082**	**0.074**
Did not prepare you for research	-0.002	-0.023	-0.012	-0.020
Students are involved in academic life	0.030	0.020	-0.004	-0.012
Students are not involved in academic life	0.067	0.088	-0.009	-0.003
Required to attend dissertation seminar	**-0.145**	**-0.135**	**-0.035**	**-0.027**
Worked as a research assistant	0.052	0.037	-0.001	-0.006
Initial job outcome[a]				
Tenure track at four-year institution		**0.408**		**0.112**
Nonacademic position		0.081		-0.028
Not employed		**-0.549**		**-0.193**

Notes: These models also include controls for the student's field and the institution at which the PhD was received. The numbers in columns 1a and 1b are the estimated marginal effects on the number of publications during the first three years after PhD receipt of changing each of the explanatory variables by one unit, holding constant all other variables. The numbers in columns 2a and 2b are the estimated marginal effects on the probability of having at least one publication during the first three years after PhD receipt of each of the explanatory variables, holding constant all of the other variables. Marginal effects in bold type are statistically significant at the 5 percent level.

[a] "Other academic position" is the omitted category.

References

American Academy of Arts and Sciences. 2008. "Doctorate Recipients in the Humanities, 1970–2007," in *Humanities Indicators, 2008*. Cambridge, MA. http://www.humanitiesindicators.org.

American Economic Association. 2000. *Newsletter of the Committee on the Status of Women in the Economics Profession*, Winter.

Andrew W. Mellon Foundation. 1991. "Foundation Announces a Major New Program in Graduate Education." Press release, March 25.

———. 1991. *Annual Report.*

Astin, Helen S. 1969. *The Woman Doctorate in America: Origins, Career, and Family.* New York: Russell Sage.

Attiyeh, Gregory, and Richard Attiyeh. 1997. "Testing for Bias in Graduate School Admissions." *Journal of Human Resources* 32 (Summer): 524–48.

Bender, Thomas, Phillip M. Katz, Colin Palmer, and the Committee on Graduate Education of the American Historical Association. 2004. *The Education of Historians for the Twenty-First Century.* Urbana: University of Illinois Press.

Berelson, Bernard. 1960. *Graduate Education in the United States.* New York: McGraw-Hill.

Bieber, Jeffery P., and Robert T. Blackburn. 1993. "Faculty Research Productivity, 1972–1988: Development and Application of Constant Units of Measure." *Research in Higher Education* 34 (October): 551–67.

Bowen, William G., and Neil L. Rudenstine. 1992. *In Pursuit of the PhD*. Princeton, NJ: Princeton University Press.

Bowen, William G., and Julie Ann Sosa. 1989. *Prospects for Faculty in the Arts and Sciences.* Princeton, NJ: Princeton University Press.

Bowen, William G., Graham Lord, and Julie Ann Sosa. 1991. "Measuring Time to the Doctorate: Reinterpretation of the Evidence." *Proceedings of the National Academy of Sciences USA* 88 (February): 713–17.

Breneman, David W. 1970. "The Ph.D. Production Process: A Study of Departmental Behavior." Ph.D. dissertation, Department of Economics, University of California at Berkeley.

Brown, David G. 1967. *The Mobile Professors.* Washington, DC: American Council on Education.

Buchmueller, Thomas C., Jeff Dominitz, and W. Lee Hansen. 1999. "Graduate Training and the Early Career Productivity of PhD Economists." *Economics of Education Review* 18 (February): 65–77.

Clemente, Frank. 1973. "Early Career Determinants of Research Productivity." *American Journal of Sociology* 79 (September): 409–19.

Clotfelter, Charles T. 2006. "Patron or Bully? The Role of Foundations in Higher Education," in Ray Bacchetti and Thomas Ehrlich, eds., *Reconnecting Education and Foundations: Turning Good Intentions into Educational Capital.* San Francisco: Jossey-Bass, 211–48.

Cole, Jonathan R., and Harriet Zuckerman. 1987. "Marriage, Motherhood and Research Performance in Science." *Scientific American* 256 (February): 119–26.

Committee on Science, Engineering, and Public Policy. 1995. *Reshaping the Graduate Education of Scientists and Engineers*. Washington, DC: National Academies Press.

———. 2007. *Beyond Bias and Barriers: Fulfilling the Potential of Women in Academic Science and Engineering*. Washington, DC: National Academies Press, April.

Council of Graduate Schools. 2003. *Ph.D. Completion/Attrition Workshop*. Airlie, VA, April.

———. 2004. *Ph.D. Completion and Attrition: Policy, Numbers, Leadership, and Next Steps*. Washington, DC.

———. 2007. *Ph.D. Completion and Attrition: Analysis of Baseline Program Data from the Ph.D. Completion Project*. Washington, DC, December.

———. 2008. *Ph.D. Completion and Attrition: Analysis of Baseline Demographic Data from the Ph.D. Completion Project*. Washington, DC.

Dare, Audrey Williams. 2008. "Graduate Students' Pay and Benefits Vary Widely, Survey Shows." *Chronicle of Higher Education*, December 5, A1.

Denecke, Daniel D., Helen S. Frasier, and Kenneth E. Redd. 2008. "The Council of Graduate Schools' Ph.D. Completion Project," in Ronald G. Ehrenberg and Charlotte V. Kuh, eds., *Doctoral Education and the Faculty of the Future*. Ithaca, NY: Cornell University Press, 35–52.

Diffley, Peter. 2005. "Selection and Attrition." *Communicator* 38 (November): 3–8.

Ehrenberg, Ronald G. 1992. "The Flow of New Doctorates." *Journal of Economic Literature* 30 (June): 830–75.

———. 2003. "Studying Ourselves: The Academic Labor Market." *Journal of Labor Economics* 21 (April): 267–87.

Ehrenberg, Ronald G., and Pangiotis G. Mavros. 1995. "Do Doctoral Students' Financial Support Patterns Affect Their Times-to-Degree and Completion Probabilities?" *Journal of Human Resources* 30 (September): 581–609.

Ehrenberg, Ronald G., George H. Jakubson, Jeffrey A. Groen, Eric So, and Joseph Price. 2007. "Inside the Black Box of Doctoral Education: What Program Characteristics Influence Doctoral Students' Attrition and Graduation Probabilities?" *Educational Evaluation and Policy Analysis* 29 (June): 134–50.

England, Paula, Paul Allison, Su Li, Noah Mark, Jennifer Thompson, Michelle J. Budig, and Han Sun. 2007. "Why Are Some Academic Fields Tipping toward Female? The Sex Composition of U.S. Fields of Doctoral Receipt, 1971–2002." *Sociology of Education* 80 (January): 23–42.

Feldman, Saul D. 1973. "Impediment or Stimulant? Marital Status and Graduate Education." *American Journal of Sociology* 78 (December): 982–94.

Ferreira, Maria. 2003. "Gender Issues Relating to Graduate Student Attrition in Two Science Departments." *International Journal of Science Education* 25 (August): 969–89.

Fleishman, Joel L. 2007. *The Foundation: A Great American Secret—How Private Wealth Is Changing the World*. New York: Public Affairs Books.

Ginther, Donna, and Shulamit Kahn. 2004. "Women in Economics: Moving Up or Falling Off the Academic Career Ladder?" *Journal of Economic Perspectives* 18 (Summer): 193–214.

Glenn, David. 2008. "Ohio State Gets Jump on Doctoral Evaluations." *Chronicle of Higher Education*, November 7, A1.

Goldberger, Marvin L., Brendan A. Maher, and Pamela E. Flattau, eds. 1995. *Research Doctorate Programs in the United States: Continuity and Change*. Washington, DC: National Academies Press.

Golde, Chris M. 1996. "How Departmental Contextual Factors Shape Doctoral Student Attrition." Ph.D. dissertation, School of Education, Stanford University.

———. 2000. "Should I Stay or Should I Go? Student Descriptions of the Doctoral Attrition Process." *Review of Higher Education* 23 (Fall): 199–227.

———. 2005. "The Role of the Department and the Discipline in Doctoral Student Attrition: Lessons from Four Departments." *Journal of Higher Education* 76 (November–December): 669–700.

———. 2006. "Preparing Stewards of the Discipline," in Chris M. Golde and George E. Walker, eds., *Envisioning the Future of Doctoral Education: Preparing Stewards of the Discipline*. San Francisco: Jossey-Bass, 3–22.

Golde, Chris M., and George E. Walker, eds. 2006. *Envisioning the Future of Doctoral Education: Preparing Stewards of the Discipline*. San Francisco: Jossey-Bass.

Goodwin, Thomas H., and Raymond D. Sauer. 1995. "Life Cycle Productivity in Academic Research: Evidence from Cumulative Publication Histories of Academic Economists." *Southern Economic Journal* 61 (January): 728–43.

Gravois, John. 2007. "In Humanities, 10 Years May Not Be Enough to Get a Ph.D." *Chronicle of Higher Education*, July 27, A1.

Groen, Jeffrey A., George H. Jakubson, Ronald G. Ehrenberg, Scott Condie, and Albert Y. Liu. 2008. "Program Design and Student Outcomes in Graduate Education." *Economics of Education Review* 27 (April): 111–24.

Grove, Wayne A., and Stephen Wu. 2007. "The Search for Economics Talent: Doctoral Completion and Research Productivity." *American Economic Review* 97 (May): 506–11.

Han, Aaron, and Jerry A. Hausman. 1990. "Flexible Parametric Estimation of Duration and Competing Risk Models." *Journal of Applied Econometrics* 5 (January–March): 1–28.

Hansen, W. Lee, Burton Weisbrod, and Robert Strauss. 1978. "Modeling the Earnings and Research Productivity of Academic Economists." *Journal of Political Economy* 86 (August): 729–41.

Harrington, Lisa. 2007. "The Parent Rap: A Conversation with Mary Ann Mason on Why Babies Matter." *The Graduate* 19: 4–8.

Hoffer, Thomas B., Vincent Welch Jr., Kimberly Williams, Mary Hess, Kristy Webber, Brian Lisek, Daniel Loew, and Isabel Guzman-Barron. 2005. *Doctorate Recipients from United States Universities: Summary Report 2004*. Chicago: National Opinion Research Center.

Hoffer, Thomas B., Vincent Welch Jr., Kristy Webber, Kimberly Williams, Brian Lisek, Mary Hess, Daniel Loew, and Isabel Guzman-Barron. 2006. *Doctorate Recipients from United States Universities: Summary Report 2005*. Chicago: National Opinion Research Center.

Hogan, Timothy. 1981. "Faculty Research Activity and the Quality of Graduate Training." *Journal of Human Resources* 16 (Summer): 400–15.

Hunt, Lynn. 1997. "Democratization and Decline? The Consequences of Demographic Changes in the Humanities," in Alvin B. Kernan, ed., *What's Happened to the Humanities?* Princeton, NJ: Princeton University Press, 17–31.

———. 1998. "The Tradition Confronts Change: The Place of the Humanities in the University," in *The Humanist on Campus*, ACLS Occasional Paper 44, 3. http://archives.acls.org/op/op44hunt.htm.

Jaeger, David A., and Marianne E. Page. 1996. "Degrees Matter: New Evidence on Sheepskin Effects in the Returns to Education." *Review of Economics and Statistics* 78 (November): 733–40.

Jaschik, Scott. 2007. "How to Cut Ph.D. Time to Degree." *Inside Higher Ed*, December 17.

———. 2008. "'Collision Course' for Graduate Education," *Inside Higher Ed*, August 28.

———. 2009. "The Impact of 'Time to Degree'," *Inside Higher Ed*, January 30.

Kalb, Laura, and Emily Dwoyer. 2004. *Evaluation of the Graduate Education Initiative: Final Report.* Princeton, NJ: Mathematica Policy Research, February 27.

Kane, Thomas J., and Cecilia E. Rouse. 1995. "Labor Market Returns to Two- and Four-Year Colleges." *American Economic Review* 85 (June): 600–14.

Kernan, Alvin B., ed. 1997. *What's Happened to the Humanities?* Princeton, NJ: Princeton University Press.

Lee, Wade M. 2000. "Publication Trends of Doctoral Students in Three Fields from 1965–1995." *Journal of the American Society for Information Science* 51 (January): 139–44.

Levin, Sharon, and Paula Stephan. 1991. "Research Productivity over the Life Cycle: Evidence for Academic Scientists." *American Economic Review* 81 (March): 114–32.

Long, J. Scott. 1978. "Productivity and Academic Positions in the Scientific Career." *American Sociological Review* 46 (December): 422–42.

———. 1992. "Measures of Sex Differences in Scientific Productivity." *Social Forces* 71 (September): 159–78.

Lovitts, Barbara E. 2001. *Leaving the Ivory Tower.* Lanham, MD: Rowman and Littlefield.

———. 2007. *Making the Implicit Explicit: Creating Performance Expectations for the Dissertation.* Sterling, VA: Stylus.

Maki, Peggy L., and Nancy A. Borkowski, eds. 2006. *The Assessment of Doctoral Education.* Sterling, VA: Stylus.

Mason, Mary Ann. 2006. "Graduate Student Parents: The Underserved Minority." Presentation to the Annual Meeting of the Council of Graduate Schools, December 9. http://www.cgsnet.org/portals/0/pdf/mtg_am06Mason.pdf.

Mason, Mary Ann, and Mark Goulden. 2004. "Do Babies Matter (Part II)? Closing the Baby Gap." *Academe* 90 (November–December): 11–16.

McDowell, John, Larry Singell Jr., and Mark Stateer. 2006. "Two to Tango? Gender Differences in the Decision to Publish and Coauthor." *Economic Inquiry* 44 (January): 153–68.

Merton, Robert K. 1936. "The Unanticipated Consequences of Purposive Social Action." *American Sociological Review* 1 (December): 894–904.

———. 1973. "Singletons and Multiples in Science," in *The Sociology of Science: Theoretical and Empirical Investigations*. Chicago: University of Chicago Press, 343–70.

Millman, Sierra. 2007. "Princeton Expands Family-Friendly Benefits for Graduate Students with Children." *Chronicle of Higher Education,* April 13, A13.

National Research Council. 1996. *The Path to the Ph.D.: Measuring Graduate Attrition in the Sciences and the Humanities*. Washington, DC: National Academies Press.

———. 1998. *Trends in the Early Careers of Life Scientists*. Washington, DC: National Academies Press.

National Research Council, Center for Education. 2005. Workshop on "STEM Doctoral Students: How Finance Mechanisms Influence the Quality of Their Education." Washington, DC: Center for Education of the National Research Council, June 22.

Nerad, Maresi. 1991. *Doctoral Education at the University of California and Factors Affecting Time-to-Degree*. Oakland, CA: Office of the President of the University of California.

———. 2008. "Confronting Common Assumptions: Designing Future-Oriented Doctoral Programs," in Ronald G. Ehrenberg and Charlotte Kuh, eds., *Doctoral Education and the Faculty of the Future*. Ithaca, NY: Cornell University Press, 80–89.

Nerad, Maresi, and Joseph Cerny. 1999. "From Rumors to Facts: Career Outcomes of English Ph.D.s." *Communicator* 32 (Fall): 1–11.

———. 2000. "Improving Doctoral Education: Recommendations from the 'Ph.D.s Ten Years Later' Study." *Communicator* 33 (March): 6.

———. 2002. "Postdoctoral Appointments and Employment Patterns of Science and Engineering Doctoral Recipients Ten-Plus Years after Ph.D. Completion: Selected Results from the 'Ph.D.s Ten Years Later' Study." *Communicator* 35 (August–September): 1–11.

Nerad, Maresi, and Debra Miller. 1996. "Increasing Student Retention in Graduate and Professional Programs." *New Directions for Institutional Research* 92 (Winter): 61–76.

———. 1997. "The Institution Cares: Berkeley's Efforts to Support Doctoral Students in the Humanities and Social Sciences with Their Dissertations." *New Directions for Higher Education* 99 (Fall): 75–90.

Nettles, Michael T., and Catherine M. Millett. 2006. *Three Magic Letters: Getting to Ph.D.* Baltimore, MD: Johns Hopkins University Press.

Nielsen, Waldemar A. 1972. *The Big Foundations*. New York: Columbia University Press.

Price, Joseph. 2005. *Marriage and Graduate Student Outcomes*. Cornell Higher Education Research Institute Working Paper 75. Ithaca, NY: Cornell Higher Education Research Institute, July.

———. 2008. "Gender Differences in Response to Competition." *Industrial and Labor Relations Review* 61 (April): 320–33.

Rapoport, Alan I. 1998. *Summary of a Workshop on Graduate Student Attrition*. Washington, DC: National Science Foundation, December.

Reskin, Barbara. 1978. "Scientific Productivity, Sex and Location in the Institution of Science." *American Journal of Sociology* 83 (March): 1235–43.

Sadrozinski, Renate, Maresi Nerad, and Joseph Cerny. 2003. *PhDs in Art History: Over a Decade Later.* Seattle: Center for Research and Innovation in Graduate Education.

Seagram, Belinda Crawford, Judy Gould, and Sandra W. Pyke. 1998. "An Investigation of Gender and Other Variables on Time to Completion of Doctoral Degrees." *Research in Higher Education* 39 (June): 319–55.

Smallwood, Scott. 2004. "Doctor Dropout." *Chronicle of Higher Education,* January 16, A10.

Somerville, Bill, with Fred Setterberg. 2008. *Grassroots Philanthropy: Notes of a Maverick Grantmaker.* Berkeley, CA: Heyday.

Stack, Steven. 2002. "Gender and Scholarly Productivity: 1970–2000." *Sociological Focus* 35 (August): 285–96.

Wadensjö, Eskil. 1992. "Recruiting a New Generation," in Lars Engwall, ed., *Economics in Sweden: An Evaluation of Swedish Research in Economics.* London: Routledge, 67–103.

Xie, Yu, and Kimberlee A. Shauman. 1998. "Sex Differences in Research Productivity: New Evidence about an Old Puzzle." *American Sociological Review* 63 (December): 847–70.

———. 2003. *Women in Science: Career Processes and Outcomes.* Cambridge, MA: Harvard University Press.

Zuckerman, Harriet, Jonathan R. Cole, and John T. Bruer, eds. 1991. *The Outer Circle: Women in the Scientific Community.* New York: W. W. Norton.

Index

Page numbers for entries occurring in figures are suffixed by an f; those for entries in notes, by an n; and those for entries in tables, by a t.

attrition rates: accuracy of estimates, 264–65; citizenship of students and, 104t, 105n; costs to universities of high, 7, 169, 170, 265; departmental expectations for dissertations and, 149, 151–53, 256; entering cohort sizes and, 103; factors affecting, 27–28; by field, 172–73, 173f; financial support effects, 5, 17, 133–35, 136–37t, 149, 253, 254–55; future research on reducing, 154–55; as GEI effectiveness measure, 3; by gender, 104t, 105n, 156–57, 160–61, 161f, 162t; GRE scores and, 103–4, 104t; in humanities fields, 5, 172, 264; impact of GEI on, 16, 55, 96, 100, 101, 101f, 110f, 151–53, 225, 251, 313t; institutional factors and, 15; by marital status, 157, 160–61, 161f, 162t, 261; measuring changes in, 27–28; overall, 169; with prior master's degree, 104–5, 104t; by race and ethnicity, 104t, 105n; reasons for enrollment and, 173–75, 174f; by stage, 109, 110f, 313t. *See also* cumulative attrition rates
AWMF. *See* Mellon Foundation

Bachetti, Ray, 9n
Bender, Thomas, 12n, 251n
Berelson, Bernard, 2n, 4
Bieber, Jeffery P., 211n
Blackburn, Robert T., 211n
Borkowski, Nancy A., 232n
Bowen, William G., 4–7, 32, 33, 36n, 37n, 156n, 169n, 229, 302n
Breneman, David W., 6n, 32n, 36n, 228n
Broh, C. Anthony, 300
Brown, David G., 211n
Bruer, John T., 211n
Buchmueller, Thomas C., 211n
Budig, Michelle J., 261n
business degrees. *See* professional degrees

candidacy: attrition after, 96, 172–73, 173f, 175, 176f; clarified deadlines, 62, 74; impact of summer support on timing of, 64; incompletes policies and, 67n; percentage of students, 96, 109, 110f; reduced time to, 53–54, 68, 309t; requirements for, 63, 75, 79–80, 237, 242n. *See also* prelims

careers: early, 187–90, 204–5; longer-run success, 201–4. *See also* academic employment; employment; occupations
Carnegie Foundation for the Improvement of Teaching, 14
Carnegie Initiative on the Doctorate (CID), 14
CARs. *See* cumulative attrition rates
Cerny, Joseph, 11n, 201n, 202n
CCRs. *See* cumulative completion rates
CGS. *See* Council of Graduate Schools
children, presence of: completion rates and, 163–64, 164t, 261; employment outcomes and, 183, 198, 320t; at entry to graduate programs, 157, 158, 163–64, 262; labor force participation rates and, 182, 320t; time-to-degree and, 158, 162–63, 164t, 261–62
CID. *See* Carnegie Initiative on the Doctorate
citizenship: attrition rates and, 104t, 105n; in departments prior to GEI, 44; discrimination in admissions process, 208–9; employment outcomes and, 198, 320t; financial support by, 124–25, 124t, 318t; of GES respondents, 209; publication rates and, 208–9, 209t, 212, 213; tenure rates and, 203, 203t
clarity of timetables: completion rates and, 19, 256; increases in, 58, 62, 80, 82, 83, 146, 151–53
"clarity of timetables" index, 144–45t, 146, 148, 152
classics departments: attrition rates in, 173, 173f; financial support in, 125; impact of GEI in, 108, 312t, 314f. *See also* fields
Clemente, Frank, 211n
Clotfelter, Charles T., 9n
cohorts. *See* entering cohort sizes
Cole, Jonathan R., 200n, 211n, 261n
Columbia University, 8, 30t, 35n, 97t
Committee on Science, Engineering, and Public Policy, 154n, 200n
comparative literature departments: attrition rates in, 172, 173f; impact of GEI in, 108, 312t, 314f. *See also* fields
comparison departments. *See* control departments

prospectuses (*continued*)
240–41; programmatic changes, 63, 71,
77, 78, 79–80, 81, 84–85, 237; required
for advancement to candidacy, 63, 75,
237; summer support for preparing, 67;
terms used for, 66n
publications, early-career: determinants of
rates, 213–14, 328–29t; by field, 207, 208t,
326t; impact of GEI, 217, 218t, 219; number of publications, 207–8, 208t; personal
characteristics and, 208–10, 209t, 326t,
328t; publication during graduate school
and, 213, 214, 218; rates of, 207, 208t;
time-to-degree and, 214–16, 215t
publications during graduate school: attrition rates and, 149, 256; departmental
expectations for, 146–47, 149, 151, 153,
212–14, 256, 327t; determinants of rates,
210–13, 327t; employment outcomes
and, 193, 194–95, 195t, 196–98, 199,
202, 264, 325t; by field, 210, 326t; impact
of GEI, 205, 216–17, 218t, 219; as predictor of early-career publications, 213,
214, 218; rates reported by students,
207–10, 208t; student characteristics
and, 208–10, 209t, 212–13, 327t; time-to-
degree and, 151, 214–16, 215t, 264; validation of self-reports, 206, 278–79
Pyke, Sandra W., 156n

qualifying exams. *See* prelims

race and ethnicity: attrition rates and, 104t,
105n; in departments prior to GEI, 44;
employment outcomes and, 198; financial support by, 124t, 125, 318t; publication rates and, 209–10, 209t, 212, 213;
tenure rates and, 203–4, 203t
Rapoport, Alan I., 14n, 169n
RAs. *See* research assistantships
recruitment: competition for gifted students, 3; competitive advantages of treatment departments, 51, 131, 139; financial support and, 114–15, 131
Redd, Kenneth E., 15n
registered time-to-degree, 5, 33, 300. *See
also* time-to-degree
regression models, 38–40
religion departments: attrition rates in,
172, 173f; financial support in, 125; im-

pact of GEI in, 108, 312t, 316f; sizes of,
127. *See also* fields
research assistantships (RAs), 117–18,
118t, 132. *See also* assistantships
research universities, 200–201. *See also*
institutions
Reskin, Barbara, 211n
romance languages departments: attrition
rates in, 173f; in GEI, 30t
Rouse, Cecilia E., 171n
Rudenstine, Neil L., 5–7, 32, 37n, 156n,
169n, 229, 302n

Sauer, Raymond D., 211n
Sadrozinski, Renate, 11n, 201n
science and engineering faculty, 200–201
science and engineering graduate programs: ages at PhD completion, 192n;
completion rates in, 173; financial
support by citizenship, 124n; financial
support levels, 259; future research on
program changes, 154; improving effectiveness of, 15
Seagram, Belinda Crawford, 156n
"seminar requirements" index, 143t, 145,
146, 148
seminars. *See* workshops
Setterberg, Fred, 9n
Shauman, Kimberlee A., 200n, 211n, 262n
Singell, Larry Jr., 211n
single students. *See* marital status
sizes of programs. *See* department sizes; entering cohort sizes
small departments. *See* department sizes
Smallwood, Scott, 173n
So, Eric, 140n, 146n, 148n
social sciences: empirical, 154; related to
humanities, 2n; trends in graduate education, 2. *See also* fields
Somerville, Bill, 9n
Sosa, Julie Ann, 4, 7n, 33n
spouses. *See* marital status
Stack, Steven, 211n
stage: attrition by, 173, 176; financial support by, 113–14, 117, 254; GEI impacts
by, 109–10; outcomes by, 47–48, 53–54,
60–63; programmatic changes by, 142,
149. *See also* advancement to candidacy;
coursework period; dissertation period
standard error, 38